THE LOEB CLASSICAL LIBRARY

FOUNDED BY JAMES LOEB, LL.D.

EDITED BY

E. H. WARMINGTON, M.A., F.R.HIST.SOC.

PREVIOUS EDITORS

† T. E. PAGE, C.H., LITT.D. † E. CAPPS, PH.D., LL.D.

† W. H. D. ROUSE, LITT.D. L. A. POST, L.H.D.

CICERO

XIII

PRO CAELIO
DE PROVINCIIS CONSULARIBUS
PRO BALBO

447

CICERO

IN TWENTY-EIGHT VOLUMES

XIII

PRO CAELIO
DE PROVINCIIS CONSULARIBUS
PRO BALBO

WITH AN ENGLISH TRANSLATION BY

R. GARDNER, M.C., M.A.

FELLOW AND BURSAR OF EMMANUEL COLLEGE, CAMBRIDGE
FORMERLY UNIVERSITY LECTURER IN CLASSICS

CAMBRIDGE, MASSACHUSETTS
HARVARD UNIVERSITY PRESS
LONDON
WILLIAM HEINEMANN LTD
MCMLXX

American
ISBN 0-674-99492-2

British
ISBN 0 434 99447 2

First printed 1958
Reprinted 1965, 1970

Printed in Great Britain

CONTENTS

CONTENTS

LIST OF CICERO'S WORKS

SHOWING THEIR DIVISION INTO VOLUMES IN THIS EDITION

VOLUME

A. RHETORICAL TREATISES. 5 VOLUMES

I. [Cicero], Rhetorica ad Herennium

II. De Inventione
De Optimo Genere Oratorum
Topica

III. De Oratore, Books I-II

IV. De Oratore, Book III
De Fato
Paradoxa Stoicorum
De Partitione Oratoria

V. Brutus
Orator

LIST OF CICERO'S WORKS

VOLUME

B. ORATIONS. 10 VOLUMES

VI. Pro Quinctio
Pro Roscio Amerino
Pro Roscio Comoedo
De Lege Agraria Contra Rullum I-III

VII. The Verrine Orations I:
In Q Caecilium
In C. Verrem Actio I
In C. Verrem Actio II, Books I-II

VIII. The Verrine Orations II:
In C. Verrem Actio II, Books III-V

IX. De Imperio Cn. Pompei (Pro Lege Manilia)
Pro Caecina
Pro Cluentio
Pro Rabirio Perduellionis Reo

X. In Catilinam I-IV
Pro Murena
Pro Sulla
Pro Flacco

XI. Pro Archia
Post Reditum in Senatu
Post Reditum ad Quirites

VOLUME

De Domo Sua
De Haruspicum Responsis
Pro Cn. Plancio

XII. Pro Sestio
In Vatinium

XIII. Pro Caelio
De Provinciis Consularibus
Pro Balbo

XIV. Pro Milone
In Pisonem
Pro Scauro
Pro Fonteio
Pro Rabirio Postumo
Pro Marcello
Pro Ligario
Pro Rege Deiotaro

XV. Philippics I-XIV

C. Philosophical Treatises. 6 Volumes

XVI. De Re Publica
De Legibus

XVII. De Finibus Bonorum et Malorum

PREFACE

Many years ago I accepted an invitation from the Editors of the Loeb Classical Library to revise and complete the five speeches of Cicero now comprised in two volumes, a work which had been left unfinished by their contributor, the late J. H. Freese, M.A., formerly Fellow of St. John's College, Cambridge, and Assistant Master at Repton School and at St. Paul's School. His earlier contributions to the Loeb Library were Aristotle's *Art of Rhetoric* (1926) and Cicero's *Pro P. Quinctio, Pro Sex. Roscio Amerino, Pro Q. Roscio Comoedo*, and *De lege agraria*, i-iii (1930).

I regret that the completion of this task has been gravely interrupted and delayed by the claims of administrative work and other duties. It is, however, possible that some advantage may have been gained by this delay. Within the last generation scholars have assiduously investigated the wealth of literary evidence that has made political and prosopographical studies of the late Roman Republic so profitable a field of inquiry. Their labours have thrown new light upon some aspects of the setting and the subject-matter of Cicero's speeches. To these recent researches and, no less, to those of earlier date, I have been under a constant obligation. The Bibliography which will be found on pp. 735-742 is, naturally, far from exhaustive ; it is no more than a list of such books and articles as have been found useful in the preparation of these volumes, and may indicate the amount of work which has been done in this field. My chief debt is to those annotated editions without whose aid I could have done nothing. Over seventy years have passed since two of them were published : J. S. Reid's edition of the *Pro Balbo* appeared in 1878, H. A. Holden's edition of the *Pro Sestio* in 1883. Two are more recent. In 1924 H. E. Butler and M. Cary published their edition of the *De provinciis consularibus*, and L. G. Pocock's edition of the *In Vatinium* is dated to 1926. The most recent commentary on the *Pro Caelio* is Professor R. G. Austin's revision (1952) of his earlier work (1933). For the guidance and help which I have received from this indispensable work I am obviously indebted and I am deeply grateful.

I have departed but rarely from the text used by the original translator, the Teubner edition (1904) by C. F. W. Müller, and then only to adopt suggestions by editors of the annotated editions. Müller's text has now been superseded by the Teubner edition of 1919 by A. Klotz and F. Schöll.

In any assessment of the qualities of the Ciceronian corpus these five speeches, taken as a whole, must be judged worthy of a high place. They not only vividly illustrate some of those literary qualities which link Cicero with Virgil as the most influential of the Romans, but they also illuminate many aspects of Cicero's amazing versatility as an orator. The *Pro Sestio* and the *In Vatinium*, with the *Pro Caelio* presenting some tantalizing glimpses of late Republican society, are a contemporary source of great value for the history of the short but crowded interlude between the bloodless revolution of 59 B.C. and the Conference of Luca. The *De provinciis consularibus* and the *Pro Balbo*, expressions of Cicero's loss of political independence, show how effectively the opposition to the coalition of Pompey, Caesar and Crassus had been paralysed, and almost point the way to the great laws of 55 B.C., the *lex Pompeia Licinia* and the *lex Trebonia*, which set up armed *principes* in control of the State.

The matter supplementary to the text and translation has been provided, possibly at the cost of treading paths already well worn, in an attempt to expound the historical setting of these speeches, to discuss some topics arising from their subject-matter, and to comment on those abundant references to earlier periods of Roman History which enhance the value of Cicero's work.

R. Gardner

Emmanuel College
Cambridge
6 *January* 1958

TABLE OF EVENTS IN ROMAN POLITICS FROM 60 B.C. TO 56 B.C.[a]

[a] Where chronology is precise, we are indebted, first and foremost, to Cicero's *Letters*, and, to a lesser degree, to the speeches delivered by him in 57 and 56 B.C. In general, the sequence of events in the years from 60 to 56 B.C. can be determined with fair accuracy, except where the sources are either silent or conflicting or variously interpreted. For a most helpful table of dates see R. G. Nisbet's edition of Cicero, *De domo sua*, pp. xxxv-xxxvii.

60 B.C.

Consuls : Q. Caecilius Metellus Celer and L. Afranius

Early months. Political deadlock arising from the Senate's refusal to ratify Pompey's settlement of the Near East and to allot lands to his veterans, and from Cato's opposition to a proposal to revise a tax-contract for the province of Asia.

P. Clodius, desirous of becoming tribune, plans to have himself declared a plebeian, a move successfully opposed by the consul Q. Metellus.

June. Caesar returns from his propraetorship in Further Spain. He abandons his claim to a triumph and appears as a candidate for the consulship. The Senate assign the province of *silvae callesque* (forests and stock-routes) for the prospective consuls of 59.

July. Caesar enters into negotiations with Pompey leading to the coalition known as "The First Triumvirate." Caesar and M. Calpurnius Bibulus elected consuls for 59.

December. Cicero, approached by Caesar's agent L. Cornelius Balbus, refuses to support Caesar's agrarian bill and so to enter into political partnership with him. Crassus enlisted by Caesar as a third partner in the Triumvirate.

TABLE OF EVENTS IN ROMAN POLITICS

59 B.C.

Consuls: C. Iulius Caesar and M. Calpurnius Bibulus

Caesar's first agrarian bill is passed by unconstitutional and violent methods, the Senate having refused to discuss it. Caesar reveals his coalition with Pompey and Crassus, disregards tribunes' vetoes and drives from the Forum his colleague Bibulus and other opponents. Bibulus, having withdrawn to his house, gives notice that he is "watching the heavens" and publishes edicts against Caesar. From January to the end of April.

Cicero criticizes the illegalities of Caesar and his partners in his unsuccessful defence of C. Antonius (consul 63 and proconsul of Macedonia 62–60) when prosecuted by M. Caelius Rufus, probably for *maiestas*. On the same day P. Clodius is transferred to plebeian status by the *comitia curiata*, under the presidency of Caesar as consul and Pontifex Maximus, and with the approval of Pompey as an augur.

Death of Q. Metellus Celer, proconsul-designate of Transalpine Gaul, and husband of Clodia, sister of P. Clodius.

Confirmation, probably by a *lex Vatinia*, of Pompey's settlement of the Near East.

Revision, probably by a *lex Vatinia*, of the tax-contract for the province of Asia.

Recognition, by a decree of the Senate and a law, of Ptolemy Auletes as King of Egypt.

Promulgation of the *lex Iulia de agro Campano*.

Marriage of Pompey and Julia, daughter of Caesar. Before 10 May.

Passing of the *lex Iulia de agro Campano*. May.

A *lex Vatinia* gives Caesar the provinces of Cisalpine Gaul and Illyricum. May (or June).

June (or July). A decree of the Senate gives Caesar the province of Transalpine Gaul.

June and July. Unpopularity of the Triumvirate: demonstrations at public festivals, *e.g.* at the Ludi Apollinares (6-13 July); the *affaire* Vettius.

July. L. Antistius, P. Clodius, Sex. Aelius Ligus, L. Ninnius Quadratus, among others, elected tribunes for 58.

Clodius begins openly to threaten Cicero.

25 July. Pompey publicly protests against the edicts of Bibulus.

18 October. L. Calpurnius Piso and A. Gabinius elected consuls for 58. Among the praetors elected are L. Domitius Ahenobarbus, L. Flavius, C. Memmius.

November. Acquittal of L. Flaccus (praetor 63 and propraetor of Asia 62) on a charge of *repetundae*, defended by Hortensius and Cicero.

10 December. P. Clodius enters tribunate and promulgates four bills.

58 B.C.

Consuls: L. Calpurnius Piso and A. Gabinius

Early in the year. Attacks on Caesar by L. Domitius Ahenobarbus and C. Memmius, praetors, and by L. Antistius, tribune.

4 January. P. Clodius passes *leges de censoria notione, de legibus Aelia et Fufia, frumentaria, de collegiis*.

Late January or February. P. Clodius promulgates bills *de capite civis Romani, de provinciis, de Cypro*.

Cicero leaves Rome. *Leges de capite civis* and *de provinciis* passed.	Early in March.
Cicero's house on the Palatine destroyed.	
Lex de Cypro passed. Caesar leaves for Gaul.	March.
Clodius promulgates bill *de exsilio Ciceronis.*	About 25 March.
Clodius promulgates bill *de Catone.*	April.
Clodius promulgates bill *de exsilio Ciceronis* in revised form.	3 April.
Leges de exsilio Ciceronis and *de Catone* passed.	24 April.
Cato leaves for Cyprus.	Soon afterwards.
Outbreak of feud between Pompey and Clodius, who contrives the release, from custody as a hostage, of an Armenian prince, Tigranes the younger.	April or May.
Pompey begins to urge the recall of Cicero. Clodius at feud with the consul Gabinius.	May.
Proposal for Cicero's recall made in the Senate by L. Ninnius Quadratus vetoed by Sex. Aelius Ligus.	1 June.
The College of Augurs having declared illegal Clodius' election as tribune, Clodius attacks Caesar's *acta* as consul.	? July (or later in the year).
P. Lentulus Spinther and Q. Metellus Nepos elected consuls for 57.	? late July.
Attempt by Clodius to intimidate, or to assassinate, Pompey, who withdraws from public life till the end of Clodius' tribunate.	11 August.
Sex. Aelius Ligus vetoes a bill for Cicero's recall promulgated by eight tribunes.	29 October.
The consuls leave for their provinces: Piso for Macedonia, Gabinius for Syria.	Before the end of the year.

Before 10 December. P. Sestius, tribune-elect, visits Caesar in Cisalpine Gaul to intercede for Cicero.

57 B.C.

Consuls : P. Lentulus Spinther and Q. Metellus Nepos. Praetorship of Appius Claudius Pulcher, brother of P. Clodius. Among the tribunes are P. Sestius, T. Annius Milo, Sex. Atilius Serranus, Numerius Quintius Rufus, Q. Fabricius, T. Fadius.

1 January. Sex. Atilius Serranus obstructs a proposal for Cicero's recall made in the Senate by the consul P. Lentulus.

23 January. Q. Fabricius prevented from submitting a bill for Cicero's recall, a meeting of the Assembly being broken up by Clodius' *operae* and by gladiators supplied by his brother, Appius Claudius, *praetor urbanus*.

Later. P. Sestius attacked in the Temple of Castor and wounded by Clodius' *operae*.

Early in the year. Clodius begins a candidature for the aedileship.

February. Failure of a first attempt by T. Annius Milo to prosecute Clodius *de vi*.

From February to July. Milo and Sestius, with *operae* and gladiators, engage in faction fights against Clodius.

Between 1 June and end July. The Senate pass a series of decrees in favour of Cicero.

End July. The Senate pass by 416 votes to 1 a proposal of P. Lentulus Spinther for the recall of Cicero.

4 August. The *comitia centuriata* sanction Cicero's recall.

4 September. Cicero returns to Rome.

5 September. Cicero delivers speech *Post reditum in senatu*.

Cicero delivers speech *Post reditum ad Quirites.*	5 September (or later)
The Senate, on the proposal of Cicero, sponsor a consular law appointing Pompey corn-controller for five years with proconsular *imperium* and fifteen legates.	6 or 7. September.
Cicero delivers speech *De domo sua ad pontifices.* Clodius' consecration of the site of Cicero's house on the Palatine declared invalid.	29 September.
The Senate order compensation to Cicero for the destruction of his town and country houses.	2 October.
Cicero, by removing from the Capitol the tablets recording the *acta* of Clodius' tribunate, displeases Cato.	? October.
Cicero proposes *supplicatio* of fifteen days for Caesar's Gallic victories of 58 and 57.	? October.
Clodius attacks the houses of M. and Q. Cicero.	3 November.
Clodius attacks Cicero's escort in *via sacra.*	11 November.
Clodius driven from an assault on Milo's house.	12 November.
The Senate debate Clodius' recent acts of violence. Milo begins a second attempt to prosecute Clodius *de vi* and, to prevent his election as an aedile, gives notice of an intention " to watch the skies."	14 November.
Milo obstructs election of aediles by *obnuntiatio.*	20 November.
C. Cato and P. Rutilius Lupus enter tribunate.	10 December.
P. Rutilius Lupus raises in the Senate the question of the *ager Campanus.*	Mid-December.
Ptolemy Auletes, expelled from Alexandria (end 58 ?), arrives in Rome to intrigue for his restoration by Pompey.	? Summer.

Later. Arrival in Rome of a large deputation from Alexandria, led by Dio, to protest against the restoration of Ptolemy Auletes.

Before end of the year. The Senate decree that P. Lentulus Spinther, proconsul-elect of Cilicia, shall restore Ptolemy.

56 B.C.

Consuls : Cn. Cornelius Lentulus Marcellinus and L. Marcius Philippus

Before 13 January. The statue of Juppiter on the Alban Mount struck by lightning. The keepers of the Sibylline Books, consulted as to expiation, announce an oracle forbidding the restoration of an Egyptian king " with a multitude." The Senate reconsider their decree commissioning P. Lentulus Spinther to restore Ptolemy and decide that Roman intervention in Egypt shall not be military.

13 and 15 January. Indecisive debates in the Senate on the proposed restoration of Ptolemy.

20 January. Clodius elected aedile.

Early in the year. L. Domitius Ahenobarbus, a candidate for the consulship of 55, announces that if elected he will as consul take steps to deprive Caesar of his provinces.

2 February. Clodius begins prosecution of Milo *de vi*, before the Assembly.

6 February. Adjournment of Milo's trial. Pompey speaks in support of him amid uproar from Clodius' *operae*. Clodius attacks Pompey as corn-controller and presses Crassus' claims to restore Ptolemy.

8 February. Pompey, attacked in the Senate by a tribune C. Cato, accuses Crassus of plotting his murder.

Trial of P. Sestius, defended by Cicero and others, when prosecuted by Cn. Nerius *de ambitu* and by P. Tullius Albinovanus *de vi*.	**10 February to 11 March.**
Cicero successfully defends L. Calpurnius Bestia when prosecuted *de ambitu* by M. Caelius Rufus.	**11 February.**
Unanimous acquittal of Sestius.	**11 March.**
Acquittal of Sextus Clodius, prosecuted by Milo at Pompey's instance.	**End of March.**
Cicero successfully defends P. Asicius, accused of murdering Dio, leader of the deputation of Alexandrians sent to protest against the restoration of Ptolemy Auletes.	**Before beginning of April.**
Cicero successfully defends M. Caelius Rufus when prosecuted (3-4 April) by L. Sempronius Atratinus.	**4 April.**
The Senate vote a grant of 40,000,000 sesterces to Pompey as corn-controller, and approve Cicero's proposal for a debate *de agro Campano* at a full meeting on 15 May. Crassus at once leaves Rome and meets Caesar at Ravenna.	**5 April.**
Cicero leaves Rome for a tour of his country houses, intending to return on 6 May.	**8 April.**
Pompey leaves Rome for a port of embarkation (Pisae or Labro) for corn-control business in Sardinia and Africa.	**11 April.**
Pompey reaches Pisae where he is joined by Caesar and Crassus.	**? 16 April.**
Conference of Pompey, Caesar, and Crassus at Luca, after which Caesar returns to Gaul and Pompey sails to Sardinia where he plans, through Q. Cicero and	**? 17 April.**

L. Vibullius Rufus, to dissuade Cicero from making his motion *de agro Campano* before his own return.

6 May. Date of Cicero's proposed return to Rome from a tour of his country houses.

Soon afterwards. Cicero, informed of Pompey's representations, composes the letter or speech [a] described as παλινῳδία in *Epp. ad Att.* iv. 5. 1.

15 and 16 May. Meetings of the Senate. No debate *de agro Campano.* The Senate refuse a *supplicatio* for Gabinius' victories in Syria.

? May (or September). Cicero delivers in the Senate his speech *De haruspicum responsis.*

Late May or early June. On Cicero's proposal, the Senate pass decrees authorizing pay for Caesar's four new legions and assigning him *decem legati.*

Late June or early July. Cicero's speech in the Senate *De provinciis consularibus.*

July. Cn. Lentulus Marcellinus, consul, refuses to accept the candidatures of Pompey and Crassus for the consulship of 55.

July to December. C. Cato, tribune, in the employment of Pompey and Crassus, maintains his veto on the election of curule magistrates.

Late summer or autumn. Cicero successfully defends L. Cornelius Balbus when prosecuted by an unknown Gaditane in respect of the citizenship conferred on him by Pompey under the *lex Gellia Cornelia* (72 B.C.).

Autumn M. Cato returns from Cyprus.

[a] T. A. Dorey, *J.R.S.* xlix (1959), p. 199. See p. 529, notes *a* and *b*.

ROMAN POLITICS FROM 63 B.C. TO 57 B.C.

Roman Politics from the breaking of the Second Catilinarian Conspiracy (63 B.C.) to Cicero's Return from Exile (September 57 B.C.).

Since the setting and much of the subject-matter of the speeches of Cicero comprised in these volumes are very closely interwoven with the political history of the previous seven years, some account of events in Rome from the breaking of the Second Catilinarian Conspiracy to Cicero's return from exile may be attempted as a preliminary.

In Cicero's consulship (63 B.C.) the Second Catilinarian Conspiracy, organized by an impoverished and ambitious patrician noble for the overthrow of the constitution, was broken by a combination of good fortune and good management. While its repercussions were to be felt in Roman public life for many years, it had immediate results for several leading men in the State. The antagonism which it induced between Caesar and Cato was to become an important determinant of Roman politics. Pompey was disappointed at being denied an opportunity of rounding-off his feats overseas by a commission to end the Catilinarian movement at home. Cicero, whose execution of the conspirators left in the city had received the moral, but not the legal, support of the Senate, was quick to see the significance of his enlistment against Catiline of those elements in Roman society that had nothing to gain from anarchy. Internal stability, in his view, could be secured by making permanent the temporary alliance of all loyal citizens (*boni*), senators, *equites* and commons, who had supported him as consul, and the commonwealth could be saved from the menace of military adventurers by setting up Pompey, then at the height of his prestige, as its defender. Having championed Pompey's interests during his long absence in the Near East, Cicero, shortly before Pompey's return, sedulously devoted himself to the task of winning the general to the cause of his *concordia ordinum*, an alliance of senators and *equites*. In one of the most important of his early letters (*Epp. ad Fam.* v. 7, of 62 B.C.) Cicero cast for Pompey the part of Scipio Aemilianus, the great conqueror of the mid-second century B.C. who practised a conservative policy, and for himself that of a joint-leader with Pompey of a coalition of all loyal citizens.

By the summer of 60 B.C. Cicero's *concordia* lay in ruins, the victim of political misfortunes and private animosities.[a] Two episodes of the year 61 B.C. opened up a rift between senators and *equites* which had grave consequences.

In December 62 B.C. a young patrician, P. Clodius, disguised as a female slave, broke into the house of Julius Caesar, Pontifex Maximus and a praetor of the year, where the worship of an archaic deity, Bona Dea, whose rites were forbidden to men, was being celebrated. Clodius was suspected of an intrigue with Pompeia, Caesar's wife. As even Cicero

[a] Cicero, *Epp. ad Att.* i. 18. 3.

could admit, this was an escapade which need not have serious consequences. But, invested by Cato and others of his kind with special significance and mismanaged by the Senate, the trial of Clodius for sacrilege became a *cause célèbre* which began the dissolution of Cicero's *concordia*. By abandoning their original plan of commissioning a praetor to try Clodius by a specially empanelled jury, the Senate permitted the jurors to be chosen in the ordinary way. This was playing into the hands of Crassus, who bribed the jury to acquit Clodius. No doubt Crassus and Caesar saw that Clodius might be useful to them. The trial had two important results. First, it marked for Cicero the beginning of a long and bitter feud with Clodius. Not only had Cicero given evidence at Clodius' trial which disproved a plea of alibi submitted by the defendant, but the orator's gibes [a] humiliated one who claimed a family connexion with the bluest blood in Rome. Clodius swore to be revenged. Secondly, a grave menace to Cicero's *concordia* was that before the end of the year, the Senate, indignant at the venality of the jury which had acquitted Clodius, and following the lead of Cato, attempted to deprive non-senatorial jurymen of a strange immunity from prosecution for corruption which they had enjoyed since the passing of C. Gracchus' jury-law, the *lex Acilia* (122 B.C.).[b]

The second episode which produced strained relations between *equites* and senators was the Senate's refusal, at the instigation of Cato and Q. Metellus Celer, consul-elect for 60 B.C., to sanction a rebate

[a] For example, in the Senate on 15 May 61 B.C. Cicero, *Epp. ad Att.* i. 16. 9-10.

[b] Cicero, *Epp. ad Att.* i. 17. 8.

for a company of *publicani* which was finding onerous the terms of its contract for the collection of the tithes payable by the province of Asia.[a] Crassus was behind the *publicani* ; Cato denounced their rapacity ; Cicero, fearful for his *concordia*, urged concessions both in this matter and in that of the non-senatorial jurors' privilege, but strove in vain. But it was on the rock of prejudice and animosity that Cicero's *concordia* foundered. Would there be a reconciliation between Pompey and the Senate ? The conqueror of the Near East was widely distrusted for his part in overthrowing the Sullan constitution and for his elevation to an unrepublican position by the Gabinian and Manilian laws. His behaviour towards contemporaries who had commanded in the Near East, such as Marcius Rex, Metellus Creticus, and L. Lucullus, had been less than creditable, and through his agent Metellus Nepos he had schemed for dominance in Italy. But Pompey's dismissal of his army on his return at the end of 62 B.C. dispelled fears of a second *Sullanum regnum*. The studied yet clumsy courtesy which he showed in public was a friendly gesture which the Senate would have been wise to welcome. This was a situation from which neither party emerged with credit : Pompey's defects of personality, acutely observed by Cicero,[b] gave an impression of a lack of sincerity and statesmanlike qualities ; many senators, too mindful of the past, allowed reason to be overruled by prejudice. The Senate therefore threw away a golden opportunity of a friendly understanding with Pompey by its reaction to two reasonable requests submitted to it

[a] Cicero, *Epp. ad Att.* i. 17. 9.
[b] Cicero, *Epp. ad Att.* i. 13. 4.

by him: the ratification of his settlement of the Near East, and the pensioning-off of his veterans by grants of land. By obstructive tactics in the Senate Pompey's opponents, instead of giving general approval to his eastern dispositions, insisted on their examination in detail, and dallied obstinately over the problem of settling his veterans on the land.

Pompey attempted to outflank the Senate by employing a tribune, L. Flavius, to present to the *concilium plebis* an agrarian bill for the benefit of the urban populace as well as of Pompey's veterans. Under it certain public lands in Italy were to be resumed and distributed; use was to be made of the new revenue from the Near East for the purchase of other land. Not only did Cicero, who strangely claimed to be rendering Pompey a service, severely criticize some provisions of the bill, but the Senate, led by the consul Q. Metellus Celer who was even imprisoned by Flavius for his obstruction, opposed the bill so vigorously that Pompey abruptly dropped it.[a]

Having thus rendered Pompey helpless, the Senate fondly imagined that Caesar could be similarly treated. About June 60 B.C. Caesar returned to Rome after a year in which as propraetor of Further Spain he had governed so successfully that Cicero could say that "the wind was now blowing full into his sails."[b] He hoped to win a triumph for his victories, a consulship, and, above all, a proconsular command for the further exercise of his abilities as a general. Refused permission by the Senate to submit by proxy his nomination as a candidate for the

[a] Cicero, *Epp. ad Att.* i. 19. 4; Dio Cassius, xxxvii. 50. 1-3.
[b] Cicero, *Epp. ad Att.* ii. 1. 6.

consulship of 59 B.C., Caesar entered the city and so forfeited his right to a triumph. Anticipating his election as consul and bent on ruining his subsequent career, the Senate made an unorthodox disposition of provinces for the prospective consuls of 59 B.C. by assigning to them the superintendency of forests and stock-routes,[a] almost a civilian function.

Pompey and Caesar, therefore, smarting over these set-backs, entered into secret negotiations which led ultimately to the coalition commonly but irregularly called "The First Triumvirate."[b] At the consular elections Caesar, backed by Crassus' wealth, won his own election, but found that his colleague was a rigid Optimate, M. Calpurnius Bibulus, whose return Caesar's enemies secured by lavish bribery, condoned even by Cato as being "in the interest of the State."

The original agreement between Pompey and Caesar provided that Caesar, with help if need be from his partner, would force the two concessions refused to Pompey by the Senate. The pact between the two men was sealed and a strong link was forged between them by Pompey's marriage early in 59 B.C. with Julia, Caesar's only child. To sound other political leaders whose relations with the Senate were strained was Caesar's next undertaking. These were Cicero and Crassus. Cicero, whose oratory in Rome and influence in Italy were highly assessed by Caesar, was lamenting the intransigence of Cato and other extremists and the ruin of the *concordia* from which

[a] Suetonius, *Div. Iul.* 19. 1: "silvae callesque." *Calles* were "routes" or "tracks" connecting winter and summer grazing-grounds. See p. 51, note *c*.

[b] See p. 382, note *c*.

he had hoped so much. He refused, however, Caesar's invitation to an alliance. Although he had toyed with the idea of winning Caesar over to the Senate,[a] he was obsessed by a suspicion, if not a growing belief, that Caesar was guilty of complicity in the Catilinarian Conspiracies. He remained, therefore, true to his instincts : an unwavering loyalty to the established constitution and a reluctance to ally himself with Caesar against the Senate.[b] Crassus, however, accepted Caesar's overtures. Financial necessity had played some part in Caesar's earlier partnership with Crassus during Pompey's absence from Italy (67–62 B.C.), and Caesar's invitation to Crassus to join his coalition was partly prompted by the large sums which Crassus had advanced to him before he left for his propraetorship in Spain. On his side, Crassus saw two positive gains in an alliance with Caesar : for himself, protection against Pompey, and, for his friends the *publicani*, a rebate from their unfavourable tax-contract.

Caesar's coalition with Pompey and Crassus has come to be known as " The First Triumvirate." [c] It sprang from the ruins of Cicero's *concordia*, dominated Roman politics for ten years and made possible warfare between armed dynasts. Asinius Pollio [d] rightly dated the origins of the Civil War to " the consulship of Metellus (60 B.C.)."

" Weak as he then was, he was stronger than the

[a] *Epp. ad Att.* ii. 1. 6.

[b] *Epp. ad Att.* ii. 3. 3 ; iv. 6. 2 ; *De prov. cons.* 41.

[c] It had neither legal nor constitutional basis, unlike the Second Triumvirate which was established by the *lex Titia* of 27 November 43 B.C.

[d] Horace, *Odes*, ii. 1. 1-7 : " Motum ex Metello consule civicum bellique causas . . . tractas."

whole State," [a] is an apt commentary on the character of Caesar's first consulship. Not only were the main objects of his compact with Pompey and Crassus secured by a determination which reduced the Senate to helplessness, but steps also were taken towards the maintenance of the legislation of the year and the perpetuation of the rule of the Triumvirate.

Caesar began by a proposal to provide land for Pompey's veterans and some of the superfluous population of Rome. The Senate having refused to discuss his first bill for the use of money provided by Pompey's conquests to buy land from private owners, Caesar submitted his measure to the Assembly and passed it into law by ruthless treatment of the opposition, both physical and constitutional, vainly offered by his colleague Bibulus, and by Cato and several tribunes. He then remained contemptuous of Bibulus' claim that, under the *lex Aelia Fufia*,[b] Caesar's land law and whatever other proposals might be passed into law during the remainder of the year were invalidated by his announcements (*obnuntiationes*) that he was " watching for something coming down from the sky " (*servare de caelo*). Shortly afterwards, a supplementary bill having been found necessary, Caesar passed with less difficulty the *lex Iulia de agro Campano* which settled Pompey's veterans and some civilians also on valuable public land around and near Capua,[c] from which sitting tenants had presumably to be evicted.

Further legislation to satisfy the Triumvirate was then carried by P. Vatinius, a tribune in Caesar's employment: *leges Vatiniae* not only ratified Pom-

[a] Cicero, *Epp. ad Att.* vii. 9. 3.
[b] See pp. 315-316. [c] Suetonius, *Div. Iul.* 20. 3.

pey's settlement of the Near East but also met Caesar's obligation to Crassus by relieving the *publicani* of one-third of the price of their Asiatic tax-contract. For himself, again through the agency of Vatinius, Caesar secured no ordinary proconsulate: the governorship of Cisalpine Gaul and of Illyricum for five years from 1 March 59 B.C. Further, a vacancy having been created in the governorship of Gallia Narbonensis by the death of Q. Metellus Celer, the Senate by its own decree assigned to Caesar that province also.[a] Magnificent as was the opportunity thus presented to Caesar for enterprise north of the Alps, it should not be overlooked that as governor of Cisalpine Gaul, called by Appian[b] the "Acropolis of Italy," Caesar was well placed also for observation and control, as in 56 B.C., of affairs in Rome. Further steps were taken to safeguard the ascendancy of the Triumvirate. At home there were designated consuls for 58 B.C. a plebeian *nobilis*, L. Calpurnius Piso, whose daughter Caesar took in marriage, and A. Gabinius, who had served as a legate under Pompey. In 57 and 56 B.C. consulships were held by adherents of the three partners. Moreover, it had become clear to Caesar, that, once he had left Rome for his provinces, his legislation would be exposed to determined attack, especially by Cicero and Cato. After refusing to enter into partnership with Caesar, Cicero temporarily quitted politics and played no part in the opposition to Caesar's earliest proceedings as consul. But his indignation soon got the better of him, for in March (or early April) 59 B.C.,

[a] Cicero, *Epp. ad Att.* viii. 3. 3; Suetonius, *Div. Iul.* 22. 1.
[b] *Bell. Civ.* iii. 27. 103. See also Cicero, *Epp. ad Att.* ii. 16. 2.

while defending C. Antonius, his former colleague as praetor (66 B.C.) and as consul (63 B.C.), on a charge of *maiestas*, probably covering treasonable conduct in Macedonia and collusion with Catiline,[a] he frankly criticized the methods of Caesar and his partners. Caesar at once saw that decisive action was required. Ever since his acquittal in 61 B.C. Clodius had been nursing a passion to revenge himself on Cicero for the incriminating evidence which he had given at the trial and for his sarcasms in the Senate. To this end he sought a tribunate, but so far had been unsuccessful in attempts to remove the disqualification of his patrician blood by adoption into a plebeian family. Cicero's indiscretion in his defence of Antonius made it clear to Caesar that Clodius, invested with plebeian status, would as a tribune be conveniently available to avert any danger which Cicero (or Cato) might threaten to the legislation of 59 B.C. Three hours, therefore, after Cicero's speech Caesar, consul and Pontifex Maximus, convened the *comitia curiata* and, with the approval of Pompey as an augur, carried a *lex curiata* which sanctioned the adoption of Clodius into a plebeian family.[b]

At first the connexion between Caesar and Clodius was not revealed; Clodius, by parading a pretended quarrel with Caesar, seems to have misled Cicero about his intentions. But after July, when he was elected a tribune, Clodius cast off the mask and

[a] Antonius was condemned and went into exile. For the case against Antonius see Cicero, *Pro Caelio*, R. G. Austin (Second Edition, 1952), Appendix vii, pp. 156-157.

[b] Suetonius, *Div. Iul.* 20. 4; Cicero, *De domo*, 41, *De prov. cons.* 42.

began to threaten Cicero openly. Cicero, however, disregarded, or claimed to disregard, danger from Clodius; he trusted in the unpopularity of the Triumvirs and in frequent assurances from Pompey. Caesar at first tried to conjure the danger anticipated from Cicero by tempting offers of honourable employment: membership of the Land Commission, a *legatio libera*, appointment to his proconsular staff in Gaul.[a] Cicero declined all these offers and, as the year was ending, enumerated to his brother Quintus [b] the resources of friendship and support by which he hoped to defy whatever attack on him might be launched by Clodius. He misjudged the danger.

On 10 December 59 B.C. Clodius brought forward four bills, to win popular support and to prepare the way for action which he proposed to take later against Cicero and Cato, the two most dangerous senatorial leaders. The first, which was perhaps intended in a general way to discourage a revival of the censorial power and, in particular, to safeguard the status as senators of himself and others, limited the censors' power of expelling members of the Senate to action only after an agreed condemnation on a specific charge. The remaining three were intended to invest his tribunate with autocratic power for the discomfiture of enemies of the Triumvirate. One of these angled for the favour of the *plebs urbana* by substituting a free distribution of public corn for the previous sales at less than half the normal market price. The second withdrew the ban which in 64 B.C. the Senate had placed upon all *collegia* or clubs, save upon a few genuine artisans' unions. In effect, Clodius' bill so

[a] Cicero, *De prov. cons.* 41.
[b] *Epp. ad Quintum fratrem*, i. 2. 16.

encouraged the growth of new *collegia* that he had ready to hand the material for that trained force of *operae*, or armed rioters, that was to make him the virtual ruler of the city for a year and a half. The scope of the fourth bill has been much disputed. Statements in Cicero's speeches delivered during the years 57–55 B.C. declare that Clodius repealed the *lex Aelia Fufia* (or *leges Aelia et Fufia*), passed about the middle of the second century B.C., which regulated the powers of curule magistrates and tribunes to obstruct the holding of legislative and elective assemblies by watching for omens (*spectio*, or *servare de caelo*) and by reporting unfavourable ones to a presiding magistrate (*obnuntiatio*). An advance was made in the interpretation of Clodius' measure by the conclusion [a] that Clodius repealed part only of the *lex Aelia Fufia*: tribunes and augurs were to retain the right of *obnuntiatio*, curule magistrates were to retain this right for elective, but to lose it for legislative, assemblies. Later a more drastic solution was proposed: that Clodius wholly repealed the *lex Aelia Fufia* in order to facilitate his legislation and, in particular, his proceedings against Cicero, but that the Senate proclaimed the nullity of his legislation on the ground that his adoption and his tribunate were illegal.[b] On 4 January 58 B.C. these *leges* were passed.

Clodius then launched his attack against Cicero. In late January or February 58 B.C. he promulgated a bill (*de capite civis Romani*) which "interdicted from fire and water anyone who had put to death, or

[a] W. F. McDonald, "Clodius and the *Lex Aelia Fufia*," in *J.R.S.* xix, pp. 164 ff.

[b] S. Weinstock, "Clodius and the *Lex Aelia Fufia*," in *J.R.S.* xxvii, pp. 215 ff. See p. 318, p. 396, note *b*.

should thereafter put to death, a Roman citizen uncondemned." Although expressed in general terms, this bill was clearly aimed at Cicero, in allusion to his summary execution of Catiline's accomplices in Rome. Cicero had been uneasy in 59 B.C., but seemed somewhat reassured as the year ended. He at once struggled desperately to avert the blow. Genuine sympathy and support came in from many sides. But the Triumvirs showed no disposition to help him, Pompey callously rebuffing his appeals, Caesar openly supporting Clodius' action. The consuls, Piso and Gabinius, were actively hostile. By a bill which was promulgated on the same day as his proposal *de capite civis Romani* Clodius defied the *lex Sempronia* by which consular provinces were assigned before the election of the consuls who were to hold them: Piso and Gabinius were to be allowed to select their own provinces and ultimately did so, the former taking Macedonia and the latter Syria. In the end, although Lucullus advised resistance, Cato and Hortensius urged surrender. So early in March Cicero left Rome for voluntary exile, and on the same day Clodius' two bills, *de capite civis Romani* and *de provinciis*, were passed. Several days later, about 25 March, Clodius published another bill which formally declared Cicero an outlaw (*de exsilio Ciceronis*), thereby making his life unsafe probably anywhere within the Roman world. But on 3 April this bill was promulgated in a revised form which limited the area of outlawry to one within five hundred miles from Italy, and was passed into law by the *concilium plebis* on 24 April. This law appears to have enacted also that Cicero's property should be confiscated and that no resolution for his recall should be submitted to the

Senate or the Assembly. Cicero's house on the Palatine was looted and demolished, but, if the orator is to be believed, Clodius was not empowered by his *lex de exsilio Ciceronis* to consecrate the house or its site. Cicero's villas at Tusculum and Formiae were destroyed. Clodius' procedure in driving Cicero from Rome may have been of doubtful legality, but it was unquestionably effective.[a]

For Caesar's purposes the removal from Rome of the inflexible Cato was no less urgent than that of Cicero. Since no ground for a prosecution of Cato could be discovered, he was not humiliated, but was entrusted with what was ostensibly an honourable commission. Since 88 B.C. the island of Cyprus had been ruled by a Ptolemy, brother of Ptolemy XI Auletes of Egypt who in 59 B.C. had purchased from Caesar and Pompey for six thousand talents the recognition of his precarious royal title. But the ruler of Cyprus showed no disposition to secure his crown by a similar insurance. Clodius therefore proposed and carried a bill under which Cyprus was declared a Roman province, the official pretext being that Ptolemy had aided piracy in the Levant. Politically, the annexation of Cyprus would round-off the bequest of Cyrene and the conquests of Syria, Cilicia and Crete. A second bill was passed into law commis-

[a] Cicero argued that Clodius' *lex de exsilio* was null and void, for two reasons: it was a capital sentence passed, not by the *comitia centuriata*, but by the *concilium plebis*; it was a *privilegium* which, since there had been no trial, could not be a formal bill of outlawry. Modern writers are divided in their views. Rice Holmes, *The Roman Republic*, i, p. 334, accepts Cicero's version of the matter; Greenidge, *Legal Procedure of Cicero's Time*, p. 363, thinks that Clodius' actions may have been legal.

sioning Cato to confiscate the royal treasures, annex the island, and restore certain exiles to Byzantium. It is said that Cato went only because the Stoic doctrines made him consider first the interest of the State. Ptolemy, on hearing that he was to lose his treasures, made away with himself. Cyprus was annexed to the province of Cilicia. Cato was thus virtually banished till his return to Rome late in 56 B.C.[a]

With the departure of Cicero and Cato the Triumvirate was freed from the danger of attack by its two most redoubtable critics. But its internal weakness was soon demonstrated by the disorderly proceedings of Clodius during the remainder of his tribunate. He was soon at feud with his nominal allies, Pompey and Gabinius. A movement which Pompey had initiated almost at once for Cicero's restoration evoked in April a hostile response from Clodius. Bribed by Tigranes, the client-king of Armenia, Clodius had contrived the escape from custody in Rome of his son, Tigranes, who had appeared as a captive at Pompey's triumph, and was detained as a hostage. Not only Pompey but Gabinius also took umbrage at this, and in the resultant street-fighting the consul had his *fasces* broken and his goods consecrated to Ceres, by act of Clodius.[b] That the incident of Tigranes' escape might lead to a rupture between Pompey and Caesar (as Clodius' employer) was a hope which by the end of May Cicero regretfully abandoned.[c] Early in August Clodius' feud with Pompey became even

[a] Cicero, *De domo*, 22 and 65 ; *Pro Sestio*, 60.
[b] Cicero, *De domo*, 125.
[c] Cicero, *Epp. ad Att.* iii. 8. 3 of 29 May.

more sensational: on the 11th of that month he introduced an armed slave into the Senate either to alarm or even to assassinate Pompey, and succeeded in driving him into seclusion for the rest of the year. Moreover, if we may believe Cicero, Clodius in the later months of his tribunate even turned upon Caesar and denounced as illegal his legislation of 59 B.C.; the College of Augurs, after hearing the evidence of Bibulus at a *contio* convened by Clodius, expressed their opinion that the tribunate of Clodius, based on his adoption, and the acts of Caesar were alike illegal.[a]

Meantime Pompey's movement for the restoration of Cicero gathered strength. As early as 1 June a tribune L. Ninnius Quadratus made in the Senate a proposal for Cicero's recall which was accepted by a full house, but vetoed by a hostile tribune, Aelius Ligus.[b] In July Cicero received from Atticus

[a] Cicero, *De domo*, 40; *De prov. cons.* 43; *De haruspicum responsis*, 48. These three passages are difficult. Interpreted literally, they suggest that in the later months of his tribunate Clodius behaved with wanton recklessness. For example, Strachan-Davidson, *Cicero*, p. 242, compares his proceedings with "the tricks of a mischievous monkey." R. G. Nisbet (Cicero, *De domo*, p. 105) thinks it very possible that Cicero's evidence is substantially true, that Caesar had ordered Clodius to halt, and that there had been some rupture between them. On the other hand, L. G. Pocock (*In Vatinium*, pp. 152 ff.) holds that this was no more than a sham attack made by Clodius upon Caesar at a time when his own position was threatened; for an offer, possibly inspired by Pompey, was made by the Optimates to Caesar that his measures should be re-enacted with due observance of the auspices (*De prov. cons.* 46), that Caesar should sever his connexion with the *populares*, and that Clodius and his offensive legislation should be sacrificed.

[b] Cicero, *Pro Sestio*, 68.

an assurance that Pompey was well disposed towards him and that as soon as Caesar had expressed his approval of Cicero's proposed recall, he would instruct some magistrate to act. Moreover, the elections for 57 B.C. turned out favourably for Cicero. Of the consuls designate, P. Lentulus Spinther was an intimate friend both of Pompey and of Cicero; his colleague, Q. Metellus Nepos, a cousin of Clodius, had as tribune been hostile to Cicero, but was to prove a placable enemy.[a] Eight of the incoming tribunes were well disposed; but Cicero's cause was to be opposed by two tribunes, Serranus and Numerius Quintius Rufus, and by a praetor, Appius Claudius, brother of Clodius. It was with Pompey's approval, or perhaps at his initiative, that P. Sestius, one of the tribunes-elect, undertook before he entered upon his tribunate a journey to Cisalpine Gaul with a view to winning Caesar's consent. What Sestius accomplished was not at first revealed,[b] but Caesar must later have expressed his approval of the measures which Pompey wished to take for Cicero's recall, the pact being sealed by Quintus Cicero, who gave certain pledges on his brother's account to the Triumvirs.[c] On 29 October eight of the tribunes in office promulgated a bill for Cicero's recall, supported by Pompey and P. Lentulus Spinther, consul-elect; this, however, was not only opposed by the consuls and vetoed by the tribune Aelius Ligus, but was also criticized by Cicero for flaws in its drafting.[d] It was withdrawn. So these uncertain prospects of recall

[a] Cicero, *De prov. cons.* 22; *Pro Sestio*, 130.

[b] Cicero, *Pro Sestio*, 71.

[c] Cicero, *Epp. ad Fam.* i. 9. 9; *De prov. cons.* 43.

[d] Cicero, *Epp. ad Att.* iii. 23.

are reflected in the despairing tone of Cicero's letters written from Dyrrhachium towards the end of the year.[a]

The year 57 B.C. opened with a determined attempt by Cicero's supporters to secure his recall. In the Senate on 1 January the consul, P. Lentulus Spinther, proposed that Cicero should be recalled; his colleague, Q. Metellus Nepos, did not demur; Appius Claudius, Cicero's only enemy among the praetors, was silent. In a discussion about procedure, an eminent jurist, L. Aurelius Cotta (consul 65 B.C.), thought that legislation was unnecessary, but Pompey advised that a resolution of the Senate should be confirmed by a vote of the Assembly. But the passing of a resolution was obstructed by Atilius Serranus, one of the two tribunes hostile to Cicero; and although discussion in the Senate was resumed whenever possible, continued obstruction prevented a resolution from being passed. Nevertheless a tribune, Q. Fabricius, made preparations to bring a bill before the Assembly on 23 January. But Clodius' *operae* were already found in occupation of "the Forum, the Comitium, and the Senate House,"[b] and with the help of gladiators borrowed from his brother, the praetor Appius Claudius, Clodius frustrated this attempt to hold an Assembly. In this murderous riot, the like of which, Cicero said, had not been seen in Rome since the civil war between Cinna and Octavius (87 B.C.),[c] Q. Cicero barely escaped with his life. In a later affray Sestius, after announcing an evil omen (*obnuntiatio*) to the consul

[a] *e.g. Epp. ad Att.* iii. 23; *Epp. ad Fam.* xiv. 3.
[b] Cicero, *Pro Sestio*, 75.
[c] The "Bellum Octavianum." Cicero, *Pro Sestio*, 77.

Metellus Nepos against some proposal or measure to Cicero's detriment, was attacked in the Temple of Castor and left for dead.[a] His assailants, having admitted their guilt before the Senate, were imprisoned by Milo but released by Atilius Serranus. Certainty as to what followed cannot be reached, and the following narrative is tentative.[b] Probably in February Milo attempted to prosecute Clodius for a breach of the peace committed on 23 January under the *lex Plautia de vi*,[c] not as a tribune before the *concilium plebis* but before a *quaestio perpetua* presided over by a praetor. But the consul Metellus Nepos, supported by the praetor Appius Claudius and by the tribune Serranus, and appealing to a general suspension of public business announced by the Senate, refused to accept Milo's charge and thus brought at least criminal jurisdiction to a standstill. Our sources say that in 57 B.C. Milo twice attempted to prosecute Clodius, but was twice baulked by Metellus Nepos. The above was the first occasion, the second occurring in November (see p. 30).

Clodius then announced his candidature for an aedileship as a precaution against a renewal of Milo's intended prosecution *de vi*, since, once elected, he

[a] Cicero, *Epp. ad Quintum fratrem*, ii. 3. 6; *Pro Sestio*, 79.

[b] The main sources are: Cicero, *Post reditum in senatu*, 6 and 19; *Pro Sestio*, 85, 89, 95; *Pro Milone*, 35, 38, 40; *Epp. ad Att.* iv. 3. 2; *Epp. ad Fam.* i. 9. 5; v. 3; Plutarch, *Cicero*, 33; Dio Cassius, xxxix. 7. 4. The above version is based on E. Meyer, *Caesars Monarchie*, 1922, pp. 109-112. See also Rice Holmes, *The Roman Republic*, ii, p. 59, and Holden, *Pro Sestio*, p. 195, both of whom stress the point that as the quaestors, who appointed the jurors, had not been elected, Metellus forbade the praetor to hear any prosecution before the jurors had been duly chosen.

[c] Or *Plotia*.

could not be tried for any offence save for one arising from his election. Milo retaliated by raising a troop of gladiators [a] and, with the help of his colleague Sestius and others, proceeded slowly to wear down Clodius' resistance so that constitutional steps could be taken to recall Cicero. Pompey also helped this movement. By inducing Capua, where he was *duumiur*, to pass a vote in Cicero's favour, he created a sympathy for him which he later fostered by going from town to town to speak on his behalf.[b]

During the early summer the Senate passed a number of decrees favourable to Cicero at three sittings which may be distinguished. In the Temple of Honos and Virtus early in July, the Senate on the motion of Lentulus commended Cicero to the protection of provincial governors and peoples and summoned citizens from all parts of Italy to vote for his recall. This was followed by a great demonstration in honour of Cicero in the theatre at the Ludi Apollinares (6–13 July).[c] Later, the Senate, meeting in the Temple of Iuppiter Capitolinus, accepted by 416 votes to Clodius' solitary dissent,[d] a written statement read by Pompey that Cicero had saved the State, and instructed the consuls to bring in a bill for his recall. At that meeting the consul Metellus Nepos declared himself reconciled to Cicero.[e] On the following day, assembled in the *curia*, the Senate resolved that whoever should attempt to block by

[a] Dio Cassius, xxxix. 8. 1.

[b] Cicero, *Post reditum in senatu*, 29; *In Pisonem*, 25 and 80; *Pro Milone*, 39.

[c] Cicero, *Pro Sestio*, 115 ff.

[d] Cicero, *Post reditum in senatu*, 26.

[e] Cicero, *Pro Sestio*, 130; *De prov. cons.* 22.

obnuntiatio or otherwise to obstruct the holding of an Assembly to order Cicero's recall, should be declared a public enemy ; also that, if such obstruction should take place on five *dies comitiales*, Cicero should be free to return with full citizen rights.[a] In fact, Cicero owed his recall to a *senatus consultum* which, it is thought, like the *lex Clodia* of 58 B.C., repealed the *lex Aelia Fufia* for a special purpose.[b] On 4 August, voters from all Italy being present, the *comitia centuriata* sanctioned Cicero's return, probably by declaring ineffective the previous acts against him on the ground that no banishment could be legal unless it followed a formal trial and condemnation. On 4 September Cicero was welcomed back to Rome as he entered by the Porta Capena.

[a] Cicero, *Pro Sestio*, 129. See p. 319.

[b] S. Weinstock, *J.R.S.* xxvii, p. 220 ; Rice Holmes, *The Roman Republic*, ii, p. 60, note 5.

An important note on Clodius' " repeal " of the *lex Aelia Fufia* was published just as these volumes had reached their penultimate stage of preparation. In *J.R.S.* xlvii (1957), pp. 15-20, " Roman History, 56–56 B.C. : Three Ciceronian Problems," J. P. V. D. Balsdon discusses (pp. 15-16) Clodius' " repeal " of the *lex Aelia Fufia.* Having pointed out objections to previous hypotheses, he cannot detect in Cicero's many attacks against Clodius after his return from exile any evidence which might support Weinstock's view (*op. cit.* p. 220) that the Senate decided against the legality of Clodius' tribunate and legislation. He makes the cogent suggestion that Clodius' bill was framed to counter any repetition of such obstructive tactics as those of Bibulus in 59 B.C., by empowering the *comitia* and the *concilium plebis* to order that *obnuntiatio*, if attempted, should be disallowed. On this interpretation, the *lex Clodia* was the model for the decree (*Pro Sestio*, 129) passed by the Senate before the *comitia centuriata* sanctioned Cicero's recall.

PRO CAELIO

I. The Early Career of M. Caelius Rufus

It may be regarded as certain that M. Caelius Rufus was born on 28 May 82 B.C.,[a] and as highly probable that his birthplace was Interamnia[b] (now Teramo), the chief town of the *ager Praetuttianus*, in the territory of Picenum. Nothing more is known of his father than that he was a Roman knight, of economical[c] habits, who owned property in Africa.[d] It is probable that originally he had not lived in Rome.

Caelius came under the tutelage of Cicero in 66 when, according to Pliny, he was sixteen, an age at which the *toga virilis* was usually assumed. He was taken to Rome by his father and put in the charge of Cicero and Crassus for his *tirocinium fori*, a period of apprenticeship for an aspirant to a public career.[e] We learn from Cicero that during this apprenticeship, which lasted as long as three years,[f] Caelius developed a remarkable flair for matters political.[g] But during Cicero's consulship Caelius broke away from him, falling a victim to the magnetism of Catiline. Although there is no evidence that Caelius joined the conspiracy, this lapse temporarily clouded his reputation and needed much special pleading from Cicero. At the end of 62 or early in 61 Caelius

[a] Pliny, *N.H.* vii. 165.
[b] *Pro Caelio*, 5.
[c] *Pro Caelio*, 36.
[d] *Pro Caelio*, 73.
[e] *Pro Caelio*, 72.
[f] *Pro Caelio*, 10.
[g] Cicero, *Epp. ad Fam.* ii. 8. 1.

joined the staff (*cohors*) of Q. Pompeius Rufus,[a] a praetor of 63, who was then due to govern the province of Africa with proconsular *imperium*. His choice of Africa, where he acquitted himself well, was perhaps influenced by the location there of his father's estates.

On his return to Rome in 60 Caelius made an impressive entry into public life by prosecuting[b] an ex-consul, C. Antonius Hybrida, who had been Cicero's colleague in 63. Since Antonius was strongly suspected of leanings towards Catiline, Cicero, to purchase his loyalty during his consulship, surrendered to him his own proconsular province of Macedonia. Antonius' proconsulship in Macedonia was disgraced by gross misgovernment. He was tried in March 59, and, though defended by Cicero, was condemned. The main charge against him was probably *maiestas* covering treasonable conduct in Macedonia and collusion with Catiline, *repetundae* being a subsidiary charge.[c] Though no friend of Antonius, Cicero defended him from a sense of obligation to his consular colleague who, officially at least, was in command of the operations which ended Catiline's career at Pistoria early in 62. The trial brought about Clodius' transference to the *plebs*, for an attack on Caesar[d] made by Cicero in his speech led three hours later on the same day to Caesar's passing of the *lex curiata* that made Clodius a plebeian.[e]

[a] *Pro Caelio*, 73.

[b] According to Dio Cassius (xxxviii. 10. 4), Cicero held Caesar responsible for the accusation brought against Antonius.

[c] Austin, *op. cit.*, Appendix vii, pp. 156-157.

[d] Dio Cassius, xxxviii. 10. 4.

[e] Cicero, *De domo*, 41. Suetonius, *Div. Iul.* 20. 4.

This victory in the courts was a turning-point in Caelius' career. Estranged from Cicero and dissatisfied with a quiet home life, he moved to a fashionable quarter of Rome by renting a house on the Palatine from P. Clodius, thus becoming a neighbour of Clodia, Clodius' sister, widowed in 59 by the death of Q. Metellus Celer.

Supplanting, in all probability, Catullus in the affections of Clodia, he began an intimacy with her lasting for about two years. Cicero catalogues the amusements [a] at Rome and Baiae of the set in which they moved. When these relations had been broken by a bitter quarrel, Clodia set about to punish her former lover.

Early in 56 Caelius indicted for *ambitus*, probably in connexion with the praetorian elections of 57, L. Calpurnius Bestia who, on 11 February, was successfully defended by Cicero.[b] Bestia is probably identical with a tribune of that name, of Catilinarian sympathies, who entered office on 10 December 63 and who was to have given a signal for an insurrection of Catilinarians in Rome.[c] It has been convincingly shown that this Bestia was none other than the father of L. Sempronius Atratinus, the formal initiator of Caelius' prosecution.[d] Bestia having begun after his acquittal a fresh candidature for the praetorship, Caelius at once formulated a second charge against him,[e] probably not only to clear himself of any suspicion of complicity with Catiline, but

[a] *Pro Caelio*, 35.
[b] *Epp. ad Quintum fratrem*, ii. 3. 6.
[c] Sallust, *Catiline*, 43.
[d] By Münzer, *Hermes*, xliv (1909), pp. 135 f.
[e] *Pro Caelio*, 76.

also to recover some loss of reputation. This second indictment, however, never came into court, since Bestia's son, the young L. Sempronius Atratinus, interposed to save his father by prosecuting Caelius.

II. The Trial of Caelius

The trial was held on 3-4 April 56 B.C., for Cicero, the closing speaker, spoke on 4 April, the first day of the *Ludi Megalenses* (4 to 10 April).[a] The accusation was framed under a *lex de vi*, probably the *lex Plautia*,[b] directed particularly against those who disturbed the public peace by armed bands. In 57 Clodius evaded trial for this offence; and less than a month before the delivery of the *Pro Caelio* Cicero had successfully defended Sestius on a like charge.

Of the five formal charges against Caelius, shortly to be mentioned, all, with the possible exception of that *de bonis Pallae*, would normally have been assigned, under other laws, to other courts. It would have been proper for charges (2), (4) and (5) to have been dealt with by the *quaestio inter veneficos et sicarios*. But the apparent irregularity of the process against Caelius may be explained in two ways. First, trials for *vis* received priority and could be held even during the games (in this case the *Ludi Megalenses*) when the other criminal courts were not in session. Secondly, the prosecution followed a growing practice at that time to extend to other offences the scope of the *lex de vi*.[c]

[a] See Austin, *op. cit.*, Appendix iv, p. 149. Passages in §§ 1 and 78 of the speech help to fix the date.

[b] See p. 32, note *c*.

[c] *Pro Caelio*, 71, with Austin's note.

There were five[a] formal charges against Caelius: (1) *de seditionibus Neapolitanis*; (2) *de Alexandrinorum pulsatione Puteolana*; (3) *de bonis Pallae*; (4) *de Dione*; (5) *de veneno in Clodiam parato*. Of these the first three were dealt with by Crassus, the remaining two by Cicero. The charge, *de seditionibus Neapolitanis*, was probably some dispute at Neapolis such as would normally have been settled by a local court. The second charge, *de Alexandrinorum pulsatione Puteolana*, must, in the silence of our sources, have been associated with the fourth, *de Dione*, an alleged attack by Caelius upon Dio. As the second and fourth charges are connected with the affair of Ptolemy Auletes of Egypt, around which much intrigue had recently gathered, the preliminary account of this which has already been given[b] may be thus amplified. When in 58 Ptolemy had been dethroned by his subjects and had fled from Alexandria to Rome with an eye to restoration by Pompey, the people of Alexandria sent a deputation of one hundred of their citizens, led by Dio, an Academic philosopher, to plead their cause to the Senate. But these envoys were waylaid and massacred by Ptolemy's orders; and it was even hinted that Pompey[c] abetted him. When, amid general indignation, Dio was summoned to make a statement, Ptolemy prevented him from obtaining a hearing by the Senate, and afterwards had him murdered by one P. Asicius. In 56, some time before Caelius' trial, Asicius was prosecuted by C. Licinius Calvus and acquitted on Cicero's defence.[d] The prosecution alleged that Caelius had been in some way implicated in an attack at Puteoli on the

[a] *Pro Caelio*, 23.
[b] See pp. 27-28.
[c] Strabo, xvii. 1. 11.
[d] *Pro Caelio*, 24.

deputation from Alexandria, whether in a casual encounter or in the actual massacre perpetrated by Ptolemy we cannot decide. Further, Caelius was said to have been involved in Asicius' murder of Dio ; and a separate charge, *de Dione*, was that he had made an independent attempt to kill Dio. Although Cicero's flow of words imparts additional obscurity to these allegations and charges, such persistent rumours cannot have been devoid of foundation. It is not impossible that the prosecution were endeavouring to make capital out of the tangled home politics of the moment and, by representing Caelius as a tool of Ptolemy, to aggravate Pompey's embarrassments.

The third charge, *de bonis Pallae*, may have been one of violent dispossession from property, and more substantially based than the other indictments. It must have had some technical importance, as it is specifically mentioned by Quintilian [a] and was dealt with by Caelius in his own speech for the defence, and also by Crassus. Palla is a woman otherwise unknown, but she may possibly be identified with a Palla mentioned by Dio Cassius [b] as the mother or stepmother of L. Gellius Poplicola (a consul of 36 B.C.) who married Sempronia Atratina, adoptive sister of Caelius' prosecutor, Atratinus. Also, it is not improbable that Poplicola is to be identified with a Gellius whom Catullus [c] attacks and who was possibly a rival of Caelius for Clodia's favours. This charge, therefore, may have been a family affair.

The fifth charge, *de veneno in Clodiam parato*, which arose out of that *de Dione*, is treated in detail by

[a] iv. 2. 27. [b] xlvii. 24.
[c] Catullus, 74.

Cicero (§§ 61-69), but in such mysterious language that the truth cannot be established. As, however, some of the detail is too circumstantial to be a complete fabrication, and as the whole affair was obviously common property, this charge must have rested on some underlying basis of fact.

The statement of St. Jerome that the prosecutor L. Sempronius Atratinus was only seventeen years old at the time is fully credible in view of Cicero's references in the speech to his extreme youth. A son of L. Calpurnius Bestia whom Cicero defended, he was probably adopted by some member of the *gens Sempronia* who had himself revived the name of Atratinus and did not wish his branch of the family to become extinct.[a] Atratinus' subsequent career was long and distinguished : augur in 40 ; *legatus pro praetore* in Greece with M. Antonius before or after 40 [b] ; consul in 34 ; *triumphator* in 21, after a proconsulship in Africa. He died in A.D. 7. St. Jerome's mention of him refers to his eminence as an orator.

Atratinus' junior counsel (*subscriptores*) were P. Clodius and L. Herennius Balbus. Clodius was probably some obscure member of the family, for P. Clodius himself, Cicero's enemy, was aedile in 56, and at the time of the trial would have been holding the *Ludi Megalenses*. L. Herennius Balbus, who spoke last for the prosecution, was an old friend of Atratinus' father, but cannot be identified with a man of that name mentioned by Asconius in his commentary on the *Pro Milone*.[c] Caelius spoke in

[a] His adoptive father may have been a Λεύκιος Ἀτρατεῖνος mentioned in an inscription from the Acropolis at Athens, see U. Köhler, *Hermes*, xxx (1895), p. 630.

[b] Dessau 9461.

[c] Asconius, p. 34 (Clark).

his own defence, probably first. He was followed by Crassus and by Cicero, who, according to his usual practice, spoke last.

Whatever lay in the background, the prosecution was certainly instigated by Clodia, with a view to driving her former lover from society.[a] She did not succeed. Although our sources are silent, Caelius' later career proves his acquittal. Save for another attack on him by the Clodii in 54 B.C.,[b] no more is heard of this vendetta. Caelius, probably out of consideration for Cicero, dropped his proposed second prosecution of Bestia.

[a] This view (Austin, *op. cit.*, p. viii) has recently been challenged by T. A. Dorey in " Cicero, Clodia and the *Pro Caelio* " (*Greece and Rome*, 2nd series, v, 1958, pp. 175-180), who suggests that Clodia's part in the case, though important, was only subsidiary and has been deliberately exaggerated by Cicero.

[b] Cicero, *Epp. ad Quintum fratrem*, ii. 13. 2.

III. PRO M. CAELIO ORATIO

1 I. Si quis, iudices, forte nunc adsit ignarus legum, iudiciorum, consuetudinis nostrae, miretur profecto, quae sit tanta atrocitas huiusce causae, quod diebus festis ludisque publicis, omnibus forensibus negotiis intermissis unum hoc iudicium exerceatur, nec dubitet, quin tanti facinoris reus arguatur, ut eo neglecto civitas stare non possit; idem cum audiat esse legem, quae de seditiosis consceleratisque civibus, qui armati senatum obsederint, magistratibus vim attulerint, rem publicam oppugnarint, cotidie quaeri iubeat: legem non improbet, crimen quod versetur in iudicio, requirat; cum audiat nullum facinus, nullam audaciam, nullam vim in iudicium vocari, sed adulescentem illustri ingenio, industria, gratia accusari ab eius filio, quem ipse in iudicium et vocet et vocarit, oppugnari

---

[a] Cicero spoke on 4 April 56 B.C., the opening day of the *Ludi Megalenses*.

[b] Caelius was being tried under the *lex Plautia de vi*, dated to 65–64 B.C. Trials under this law were not subject to adjournment owing to public holidays. On the latest interpretation, its operation was limited to cases of *vis contra privatos*; the *lex Lutatia de vi* (78 B.C.) dealt with *vis contra rem publicam*. See J. Cousin, "*Lex Lutatia de Vi*" (*Revue historique de Droit français et étranger* 1943, pp. 88-94). See also p. 32.

[c] L. Sempronius Atratinus, seventeen-year-old son of

III. A SPEECH IN DEFENCE OF MARCUS CAELIUS

I. If, gentlemen, anyone should happen to be 1
present who is ignorant of our laws, our tribunals and customs, he would, in my opinion, wonder what special gravity there is in this case, in that this trial alone is being held amid festivities and public games, at a time when all legal business is suspended [a]; and he would have no doubt that the defendant is guilty of a crime so heinous that, if it were treated with indifference, the constitution could not survive. The same person when he hears that there is a law, which, when seditious and wicked citizens have made armed onslaught against the Senate, have laid violent hands on magistrates, and have attacked the State, prescribes that an inquiry be held on any and every day,[b] while he would not disapprove of the law, he would seek to know the kind of charge that was before the court. When he hears that no crime, no reckless act, no deed of violence is being tried, but that a young man of brilliant intellect, remarkable application, and influential position, is accused by the son [c] of a man whom he both is preparing to prosecute and has already prosecuted, and that above all he is being attacked

L. Calpurnius Bestia, who was successfully defended by Cicero when prosecuted by Caelius on 11 Feb. 56 B.C. Caelius then began fresh proceedings against Bestia.

autem opibus meretriciis : [Atratini][1] illius pietatem non reprehendat, muliebrem libidinem comprimendam putet, vos laboriosos existimet, quibus otiosis
2 ne in communi quidem otio liceat esse. Etenim si attendere diligenter, existimare vere de omni hac causa volueritis, sic constituetis, iudices, nec descensurum quemquam ad hanc accusationem fuisse, cui, utrum vellet, liceret, nec, cum descendisset, quicquam habiturum spei fuisse, nisi alicuius intolerabili libidine et nimis acerbo odio niteretur. Sed ego Atratino, humanissimo atque optimo adulescenti meo necessario, ignosco, qui habet excusationem vel pietatis vel necessitatis vel aetatis. Si voluit accusare, pietati tribuo, si iussus est, necessitati, si speravit aliquid, pueritiae. Ceteris non modo nihil ignoscendum, sed etiam acriter est resistendum.

3 II. Ac mihi quidem videtur, iudices, hic introitus defensionis adulescentiae M. Caeli maxime convenire, ut ad ea, quae accusatores deformandi huius causa, detrahendae spoliandaeque dignitatis gratia dixerunt, primum respondeam. Obiectus est pater varie, quod aut parum splendidus ipse aut parum pie tractatus a filio diceretur. De dignitate M. Caelius notis ac maio-

[1] Atratini illius *MSS.*: *Klotz, following Muretus, regards* Atratini *as a gloss*: Atratini ipsius *Clark*: *Austin* (*op. cit.* p. 41) *prefers Klotz's text.*

[a] Clodia.

by the wealth of a courtesan,[a] what will he think? that the accuser's sense of duty is excusable, that woman's passions must be checked, and that you, gentlemen, are worked too hard, since even on a public holiday there is no holiday for you. In fact, 2
if you wish to attend carefully, and to form a correct idea of this case as a whole, you will understand, gentlemen, that no one would ever have ventured to take up this case if he had been allowed any choice in the matter; nor, when he had thus demeaned himself, would he have expected a favourable result, unless he were supported by the intolerable passions and unnatural hatred of someone else.[a] As for myself, I pardon Atratinus, who is a most accomplished and excellent young man and a friend of mine; he can plead as an excuse either filial affection, or necessity,[a] or his age. If he was willing to bring the accusation, I put it down to affection; if he was under orders, to necessity; if he had any hopes, to his boyhood. The other accusers have no claim to indulgence; they deserve a most vigorous resistance.

II. I think, gentlemen, that the defence of a 3
young man like Marcus Caelius can best be introduced if I begin by answering what his accusers have said to disgrace my client and to strip him and despoil him of his good name. His father has been made a matter of reproach to him in differing ways, either as himself not living in suitable style,[b] or as having been treated with insufficient respect by his son.[c] In regard to the position he holds, Marcus Caelius,[d] to those who are known to him and to men older

[b] Not befitting his rank as a Roman Knight.

[c] See § 18.

[d] This is M. Caelius the elder.

ribus natu et sine mea oratione et tacitus facile ipse respondet; quibus autem propter senectutem, quod iam diu minus in foro nobiscumque versatur, non aeque est cognitus, ii sic habeant, quaecumque in equite Romano dignitas esse possit, quae certe potest esse maxima, eam semper in M. Caelio habitam esse summam hodieque haberi non solum a suis, sed etiam ab omnibus, quibus potuerit aliqua de causa esse notus.
4 Equitis Romani autem esse filium criminis loco poni ab accusatoribus neque his iudicantibus oportuit neque defendentibus nobis. Nam quod de pietate dixistis, est quidem ista nostra existimatio, sed iudicium certe parentis; quid nos opinemur, audietis ex iuratis; quid parentes sentiant, lacrimae matris incredibilisque maeror, squalor patris et haec praesens maestitia,
5 quam cernitis, luctusque declarat. Nam quod est obiectum municipibus esse adulescentem non probatum suis, nemini umquam praesenti †praetoriani†[1] maiores honores habuerunt quam absenti M. Caelio; quem et absentem in amplissimum ordinem cooptarunt et ea non petenti detulerunt, quae multis petentibus denegarunt; idemque nunc lectissimos viros et nostri ordinis et equites Romanos cum legatione ad

[1] Puteolani *older editions*; *other conjectures are*: Tusculani *Baiter*: Praestutiani *Clark following* Σ: Praetuttiani *Gruter which is probably the correct reading*: Praenestini *Orelli.* *P has* praetoriani, *but the letters* -tori- *have been added later over an erasure.*

---

[a] Because the jury was largely composed of *equites* and Cicero was the son of one.

[b] The reading †*Praestutiani*† of Σ strongly suggests that Praetuttiani is the correct reading and that Caelius' birthplace was Interamnia Praetuttiorum in Picenum.

[c] The municipal Senate, the *decuriones*.

among us, without any defence of mine, and without his saying a word, easily makes answer by being himself; but as for those who are not so well acquainted with him, since his age has for a long time now prevented him from associating with us either in the Forum or privately, let them be assured, that whatever high position a Roman Knight may possess—and it certainly can be very high—that has always been found in the highest degree in Marcus Caelius, and is found there at the present time, not only by his friends but also by all to whom he may for some reason or other have become known. But to be the 4
son of a Roman Knight ought not to have been used as ground for a charge by any accusers, nor before these judges, nor when I speak in defence.[a] For what you have said in reference to filial affection is a matter on which we may form an opinion, but it is the parent who is certainly the judge. What we think, you will learn from the evidence of witnesses on oath; what his parents feel, is plainly shown by the tears and indescribable sorrow of his mother, by the mourning garments of his father, and his misery that you see before you, and by all these signs of grief. As for your reproach that my young client 5
is not esteemed by his fellow-townsmen, there is none of their own burgesses upon whom they[b] have ever conferred higher honours when he was with them, than upon Marcus Caelius when he was away from them. It was during his absence that he was elected into the highest body of men[c] in his town, and they offered him, without his asking, those honours which they refused to many who did ask; they also sent a deputation including very distinguished members of the Order to which I belong and Roman Knights to

hoc iudicium et cum gravissima atque ornatissima laudatione miserunt. Videor mihi iecisse fundamenta defensionis meae, quae firmissima sunt, si nituntur iudicio suorum. Neque enim vobis satis commendata huius aetas esse posset, si non modo parenti tali viro, verum etiam municipio tam illustri ac tam gravi displiceret.

6 III. Equidem, ut ad me revertar, ab his fontibus profluxi ad hominum famam, et meus hic forensis labor vitaeque ratio dimanavit ad existimationem hominum paulo latius commendatione ac iudicio meorum.

Nam quod obiectum est de pudicitia, quodque omnium accusatorum non criminibus, sed vocibus maledictisque celebratum est, id numquam tam acerbe feret M. Caelius, ut eum paeniteat non deformem esse natum. Sunt enim ista maledicta pervulgata in omnes, quorum in adulescentia forma et species fuit liberalis. Sed aliud est male dicere, aliud accusare. Accusatio crimen desiderat, rem ut definiat, hominem ut notet, argumento probet, teste confirmet; maledictio autem nihil habet propositi praeter contumeliam quae si petulantius iactatur, convicium, si facetius
7 urbanitas nominatur. Quam quidem partem accusationis admiratus sum et moleste tuli potissimum esse Atratino datam. Neque enim decebat neque aetas illa postulabat neque, id quod animadvertere poteratis,

attend this trial, and to offer a testimony to his character that was most impressive and most eloquent. I think that I have laid the foundations of my defence, which are most surely laid if they rest upon the judgment of his own townsmen. For you would not consider this young man sufficiently recommended to you, if he had incurred the disapproval not only of such a man as his father but also of a town so distinguished and so important.

III. For my part, if I may pass to my own case, it is 6
from like springs that my life's stream has flowed into widespread repute, and my labours here in the Forum and the conduct of my career have slowly found a somewhat wider entry into general recognition, thanks to the commendation and support of my friends.

Now as to the reproaches cast on his morals, as to all the clamour made by his accusers, not criminal charges but abuse and slander, Marcus Caelius will never feel this so bitterly as to regret that he was born not unhandsome. For such slanders are commonly uttered against all who in their youth have been distinguished by a becoming figure and noble appearance. But abuse is one thing, accusation is another. Accusation requires ground for a charge, to define a fact, to mark a man, to prove by argument, to establish by testimony. The only object of slander, on the other hand, is to insult; if it has a strain of coarseness, it is called abuse; if one of wit, it is called elegance. I was both surprised and annoyed that this 7
part of the accusation was entrusted to Atratinus of all people; for it was not in keeping with him, nor did his age [a] call for it, nor, as you could see for your-

[a] Atratinus was then in his eighteenth year; an older man might be supposed to brazen out such a tone better.

pudor patiebatur optimi adulescentis in tali illum oratione versari. Vellem aliquis ex vobis robustioribus hunc male dicendi[1] locum suscepisset; aliquanto liberius et fortius et magis more nostro refutaremus istam male dicendi licentiam. Tecum, Atratine, agam lenius, quod et pudor tuus moderatur orationi meae et meum erga te parentemque tuum beneficium tueri
8 debeo. Illud tamen te esse admonitum volo, primum ut qualis es talem te esse omnes existiment[2] ut, quantum a rerum turpitudine abes, tantum te a verborum libertate seiungas; deinde ut ea in alterum ne dicas, quae cum tibi falso responsa sint, erubescas. Quis est enim, cui via ista non pateat, qui isti aetati atque etiam isti dignitati non possit quam velit petulanter, etiamsi sine ulla suspicione, at non sine argumento male dicere? Sed istarum partium culpa est eorum, qui te agere voluerunt; laus pudoris tui, quod ea te invitum dicere videbamus, ingenii, quod ornate politeque dixisti.

9 IV. Verum ad istam omnem orationem brevis est defensio. Nam quoad aetas M. Caeli dare potuit isti suspicioni locum, fuit primum ipsius pudore, deinde etiam patris diligentia disciplinaque munita. Qui ut huic virilem togam dedit—nihil dicam hoc loco

[1] *Schöll brackets* male dicendi, *in view of* male dicendi licentiam *that follows.*

[2] primum ut qualis es talem te esse omnes existiment *Klotz. This emendation is translated.*

---

[a] Cicero defended Atratinus' father (Bestia) on 11 Feb. 56 B.C. and may have taught the son public speaking.

[b] The reading is uncertain, but the meaning is clear. He is to take care that men judge him to be the man he actually is, and so he may escape censure.

self, did this excellent young man's sense of propriety make him at home with language of this sort. I could wish that one of the more hardened among you accusers had taken upon himself the part of slanderer; we should have rather more freedom and force, and feel far more natural, in retorting upon such licence of an evil tongue. With you, Atratinus, I will deal more leniently, since your scruples restrain my language, and I feel bound also not to undo the kindness I have done you and your father.[a] I should like, however, to give you a hint: 8
first, in order that all may form a correct view of you,[b] that, just as you are far from baseness in deed, you should keep yourself free from licence in word; next, that you should not bring charges against another which you would blush to hear brought falsely against yourself. For who is there who does not find that road open? Who is there who cannot make some scandalous attack as impudently as he pleases against one of your years, and also of your personal charm, even if with no ground for suspicion, yet not without some basis of accusation? But the blame for the part you have played rests with those who desired you to play it; the credit belongs to your scruples, because we saw with what reluctance you spoke, and to your ability, because you spoke with such grace and refinement.

IV. But to everything you have said, my answer 9
is brief. So far as the age of Marcus Caelius might have given room for such suspicion, it was protected, first by his own conscience, and in the second place by his father's carefulness and severe training. As soon as his father had given him the gown of manhood [c]—

[c] See *Pro Sestio*, 6.

de me; tantum sit, quantum vos existimatis; hoc dicam, hunc a patre continuo ad me esse deductum; nemo hunc M. Caelium in illo aetatis flore vidit nisi aut cum patre aut mecum aut in M. Crassi castissima domo, cum artibus honestissimis erudiretur.

10 Nam quod Catilinae familiaritas obiecta Caelio est, longe ab ista suspicione abhorrere debet. Hoc enim adulescente scitis consulatum mecum petisse Catilinam. Ad quem si accessit aut si a me discessit umquam (quamquam multi boni adulescentes illi homini nequam atque improbo studuerunt), tum existimetur Caelius Catilinae nimium familiaris fuisse. At enim postea scimus et vidimus esse hunc in illius amicis. Quis negat? Sed ego illud tempus aetatis, quod ipsum sua sponte infirmum aliorum libidine infestum est, id hoc loco defendo. Fuit adsiduus mecum praetore me; non noverat Catilinam; Africam tum praetor ille obtinebat. Secutus est tum annus, causam de pecuniis repetundis Catilina dixit. Mecum erat hic; illi ne advocatus quidem venit umquam. Deinceps fuit annus, quo ego consulatum

---

[a] After a young man had assumed the *toga virilis* he was taken to some person of distinction to be taught or trained in public affairs. Such a period was called *tirocinium fori*, a probationary interlude between home and public life.

[b] In 64 B.C.

[c] For this special meaning of *amici* ("political adherents") see R. Syme, *The Roman Revolution*, p. 12; Cicero, *Epp. ad Fam.* v. 7. 1 and 3.

[d] In 66 B.C.

[e] Catiline, back from Africa in summer 66 B.C., was threatened with prosecution for extortion and was prevented by a decision of the presiding consul (L. Volcacius Tullus) from being a candidate at supplementary consular elections

and here I will say nothing about myself (I would be content to leave that to your estimation)—I will only say that he was brought to me at once by his father.[a] No one ever saw this young Marcus Caelius, while he was in that early youth, in the company of anyone but his father or myself, or in the irreproachable household of Marcus Crassus, while he was being trained in the most honourable pursuits.

For as to the reproach of intimacy with Catiline, 10
Caelius has a right to stand wholly clear of any such suspicion. You know that he was still a young man when Catiline was a candidate for the consulship along with myself.[b] If Caelius attached himself to Catiline, or ever separated himself from me—although I admit that many estimable young men were devoted to that wicked and vicious man—then let him be suspected of too great intimacy with Catiline. "Well," you say, "but afterwards we know and have seen that he was among his political adherents." [c] Who denies it? But here I am only defending that period of his youth, which, being so weak in itself, is endangered by the selfish passions of others. Caelius was always with me during my praetorship [d]; he did not know Catiline, who was at that time praetor in Africa.[e] A year passed; Catiline met a charge of extortion; Caelius was with me, and did not even appear to support Catiline in court.[f] Next came the year in which I was a candidate for the

held later in 66 B.C. This refusal was not based on any technical objection but on political grounds.

[f] Catiline was acquitted soon after July 65 B.C., his prosecutor being P. Clodius. Cicero, *Epp. and Att.* i. 2, says that he dallied with the idea of defending him, as an electioneering manœuvre. Catiline's second candidature for the consulship was in 63 B.C.

petivi ; petebat Catilina mecum. Numquam ad illum accessit, a me numquam recessit.

11 V. Tot igitur annos versatus in foro sine suspicione, sine infamia studuit Catilinae iterum petenti. Quem ergo ad finem putas custodiendam illam aetatem fuisse ? Nobis quidem olim annus erat unus ad cohibendum brachium toga constitutus, et ut exercitatione ludoque campestri tunicati uteremur, eademque erat, si statim mereri stipendia coeperamus, castrensis ratio ac militaris. Qua in aetate nisi qui se ipse sua gravitate et castimonia et cum disciplina domestica, tum etiam naturali quodam bono defenderet, quoquo modo a suis custoditus esset, tamen infamiam veram[1] effugere non poterat. Sed qui prima illa initia aetatis integra atque inviolata praestitisset, de eius fama ac pudicitia, cum is iam se corroboravisset ac vir inter viros esset, nemo
12 loquebatur. At[2] studuit Catilinae, cum iam aliquot annos esset in foro, Caelius ; et multi hoc idem ex omni ordine atque ex omni aetate fecerunt. Habuit enim ille, sicuti meminisse vos arbitror, permulta maxi marum non expressa signa, sed adumbrata lineamenta[3] virtutum. Utebatur hominibus improbis multis ; et quidem optimis se viris deditum esse

[1] *There are various conjectures instead of* veram, *which does not require alteration* : meritam *Francken*, adversam *Halm*, metam *Kayser*, morum *Bährens*.

[2] At *is Clark's conjecture, accepted by Klotz.*

[3] lineamenta *added by Francken* : simulacra *Koch*.

---

[a] 63 B.C.

[b] " A picturesque way of putting ' for being on probation.' Literally taken, it means that at this stage extravagant gesture was forbidden " (Austin, *op. cit.* p. 58). *Cf.* Seneca, *Contr. Excerpt.* v. 6 : " apud patres nostros, qui forensia

consulship, together with Catiline; Caelius never attached himself to him, never separated himself from me.

V. It was only after he had constantly for so many 11 years frequented the Forum without reproach or dishonour that he attached himself to Catiline, then[a] a second time a candidate for the consulship. How long then do you think that his youth should have been protected? When I was young, we usually spent a year "keeping our arms in our gown"[b] and, in tunics, undergoing our physical training on the Campus, and, if we began our military service at once, the same practice was followed for our training in camp and in operations. At that age, unless anyone could defend himself by his own strength of character and clean living, by good home training and also by some inborn virtue, however carefully he might be guarded by his own friends he could not escape a scandal backed by truth.[c] But anyone who had kept those first beginnings of youth pure and undefiled, by the time he had grown up and become a man among men, no one would speak evil of his reputation and morals. Yes, Caelius did support Catiline, after he 12 had had several years' training in public life; and many, of all ranks and ages, have done the same. For this Catiline, as I think you remember, showed in himself numerous features of excellence, if not firmly modelled, at least drawn in outline. He associated with many depraved persons. Yes, but he pretended that he was devoted to men of excellent character.

stipendia auspicebantur, nefas putabatur bracchium extra togam exserere."

[c] *i.e.* scandal for which there was some genuine foundation.

simulabat. Erant apud illum illecebrae libidinum multae; erant etiam industriae quidam stimuli ac laboris. Flagrabant vitia libidinis apud illum; vigebant etiam studia rei militaris. Neque ego umquam fuisse tale monstrum in terris ullum puto, tam ex contrariis diversisque et inter se pugnantibus naturae studiis cupiditatibusque conflatum.

13 VI. Quis clarioribus viris quodam tempore iucundior, quis turpioribus coniunctior? quis civis meliorum partium aliquando, quis taetrior hostis huic civitati? quis in voluptatibus inquinatior, quis in laboribus patientior? quis in rapacitate avarior, quis in largitione effusior? Illa vero, iudices, in illo homine mirabilia fuerunt, comprehendere multos amicitia, tueri obsequio, cum omnibus communicare, quod habebat, servire temporibus suorum omnium pecunia, gratia, labore corporis, scelere etiam, si opus esset, et audacia, versare suam naturam et regere ad tempus atque huc et illuc torquere ac flectere, cum tristibus severe, cum remissis iucunde, cum senibus graviter, cum iuventute comiter, cum facinerosis au-
14 daciter, cum libidinosis luxuriose vivere. Hac ille tam varia multiplicique natura cum omnes omnibus ex terris homines improbos audacesque collegerat, tum etiam multos fortes viros et bonos specie quadam virtutis assimulatae tenebat. Neque umquam ex illo delendi huius imperii tam consceleratus impetus exstitisset, nisi tot vitiorum tanta imma-

[a] Cicero may be hinting at Catiline's connexion with Crassus and Caesar in 66–65 B.C.

Men found in him many allurements to debauchery; also certain qualities that were incentives to unflagging toil. The fires of profligacy blazed within him; yet he had a keen interest in the art of war. No, I do not believe that there has ever existed on earth so strange a portent, such a fusion of natural tastes and desires that were contradictory, divergent, and at war amongst themselves.

VI. Who, at one time, could make himself more 13
agreeable to more illustrious persons,[a] who was more closely intimate with baser men? What citizen has at times been a member of a nobler party, or has been a fouler enemy of this State? Who has been more depraved in his sensuality, or more enduring in his toils? Who more covetous in his greed, who more lavish in his generosity? Indeed, gentlemen, there were paradoxical qualities in this man: to attach many by friendship, to retain them by devotion; to share what he possessed with all, to be at the service of all his friends in time of need, with money, influence, personal exertion, and, if it were needful, with reckless crime; to guide and rule his natural disposition as occasion required, and to bend and turn it this way and that; to be serious with the austere, gay with the lax, grave with the old, amiable with the young, daring with criminals, dissolute with the depraved. And so this complex and versatile spirit, at 14
the very time when he had gathered round him every wicked and reckless man from every land, still held fast many good men and true by a kind of semblance of pretended virtue. Nor would that abominable impulse to destroy this Empire ever have broken out from him, had not all those monstrous vices of his been rooted and grounded in certain

nitas quibusdam facultatis[1] et patientiae radicibus niteretur. Quare ista condicio, iudices, respuatur, nec Catilinae familiaritatis crimen haereat; est enim commune cum multis et cum quibusdam etiam bonis. Me ipsum, me, inquam, quondam paene ille decepit, cum et civis mihi bonus et optimi cuiusque cupidus et firmus amicus ac fidelis videretur; cuius ego facinora oculis prius quam opinione, manibus ante quam suspicione deprehendi. Cuius in magnis catervis amicorum si fuit etiam Caelius, magis est ut ipse moleste ferat errasse se, sicuti non numquam in eodem homine me quoque erroris mei paenitet, quam ut istius amicitiae crimen reformidet.

15 VII. Itaque a maledictis pudicitiae[2] ad coniurationis invidiam oratio est vestra delapsa. Posuistis enim, atque id tamen titubanter et strictim, coniurationis hunc propter amicitiam Catilinae participem fuisse; in quo non modo crimen non haerebat, sed vix diserti adulescentis cohaerebat oratio. Qui enim tantus furor in Caelio, quod tantum aut in moribus naturaque volnus aut in re atque fortuna? ubi denique est in ista suspicione Caeli nomen auditum? Nimium multa de re minime dubia loquor; hoc tamen dico: Non modo si socius coniurationis, sed nisi inimicissimus

[1] facilitatis *MSS.*: facultatis *Madvig.*
[2] impudicitiae *Garatoni* (*see Quintil. Inst. Orat. iv. 2. 27*).

[a] *Facultatis*, Madvig's conjecture, is followed.

[b] *Condicio*: the assumption that anyone who was a friend of Catiline must be *infamis*.

[c] In *Epp. ad Att.* i. 1 and 2 Cicero states that in 65 B.C. he was meditating the defence of Catiline for *repetundae*, although he was convinced of his guilt. Asconius (p. 76 Clark) disbelieves the statement of Fenestella that Cicero defended Catiline.

[d] *i.e.* the counsel for the prosecution.

qualities of ability [a] and endurance. Therefore, gentlemen, reject the whole assumption [b] of the prosecution, and let not Caelius' association with Catiline cleave to him as a ground for charge ; for he shares that with many others, and even some of the loyal. I myself, yes, I say, I was once myself nearly deceived by him,[c] when I took him for a loyal citizen, eager for the acquaintance of all the best men, and for a true and faithful friend. I had to see his crimes before I believed them, and to have my hands on them before I even suspected them. If Caelius also was among his crowds of friends, there is more reason why he should himself be troubled at his mistake, just as I too sometimes regret my own with regard to this same man, than that he should be in fear of such a friendship being made a matter of accusation.

VII. And so, beginning with slander against 15
morals, you gentlemen [d] have glided into creating prejudice in the matter of the Conspiracy. For you have alleged—although indeed with hesitation and hints—that Caelius' friendship for Catiline had made him a partner in the Conspiracy ; and as to that, so far from any charge holding good, the speech of our talented young friend hardly held together. Was Caelius such a mad revolutionary, was he so maimed either in character and nature, or in position and fortune ? [e] When, in fact, the suspicion was abroad, where was the name of Caelius heard ? I am wasting words on a matter where there is not the slightest doubt ; but none the less I say this : if Caelius had been privy to the Conspiracy, or even if he had not been bitterly

[e] The contention is that his condition was too sound and healthy to make him join the Catilinarian Conspiracy.

istius sceleris fuisset, numquam coniurationis accusatione adulescentiam suam potissimum commendare
16 voluisset. Quod haud scio an de ambitu et de criminibus istis sodalium ac sequestrium, quoniam huc incidi, similiter respondendum putem. Numquam enim tam Caelius amens fuisset, ut, si se isto infinito ambitu commaculasset, ambitus alterum accusaret, neque eius facti in altero suspicionem quaereret, cuius ipse sibi perpetuam licentiam optaret, nec, si sibi semel periculum ambitus subeundum putaret, ipse alterum iterum ambitus crimine arcesseret. Quod quamquam nec sapienter et me invito facit, tamen est eius modi cupiditas, ut magis insectari alterius innocentiam quam de se timide cogitare videatur.

17 Nam quod aes alienum obiectum est, sumptus reprehensi, tabulae flagitatae, videte, quam pauca respondeam. Tabulas, qui in patris potestate est, nullas conficit. Versuram numquam omnino fecit ullam. Sumptus unius generis obiectus est, habita-

---

[a] For Caelius' prosecution of C. Antonius see pp. 385 and 399, with Austin's Appendix *ad loc.* Alleged complicity with Catiline in 63 B.C. was probably part of the main charge of *maiestas.*

[b] For this rendering of *haud scio an . . . putem* see H. A. Holden, *Cicero, De officiis*, iii. 2. 6, p. 320, note, and Austin, *op. cit.* p. 64, note.

[c] Such a charge was probably based on Caelius' support of the candidature of some friend for office, perhaps that of Bestia in 57 B.C. for the praetorship.

[d] *Sodales* were members of private political clubs formed for purposes of political corruption ; *sequestres* were agents

opposed to that crime, he would never have sought to make a charge of conspiracy the special means of recommending his youthful talents.[a] In this con- 16
nexion I am inclined to think[b] that, since I have reached this point, the same kind of reply is to be made about corruption[c] and these charges concerning political clubs and bribery-agents.[d] For Caelius, had he defiled himself with the "unstinted bribery" you speak of, would never have been so mad as to accuse someone else[e] of bribery, nor would he seek to throw upon another the suspicion of being guilty of such an offence, for which he might wish to enjoy a perpetual licence himself; nor, if he thought that he would have to face the risk of being himself charged with bribery once, would he be likely to accuse another man a second time of the same offence. And, although in this matter he is acting imprudently and against my advice, yet his ambition is such that he seems rather to be attacking the innocence of another than to be apprehensive about himself.

As for the reproach that he is in debt, his ex- 17
penditure blamed, his account-books demanded,[f] see how brief is my reply. One who is still subject to his father's authority does not keep accounts. He has never borrowed any money.[g] He is reproached for extravagance of one kind—his house-

with whom cash for bribery was deposited. These clubs, banned by decree of the Senate on 10 Feb. 56 B.C. (Cic. *Epp. ad Quintum fratrem*, ii. 3. 5), were the subject of a *lex Licinia de sodaliciis* of 55 B.C.

[e] L. Calpurnius Bestia.

[f] See Cicero, *Pro Roscio Comoedo*, 2, 7.

[g] *Versuram facere*, to make a change of creditor by borrowing money from a new, in order to meet an old, creditor.

tionis; triginta milibus dixistis eum habitare. Nunc demum intellego P. Clodi insulam esse venalem, cuius hic in aediculis habitat decem, ut opinor, milibus. Vos autem dum illi placere voltis, ad tempus eius mendacium vestrum accommodavistis.

18 Reprehendistis, a patre quod semigrarit. Quod quidem iam in hac aetate minime reprehendendum est.[1] Qui cum et ex publica causa[2] iam esset mihi quidem molestam, sibi tamen gloriosam victoriam consecutus et per aetatem magistratus petere posset, non modo permittente patre, sed etiam suadente ab eo semigravit et, cum domus patris a foro longe abesset, quo facilius et nostras domus obire et ipse a suis coli posset, conduxit in Palatio non magno domum.

VIII. Quo loco possum dicere id, quod vir clarissimus, M. Crassus, cum de adventu regis Ptolemaei quereretur, paulo ante dixit:

Utinam ne in nemore Pelio—

Ac longius quidem mihi contexere hoc carmen liceret:

Nam numquam era errans

[1] Quod . . . est *bracketed by Schöll.*
[2] ex publica causa *Francken's conjecture confirmed by* Σ.

---

[a] He lodged in a block of houses on the Palatine belonging to P. Clodius.

[b] "Clodius wants people to believe that his block is worth more than it is, and therefore you said that the rent paid by Caelius was thirty thousand." The late Republic saw a great increase in rents, especially on fashionable quarters like the Palatine.

[c] His prosecution of C. Antonius.

[d] No more is meant than that Caelius had entered public life and could embark on the *cursus honorum.*

[e] Those of Cicero and Crassus.

rent,[a] which you said he paid at the rate of thirty thousand sesterces. So now I see why Clodius' block is for sale; the small apartment which Caelius rents from him is let, I believe, for ten thousand. But you, in order to oblige Clodius, have adapted your false statement to suit his turn.[b]

You reproached him for living apart from his father. 18
This cannot now be made a matter of reproach to him at his time of life. He had just won, in a political case, a victory that was annoying to me [c] yet glorious to himself, and, besides, his age allowed him to aspire to public offices [d]; then, not only with the permission of his father, but even with his advice, he separated from him, and since his father's house was a long way from the Forum, in order to be able to visit our houses [e] more easily, and to keep in touch with his own friends, he took a house on the Palatine at a moderate rent.

VIII. On this topic I may repeat what the illustrious Marcus Crassus [f] said just recently, when complaining about the arrival of King Ptolemy:

> Would that in the forest of Pelion (the ship) had not . . .

And if I wished, I could continue the quotation:

> For never would a misled mistress

[f] Crassus spoke second. At the end of 58 B.C. Ptolemy Auletes, who had purchased recognition as king of Egypt in 59 B.C., was expelled from Alexandria and, on arrival in Rome, pressed for reinstatement by Pompey. A deputation from Alexandria led by Dio, an Academic philosopher, followed to present a counterplea to the Senate. Ptolemy, however, had many of the envoys murdered, including Dio. Caelius was alleged by the prosecutors to have been involved in an attack on the deputation at Puteoli and in the murder of Dio in 57 B.C. by P. Asicius. See pp. 402-403.

hanc molestiam nobis exhiberet

> Medea animo aegra, amore saevo saucia.

Sic enim, iudices, reperietis, quod, cum ad id loci venero, ostendam, hanc Palatinam Medeam migrationemque hanc[1] adulescenti causam sive malorum omnium sive potius sermonum fuisse.

19 Quam ob rem illa, quae ex accusatorum oratione praemuniri iam et fingi intellegebam, fretus vestra prudentia, iudices, non pertimesco. Aiebant enim fore testem senatorem, qui se pontificiis comitiis pulsatum a Caelio diceret. A quo quaeram, si prodierit, primum cur statim nihil egerit, deinde, si id queri quam agere maluerit, cur productus a vobis potius quam ipse per se, cur tanto post potius quam continuo queri maluerit. Si mihi ad haec acute arguteque responderit, tum quaeram denique, ex quo iste fonte senator emanet. Nam si ipse orietur et nascetur ex sese, fortasse, ut soleo, commovebor; sin autem est rivolus accersitus

[1] migrationemque huic MS.: migrationemque hanc *Clark*.

---

[a] The verses are from the beginning of the *Medea exsul* of Ennius adapted from the play of Euripides. They are the following (*Remains of Old Latin*, L.C.L., i, pp. 312-313):

> utinam ne in nemore Pelio securibus
> caesa accidisset abiegna ad terram trabes,
> neve inde navis incohandae exordium
> coepisset, quae nunc nominatur nomine
> Argo, quia Argivi in ea delecti viri
> vecti petebant pellem inauratam arietis
> Colchis, imperio regis Peliae, per dolum.
> nam nunquam era errans mea domo ecferret pedem
> Medea, animo aegra, amore saevo saucia.

Crassus quoted the lines to show what a calamity it was that the deputation led by Dio had ever reached Italy.

have caused us this trouble,

> Medea, sick at heart, wounded by cruel love.[a]

Thus, gentlemen, you will learn what I will show when I have reached that point in my speech,[b] that this Medea of the Palatine [c] and his change of residence have been for a young man the cause of all his misfortunes, or rather of all the gossip.

Wherefore, relying upon your good sense, gentlemen, I am not alarmed by the allegations which from the words of the accusers I gather are now being fabricated[d] to support their case. For they asserted that a senator would give evidence to say that he had been assaulted by Caelius at the pontifical elections.[e] I will ask him, in the first place, if he comes forward, why he did not prosecute the matter legally at once; secondly, if he preferred to make a complaint about that rather than to prosecute, why he was brought forward by you rather than came of his own accord, and why he preferred to put off his complaint so long instead of making it at once. If he answers my questions with shrewdness and point, I will then ask, finally, what was the source and origin of that senator? For if he proves to be himself his own source and origin, possibly I may be impressed, as usual; but if he is just a rivu- 19

[b] § 37.

[c] Clodia.

[d] For *praemunitio* see Quintilian, ix. 1. 30: "praemunitio etiam est ad id quod aggrediare" (*i.e.* the building-up of a preliminary position before the main point of a case is reached).

[e] Under the *lex Domitia* (104 B.C.), repealed by Sulla and re-enacted by Caesar (63 B.C.), vacancies in the pontifical and augural colleges were filled by candidates receiving a majority vote of seventeen tribes chosen by lot.

et ductus ab ipso capite accusationis vestrae, laetabor, cum tanta gratia tantisque opibus accusatio vestra nitatur, unum senatorem solum esse, qui vobis gra-
20 tificari vellet, inventum. Nec tamen[1] illud genus alterum nocturnorum testium pertimesco. Est enim dictum ab illis fore, qui dicerent uxores suas a cena redeuntes attrectatas esse a Caelio. Graves erunt homines, qui hoc iurati dicere audebunt, cum sit iis confitendum numquam se ne congressu quidem et constituto coepisse de tantis iniuriis experiri.

IX. Sed totum genus oppugnationis huius, iudices, et iam prospicitis animis et, cum inferetur, propulsare debebitis. Non enim ab isdem accusatur M. Caelius, a quibus oppugnatur; palam in eum tela iaciuntur,
21 clam subministrantur. Neque id ego dico, ut invidiosum sit in eos, quibus gloriosum etiam hoc esse debet. Funguntur officio, defendunt suos, faciunt, quod viri fortissimi solent; laesi dolent, irati efferuntur, pugnant lacessiti. Sed vestrae sapientiae tamen est, iudices, non, si causa iusta est viris fortibus oppugnandi M. Caelium, ideo vobis quoque vos causam putare esse iustam alieno dolori potius quam vestrae fidei consulendi. Nam[2] quae sit multitudo in foro, quae genera, quae studia, quae varietas hominum, videtis.

[1] tantum *MS.*
[2] Nam, *Klotz' reading, is adopted*: iam *Clark.*

---

[a] Clodia.
[b] The senator was probably Q. Fufius Calenus, who as tribune in 61 B.C. contributed to the acquittal of Clodius by persuading the Senate to tactics which resulted in the mismanagement of the case.

let led trickling hither from the very fountain-head [a] of your case, I shall rejoice that, although your case has such influence and such resources to rely on, only one senator [b] has been found willing to oblige you.
Nor, in any case, do I fear that other variety of wit- 20
nesses, gentlemen of the night. For it was said that there will be some ready to declare that their wives, returning from a dinner-party, were indecently handled by Caelius. Men of character will they be who will dare to make such a declaration on oath, though they will have to confess that they have never, not even by any meeting and arrangement, attempted to reach a settlement about such grave wrongs! [c]

IX. But you can already foresee the whole nature of this attack, gentlemen, and when it is launched it will be your duty to repel it. For the real accusers of Marcus Caelius are not those who attack him. The shafts are let fly at him openly: they are furnished by a hidden
hand. Nor do I say this to bring odium upon those [d] 21
to whom this prosecution ought even to be a matter of pride. They are performing a duty, they are defending their friends, they act as men of spirit are wont to act; when injured they are indignant, when angry they fly out, when challenged they fight. But none the less your intelligence, gentlemen, demands that, even if men of spirit have just reason for attacking Marcus Caelius, you also ought not on that account to consider that you have a good reason to pay regard to the resentment of others rather than to your own honour. For you see what crowds of men of all classes, of all pursuits, of many kinds, fill the Forum. Of all

[c] So far from bringing Caelius into court, they make no attempt to reach a settlement out of it.

[d] Cicero means the prosecutor Atratinus.

Ex hac copia quam multos esse arbitramini, qui hominibus potentibus, gratiosis, disertis, cum aliquid eos velle arbitrentur, ultro se offerre soleant, operam
22 navare, testimonium polliceri? Hoc ex genere si qui se in hoc iudicium forte proiecerint, excluditote eorum cupiditatem, iudices, sapientia vestra, ut eodem tempore et huius saluti et religioni vestrae et contra periculosas hominum potentias condicioni omnium civium providisse videamini. Equidem vos abducam a testibus neque huius iudicii veritatem, quae mutari nullo modo potest, in voluntate testium collocari sinam, quae facillime fingi, nullo negotio flecti ac detorqueri potest. Argumentis agemus, signis luce omni clarioribus crimina refellemus; res cum re, causa cum causa, ratio cum ratione pugnabit.

23 X. Itaque illam partem causae facile patior graviter et ornate a M. Crasso peroratam de seditionibus Neapolitanis, de Alexandrinorum pulsatione Puteolana, de bonis Pallae. Vellem dictum esset ab eodem etiam de Dione. De quo ipso tamen quid est quod exspectetis? quod is, qui fecit, aut non timet aut etiam fatetur; est enim rex; qui autem dictus est adiutor

[a] Nothing is known of Caelius' connexions with disturbances at Neapolis or with an attack on the Alexandrian envoys at Puteoli.

[b] Of Palla we have no certain knowledge. But there is some evidence which suggests that she was the mother or stepmother of L. Gellius Poplicola, husband of Sempronia Atratina, adoptive sister of Caelius' prosecutor Atratinus. This Gellius Poplicola was half-brother of L. Marcius Philippus (consul 56 B.C.) and as a witness against P. Sestius in Feb.-Mar. 56 B.C. was fiercely attacked by Cicero (see *Pro Sestio*, 110-112). Ellis' identification of him (*Commentary on Catullus*, p. 443) with the Gellius of Catullus makes him a rival of Caelius and reveals Caelius' prosecution as a family affair. Gellius was consul in 36 B.C.

this number, how many do you think there are ready to offer their services voluntarily, to exert themselves, to promise their evidence to men of power, influence and volubility, when they think they want to obtain something? If, among people of this class, 22
there may be some who have by chance pushed themselves into this trial, do you, gentlemen, shut out their greed by your wisdom, that you may show yourselves to have had a careful regard at one and the same time for the welfare of my client, for your conscience, and for the security of all citizens against dangerous and powerful individuals. For my part I shall not trouble you with witnesses, nor in this case will I allow the real facts, which cannot in any way be changed, to depend on what witnesses choose to say, statements which can be so readily manipulated, so easily bent and distorted from the truth. We will proceed by arguments; we will refute the charges against us by proofs that are clearer than daylight; we will meet facts with facts, cause with cause, reason with reason.

X. Accordingly I am quite content that part of 23
the case has been fully dealt with by Marcus Crassus with such weight and eloquence, that is, the disturbances at Neapolis, the assault on the Alexandrians at Puteoli,[a] the property of Palla.[b] I could wish that he had also spoken of Dio.[c] Yet what more is there that you could expect to hear about him, considering that the author of the deed is either unafraid or even admits responsibility—for he is a king?[d] But the man who was said to have co-

[c] See p. 427, note *f*, and pp. 402-403.

[d] Ptolemy Auletes had admitted responsibility for Dio's murder.

fuisse et conscius, P. Asicius, iudicio est liberatus. Quod igitur est eius modi crimen, ut, qui commisit, non neget, qui negavit, absolutus sit, id hic pertimescat, qui non modo a facti, verum etiam a conscientiae suspicione afuit? Et, si Asicio causa[1] plus profuit quam nocuit invidia, huic oberit tuum maledictum, qui istius facti non modo suspicione, sed ne infamia
24 quidem est aspersus? At praevaricatione est Asicius liberatus. Perfacile est isti loco respondere, mihi praesertim, a quo illa causa defensa est. Sed Caelius optimam causam Asici esse arbitratur; cuicuimodi autem sit, a sua putat eius esse seiunctam. Neque solum Caelius, sed etiam adulescentes humanissimi et doctissimi, rectissimis studiis atque optimis artibus praediti, Titus Gaiusque Coponii, qui ex omnibus maxime Dionis mortem doluerunt, qui cum doctrinae studio atque humanitatis tum etiam hospitio Dionis tenebantur. Habitabat apud Titum, ut audistis, Dio, erat ei cognitus Alexandriae.[2] Quid aut hic aut summo splendore praeditus frater eius de M. Caelio existimet ex ipsis, si producti erunt, audietis.

[1] causa *omitted by Schöll*; in *inserted by Müller before* causa.

[2] *The reading of* Σ *is adopted.*

---

[a] P. Asicius was prosecuted by C. Licinius Calvus and successfully defended by Cicero.

[b] *Praevaricatio*: a technical term for collusion between prosecutor and defendant to secure an acquittal.

[c] As translated by Austin (*op. cit.* pp. 75-76), who suggests as an alternative (p. 77) " men of the highest possible culture and learning, with the advantage of the finest kind of literary training and liberal studies."

[d] In *Pro Balbo*, 53 we learn that they were the grandsons

operated with him and to have been his accomplice, Publius Asicius,[a] has been tried and acquitted. Should, then, an accusation, which is of such a kind that the man who committed the crime does not deny it, while the man who denied it has been acquitted, be dreaded by Caelius who was free from any suspicion not only of guilt, but also of complicity? And, if Asicius derived more benefit from his trial than disadvantage from the odium attaching to it, what harm will your slander do to Caelius, who, in this affair, has not only not been suspected, but not even tainted with aspersion? But, it is argued, Asicius was acquitted 24
through collusion.[b] It is very easy for me to answer upon this point; especially for me, who defended him. But Caelius, although he thinks that Asicius has a very good case, yet, of whatever nature it be, he thinks that Asicius' case is unconnected with his own. And this is not only the opinion of Caelius, but also that of two young men of the highest possible sensibility and scholarship, with the advantages of the finest kind of literary training and the most virtuous principles,[c] Titus and Gaius Coponius,[d] who more than anyone else were deeply affected by the death of Dio, and were attached to him as much by his devotion to learning and to the principles of human conduct as by ties of hospitality. Dio, as you have heard, lodged with Titus, who had made his acquaintance at Alexandria. What he or his most distinguished brother thinks of Marcus Caelius, you will hear from themselves if they appear as witnesses. So then let us 25

of T. Coponius, *civis summa virtute et dignitate.* It is possible that C. Coponius was praetor in 49 B.C. Cicero, *Epp. ad Att.* viii. 12a. 4. A clause, *i.e. seiunctam esse causam putant*, must be supplied from the previous sentence.

25 Ergo haec removeantur, ut aliquando, in quibus causa nititur, ad ea veniamus.

XI. Animadverti enim, iudices, audiri a vobis meum familiarem, L. Herennium, perattente. In quo etsi magna ex parte ingenio eius et dicendi genere quodam tenebamini, tamen non numquam verebar, ne illa subtiliter ad criminandum inducta[1] oratio ad animos vestros sensim ac leniter accederet.[2] Dixit enim multa de luxurie, multa de libidine, multa de vitiis iuventutis, multa de moribus et, qui in reliqua vita mitis esset et in hac suavitate humanitatis, qua prope iam delectantur omnes, versari periucunde soleret, fuit in hac causa pertristis quidam patruus, censor, magister; obiurgavit M. Caelium, sicut neminem umquam parens; multa de incontinentia intemperantiaque disseruit. Quid quaeritis, iudices? ignoscebam vobis attente audientibus, propterea quod egomet tam triste illud et tam asperum genus orationis horrebam.
26 Ac prima pars fuit illa, quae me minus movebat, fuisse meo necessario Bestiae Caelium familiarem, cenasse apud eum, ventitasse domum, studuisse praeturae. Non me haec movent; quae perspicue falsa sunt; etenim eos una cenasse dixit, qui aut absunt, aut quibus necesse est idem dicere. Neque vero illud

[1] instructa *Vollgraf.*
[2] accenderet MS.: accederet (*Clark*) *is preferred.*

[a] Cicero passes to Atratinus' *subscriptor*, L. Herennius Balbus, perhaps a *subscriptor* at the trial of L. Valerius Flaccus (59 B.C.), and a relative of C. Herennius who in 60 B.C. tried to transfer Clodius to the *plebs*. Herennius'

put aside such matters, that we may come at length to those on which the case turns.

XI. Now I noticed, gentlemen, that you listened to my friend, Lucius Herennius,[a] with very great attention. Although, in this connexion, you were markedly influenced by his ability and a particular style in his oratory, still I at times was afraid that his speech, carefully presented[b] to suggest guilt, might imperceptibly and gently steal into your minds. He spoke at length on profligacy, on lust, on the vices of youth, on morals. And, although he was usually a gentle soul and most pleasing in his display of those courteous manners which are now so widely admired, yet in court here he was the grimmest kind of uncle, moralist, mentor. He rebuked Marcus Caelius as a son has never been rebuked by his father : he discoursed at length on wildness and excess. In short, gentlemen, I began to excuse your careful attention, because I myself was listening with horror to his most glum and bitter manner of speech. Well, the first 26
part of it, which affected me but little, was his allegation that Caelius was intimate with my friend Bestia,[c] dined with him, frequently visited him, helped him in his candidature for the praetorship. These allegations do not trouble me ; they are quite evidently false. For he said that certain persons dined with Caelius, and these are either persons who are not here, or who are obliged to tell the same tale.

speech was probably (*a*) a discourse on vices, (*b*) a personal attack on Caelius.

[b] *Inducta* is a metaphor from the theatre, "brought on the scene." See Cicero, *Laelius*, 4 and 59, with Reid's notes *ad loc.*

[c] Father of Atratinus. Caelius is accused of betraying his former friend Bestia by his double prosecution.

me commovet, quod sibi in Lupercis sodalem esse Caelium dixit. Fera quaedam sodalitas et plane pastoricia atque agrestis germanorum Lupercorum, quorum coitio illa silvestris ante est instituta quam humanitas atque leges, siquidem non modo nomina deferunt inter se sodales, sed etiam commemorant sodalitatem in accusando, ut, ne quis id forte nesciat,
27 timere videantur! Sed haec omittam; ad illa, quae me magis moverunt, respondebo.

Deliciarum obiurgatio fuit longa, etiam lenior,[1] plusque disputationis habuit quam atrocitatis, quo etiam audita est attentius. Nam P. Clodius, amicus meus, cum se gravissime vehementissimeque iactaret et omnia inflammatus ageret tristissimis verbis, voce maxima, tametsi probabam eius eloquentiam, tamen non pertimescebam; aliquot enim in causis eum videram frustra litigantem. Tibi autem, Balbe, respondeo primum precario, si licet, si fas est defendi a me eum, qui nullum convivium renuerit, qui in hortis fuerit, qui unguenta sumpserit, qui Baias viderit.[2]

28 XII. Equidem multos et vidi in hac civitate et audivi, non modo qui primoribus labris gustassent

[1] et ea lenior *MSS.*: etiam lenior *Clark.*
[2] viserit *Müller.*

[a] Cicero's account of the origin of the Luperci is not to be taken seriously; he is merely distorting for his own purposes the charge against Caelius, probably one of improper behaviour at the Lupercalia. Caelius and Herennius were members of the college of the Luperci. In the late Republic the prestige of the college of the Luperci was low, even freedmen being eligible for admission. For a further contemptuous reference see Cicero, *Second Philippic*, 85. For full discussions see Frazer, *The Fasti of Ovid*, ii, pp. 327 ff., and Warde Fowler, *The Roman Festivals*, pp. 310 ff.

Nor does it trouble me much that he said that Caelius was a fellow-member of his in the Luperci.[a] The genuine wolf-men were a sort of savage fraternity, quite rude and rustic, who banded together in that woodland pack of theirs before the time of civilization and laws. In fact its members do not merely prosecute one another, but in their indictments even harp on their fraternity, seemingly for fear, I suppose, lest anyone should know nothing of it! But I will say 27
nothing about these matters; I will answer allegations which moved me more deeply.

His rebuking of dissipation was long, also less severe. It was a sermon rather than a diatribe, and so it was listened to with greater attention. As for my friend,[b] Publius Clodius, although he threw himself into most impressive attitudes with the greatest energy, although he was full of fire, and used the sternest language, and taxed his lungs to their loudest, while I thought well of his eloquence, I had no great fear of its effects, for in a good many suits I had seen him unsuccessful as a litigant. But it is you, Balbus,[c] I answer first of all, with your kind permission, if it is lawful or right that I should defend a man who has never refused a dinner, who has been in a park, who has used unguents, and has been to see Baiae.[d]

XII. I have indeed known and heard of many in 28
this country who had not only taken a little sip of this

[b] Cicero's language here suggests that this P. Clodius was not Clodia's brother and his own arch-enemy; more probably he was a less prominent member of the same *gens*.

[c] L. Herennius Balbus.

[d] A fashionable watering-place on the coast of Campania, between Cumae and Puteoli, see § 35. Cicero, *Att.* ii. 8. 2, calls it "cratera illud delicatum."

genus hoc vitae et extremis, ut dicitur, digitis attigissent, sed qui totam adulescentiam voluptatibus dedissent, emersisse aliquando et se ad frugem bonam, ut dicitur, recepisse gravesque homines atque illustres fuisse. Datur enim concessu omnium huic aliqui ludus aetati, et ipsa natura profundit adulescentiae cupiditates. Quae si ita erumpunt, ut nullius vitam labefactent, nullius domum evertant,
29 faciles et tolerabiles haberi solent. Sed tu mihi videbare ex communi infamia iuventutis aliquam invidiam Caelio velle conflare; itaque omne illud silentium, quod est orationi tributum tuae, fuit ob eam causam, quod uno reo proposito de multorum vitiis cogitabamus. Facile est accusare luxuriem. Dies iam me deficiat, si, quae dici in eam sententiam possunt, coner expromere; de corruptelis, de adulteriis, de protervitate, de sumptibus immensa oratio est. Ut tibi reum neminem, sed vitia ista[1] proponas, res tamen ipsa et copiose[2] et graviter accusari potest. Sed vestrae sapientiae, iudices, est non abduci ab reo nec, quos aculeos habeat severitas gravitasque vestra, cum eos accusator erexerit in rem, in vitia, in mores, in tempora, emittere in hominem et in reum, cum is non suo crimine, sed multorum vitio sit in quoddam
30 odium iniustum vocatus. Itaque severitati tuae, ut oportet, ita respondere non audeo; erat enim meum

[1] *Clark's reading of* vitia ista *for* vitia ipsa *of* Σ *is adopted.*
[2] et copiose, *found in* Σ, *was inserted by Naugerius.*

[a] For *conflare* see note on *Pro Sestio*, 66.

kind of life, and touched it, as the proverb says, with the tips of their fingers, but who had given up their youth entirely to sensuality, who have at length risen to the surface and, as they say, turned over a new leaf and have become respectable and distinguished men. For by common consent a young man is allowed some dalliance, and nature herself is prodigal of youthful passions; and if they do find a vent so as not to shatter anyone's life, nor to ruin anyone's home, they are generally regarded as easy to put up
with. But what I thought was that you were using 29
the charges which are made against young men in general to trump up [a] prejudice against Caelius; and so all that silent attention which was accorded to your speech had this for its reason, that, while there was only one defendant brought forward, we were thinking of the vices of many. It is easy to inveigh against profligacy; daylight would soon fail me if I were to endeavour to expose everything which could be said upon that topic: seduction, adultery, wantonness, extravagance, the topic is illimitable. Even with no defendant, but these vices to indict, you yet have ample material for a serious attack against their existence. But your good sense, gentlemen, must not allow you to be diverted from the defendant. Your ideals of strictness and responsibility provide you with a sting; and, since the prosecutor has aroused it against a *topic*, against vices, morals and this age, you must not direct it against a *person* who is facing a charge, when undeserved odium has been called down upon his head, through no fault of his
own but through the failings of many others. And 30
therefore I do not venture to reply as is fitting to your severe remarks—for my answer might have been

deprecari vacationem adulescentiae veniamque petere; non, inquam, audeo; perfugiis non utor aetatis, concessa omnibus iura dimitto; tantum peto, ut, si qua est invidia communis hoc tempore aeris alieni, petulantiae, libidinum iuventutis, quam video esse magnam, ne huic aliena peccata, ne aetatis ac temporum vitia noceant. Atque ego idem, qui haec postulo, quin criminibus, quae in hunc proprie conferuntur, diligentissime respondeam, non recuso.

XIII. Sunt autem duo crimina, auri et veneni; in quibus una atque eadem persona versatur. Aurum sumptum a Clodia, venenum quaesitum, quod Clodiae daretur, ut dicitur. Omnia sunt alia non crimina, sed maledicta, iurgi petulantis magis quam publicae quaestionis. "Adulter, impudicus, sequester" convicium est, non accusatio; nullum est enim fundamentum horum criminum, nulla sedes; voces sunt contumeliosae temere ab irato accusatore nullo auc-
31 tore emissae. Horum duorum criminum video auctorem, video fontem,[1] video certum nomen et caput. Auro opus fuit; sumpsit a Clodia, sumpsit sine teste, habuit, quamdiu voluit. Maximum video signum cuiusdam egregiae familiaritatis. Necare eandem voluit; quaesivit venenum, sollicitavit quos potuit, paravit, locum constituit, attulit.[2] Magnum rursus

[1] *The reading of Σ is followed, as against that of those* MSS. *giving* video fontem, video auctorem.

[2] *Müller's text. For the difficulties see Austin, op. cit. p. 88. The translation follows Austin's reading*: quaesivit venenum, paravit, sollicitavit quos potuit; *and Housman's conjecture*: horam locum constituit, attulit.

---

[a] See § 51 note.

to plead the indulgence allowed to youth and to ask you to pardon it—I say, I do not venture to do that; I do not seek refuge in the plea of his youth; I renounce the rights which are granted to all. All I ask is that, however discreditable young men's debts, excesses and profligacy may be generally regarded at this present time (and I see this feeling is a strong one), the offences of others and the vices of his age and of the times may not damnify Caelius. And yet, while making this claim, I do not object to reply with the most scrupulous care to the particular charges which are brought against him in person.

XIII. Now there are two charges,[a] one about some gold, one about some poison, in which one and the same character is concerned. It is alleged that the gold was taken from Clodia, the poison procured to be given to Clodia. All the other matters complained of are not accusations, but slanders; they smack rather of vulgar vituperation than of a court of justice. To call Caelius an adulterer, a lewd fellow, a dealer in bribes, is abuse, not accusation; there is no foundation for these charges, no ground; they are insulting taunts hurled at random by an accuser who is in a rage and who speaks without any authority.
But as for the two charges I have mentioned, I can 31
see that there is someone in the background, I can see that they have a source, I can see a definite individual as their fountain-head. "Caelius wanted gold, he took it from Clodia, took it without witnesses, and kept it as long as he wanted." I see in this strong evidence of a quite remarkable intimacy. "He wanted to put her to death; he procured poison, prepared it, incited whom he could, fixed on a time and place, brought it." Here, again, I see violent

odium video cum crudelissimo discidio exstitisse. Res est omnis in hac causa nobis, iudices, cum Clodia, muliere non solum nobili, sed etiam nota; de qua ego
32 nihil dicam nisi depellendi criminis causa. Sed intellegis pro tua praestanti prudentia, Cn. Domiti, cum hac sola rem esse nobis. Quae si se aurum Caelio commodasse non dicit, si venenum ab hoc sibi paratum esse non arguit, petulanter facimus, si matrem familias secus, quam matronarum sanctitas postulat, nominamus. Sin ista muliere remota nec crimen ullum nec opes ad oppugnandum Caelium illis relinquuntur, quid est aliud quod nos patroni facere debeamus, nisi ut eos, qui insectantur, repellamus? Quod quidem facerem vehementius, nisi intercederent mihi inimicitiae cum istius mulieris viro—fratre volui dicere; semper hic erro. Nunc agam modice nec longius progrediar quam me mea fides et causa ipsa coget. Neque enim muliebres umquam inimicitias mihi gerendas putavi, praesertim cum ea quam omnes semper amicam omnium potius quam cuiusquam inimicam putaverunt.

33 XIV. Sed tamen ex ipsa quaeram prius utrum me secum severe et graviter et prisce agere malit an remisse et leniter et urbane. Si illo austero more ac

[a] Cn. Domitius Calvinus, a praetor, was president of the court. He had already presided at the trial of L. Calpurnius Bestia *de ambitu* on 11 February. Since the trial of P. Sestius *de vi* (10 February to 11 March) was presided over by M. Aemilius Scaurus, a certain latitude was apparently permissible in the allocation of courts to presidents even after arrangements for the year had been completed. An enigmatic figure, Domitius when tribune in 59 B.C. supported Bibulus against Caesar, but after his consulship in 53 B.C. became a prominent Caesarian.

hatred had taken shape with a most distressing rupture. In this case, gentlemen, we are concerned entirely with Clodia, a woman not only of noble birth, but also of notoriety, of whom I will say no more than what is necessary to repel the charge. But you, with your great wisdom, Gnaeus Domitius,[a] 32
understand that it is with this woman alone that we have to deal. If she denies that she lent Caelius gold, if she does not allege that he tried to poison her, we are behaving disgracefully in using a matron's name otherwise than as a matron's virtue demands.[b] But if with this woman removed from the case, our enemies have no accusation left nor means to attack Caelius, what other course is open to us who are his counsel than to refute those who attack him? And that I should do with all the more vehemence, were I not hindered by my personal enmity to that woman's husband—I meant to say brother [c]; I always make that slip. As it is, I will act with moderation, and go no farther than my duty to my client and the case itself compel me. For indeed I never thought that I should have to engage in quarrels with women, still less with a woman whom everyone has always thought to be everyone's friend rather than anyone's enemy.[d]

XIV. Nevertheless I will first inquire of herself, 33
whether she prefers me to deal with her severely, solemnly, and in an old-fashioned manner, or mildly, gently, and in a modern way. If in the old grim

[b] Clodia's behaviour is quite inconsistent with her position as a *matrona*.

[c] Cicero's enmity with P. Clodius dated from the latter's trial for impiety in 61 B.C.

[d] See Quintilian, ix. 2. 29. The word *amica* means either "mistress" or "friend."

modo, aliquis mihi ab inferis excitandus est ex barbatis illis non hac barbula, qua ista delectatur, sed illa horrida, quam in statuis antiquis atque imaginibus videmus, qui obiurget mulierem et pro me loquatur, ne mihi ista forte suscenseat. Exsistat igitur ex hac ipsa familia aliquis ac potissimum Caecus ille; minimum enim dolorem capiet, qui istam non videbit.
34 Qui profecto, si exstiterit, sic aget ac sic loquetur: "Mulier, quid tibi cum Caelio, quid cum homine adulescentulo, quid cum alieno? Cur aut tam familiaris huic fuisti, ut aurum commodares, aut tam inimica, ut venenum timeres? Non patrem tuum videras, non patruum, non avum, non proavum, non abavum, non[1] atavum audieras consules fuisse; non denique modo te Q. Metelli matrimonium tenuisse sciebas, clarissimi ac fortissimi viri patriaeque amantissimi, qui simul ac pedem limine extulerat, omnes prope cives virtute, gloria, dignitate superabat? Cum ex amplissimo genere in familiam clarissimam nupsisses, cur tibi Caelius tam coniunctus fuit? cognatus, adfinis, viri

[1] non atavum non ΣB: atavum *cett.* non abavum, non atavum *Clark*.

---

[a] The following passage, a variety of the rhetorical figure known as προσωποποιία, a "speech in character," by which an impersonation of Appius Claudius Caecus was given, not only aroused the admiration of ancient critics (*e.g.* Quintilian, iii. 8. 54; xii. 10. 61) but also was so skilfully introduced that Cicero must soon have known that his case was won.

[b] Appius Claudius Caecus, builder as censor in 312 B.C. of the first stretch of the Via Appia and of the Aqua Appia, was consul in 307 and 296 B.C. In 280 B.C. he persuaded the Senate to reject Pyrrhus' offer of peace (Plutarch, *Pyrrh.* 19).

[c] *i.e.* of any of the family.

mode and method, then I must call up from the dead [a] one of those full-bearded men of old—not with a trim modern beardlet that she delights in, but a rough one, like those we see on old statues and busts—to rebuke the woman and speak instead of me, so that she may not perhaps be angered with me. Let me therefore call up some member of this very family, above all Appius Claudius the Blind,[b] for he will feel the least [c] sorrow since he will not be able to see her.
If he appears, this assuredly is how he will plead, 34
this is how he will speak : " Woman, what hast thou to do with Caelius, with a stripling, with a stranger ? Why hast thou been either so intimate with him as to lend him gold, or such an enemy as to fear poison ? Hadst thou not seen that thy father, hadst thou not heard that thy uncle, thy grandfather, thy great-grand-father, thy great-great-grandfather and his father were consuls ? [d] Lastly, didst thou not know that lately thou hadst in marriage Quintus Metellus, a most illustrious and most courageous man, most devoted to his country, who had only to step outside his own door to surpass nearly all his fellow-citizens in courage, in glory and in prestige ? [e] When thou hadst passed, by marriage, from a family of high nobility into a most illustrious house, why was Caelius so closely connected with thee ? Kinsman ? Relative by marriage ? Friend of thine husband ?

[d] In 79, 92, 143, 177, 212, and 249 B.C.

[e] Q. Metellus Celer, praetor 63, consul 60 B.C., died in March or April 59 B.C. as governor designate of Gallia Narbonensis. His wife and cousin, Clodia, with whom he was on bad terms, was suspected of having poisoned him. When consul he opposed Clodius' attempt to secure plebeian status.

tui familiaris? Nihil eorum. Quid igitur fuit nisi quaedam temeritas ac libido? Nonne te, si nostrae imagines viriles non commovebant, ne progenies quidem mea, Q. illa Claudia, aemulam domesticae laudis in gloria muliebri esse admonebat, non virgo illa Vestalis Claudia, quae patrem complexa triumphantem ab inimico tribuno plebei de curru detrahi passa non est? Cur te fraterna vitia potius quam bona paterna et avita et usque a nobis cum in viris tum etiam in feminis repetita moverunt? Ideone ego pacem Pyrrhi diremi, ut tu amorum turpissimorum cotidie foedera ferires, ideo aquam adduxi, ut ea tu inceste uterere, ideo viam munivi, ut eam tu alienis viris comitata celebrares?"

35 XV. Sed quid ego, iudices, ita gravem personam induxi, ut verear, ne se idem Appius repente convertat et Caelium incipiat accusare illa sua gravitate cen-

---

[a] Perhaps a granddaughter of Appius Claudius Caecus and daughter of Publius Claudius Pulcher (consul 249 B.C.), a Roman matron. When the image of Cybele was being removed from Pessinus to Rome, the vessel grounded in a shallow at the mouth of the Tiber. Claudia, who had been suspected of immorality, proved her innocence by drawing it free. (See Livy xxix. 14; Ovid, *Fasti*, iv. 305; Cicero, *De haruspicum responsis*, xiii. 27.)

[b] The daughter or sister of Appius Claudius Pulcher, consul 143 B.C. Her protection of her father from the menacing populace enabled him to triumph, *minore dignitate* it would seem, over the Salassi, a semi-Alpine tribe in the north-west of Cisalpine Gaul (Livy, *Per.* 53).

[c] His speech which moved the Senate to refuse peace with

None of these. What then was thy reason, if it was not some reckless passion? If the images of the men of our family did not touch thine heart, did not even the famous Quinta Claudia,[a] a daughter of my own race, rouse thee to show thyself a rival of those virtuous women who have brought glory upon our house? Wast thou not roused by Claudia, that famous Vestal who, at her father's triumph, held him in her embrace and did not suffer him to be dragged down from his chariot by a hostile tribune of the commons?[b] Why did thy brother's vices move thee rather than the virtues of thy father and of thine ancestors, kept alive since my time not only by the men but also by the women of our family? Was it for this that I tore up the peace with Pyrrhus,[c] that thou mightest daily strike bargains about thine infamous amours? Was it for this that I brought water[d] to Rome, that thou mightest use it after thy incestuous debauches? Was it for this that I built up a road,[e] that thou mightest frequent it with a train of other women's husbands?"

XV. But why, gentlemen, have I introduced a 35
personage so austere, that I am afraid lest that same Appius should suddenly turn and begin to accuse Caelius with that severity of his befitting a censor?

Pyrrhus was extant in Cicero's time, see *De Senectute*, vi. 16; *Brutus*, 61; Quintilian, ii. 16. 7.

[d] The first Roman aqueduct was constructed by Appius Claudius Caecus in 312 B.C. The intake, from springs never satisfactorily identified, was about seven Roman miles to the E. of the city. See Platner and Ashby, *op. cit.* p. 21.

[e] Appius Claudius Caecus in 312 B.C. began the construction of the Via Appia from Rome to Capua (Livy, ix. 29). By 244 B.C., possibly, it had been extended to Brundisium, through Beneventum, Venusia and Tarentum.

soria? Sed videro hoc posterius, atque ita, iudices, ut vel severissimis disceptatoribus M. Caeli vitam me probaturum esse confidam. Tu vero, mulier, (iam enim ipse tecum nulla persona introducta loquor) si ea, quae facis, quae dicis, quae insimulas, quae moliris, quae arguis, probare cogitas, rationem tantae familiaritatis, tantae consuetudinis, tantae coniunctionis reddas atque exponas necesse est. Accusatores quidem libidines, amores, adulteria, Baias, actas, convivia, comissationes, cantus, symphonias, navigia iactant, idemque significant nihil se te invita dicere. Quae tu quoniam mente nescio qua effrenata atque praecipiti in forum deferri iudiciumque voluisti, aut diluas oportet ac falsa esse doceas aut nihil neque crimini tuo neque testimonio credendum esse fateare.

36 Sin autem urbanius me agere mavis, sic agam tecum; removebo illum senem durum ac paene agrestem; ex his igitur tuis sumam aliquem ac potissimum minimum fratrem, qui est in isto genere urbanissimus; qui te amat plurimum, qui propter nescio quam, credo, timiditatem et nocturnos quosdam inanes metus tecum semper pusio cum maiore sorore cubitavit. Eum putato tecum loqui: "Quid tumultuaris, soror? quid insanis?

Quid clamorem exorsa verbis parvam rem magnam facis?

---

[a] For some aspects of life at Baiae see Seneca, *Epp.* 51. 4 and 12.

[b] *i.e.* because Clodia had taken part in them all and so was discredited.

[c] A verse from some comic poet—perhaps Caecilius Statius, writer of comedies (*c.* 219–168 B.C.), many adapted from Menander. Cicero (*De optimo genere oratorum*, i. 2)

But I will attend to this later, and in such a manner, gentlemen, that I feel confident I shall be able to justify the life of Marcus Caelius even to the severest judges. But as for you, woman (for now it is myself alone and not an imaginary person who addresses you), if you have an intention of proving your deeds, your words, your assertions, your intrigues, your allegations, you will have to render an account of and explain such intimacy, such familiarity, such a close connexion. The accusers are dinning into our ears the words debauchery, amours, misconduct, trips to Baiae,[a] beach-parties, feasts, revels, concerts, musical parties, pleasure-boats; they also inform us that they say nothing of which you do not approve. And since in some mad and reckless frame of mind you have desired that these matters should be brought into the Forum and into court, you must either disprove them, and show that they are false, or else you must confess that neither your accusation nor your evidence is to be believed.[b]

But if you prefer that I should take a more refined 36
tone, I will proceed with you in this way. I will dismiss that uncouth and almost rustic old man, and accordingly take one of your present relatives, and by choice your youngest brother, who is in that respect a perfect man of the world; who loves you most dearly; who, I suppose, being a prey to a sort of nervousness and certain idle terrors at night, always when a little fellow went to bed with you, his elder sister. Imagine him saying to you, "Sister, why are you making such a to-do? Why have you lost your senses?

Why do you shout so loud, why do you fuss about a trifle?[c]

calls him *fortasse summus comicus*, and in his speeches delivered between 56 and 54 B.C. quotes frequently from him.

Vicinum adulescentulum aspexisti; candor huius te et proceritas, vultus oculique pepulerunt; saepius videre voluisti; fuisti non numquam in isdem hortis; vis nobilis mulier illum filium familias patre parco ac tenaci habere tuis copiis devinctum; non potes; calcitrat, respuit, non putat tua dona esse tanti; confer te alio. Habes hortos ad Tiberim ac diligenter eo loco paratos,[1] quo omnis iuventus natandi causa venit; hinc licet condiciones cotidie legas; cur huic, qui te spernit, molesta es?"

37 XVI. Redeo nunc ad te, Caeli, vicissim ac mihi auctoritatem patriam severitatemque suscipio. Sed dubito, quem patrem potissimum sumam, Caecilianumne aliquem vehementem atque durum:

> Nunc enim demum mi animus ardet, nunc meum cor cumulatur ira

aut illum:

> O infelix, o sceleste!

Ferrei sunt isti patres:

> Egon quid dicam, quid velim? quae tu omnia
> Tuis foedis factis facis ut nequiquam velim,

vix ferendi.[2] Diceret talis pater: "Cur te in istam vicinitatem meretriciam contulisti? cur illecebris cognitis non refugisti?

paratos (*ZB*) *is to be preferred to* parasti (*P*).
[2] *Clark's text is adopted.*

---

[a] For this meaning of *condicio* see Tyrrell and Purser on Cicero, *Epp. ad Brutum*, i. 17. 7 (vol. vi, p. 166); Reid on Cicero, *Laelius*, 34.

[b] Old men in the comedies of Caecilius were notoriously ill-tempered (Cicero, *Pro Roscio Amerino*, 46).

A neighbour, a young man, caught your eye; his beauty, his tall figure, his looks and eyes took you by storm; you wanted to see him often; you were sometimes with him in the same park; you are a great lady, and by your wealth you want to keep hold of a young fellow who has a mean and niggardly father; you cannot do it; he kicks, treats you with contempt; he does not think your gifts are worth so much; well, try a choice elsewhere. You have grounds by the Tiber purposely procured just at the place where all the young men come to bathe; from there you may pick up marriage proposals[a] any day; why do you worry this man who disdains your advances?"

XVI. I come now to you in turn, Caelius, and myself assume the authority and severity of a father. 37
But I doubt which father above all I am to choose—a rough and unfeeling one, like the one in Caecilius?[b]

> For now at last my mind's afire,
> My heart is full of wrath—

or this one:

> O miserable villain![c]

Those fathers have hearts of iron:

> What am I to say? What am I to wish? Whate'er you do,
> By your disgraceful deeds you make my wishes vain.

They are almost unendurable. Such a father would say: "Why have you betaken yourself to the neighbourhood of that courtesan? Why did you not flee as soon as you found out her allurements?

[c] See Austin, *op. cit.* p. 99 for a statement of the textual and metrical difficulties in this and the following lines.

Cur alienam ullam mulierem nosti? Dide ac disice;
Per me tibi licet. Si egebis, tibi dolebit, non mihi.
Mihi sat est qui aetatis quod relicuom est oblectem meae."

38 Huic tristi ac derecto seni responderet Caelius se nulla cupiditate inductum de via decessisse. Quid signi? Nulli sumptus, nulla iactura, nulla versura. At fuit fama. Quotus quisque istam effugere potest in tam maledica civitate? Vicinum eius mulieris miraris male audisse, cuius frater germanus sermones iniquorum effugere non potuit? Leni vero et clementi patre, cuius modi ille est:

Fores ecfregit, restituentur; discidit
Vestem, resarcietur,

Caeli[1] causa est expeditissima. Quid enim esset, in quo se non facile defenderet? Nihil iam in istam mulierem dico; sed, si esset aliqua dissimilis istius, quae se omnibus pervolgaret, quae haberet palam decretum semper aliquem, cuius in hortos, domum, Baias iure suo libidines omnium commearent, quae etiam aleret adulescentes et parsimoniam patrum suis sumptibus sustentaret; si vidua libere, proterva petulanter, dives effuse, libidinosa meretricio more viveret, adulterum ego putarem, si quis hanc paulo liberius salutasset?

39 XVII. Dicet aliquis: "Haec est igitur tua disci-

[1] MSS. fili: Caeli *Angelius*.

---

[a] See § 17.
[b] The words of a kind father in Terence, *Adelphi* 120-121
[c] Clodia.

Why have you become acquainted with a strange woman?
Scatter and squander;
You may do as you please for all I care. 'Tis you, not I, who'll rue your poverty.
I have enough whereon to live what remains of my life in comfort."

To this glum and outspoken old man Caelius 38 would reply that no mad passion caused him to stray from the right path. What proof of this would he give? No extravagance, no waste, no borrowing to pay his debts.[a] "But it was reported that there was." How few are there who can avoid such reports in so slanderous a city! Are you surprised that a neighbour of this woman gained a bad repute, when her own brother has been unable to escape slanderous tongues? But if I take a mild and indulgent father like this one, who would say:

He has broken a door, the wreck shall be made good;
He has torn your clothes, they shall be mended up,[b]

Caelius' case is quite without difficulty. For what charge could there be on which he would not find it easy to defend himself? I am not now saying anything against that woman,[c] but suppose it were someone quite unlike her—a woman who made herself common to all, who openly had some special lover every day, into whose grounds, house and place at Baiae every rake had a right of free entry, who even supported young men, and made their fathers' stinginess bearable at her own expense; if a widow were casting off restraints, a frisky widow living frivolously, a rich widow living extravagantly, an amorous widow living a loose life, should I regard any man guilty of misconduct if he had been somewhat free in his attentions to her?

XVII. But someone will say: "Is this then your 39

plina? sic tu instituis adulescentes? ob hanc causam tibi hunc puerum parens commendavit et tradidit, ut in amore atque in voluptatibus adulescentiam suam collocaret, et ut hanc tu vitam atque haec studia defenderes?" Ego, si quis, iudices, hoc robore animi atque hac indole virtutis atque continentiae fuit, ut respueret omnes voluptates omnemque vitae suae cursum in labore corporis atque in animi contentione conficeret, quem non quies, non remissio, non aequalium studia, non ludi, non convivia delectarent,[1] nihil in vita expetendum putaret, nisi quod esset cum laude et cum dignitate coniunctum, hunc mea sententia divinis quibusdam bonis instructum atque ornatum puto. Ex hoc genere illos fuisse arbitror Camillos, Fabricios, Curios omnesque eos, qui haec ex minimis tanta fecerunt. Verum haec genera virtutum non solum in moribus nostris, sed vix iam in libris reperiuntur. Chartae quoque, quae illam pristinam severitatem continebant, obsoleverunt; neque solum apud nos, qui hanc sectam rationemque vitae re magis quam verbis secuti sumus, sed etiam apud Graecos, doctissimos homines, quibus, cum facere non possent, loqui tamen et scribere honeste et magnifice licebat, alia quaedam mutatis Graeciae temporibus prae-

[1] convivium delectaret *Clark*: convivia delectarent *Klotz.*

---

[a] For the meaning of *ludi* in such a context see Austin, *op. cit.*, note on § 28, p. 84.

[b] M. Furius Camillus, as dictator, captured Veii in 396 B.C. and saved Rome after the Gallic invasion (387 B.C.). C. Fabricius Luscinus (consul 282 B.C.) saved Thurii from the Lucanians; was consul (278 B.C.) in the Pyrrhic War, and

code of morality? Is this the way you train young
men? Was this the reason why his father recommended and entrusted this lad to you, that he might
spend his youth in love and pleasures, and that you
yourself should defend such a life and such pursuits?"
For myself, gentlemen, if there ever was a man of
mind strong enough, of character sufficiently virtuous
and self-controlled, to despise all pleasures and spend
the whole course of his life in bodily labour and mental
exertion; to be insensible to the attractions of rest, of
relaxation, of the pursuits of his friends, of love-affairs[a]
and festivities; to think that nothing in life was
worth striving for unless it was united with glory and
honour—such a man, in my judgment, I hold to have
been endowed and blessed with virtues greater than
human. Such I think were those famous Camilli,
Fabricii, Curii,[b] and all those who made Rome so
great that was once so small. But virtues of this kind 40
are no longer to be found in our manners, indeed but
rarely in our books. The papers [c] also that recorded
this old-world austerity have gone out of fashion;
and not only among us who have followed this path
and rule of life in practice rather than in theory, but
also among the Greeks, men of profound learning,
who in their speech and in their writing, but not in
their actions, could reach honour and brilliance,
have precepts of another kind come into fashion now

in the winter of 278–277 B.C. triumphed over Lucanians, Samnites, Tarentines and Bruttians. M'. Curius Dentatus (consul 290, 284 (*suffectus*), 275, 274 B.C.) conquered Samnites, Sabines and Lucanians; defeated Pyrrhus near Malventum (later Beneventum); retired to a Sabine farm. These were typical early Republican heroes of Roman rhetoric.

[c] Possibly by *libri* Cicero refers to works in actual circulation, by *chartae* to the original parchments.

41 cepta exstiterunt. Itaque alii voluptatis causa omnia sapientes facere dixerunt, neque ab hac orationis turpitudine eruditi homines refugerunt; alii cum voluptate dignitatem coniungendam putaverunt, ut res maxime inter se repugnantes dicendi facultate coniungerent; illud unum derectum iter ad laudem cum labore qui probaverunt, prope soli iam in scholis sunt relicti. Multa enim nobis blandimenta natura ipsa genuit, quibus sopita virtus coniveret interdum; multas vias adulescentiae lubricas ostendit, quibus illa insistere aut ingredi sine casu aliquo aut prolapsione vix posset; multarum rerum iucundissimarum varietatem dedit, qua non modo haec aetas, sed
42 etiam iam corroborata caperetur. Quam ob rem si quem forte inveneritis, qui aspernetur oculis pulchritudinem rerum, non odore ullo, non tactu, non sapore capiatur, excludat auribus omnem suavitatem, huic homini ego fortasse et pauci deos propitios, plerique autem iratos putabunt.

XVIII. Ergo haec deserta via et inculta atque interclusa iam frondibus et virgultis relinquatur; detur aliquid aetati[1]; sit adulescentia liberior; non omnia voluptatibus denegentur; non semper superet vera illa et derecta ratio; vincat aliquando cupiditas

[1] detur aliqui ludus aetati *Clark.*

---

[a] Greek independence was lost in 146 B.C. after war between Rome and the Achaean League.

[b] The Epicureans, whose theory of "pleasure," disliked by Cicero, was often misinterpreted. Seneca, *Contr.* ii. 6. 2: "quidam summum bonum dixerunt voluptatem et omnia ad corpus rettulerunt."

that the times have changed for Greece.[a] And so, 41
some [b] have said that the wise do everything for the sake of pleasure, and learned men have not shrunk from this disgraceful statement; others [c] have imagined that virtue could be combined with pleasure, so as to unite by the wit of words two things that are eminently incompatible; and those [d] who have shown that the only straightforward path to glory is the path of toil, are now left almost deserted in their lecture-rooms. For many are the allurements to which nature of her own accord has given birth, such as can lull virtue to rest at times and cause her to relax her vigilance; she has put before the young many slippery paths, on which they can scarcely keep their footing or even enter without falling or stumbling; she has presented them with a variety of delightful things, adapted to charm not only youth, but even
the settled strength of maturity. And so, if by chance 42
you find anyone who despises the sight of beautiful things, whom neither scent nor touch nor taste seduces, whose ears are deaf to all sweet sounds—such a man I, perhaps, and some few will account heaven's favourite, but most the object of its wrath.

XVIII. Let us therefore forsake this abandoned and neglected track now blocked by branches and undergrowth; let some allowance be made to age; let youth be allowed greater freedom; let not pleasures always be forbidden; let not that upright and unbending reason always prevail; let desire and

[c] The doctrine of the Academics and Peripatetics, midway between that of the Stoics and Epicureans, was that the chief good lay in joining virtue to bodily pleasure.

[d] The Stoics held the supreme good to be *honesta actio*, the rational selection of things in themselves agreeable to nature (*i.e.* to reason).

voluptasque rationem, dum modo illa in hoc genere praescriptio moderatioque teneatur: parcat iuventus pudicitiae suae, ne spoliet alienam, ne effundat patrimonium, ne faenore trucidetur, ne incurrat in alterius domum atque famam, ne probrum castis, labem integris, infamiam bonis inferat, ne quem vi terreat, ne intersit insidiis, scelere careat; postremo, cum paruerit voluptatibus, dederit aliquid temporis ad ludum aetatis atque ad inanes hasce adulescentiae cupiditates, revocet se aliquando ad curam rei domesticae, rei forensis reique publicae, ut ea, quae ratione antea non perspexerat, satietate abiecisse, experiendo contempsisse videatur.

43 Ac multi et nostra et patrum maiorumque memoria, iudices, summi homines et clarissimi cives fuerunt, quorum cum adulescentiae cupiditates defervissent, eximiae virtutes firmata iam aetate exstiterunt. Ex quibus neminem mihi libet nominare; vosmet vobiscum recordamini. Nolo enim cuiusquam fortis atque illustris viri ne minimum quidem erratum cum maxima laude coniungere. Quod si facere vellem, multi a me summi atque ornatissimi viri praedicarentur, quorum partim nimia libertas in adulescentia, partim profusa luxuries, magnitudo aeris alieni, sumptus, libidines nominarentur, quae multis postea virtutibus obtecta adulescentiae, qui vellet, excusatione defenderet.

---

[a] Perhaps an allusion to Julius Caesar.

[b] According to Aulus Gellius (vi. 8) it was rumoured that Scipio Africanus Major in his youth had not an untarnished reputation, and Polybius says (x. 19) of him *φιλογύνην ὄντα Πόπλιον*.

pleasure sometimes triumph over reason, provided that in such matters the following rule and limitation is observed: let a young man be mindful of his own repute and not a despoiler of another's; let him not squander his patrimony; nor be crippled by usury; nor attack the home and reputation of another; nor bring shame upon the chaste, taint upon the virtuous, disgrace upon the upright; let him frighten none by violence, quit conspiracy, keep clear of crime. Lastly, when he has listened to the voice of pleasure and given some time to love-affairs and these empty desires of youth, let him at length turn to the interests of home life, to activity at the bar and in public affairs, so that all those pursuits the vanity of which reason had previously failed to reveal, he may show that he has abandoned from satiety and found contemptible through experience.

And, gentlemen, both in our own days and within 43
the memory of our fathers and ancestors, there have been many great men and illustrious citizens who, after the passions of youth had simmered down, have in their maturer years been eminently conspicuous for their virtues.[a] I do not care to mention any of them by name; do you recall them for yourselves.[b] For I do not wish to associate the high renown of any brave and illustrious citizen with even the slightest fault. Were that my wish I could bring forward the names of many men of the highest rank and distinction who were notorious, some for gross licentiousness in youth, some for utter profligacy, vast debts, extravagances, sensual excesses, but whose failings were afterwards so covered over by numerous virtues, that anyone who wished could excuse them on the plea of youth.

44 XIX. At vero in M. Caelio (dicam enim iam confidentius de studiis eius honestis, quoniam audeo quaedam fretus vestra sapientia libere confiteri) nulla luxuries reperietur, nulli sumptus, nullum aes alienum, nulla conviviorum ac lustrorum libido : quod quidem vitium ventris et gurgitis non modo non minuit aetas hominibus, sed etiam auget. Amores autem et hae deliciae, quae vocantur, quae firmiore animo praeditis diutius molestae non solent esse (mature enim et celeriter deflorescunt), numquam hunc occupatum
45 impeditumque tenuerunt. Audistis, cum pro se diceret, audistis antea, cum accusaret (defendendi haec causa, non gloriandi eloquor) ; genus orationis, facultatem, copiam sententiarum atque verborum, quae vestra prudentia est, perspexistis ; atque in eo non solum ingenium elucere eius videbatis, quod saepe, etiamsi industria non alitur, valet tamen ipsum suis viribus, sed inerat, nisi me propter benevolentiam forte fallebat, ratio et bonis artibus instituta et cura et vigiliis elaborata. Atqui scitote, iudices, eas cupiditates, quae obiciuntur Caelio, atque haec studia, de quibus disputo, non facile in eodem homine esse posse. Fieri enim non potest, ut animus libidini deditus, amore, desiderio, cupiditate, saepe nimia copia, inopia etiam non numquam impeditus hoc, quicquid est, quod nos facimus in dicendo, quoquo

---

[a] Caelius opened his own defence.

[b] Either of C. Antonius, Cicero's colleague as consul in

XIX. But in Marcus Caelius—for I now intend to 44 speak more boldly of his honourable pursuits, since in reliance on your wisdom I venture freely to make certain confessions—you will find no profligacy, no extravagance, no debts, no passion for gluttony and evil haunts—that vice of greed and guzzling, which men find that age not only does not lessen but even increases. But love-making, and these "affairs" as they are called, which as a rule do not long trouble those of stronger minds—for they lose their bloom early and quickly—have never held my client entangled in their grasp. You have heard him when 45 pleading for himself [a]; you have already heard him as an accuser [b] (I freely say this in defence of my client, not to make any boast of it [c]); you have recognized his style, his gift of language, his wealth of thought and expression, with your usual sagacity; and in his style you saw not only his natural talent shine forth, which often, although not assisted by industry, yet asserts itself alone by its own power. But there was also, unless possibly I was misled by affection, a method based on liberal studies and brought to perfection by painstaking and tireless application. And yet be assured, gentlemen, that those excesses with which Caelius is reproached, and these pursuits which I am discussing, cannot easily be found in the same man. For it is impossible that a mind given up to the allurements of passion, hampered by love, longing, desire, often by excessive wealth, sometimes also by the lack of it, can sustain the efforts, whatever they may be, which we make

63 B.C., prosecuted by Caelius in 59 B.C., or of L. Calpurnius Bestia in 56 B.C.

[c] Cicero had instructed Caelius in oratory.

modo facimus[1] non modo agendo, verum etiam cogi-
46 tando possit sustinere. An vos aliam causam esse ullam putatis, cur in tantis praemiis eloquentiae, tanta voluptate dicendi, tanta laude, tanta gratia, tanto honore tam sint pauci semperque fuerint, qui in hoc labore versentur? Obterendae sunt omnes voluptates, relinquenda studia delectationis, ludus, iocus, convivium, sermo paene est familiarum deserendus. Quare in hoc genere labor offendit homines a studioque deterret, non quo aut ingenia deficiant aut doctrina
47 puerilis. An hic, si sese isti vitae dedidisset, consularem hominem admodum adulescens in iudicium vocavisset? hic, si laborem fugeret, si obstrictus voluptatibus teneretur, in hac acie cotidie versaretur, appeteret inimicitias, in iudicium vocaret, subiret periculum capitis, ipse inspectante populo Romano tot iam menses aut de salute aut de gloria dimicaret?

XX. Nihilne igitur illa vicinitas redolet, nihilne hominum fama, nihil Baiae denique ipsae loquuntur? Illae vero non loquuntur solum, verum etiam personant, huc unius mulieris libidinem esse prolapsam, ut ea non modo solitudinem ac tenebras atque haec flagitiorum integumenta non quaerat, sed in turpissimis rebus frequentissima celebritate et clarissima luce laetetur.
48 Verum si quis est, qui etiam meretriciis amoribus interdictum iuventuti putet, est ille quidem valde

[1] *Madvig inserts* quoquo modo facimus *after* dicendo.

[a] C. Antonius, in 59 B.C.
[b] Caelius lived on the Palatine near Clodia.

in speaking, in whatever way we make them, not only the bodily exertion but also the mental labour. Do you think that there is any other reason, when 46
there are such great rewards for eloquence,—such delight in speaking, such credit, such influence and such honour,—why there are and always have been so few who make the art of oratory the object of their toil? All pleasures must be trodden under foot, the pursuit of amusement, love-affairs, pleasantry, dining-out, must be renounced, even conversation with intimate friends must almost be abandoned. That is why the effort that eloquence requires disgusts men and scares them from studying it, not that they either lack natural ability or training in boyhood. Or would Caelius, if he had given himself to 47
such a life as his accusers have described, while still quite a youngster, have brought to trial a man of consular rank?[a] If he shrunk from labour, if he were fast bound in the fetters of pleasure, would he day by day be active here in combat, brave hostilities, prosecute, or risk the issue of a criminal trial, would he himself, under the eyes of the people of Rome, maintain, now for so many months, a struggle either for salvation or for glory?

XX. Does not then that notorious neighbourhood[b] put us on the scent? Does public rumour, does Baiae itself say nothing? Yes, Baiae does not merely talk, but even cries aloud that there is one woman whose amorous passions are so degraded that, far from seeking privacy and darkness and the usual screens for vice, she revels in her degraded lusts amid the most open publicity and in the broadest daylight.

However, if there is anyone who thinks that youth 48
should be forbidden affairs even with courtesans, he is

severus (negare non possum), sed abhorret non modo ab huius saeculi licentia, verum etiam a maiorum consuetudine atque concessis. Quando enim hoc non factitatum[1] est, quando reprehensum, quando non permissum, quando denique fuit, ut, quod licet, non liceret? Hic ego iam rem[2] definiam, mulierem nullam
49 nominabo; tantum[3] in medio relinquam. Si quae non nupta mulier domum suam patefecerit omnium cupiditati palamque sese in meretricia vita collocarit, virorum alienissimorum conviviis uti instituerit, si hoc in urbe, si in hortis, si in Baiarum illa celebritate faciat, si denique ita sese gerat non incessu solum, sed ornatu atque comitatu, non flagrantia oculorum, non libertate sermonum, sed etiam complexu, osculatione, actis, navigatione, conviviis, ut non solum meretrix, sed etiam proterva meretrix procaxque videatur: cum hac si qui adulescens forte fuerit, utrum hic tibi, L. Herenni, adulter an amator, expugnare pudicitiam an explere libidinem voluisse
50 videatur? Obliviscor iam iniurias tuas, Clodia, depono memoriam doloris mei; quae abs te crudeliter in meos me absente facta sunt, neglego; ne sint haec in te dicta, quae dixi. Sed ex te ipsa requiro, quoniam et crimen accusatores abs te et testem eius criminis te ipsam dicunt se habere. Si quae mulier sit eius modi, qualem ego paulo ante descripsi, tui

[1] Σ, *Lambinus*: factum *other* MSS.
[2] *Clark, with Halm* ipsam rem.
[3] totum *Klotz following Koch.*

---

[a] L. Herennius Balbus, one of the joint accusers (*subscriptores*) of Caelius.

[b] See on *Pro Sestio*, 54: the behaviour of Clodius, brother of Clodia, towards Cicero's family during his exile.

doubtless eminently austere (I cannot deny it), but his view is contrary not only to the licence of this age, but also to the custom and concessions of our ancestors. For when was this not a common practice? When was it blamed? When was it forbidden? When, in fact, was it that what is allowed was not allowed? Here and now I will explain a topic; I will mention no woman by name; I will leave just so much open. If a woman without a husband opens 49
her house to all men's desires, and publicly leads the life of a courtesan; if she is in the habit of attending dinner-parties with men who are perfect strangers; if she does this in the city, in her park, amid all those crowds at Baiae; if, in fact, she so behaves that not only her bearing but her dress and her companions, not only the ardour of her looks and the licentiousness of her gossip but also her embraces and caresses, her beach-parties, her water-parties, her dinner-parties, proclaim her to be not only a courtesan, but also a shameless and wanton courtesan; if a young man should happen to be found with this woman, would you, Lucius Herennius,[a] consider him to be an adulterer or a lover? Would you think that he desired to ravage her chastity, or only to satisfy his passion? I am now forgetting, Clodia, the wrongs 50
you have done me; I am putting aside the memory of what I have suffered; I pass over your cruel actions towards my family during my absence[b]; pray do not imagine that what I have said was meant against you. But I ask you yourself, since the accusers assert that you are the source of this charge and that they have you yourself as a witness to this charge, I ask you, if there existed a woman such as I painted a short while ago, one quite unlike you, with

dissimilis, vita institutoque meretricio, cum hac aliquid adulescentem hominem habuisse rationis num tibi perturpe aut perflagitiosum esse videatur? Ea si tu non es, sicut ego malo, quid est, quod obiciant Caelio? Sin eam te volunt esse, quid est, cur nos crimen hoc, si tu contemnis, pertimescamus? Quare nobis da viam rationemque defensionis. Aut enim pudor tuus defendet nihil a M. Caelio petulantius esse factum, aut impudentia et huic et ceteris magnam ad se defendendum facultatem dabit.

51 XXI. Sed quoniam emersisse iam e vadis et scopulos praetervecta videtur oratio mea, perfacilis mihi reliquus cursus ostenditur. Duo sunt enim crimina una in muliere summorum facinorum, auri, quod sumptum a Clodia dicitur, et veneni, quod eiusdem Clodiae necandae causa parasse Caelium criminantur. Aurum sumpsit, ut dicitis, quod L. Luccei servis daret, per quos Alexandrinus Dio, qui tum apud Lucceium habitabat, necaretur. Magnum crimen vel in legatis insidiandis vel in servis ad hospitem domini necandum sollicitandis, plenum sceleris consilium, plenum auda-
52 ciae! Quo quidem in crimine primum illud requiro,

---

[a] A wealthy Roman who was a friend of Cicero. In 64 B.C. he brought a charge of murder against Catiline whose acquittal was secured through Caesar. He was an unsuccessful candidate for the consulship of 59 B.C. (*Epp. ad Att.* i. 17. 11; Suetonius, *Div. Iul.* 19). He is better known as the recipient of a letter from Cicero (*Epp. ad Fam.* v. 12) requesting him to allow the insertion in his *History of Rome* of a chapter on Cicero's consulship.

[b] Dio was one of a deputation of one hundred Alexandrians who in 57 B.C. set out for Rome to complain to the Senate of the violence of Ptolemy Auletes, who at the end of 58 B.C. had

the life and manners of a courtesan—would you think it very shameful or disgraceful that a young man should have had some dealings with such a woman? If you are not this woman, as I prefer to think, for what have the accusers to reproach Caelius? But if they will have it that *you* are such a person, why should we be afraid of this accusation, if you despise it? Then it is for you to show us our way and method of defence; for either your sense of propriety will disprove any vicious behaviour by Caelius, or your utter impropriety will afford both him and the rest a fine opportunity for self-defence.

XXI. But since my speech now seems to have made 51
its way out of the shallows and to have escaped the reefs, the rest of my course presents itself as quite easy. Two indictments, for the gravest crimes, are brought against Caelius, and in both the name of one woman appears: he is charged with having taken some gold from Clodia, and with having prepared poison to murder this same Clodia. The gold, according to you, he took to give to the slaves of Lucius Lucceius,[a] to procure the assassination of Dio of Alexandria,[b] who at the time was living with Lucceius. It is a grave charge against a man, that he either plotted against the life of an ambassador,[c] or incited slaves to murder their master's guest—it is a plot rich in villainy, rich in daring! And in regard 52
to this charge, I first ask, whether he told Clodia for

fled to Rome to press upon Pompey a claim for reinstatement. See pp. 402-403.

[c] See Caesar, *Bell. Gall.* iii. 9: "legatos, quod nomen ad omnes nationes sanctum inviolatumque semper fuisset"; also Cicero, *In Verrem*, ii. 1. 85: "etenim nomen legati eiusmodi esse debet quod non modo inter sociorum iura sed etiam inter hostium tela incolume versetur."

dixeritne Clodiae, quam ad rem aurum sumeret, an non dixerit. Si non dixit, cur dedit? Si dixit, eodem se conscientiae scelere devinxit. Tune aurum ex armario tuo promere ausa es, tune Venerem illam tuam spoliare ornamentis, spoliatricem ceterorum, cum scires, quantum ad facinus aurum hoc quaereretur, ad necem legati, ad L. Luccei, sanctissimi hominis atque integerrimi, labem sceleris sempiternam? Huic facinori tanto tua mens liberalis conscia, tua domus popularis ministra, tua denique hospitalis illa Venus
53 adiutrix esse non debuit. Vidit hoc Balbus; celatam esse Clodiam dixit, atque ita Caelium ad illam attulisse, se ad ornatum ludorum aurum quaerere. Si tam familiaris erat Clodiae, quam tu esse vis, cum de libidine eius tam multa dicis, dixit profecto, quo vellet aurum; si tam familiaris non erat, non dedit. Ita, si verum tibi Caelius dixit, o immoderata mulier, sciens tu aurum ad facinus dedisti; si non est ausus dicere, non dedisti.

XXII. Quid ego nunc argumentis huic crimini, quae sunt innumerabilia, resistam? Possum dicere mores M. Caeli longissime a tanti sceleris atrocitate esse disiunctos; minime esse credendum homini tam ingenioso tamque prudenti non venisse in mentem rem tanti sceleris ignotis alienisque servis non esse cre-

---

[a] Later in this paragraph mentioned as *ornamenta*.

[b] *i.e.* Clodia. Cicero pretends that she has a statue of Venus which she decks with the spoils of her other lovers. *Spoliatrix* is perhaps here used as a mock cult-title, like *Venus Victrix*. See Martial, iv. 29. 5.

[c] The adjectives *conscia*, *liberalis*, *hospitalis* are used sarcastically in reference to her promiscuous amours.

[d] L. Herennius Balbus, Atratinus' *subscriptor*. See § 25.

[e] These games cannot have been celebrated by Caelius

what purpose he took the gold,[a] or whether he did not. If he did not tell her, why did she hand it over? If he did tell her, she made herself his accomplice in this crime. Did you[b] venture to fetch this gold from your chest, to despoil of her ornaments that Venus of yours, the despoiler of your other lovers, when you knew for how great a crime this gold was wanted—to assassinate an ambassador, to bring on a most virtuous and upright man, Lucius Lucceius, an everlasting stain of guilt? To an outrage so great your generous heart should never have been privy, that open house of yours should never have lent its aid, that hospitable Venus of yours should never have been an accomplice.[c] Balbus[d] had this point in mind; 53
he said that Clodia was not in the secret, and that Caelius told her another story—that he wanted the gold for the expenses of some games.[e] But if he was as intimate with Clodia as you[f] claim that he was, since you harp so much on his profligacy, he would certainly have told her why he wanted the gold; if he was not so intimate, she never gave it. Thus, if Caelius told you the truth, you abandoned woman!, you knowingly gave him the gold to commit a crime; if he did not venture to tell you, you did not give it.

XXII. Why then need I now oppose this charge with endless arguments? I might say that the character of Caelius was utterly incompatible with so horrible a crime: that it is incredible that it did not occur to a man naturally so clever and of such sound judgment, that the execution of so great a crime should not be entrusted to unknown slaves who

as a magistrate; possibly he was assisting a friend's candidature for office.

[f] Herennius Balbus.

dendam. Possum etiam illa et ceterorum patronorum et mea consuetudine ab accusatore perquirere, ubi sit congressus cum servis Luccei Caelius, qui ei fuerit aditus; si per se, qua temeritate; si per alium, per quem? Possum omnes latebras suspicionum peragrare dicendo; non causa, non locus, non facultas, non conscius, non perficiendi, non occultandi maleficii spes, non ratio ulla, non vestigium maximi facinoris
54 reperietur. Sed haec, quae sunt oratoris propria, quae mihi non propter ingenium meum, sed propter hanc exercitationem usumque dicendi fructum aliquem ferre potuissent, cum a me ipso elaborata proferri viderentur, brevitatis causa relinquo omnia. Habeo enim, iudices, quem vos socium vestrae religionis iurisque iurandi facile esse patiamini, L. Lucceium, sanctissimum hominem et gravissimum testem, qui tantum facinus in famam atque fortunas suas neque non audisset illatum a Caelio neque neglexisset neque tulisset. An ille vir illa humanitate praeditus, illis studiis, illis artibus atque doctrina illius ipsius periculum, quem propter haec ipsa studia diligebat, neglegere potuisset et, quod facinus in alienum hominem intentum severe acciperet, id omisisset curare in hospitem? quod per ignotos actum cum com-

[a] The points just enumerated by Cicero are technically called ἔντεχνοι πίστεις, "artificial" proofs deduced from within the case itself. They are opposed to ἄτεχνοι πίστεις, "inartificial" proofs, facts which do not depend upon a counsel's own powers of discovery. See Austin's note, *op cit.* p. 115.

belonged to another master. Again, following the custom of other counsel for the defence and my own, I might ask the accuser those usual questions: where did the meeting between Caelius and the slaves of Lucceius take place, what means of access had he to them; if in person, how rash it was; if by proxy, who was it? I might in my speech search every nook and corner where suspicion could lurk; no motive, no place, no opportunity, no accomplice, no hope of carrying out and concealing a crime, no reason for it, not a single trace of so terrible a crime will be
discovered. But all these points, which are the pro- 54
vince of an orator,[a] and which, not because of any talent of my own, but because of my experience and practice in speaking here, might have brought me some advantage, since they would seem to have been already worked up on my own responsibility and submitted as evidence—these I abandon for the sake of brevity, every one of them. For I can produce, gentlemen, a man whom you would readily allow to be associated with you in the sanctity of your oath, Lucius Lucceius, a most virtuous man and a most honourable witness, who, if such an outrage so compromising to his fortune and reputation had been attempted by Caelius, could not have failed to hear of it, could not have treated it with indifference, and could not have allowed it to take place. Could such a man, so high-principled, so scholarly, so cultured, so learned, have disregarded the danger threatening that very friend who was endeared to him through just those very interests? Could he have failed to deal with a crime committed against a guest such as would rouse his stern indignation if he heard of it as committed against a stranger? Would he have been

perisset, doleret, id a suis servis temptatum esse neglegeret? quod in agris locisve publicis factum reprehenderet, id in urbe ac suae domi coeptum esse leniter ferret? quod in alicuius agrestis periculo non praetermitteret, id homo eruditus in insidiis
55 doctissimi hominis dissimulandum putaret? Sed cur diutius vos, iudices, teneo? Ipsius iurati religionem auctoritatemque percipite atque omnia diligenter testimonii verba cognoscite. Recita. L. Lvccei testimonivm. Quid exspectatis amplius? an aliquam vocem putatis ipsam pro se causam et veritatem posse mittere? Haec est innocentiae defensio, haec ipsius causae oratio, haec una vox veritatis. In crimine ipso nulla suspicio est, in re nihil est argumenti, in negotio, quod actum esse dicitur, nullum vestigium sermonis, loci, temporis; nemo testis, nemo conscius nominatur, totum crimen profertur ex inimica, ex infami, ex crudeli, ex facinerosa, ex libidinosa domo; domus autem illa, quae temptata esse scelere isto nefario dicitur, plena est integritatis, dignitatis, officii religionis; ex qua domo recitatur vobis iure iurando devincta auctoritas, ut res minime dubitanda in contentione ponatur, utrum temeraria, procax, irata

---

[a] *Auctoritas* is here used of a written statement of evidence, deposed on oath, and read in court during the *actio.*
[b] Addressed to the clerk of the court.
[c] With the slaves of Lucceius.

grieved had he found it perpetrated by strangers, and have paid no attention when it was attempted by his own slaves? Would he have denounced such a deed if done in open country or in a public place, and have treated it mildly if planned in the city and at his own home? What he would not have passed over had some rustic been in danger, would he have thought proper to hide, when a plot was afoot against a great scholar, and he himself was a man of learning?
But why do I detain you longer, gentlemen? He 55
himself has given evidence on oath; observe the solemnity of his sworn statement,[a] carefully attend to every word of his testimony. Read it out.[b]

[The Deposition of Lucius Lucceius is read out.]

What more do you expect? Or do you think that the case itself, that truth itself, can find a voice to plead on their own behalf? Here is a justification of innocence, here is a plea submitted by the case itself, here is truth's only voice. The charge itself is not based upon any ground of suspicion, nor the fact upon any proof; the dealings which are alleged to have taken place [c] show no trace of what was said, nor of where and when; no witness, no accomplice is mentioned. The whole charge arises from a hostile, infamous, merciless, crime-stained, lust-stained house; whereas that house which is said to have been tempted to commit so foul a crime is the home of innocence, of honour, of duty, of piety; and from it you have heard read a statement deposed under a sworn oath, so that the question to be decided is easy to settle—whether you think that an unstable and angry wanton of a woman has forged this charge, mulier finxisse crimen, an gravis sapiens moderatusque vir religiose testimonium dixisse videatur.

56 XXIII. Reliquum est igitur crimen de veneno; cuius ego nec principium invenire neque evolvere exitum possum. Quae fuit enim causa, quam ob rem isti mulieri venenum dare vellet Caelius? Ne aurum redderet? Num petivit? Ne crimen haereret? Numquis obiecit? num quis denique fecisset mentionem, si hic nullius nomen detulisset? Quin etiam L. Herennium dicere audistis verbo se molestum non futurum fuisse Caelio, nisi iterum eadem de re suo familiari absoluto nomen hic detulisset. Credibile est igitur tantum facinus ob nullam causam esse commissum? et vos non videtis fingi sceleris maximi crimen, ut alterius causa sceleris suscipiendi fuisse
57 videatur? Cui denique commisit, quo adiutore usus est, quo socio, quo conscio, cui tantum facinus, cui se, cui salutem suam credidit? Servisne mulieris? Sic enim obiectum est. Et erat tam demens hic, cui vos ingenium certe tribuitis, etiamsi cetera inimica oratione detrahitis, ut omnes suas fortunas alienis servis committeret? At quibus servis? Refert enim magnopere id ipsum. Iisne, quos intellegebat non communi condicione servitutis uti, sed licentius, liberius, familiarius cum domina vivere? Quis enim hoc non videt, iudices,

---

[a] The charge of murdering Dio by the agency of the slaves of Lucceius.

[b] The reference is to Caelius' institution of fresh proceedings for *ambitus* against L. Calpurnius Bestia immediately after his acquittal on that charge on 11 February 56 B.C. See pp. 400-401.

[c] The alleged poisoning of Clodia.

[d] The alleged attempt upon Dio was, Cicero says, trumped up to give colour to Caelius' alleged attempt upon Clodia.

or whether a man of sobriety, learning, and restraint has given conscientious evidence.

XXIII. So then there remains the charge of 56
poisoning, of which I can neither discover the origin nor unravel the end. For what motive could Caelius have had for wanting to poison this woman? That he might not have to return the gold? But did she ask for its return? To prevent a charge from lying against him?[a] But did anyone accuse him of it? Would, in fact, anyone have mentioned it if Caelius had accused no one? Moreover, you heard Lucius Herennius declare that he would not have said an unfavourable word against Caelius, had he not a second time brought against his friend an action on the same charge of which he had been already acquitted.[b] Is it credible, then, that so great a crime[c] was committed without a motive? And do you not see that an accusation involving an outrageous crime was invented that there might appear to be a motive
for committing a second?[d] Lastly, in whom did he 57
confide, whom did he have to assist him, who was his partner, his accomplice, to whom did he entrust so great a crime, entrust himself, entrust his own life? To the slaves of this woman? For this has been alleged against him. And was this man, whom you certainly credit with some ability, although your hostile language deprives him of other qualities—was he so great a fool as to entrust all his fortunes to another person's slaves? But, I ask, what kind of slaves? This very point is most important. Were they slaves whom he knew not as subject to the ordinary conditions of servitude, but as living a life of more licence, liberty, and intimacy with their mistress? For who does not see, gentlemen, or who

aut quis ignorat, in eius modi domo, in qua mater familias meretricio more vivat, in qua nihil geratur, quod foras proferendum sit, in qua inusitatae, libidines, luxuries, omnia denique inaudita vitia ac flagitia versentur, hic servos non esse servos, quibus omnia committantur, per quos gerantur, qui versentur isdem in voluptatibus, quibus occulta credantur, ad quos aliquantum etiam ex cotidianis sumptibus ac luxurie
58 redundet? Id igitur Caelius non videbat? Si enim tam familiaris erat mulieris, quam vos vultis, istos quoque servos familiares esse dominae sciebat. Sin ei tanta consuetudo, quanta a vobis inducitur, non erat, quae cum servis potuit familiaritas esse tanta?

XXIV. Ipsius autem veneni quae ratio fingitur? ubi quaesitum est, quem ad modum paratum, quo pacto, cui, quo in loco traditum? Habuisse aiunt domi vimque eius esse expertum in servo quodam ad eam rem ipsam parato; cuius perceleri interitu esse
59 ab hoc comprobatum venenum. Pro di immortales! cur interdum in hominum sceleribus maximis aut conivetis aut praesentis fraudis poenas in diem reservatis? Vidi enim, vidi et illum hausi dolorem vel acerbissimum in vita, cum Q. Metellus abstraheretur e sinu gremioque patriae, cumque ille vir, qui se natum huic imperio putavit, tertio die post quam in

---

[a] The prosecution.

[b] Cicero makes no comment on such an act. See *Epp. ad Att.* i. 12. 4, and Tac. *Ann.* iv. 54.

[c] Q. Metellus Celer (consul 60 B.C.), cousin and husband of Clodia, by whom he was said (on the evidence of *Schol. Bob.* ad Cic. *pro Sestio*, 131) to have been poisoned (59 B.C.). T. Frank, *Catullus and Horace*, p. 49, regards this story as mere rumour.

is ignorant that in a house of that kind, in which the mistress lives the life of a courtesan, in which nothing is done which is fit to be published abroad, in which strange lusts, profligacy, in fact, all unheard-of vices and immoralities, are rife—who does not know that in such a house those slaves are slaves no longer? when all confidence is placed in them, everything is done by their agency, when they play their part with her in her excesses, when secrets are entrusted to them, and when they benefit considerably even from her daily extravagant expenditure. Was Caelius then ignorant of that? For if he was so intimate with the woman 58
as you [a] will have it, he knew that those slaves also were on intimate terms with their mistress. But if an association as close as you allege did not exist between the two, how could there have been such close intimacy between him and the slaves?

XXIV. But as to the poison itself, what theory is invented about that? Where was it procured, how was it prepared? In what way, to whom was it handed over, and where? It is said that Caelius had it at home and tried its effect on a slave [b] who had been procured for that very purpose; and that his very speedy death proved to Caelius the efficacy of the poison. Why, Immortal Gods, when men commit 59
the greatest crimes do ye sometimes overlook them or reserve to some future day punishment for a crime of the present? I witnessed, yes, I witnessed what was perhaps the most bitter sorrow of my life and I drained the cup of misery to its end on that day when Q. Metellus [c] was snatched from the bosom and embrace of his country, and when that great man, who in his own regard was destined from his birth for the service of our Empire, two days after he had displayed

curia, quam in rostris, quam in re publica floruisset, integerrima aetate, optimo habitu, maximis viribus eriperetur indignissime bonis omnibus atque universae civitati. Quo quidem tempore ille moriens, cum iam ceteris ex partibus oppressa mens esset, extremum sensum ad memoriam rei publicae reservabat, cum me intuens flentem significabat interruptis ac morientibus vocibus, quanta impenderet procella mihi, quanta tempestas civitati, et cum parietem saepe feriens eum, qui cum Q. Catulo fuerat ei communis, crebro Catulum, saepe me, saepissime rem publicam nominabat, ut non tam se emori quam spoliari suo praesidio cum
60 patriam, tum etiam me doleret. Quem quidem virum si nulla vis repentini sceleris sustulisset, quonam modo ille furenti fratri suo consularis restitisset, qui consul incipientem furere atque tonantem[1] sua se manu interfecturum audiente senatu dixerit? Ex hac igitur domo progressa ista mulier de veneni celeritate dicere audebit? Nonne ipsam domum metuet, ne

[1] tonantem *Clark for* MSS. conantem, *which is preferred by Klotz and Austin.*

---

[a] Referring to Cicero's banishment and to the consulships of Piso and Gabinius and the tribunate of Clodius in 58 B.C.

[b] The party-wall common to Metellus' house and that of Q. Lutatius Catulus, who was dead by the previous year (60 B.C.). Catulus' death was lamented by Cicero as a great loss to the Optimate cause (*Epp. ad Att.* i. 20. 3). A son of the consul of 102 B.C., Catulus was consul in 78 B.C. and died as *princeps senatus*: a leading and upright Optimate, in 67 B.C. he opposed the *lex Gabinia*, and in 63 B.C. he spoke against Caesar in the debate on the Catilinarian conspirators.

[c] The MSS. needlessly add *patrueli* after *fratri suo. Fra-*

his full vigour in the Senate, on the Rostra, and in public life, was snatched away, a most cruel loss to all loyal citizens and to the whole State, when in the prime of his years, in the best of health, and in the fullness of his strength. At that moment, at the point of death, when in all other ways his mind had by then become enfeebled, he remembered the State with his last thoughts, and fixing his gaze upon me, amid my tears, he strove in broken and dying words to tell how great a storm was hanging over me, and how great a tempest threatened the State[a]; then knocking several times on the wall which had stood between him and Quintus Catulus,[b] he frequently called on the name of Catulus, often on mine, and most often on that of the State; so that he grieved not so much that he was dying as that his country and I also should be bereft of his aid. And being the man he was, had the 60
violence of a sudden crime not removed him, in what fashion would he as a man of consular rank have resisted his cousin's[c] revolutionary madness, seeing that amid his early ravings and his thunderings[d] he said when consul, in the hearing of the Senate, that he would slay him with his own hand? Shall, then, that woman who comes from a house like this venture to speak about the speedy effect of a draught of poison? Will she not dread the house itself, lest it utter some

ter alone can mean cousin. Clodius' mother was a sister of Celer's father. In Cicero, *Epp. ad Att.* iv. 3. 4 Q. Metellus Nepos (brother of Metellus Celer), Ap. Claudius and Clodius are called *fratres*.

[d] *i.e.* at the time (60 B.C.) when Clodius was seeking to acquire plebeian status (Cicero, *Epp. ad Att.* i. 19. 5). The term *furens* is used by the constitutionalists (*boni*, *optimates*) to denote their "left-wing" opponents (*improbi*, *populares*).

quam vocem eiciat, non parietes conscios, non noctem illam funestam ac luctuosam perhorrescet?

Sed revertor ad crimen; etenim haec facta illius clarissimi ac fortissimi viri mentio et vocem meam fletu debilitavit et mentem dolore impedivit.

61 XXV. Sed tamen venenum unde fuerit, quem ad modum paratum sit, non dicitur. Datum esse aiunt huic P. Licinio, pudenti adulescenti et bono, Caeli familiari; constitutum esse cum servis, ut venirent ad balneas Senias; eodem Licinium esse venturum atque iis veneni pyxidem traditurum. Hic primum illud requiro, quid attinuerit ferri in eum locum constitutum, cur illi servi non ad Caelium domum venerint. Si manebat tanta illa consuetudo Caeli, tanta familiaritas cum Clodia, quid suspicionis esset, si apud Caelium mulieris servus visus esset? Sin autem iam suberat simultas, exstincta erat consuetudo, discidium exstiterat, "hinc illae lacrimae" nimirum, et haec causa est omnium horum scelerum
62 atque criminum. "Immo," inquit, "cum servi ad dominam rem totam et maleficium Caeli detulissent, mulier ingeniosa praecepit his ut omnia Caelio pollicerentur; sed ut venenum, cum a Licinio traderetur, manifesto comprehendi posset, constitui locum iussit balneas Senias, ut eo mitteret amicos, qui delitiscerent, deinde repente, cum venisset Licinius

---

[a] Of Clodia.

[b] Mentioned here only; there is no clue to a site. It is possible that the name of the builder or manager may be concealed in the adjective.

[c] "Hinc illae lacrimae," quoted from Terence, *Andria*, 126. Cicero says that if Caelius and Clodia had quarrelled this would explain everything. It is a proverbial expression, *cf.* Juvenal, i. 168: "inde irae et lacrimae."

cry against her? Will she not shudder at the walls that know her guilt, at the memory of that night of death and grief?

But I return to the accusation; indeed the mention I have made of that illustrious and gallant man has choked my voice with tears and dazed my mind with sorrow.

XXV. But it is still not stated whence the poison 61
was procured, nor how it was prepared. It is said to have been given to Publius Licinius here, a decent and worthy young man and a friend of Caelius; that an arrangement was made with the slaves [a] that they should come to the Senian Baths,[b] where Licinius would meet them and hand over the box of poison. At this point I first ask what was the good of arranging for the poison to be brought to that place? Why did not those slaves go to Caelius at his house? If there still existed between Caelius and Clodia such intimacy and such close association, what suspicion could arise if one of the lady's slaves had appeared at Caelius' house? But if some disagreement now lurked between them, if their association had been broken off, if a rupture had taken place, "the cat," assuredly, "is out of the bag," [c] and we have the reason for all these crimes and accusations. "No," 62
says the accuser, "after the slaves had revealed to their mistress the whole affair and the villainy of Caelius, this crafty lady ordered them to make every promise to Caelius, but, so that Licinius, when handing over the poison, might be caught in the act, she ordered the Senian Baths to be arranged as a meeting-place, where she might send some friends to hide, and suddenly, when Licinius had

venenumque traderet, prosilirent hominemque comprenderent."

XXVI. Quae quidem omnia, iudices, perfacilem rationem habent reprehendendi. Cur enim potissimum balneas publicas constituerat? in quibus non invenio quae latebra togatis hominibus esse posset. Nam si essent in vestibulo balnearum, non laterent; sin se in intimum conicere vellent, nec satis commode calceati et vestiti id facere possent et fortasse non reciperentur, nisi forte mulier potens quadrantaria illa permutatione familiaris facta erat balneatori.

63 Atque equidem vehementer exspectabam, quinam isti viri boni testes huius manifesto deprehensi veneni dicerentur; nulli enim sunt adhuc nominati. Sed non dubito, quin sint pergraves, qui primum sint talis feminae familiares, deinde eam provinciam susceperint, ut in balneas contruderentur, quod illa nisi a viris honestissimis ac plenissimis dignitatis, quam velit sit potens, numquam impetravisset. Sed quid ego de dignitate istorum testium loquor? virtutem eorum diligentiamque cognoscite. "In balneis delituerunt." Testes egregios! "Dein temere prosiluerunt." Homines temperantes! Sic enim fingunt, cum Licinius venisset, pyxidem teneret in manu, conaretur tradere, nondum tradidisset, tum repente evolasse istos praeclaros testes sine nomine;

---

[a] By the phrase *quadrantaria illa permutatione* Cicero means that Clodia paid the usual admission fee, but for the men's bath (a *quadrans*), and implies further, in the word *permutatione*, that Clodia had herself first received the fee from the bathman, in return for a favour. This is an allusion to the story (Plutarch, *Cicero*, 29) that Clodia admitted her lovers for a *quadrans*. Also there is an echo here of Caelius' nickname for Clodia of *quadrantaria Clytaemnestra* (Quin-

arrived and was handing over the poison, they might dart out and seize him."

XXVI. All this, gentlemen, is perfectly easy to refute. For why had she specially fixed on the public baths, where I do not see that there could be any hiding-place for men in their togas ? For if they were in the forecourt they would not be hidden ; but if they wanted to pack themselves away inside, they could not conveniently do so in their shoes and outdoor dress, and perhaps would not be admitted—unless possibly that lady of influence had bought the favour of the bathman by her usual farthing deal.[a]
I assure you, I was eagerly waiting to hear the names 63
of those honest gentlemen who were alleged to have witnessed the discovery of this poison in Licinius' hands ; no names, in fact, have yet been mentioned. But I have no doubt that they are extremely respectable persons, in the first place because they are intimates of such a lady ; secondly, because they accepted the part of being packed away in the baths, one which she could never have imposed upon them, however influential she might be, had they not been most honourable and worthy persons. But why do I speak of the worthy character of these witnesses ? Let me tell you what brave, painstaking fellows they were. "They concealed themselves in the baths." Remarkable witnesses ! "Then they darted out accidentally." Wonderful self-control ! For they pretend that after Licinius had arrived, holding the box in his hand, and was on the point of handing it over, although he had not yet done so—then suddenly these splendid witnesses with no names flew out from their

tilian, viii. 6. 53) based on the story that she murdered her husband Q. Metellus Celer.

Licinium autem, cum iam manum ad tradendam pyxidem porrexisset, retraxisse atque illo repentino hominum impetu se in fugam coniecisse. O magna vis veritatis, quae contra hominum ingenia, calliditatem, sollertiam contraque fictas omnium insidias facile se per se ipsa defendat!

64 XXVII. Velut haec tota fabella veteris et plurimarum fabularum poetriae quam est sine argumento, quam nullum invenire exitum potest! Quid enim? isti tot viri (nam necesse est fuisse non paucos, ut et comprehendi Licinius facile posset et res multorum oculis esset testatior) cur Licinium de manibus amiserunt? Qui minus enim Licinius comprehendi potuit, cum se retraxit, ne pyxidem traderet, quam si tradidisset? Erant enim illi positi, ut comprehenderent Licinium, ut manifesto Licinius teneretur, aut cum retineret venenum aut cum tradidisset. Hoc fuit totum consilium mulieris, haec istorum provincia, qui rogati sunt; quos quidem tu quam ob rem "temere prosiluisse" dicas atque ante tempus, non reperio. Fuerant ad hoc rogati, fuerant ad hanc rem collocati, ut venenum, ut insidiae, facinus denique ipsum ut manifesto comprehenderetur.
65 Potueruntne magis tempore prosilire, quam cum Licinius venisset, cum in manu teneret veneni pyxidem? Quae cum iam erat tradita servis, si[1] evasissent subito ex balneis mulieris amici Liciniumque comprehendissent, imploraret hominum fidem atque a se

[1] si *inserted by Ernesti.*

---

[a] The word *fabula* could variously hint that Clodia wrote plays, that she was "up to her tricks" (cf. *Epp. ad Att.* iv. 2. 4), or that tales were told about her (*e.g.* the *fabula* in § 69).

hiding-place, but that Licinius, who had already stretched out his hand to give over the box, drew it back at the sudden onset of these fellows, and took to flight. How great is the power of truth, which when opposed to human ingenuity, cunning and craft, and opposed to all the falsehood and treachery in the world, is easily able to defend itself unaided !

XXVII. For example : the whole of this little play, 64
by a poetess of experience who had already composed many comedies [a]—how devoid it is of plot, how utterly it fails to find an ending ! For how did it happen that all those fellows (for they must have been many in number, so that Licinius could be easily seized, and that what took place might be attested by many eye-witnesses) allowed Licinius to escape from their hands ? How could it have been more difficult to seize him when he drew back to avoid handing over the box, than it would have been if he had handed it over ? For they had been posted in readiness to seize Licinius, to catch him in the act, either when he had the poison in his hands, or when he had handed it over. This was the lady's whole idea, this was the part of those who were asked to carry it out ; why you say that "they darted out accidentally," and too soon, I cannot understand. They had been asked to do this, they had been stationed there just on purpose that the poison, the plot, in fact the crime itself, might be palpably demonstrated. Could they have chosen a better time to dart 65
out than after Licinius had arrived, while holding in his hand the box of poison ? For when it had been already handed over to the slaves, if the lady's friends had suddenly left their hiding-place inside the baths, and seized Licinius, he would have been found im-

illam pyxidem traditam pernegaret. Quem quo modo illi reprehenderent? vidisse se dicerent? Primum ad se revocarent[1] maximi facinoris crimen; deinde id se vidisse dicerent, quod, quo loco collocati fuerant, non potuissent videre. Tempore igitur ipso se ostenderunt, cum Licinius venisset, pyxidem expediret, manum porrigeret, venenum traderet. Mimi ergo est iam exitus, non fabulae; in quo cum clausula non invenitur, fugit aliquis e manibus, deinde scabilla concrepant, aulaeum tollitur.

66 XXVIII. Quaero enim, cur Licinium titubantem, haesitantem, cedentem, fugere conantem mulieraria manus ista de manibus amiserit, cur non comprenderint, cur non ipsius confessione, multorum oculis, facinoris denique voce tanti sceleris crimen expresserint. An timebant, ne tot unum, valentes imbecillum, alacres perterritum superare non possent?

Nullum argumentum in re, nulla suspicio in causa, nullus exitus criminis reperietur. Itaque haec causa ab argumentis, a coniectura, ab iis signis, quibus veritas illustrari solet, ad testes tota traducta est.

[1] ad se vocarent *Clark*.

---

[a] They would be bringing on themselves the suspicion that had previously fallen on Licinius, *i.e.* that they themselves had handed over the poison to Clodia's slaves.

[b] Reference to a mime is here appropriate, because of their improbable situations and of the frequent playing of women's parts by *meretrices*. A mime was also silent.

[c] The word *scabillum* means a clapper fastened to the feet like a shoe or sandal, used in marking the time for dancers or pantomimists, and (in this context) in prompting the man who worked the curtain.

ploring protection, denying that he had handed over that box to them. And how were they to refute him? Were they to say that they saw him? In the first place, they would be bringing on their own heads a charge of a most serious crime[a]; secondly, they would have to say that they saw what they could not have seen from the place where they had been posted. They therefore showed themselves just at the very moment after Licinius had arrived, when he was getting out the box, stretching forth his hand, handing over the poison. So, then, we have the finale of a mime,[b] not of a proper play; the sort of thing where, when no fit ending can be found, someone escapes from someone's clutches, off go the clappers,[c] and we get the curtain.[d]

XXVIII. Why was it, I ask, that when Licinius 66
was faltering, retreating, striving to escape, those warriors under their feminine orders allowed him to give them the slip? Why did they not seize him, why did they not on his own confession, in the sight of so many witnesses, and by the cry of the deed, firmly model[e] a charge of an outrageous crime? Perhaps they were afraid that so many of them could not overpower a single man, they strong and he weak, they alert and he terrified?

There is no argument in the facts, no suspicion in the case, no conclusion in the charge that can possibly be discovered. So this case, without any argument, or inference, or those indications by which light is usually thrown upon truth, is left entirely to the wit-

[d] The drop-curtain in a Roman theatre was lowered for a performance to begin, and raised at the end of a show. See Beare, *The Roman Stage*, pp. 259 ff.

[e] *Expresserint* is a metaphor from statuary. See § 12.

Quos quidem ego, iudices, testes non modo sine ullo timore, sed etiam cum aliqua spe delectationis ex-
67 specto. Praegestit animus iam videre primum lautos iuvenes mulieris beatae ac nobilis familiares, deinde fortes viros ab imperatrice in insidiis atque in praesidio balnearum collocatos; ex quibus requiram, quem ad modum latuerint aut ubi, alveusne ille an equus Troianus fuerit, qui tot invictos viros muliebre bellum gerentes tulerit ac texerit. Illud vero respondere cogam, cur tot viri ac tales hunc et unum et tam imbecillum, quam videtis, non aut stantem comprenderint aut fugientem consecuti sint; qui se numquam profecto, si in istum locum processerint, explicabunt. Quam volent in conviviis faceti, dicaces, non numquam etiam ad vinum diserti sint, alia fori vis est, alia triclinii, alia subselliorum ratio, alia lectorum; non idem iudicum comissatorumque conspectus; lux denique longe alia est solis, alia lychnorum. Quam ob rem excutiemus omnes istorum delicias, omnes ineptias, si prodierint. Sed me audiant, navent aliam operam, aliam ineant gratiam, in aliis se rebus ostentent, vigeant apud istam mulierem venustate, dominentur sumptibus, haereant, iaceant, deserviant; capiti vero innocentis fortunisque parcant.

68 XXIX. At sunt servi illi de cognatorum sententia,

---

[a] *Excutere*, "shake out," "ransack," "rummage"; *cf.* Cicero, *Pro Sulla*, 24; *De Officiis*, iii. 81.

nesses. These witnesses, gentlemen, I now wait for, not only without alarm, but even with some hope of amusement. My mind is athrill at the idea 67
of seeing, in the first place, these young dandies, intimate friends of a rich and high-born lady, and, then again, those valiant warriors, posted by their commandress in ambush and in garrison at the Baths. I intend to ask them how or where they concealed themselves; whether it was a bath-tub, or a "Trojan Horse," which received and protected so many invincible warriors, waging war for a woman. In truth, I will force them to answer this question, why so many strong men did not either seize him where he stood or overtake him in his flight, a man alone and so weak, as you see; in my opinion they will never disentangle themselves if they come forward into the witness-box. Although at dinner-parties they are humorous, witty, sometimes glib over their cups, the idea of a court is one thing, that of a dining-room is another; benches here and couches there have different meanings; to face judges and fellow-revellers is not the same thing; in short, the light of the sun is far different from the light of lamps. And so we will shake out [a] all their pretty ways, all their follies, if they come forward. But let them listen to me: let them busy themselves elsewhere, let them curry favour by other means, let them show themselves off in other ways, let them ingratiate themselves with their lady by their elegant manners, outdo the rest by their extravagance, be always by her side, lie at her feet, be her humble servants; but let them spare the life and fortunes of an innocent man.

XXIX. But, the accusers say, these slaves have 68

nobilissimorum et clarissimorum hominum, manu missi. Tandem aliquid invenimus, quod ista mulier de suorum propinquorum fortissimorum virorum sententia atque auctoritate fecisse dicatur. Sed scire cupio, quid habeat argumenti ista manumissio; in qua aut crimen est Caelio quaesitum aut quaestio sublata[1] aut multarum rerum consciis servis cum causa praemium persolutum. "At propinquis" inquit "placuit." Cur non placeret, cum rem tute ad eos non ab aliis tibi adlatam, sed a te ipsa com-
69 pertam deferre diceres? Hic etiam miramur, si illam commenticiam pyxidem obscenissima sit fabula consecuta? Nihil est, quod in eius modi mulierem non cadere videatur. Audita et percelebrata sermonibus res est. Percipitis animis, iudices, iam dudum, quid velim vel potius quid nolim dicere. Quod etiamsi est factum, certe a Caelio non est factum (quid enim attinebat?); est enim ab aliquo adulescente fortasse non tam insulso quam non verecundo. Sin autem est fictum, non illud quidem modestum, sed tamen est non infacetum mendacium; quod profecto numquam hominum sermo atque opinio comprobasset, nisi omnia, quae cum turpitudine aliqua dicerentur, in istam quadrare apte viderentur.

[1] sublata: *Manutius' correction for the* MS. sublevata.

---

[a] A family council was normally held to consider important matters of family policy. Clodia, being a widow in *tutela*, could not of her own right manumit her slaves.

[b] That is, the slaves had helped Clodia to fabricate a charge against Caelius.

[c] So that the slaves could not be forced to give evidence under torture.

been manumitted with the approval[a] of her kinsmen, most noble and illustrious persons. At last, then, we have found something which that lady may be said to have done with the approval and with the sanction of those gallant gentlemen, her relatives. But I desire to know what is the drift of that manumission ; for it either means that a charge had been concocted against Caelius[b] or that a possibility of examination[c] had been eliminated or that a justification was found for rewarding slaves who shared so many of her secrets. " But," I am told, " her kinsmen approved." Why should they not, since you said that you reported to them facts not brought to you by others, but discovered by you yourself ? And at this point do we 69
really wonder if this imaginary box has given rise to a most improper story ?[d] There is nothing which does not seem to fit into the acts of such a lady. The story has been heard of, and is in all men's mouths. You have long since understood, gentlemen, what I wish, or rather, what I do not wish to say. However, even if the story is true, it is not true of Caelius (for what had it to do with him ?) ; it was perhaps a trick played by some young man with less modesty than wit. But if it is an invention, although not decent, yet it is a lie not without humour. In my opinion, it would not have been accepted in general talk and opinion, did not every story, which could not be told without a blush, seem perfectly to square nicely with that lady's reputation.[e]

[d] This story, which is the key to much of the mystery of §§ 61-69, cannot be explained. But Clodia was clearly the victim of some improper practical joke. See Quintilian, vi. 3. 25.

[e] Possibly with a play on *quadrantaria* (§ 62).

70 Dicta est a me causa, iudices, et perorata. Iam intellegitis, quantum iudicium sustineatis, quanta res sit commissa vobis. De vi quaeritis. Quae lex ad imperium, ad maiestatem, ad statum patriae, ad salutem omnium pertinet, quam legem Q. Catulus armata dissensione civium rei publicae paene extremis temporibus tulit, quaeque lex sedata illa flamma consulatus mei fumantes reliquias coniurationis exstinxit, hac nunc lege Caeli adulescentia non ad rei publicae poenas, sed ad mulieris libidines et delicias deposcitur?

71 XXX. Atque hoc etiam loco M. Camurti et C. Caeserni damnatio praedicatur. O stultitiam! stultitiamne dicam an impudentiam singularem! Audetisne, cum ab ea muliere veniatis, facere istorum hominum mentionem? audetis excitare tanti flagitii memoriam non exstinctam illam quidem, sed repressam vetustate? Quo enim illi crimine peccatoque perierunt? Nempe quod eiusdem mulieris dolorem et iniuriam Vettiano nefario stupro sunt persecuti. Ergo ut audiretur Vetti nomen in causa, ut illa vetus

---

[a] See note on § 1 and p. 401.

[b] The serious disturbances arising from an attack on the government by M. Aemilius Lepidus, colleague of Catulus in the consulship of 78 B.C.

[c] The otherwise unknown case of Camurtius and Caesernius, in which Clodia was concerned, was probably brought up by the prosecution as a precedent for making the *lex de vi* applicable to a case of immorality.

[d] Clodia.

[e] How the Vettius mentioned here was connected with

I have pleaded my case, gentlemen, and my task is finished. You can now appreciate how great is the responsibility of your judgment, how serious a matter has been entrusted to your decision. You are inquiring into a question of violence. The law [a] which has to do with the rule, the high estate, the stability of our country, and the welfare of all; the law which Quintus Catulus carried at a time of armed civil strife, when the State was at almost the last extremity [b]; the law which, after the conflagration which raged during my consulship had been checked, extinguished the smouldering embers of the Conspiracy—is it under this law that there is now a demand for the sacrifice of Caelius' youth, not for punishment in the interests of the State, but to satisfy the wanton whims of a woman? 70

XXX. And here also we are informed of the condemnation of Marcus Camurtius and Gaius Caesernius.[c] What an absurdity! Am I to call it absurdity or amazing impudence! Do you dare, when you come from that woman, to mention the names of these two men? Do you dare to revive the memory of that great crime, which though possibly not wholly dead, time had at least kept out of view? For what was the charge, what was the offence, for which those two men were condemned? No doubt because they avenged the spite and resentment of this same woman [d] by an infamous Vettian assault. Was it therefore that the name of Vettius [e] might be heard in this case, and that old story about the 71

Clodia or with the case of Camurtius and Caesernius is unknown. There is no evidence for regarding him as the author of the trick played on Clodia (Plutarch, *Cicero*, 29) or as the informer Vettius (Cicero, *In Vat.* 25 ff.).

aeraria[1] fabula referretur, idcirco Camurti et Caeserni est causa renovata? qui quamquam lege de vi certe non tenebantur, eo maleficio tamen erant implicati, ut ex nullius legis laqueis eximendi viderentur.
72 M. vero Caelius cur in hoc iudicium vocatur? cui neque proprium quaestionis crimen obicitur nec vero aliquod eius modi, quod sit a lege seiunctum, cum vestra severitate coniunctum; cuius prima aetas dedita disciplinae fuit iisque artibus, quibus instituimur ad hunc usum forensem, ad capessendam rem publicam, ad honorem, gloriam, dignitatem; iis autem fuit amicitiis maiorum natu, quorum imitari industriam continentiamque maxime vellet, iis aequalium studiis,[2] ut eundem quem optimi ac nobilissimi
73 petere cursum laudis videretur. Cum autem paulum iam roboris accessisset aetati, in Africam profectus est Q. Pompeio pro consule contubernalis, castissimo homini atque omnis officii diligentissimo; in qua provincia cum res erant et possessiones paternae, tum etiam usus quidam provincialis non sine causa a maioribus huic aetati tributus. Decessit illinc Pompei iudicio probatissimus, ut ipsius testimonio cognoscetis. Voluit vetere instituto eorum adulescentium exemplo,

[1] *Garatoni's conjecture, confirmed by* Σ.
[2] maxime velitis, is aequalium studiis *Klotz: Madvig inserts* eum *after* quorum, *reading* velitis.

---

[a] The *fabula* is unknown, unless it is the story quoted in Plutarch, *Cicero*, 29.
[b] Cicero and Crassus.
[c] *Contubernalis*: it was common for a young man after his *tirocinium fori* to go as an *aide-de-camp* or companion (*comes*) to a provincial governor to gain knowledge of war, or experience in administration. This attachment was called *contubernium militare*.

copper [a] be quoted again, that the case of Camurtius and Caesernius has been brought up once more? Although they certainly could not be proceeded against by the law *de vi*, they were yet implicated in such a crime that they did not seem likely to escape the meshes of any law. But as for Marcus Caelius, why 72 is he summoned before this court? No charge is brought against him that is pertinent to this court, nor in fact any kind of charge upon which, though outside the scope of the law *de vi*, you are competent to pass condemnation. His early years were devoted to training, and those exercises by which we are prepared for practice at the bar, for entering upon a public career, for office, honour and prestige; moreover he so enjoyed the friendships of older men [b] whose industry and sobriety of conduct he would most desire to imitate, so shared the pursuits of his contemporaries, that he seemed to be pursuing the same course of distinction as the best and noblest. But when years had brought some development to his 73 strength, he went to Africa as an *aide-de-camp* [c] to the governor Quintus Pompeius,[d] a man of the highest moral character and most conscientious in the performance of all his duties. In this province his father had business and lands; and he also had opportunities for experience of provincial administration, at an age which our ancestors wisely thought fit for it. He left Africa, highly esteemed by Pompeius, as you will learn by his personal testimony. It was his wish that, according to an old practice, and following the example of young men who rose to eminence in the

[d] Quintus Pompeius Rufus, praetor (63 B.C.) and proconsular governor of Africa (61 B.C.). He is not to be confused with a tribune of 52 B.C. bearing the same name.

qui post in civitate summi viri et clarissimi cives exstiterunt, industriam suam a populo Romano ex aliqua illustri accusatione cognosci.[a]

74 XXXI. Vellem alio potius eum cupiditas gloriae detulisset; sed abiit huius tempus querellae. Accusavit C. Antonium,[b] collegam meum, cui misero praeclari in rem publicam beneficii[c] memoria nihil profuit, nocuit opinio maleficii cogitati.[d] Postea nemini umquam concessit aequalium, plus ut in foro, plus ut in negotiis versaretur causisque amicorum, plus ut valeret inter suos gratia. Quae nisi vigilantes homines, nisi sobrii, nisi industrii consequi non possunt, omnia labore et diligentia est

75 consecutus. In hoc flexu quasi aetatis (nihil enim occultabo fretus humanitate ac sapientia vestra) fama adulescentis paulum haesit ad metas notitia nova mulieris et infelici vicinitate et insolentia voluptatum, quae cum inclusae diutius et prima aetate compressae et constrictae fuerunt, subito se non numquam profundunt atque eiciunt universae. Qua ex vita vel dicam quo ex sermone (nequaquam enim tantum erat,

---

[a] Young aspirants for political honours began by prosecuting someone who had attained such honours and rendered himself liable to the penalties of the law. Tacitus, *Dialogus*, 34, mentions early prosecutions by L. Licinius Crassus (cos. 95 B.C.), Julius Caesar, C. Asinius Pollio and C. Licinius Calvus. See Cicero, *De officiis*, ii. 47 ff.

[b] Antonius was accused by Caelius, probably of *maiestas*. See pp. 385, 399, 424.

[c] As a matter of fact, though Cicero gives the credit of the defeat of Catiline at Pistoria early in 62 B.C. to Antonius, who was officially in command, the victory was won by M. Petreius, a propraetor, Antonius being ill on the day of battle. See *Pro Sestio*, 12, p. 50, note *b*.

[d] He was suspected of being implicated in the Conspiracy of 63 B.C. See Cicero, *Pro Sestio*, 8.

State as its most illustrious citizens, his industry should be made known to the people of Rome by the outcome of some striking prosecution.[a]

XXXI. I could wish that his passion for glory had 74
rather taken him in another direction; but the time for such a lament is past. He accused Gaius Antonius,[b] my colleague, that unfortunate man, to whom the recollection of a signal service rendered to the State was of no avail,[c] while the suspicion of an intended crime did him great harm.[d] From that time Caelius never showed himself inferior to any of his own age in his constant attendance in the Forum, in his application to court-cases and the defence of his friends, or in the favour with which his associates regarded him. All the advantages which men cannot obtain, unless they are careful, sober and industrious, he has acquired by work and application. At what 75
may be called the turning-point of his age (for I will hide nothing from you, gentlemen, relying upon your sympathy and good sense) his youthful reputation came for a while to grief[e] through his recent acquaintance with this lady, his unfortunate proximity to her and his inexperience of pleasures which, after they have been under somewhat long restraint and during early youth curbed and controlled, quite often suddenly break loose and burst out in a flood. But from such a life, or shall I say from such gossip (for the reality was by no means so bad as people

[e] *Haesit ad metas.* A metaphor from chariot-racing. The chariots, when rounding the *metae* (short conical columns at each end of the *spina*, a low wall running lengthwise down the middle of the course), were often stopped or upset. Cicero means that when Caelius became a neighbour of Clodia his reputation suffered a temporary "set-back."

quantum homines loquebantur)—verum ex eo, quicquid erat, emersit totumque se eiecit atque extulit, tantumque abest ab illius familiaritatis infamia, ut eiusdem nunc ab sese inimicitias odiumque propulset.
76 Atque ut iste interpositus sermo deliciarum desidiaeque moreretur (fecit me invito mehercule et multum repugnante, sed tamen fecit), nomen amici mei de ambitu detulit; quem absolutum insequitur, revocat; nemini nostrum obtemperat, est violentior, quam vellem. Sed ego non loquor de sapientia, quae non cadit in hanc aetatem; de impetu animi loquor, de cupiditate vincendi, de ardore mentis ad gloriam; quae studia in his iam aetatibus nostris contractiora esse debent, in adulescentia vero tamquam in herbis significant, quae virtutis maturitas et quantae fruges industriae sint futurae. Etenim semper magno ingenio adulescentes refrenandi potius a gloria quam incitandi fuerunt; amputanda plura sunt illi aetati, siquidem efflorescit ingenii laudibus, quam inserenda.
77 Quare, si cui nimium effervisse videtur huius vel in suscipiendis vel in gerendis inimicitiis vis, ferocitas, pertinacia, si quem etiam minimorum horum aliquid offendit, si purpurae genus, si amicorum catervae, si splendor, si nitor, iam ista deferverint, iam aetas omnia, iam usus, iam dies mitigarit.

XXXII. Conservate igitur rei publicae, iudices,

---

[a] The elder Atratinus (L. Calpurnius Bestia). See p. 400.
[b] See Quintilian, i. 3. 3 ff.
[c] See Cicero, *De finibus*, v. 61.
[d] He did not wear the ordinary purple, which was almost black, but the Tyrian or Tarentine of finer dye (*cf. Pro Sestio*, 19).

maligned)—from this, whatever it was, he emerged and completely broke loose and escaped, and he is so far from the disgrace of being intimate with that woman, that he now has to defend himself against her enmity and hatred. And to silence all 76
the gossip about loose living and idleness that intervened—he did this absolutely against my wishes and in spite of my opposition, but still he did it—he brought an action for bribery against a friend of mine.[a] Although he was acquitted, Caelius returned to the charge and indicted him again; he refused to listen to any of us, and showed himself more violent than I could wish. But I am not speaking about good sense, a quality which does not belong to his years; I am speaking about his impetuosity, his eagerness to win, his ardent desire for glory. Such passions, in men who have reached our time of life, ought to be somewhat restrained, but in youth, as with plants, they give promise of what virtue in its ripeness and how great the fruits of industry will some day be.[b] Why, young men of great talent always need to be checked rather than encouraged in the quest of distinction; youth is an age when, if it is beginning to display exuberance in its intellectual gifts, pruning rather than grafting is needed.[c]
Wherefore, if anyone thinks that Caelius' energy, 77
spirit, obstinacy, either in beginning or in carrying on his enmities, have been too ardent, or if any of even these trifles give some offence, his shade of purple,[d] his hosts of friends, his sparkle, his brilliance—all this feverishness, you will find, will soon have cooled down; age, experience and time will have mellowed all.

XXXII. Save then, gentlemen, for the State, a

civem bonarum artium, bonarum partium, bonorum virorum.[1] Promitto hoc vobis et rei publicae spondeo, si modo nos ipsi rei publicae satis fecimus, numquam hunc a nostris rationibus seiunctum fore. Quod cum fretus nostra familiaritate promitto, tum
78 quod durissimis se ipse legibus iam obligavit. Non enim potest, qui hominem consularem, cum ab eo rem publicam violatam esse diceret, in iudicium vocarit, ipse esse in re publica civis turbulentus ; non potest, qui ambitu ne absolutum quidem patiatur esse absolutum, ipse impune umquam esse largitor. Habet a M. Caelio res publica, iudices, duas accusationes vel obsides periculi vel pignora voluntatis. Quare oro obtestorque vos, iudices, ut, qua in civitate paucis his diebus Sex. Cloelius absolutus sit, quem vos per biennium aut ministrum seditionis aut ducem vidistis, hominem sine re, sine fide, sine spe, sine sede, sine fortunis, ore, lingua, manu, vita omni inquinatum,[2] qui aedes sacras, qui censum populi Romani, qui memoriam publicam suis manibus incendit, qui Catuli

[1] studiosum *is added by Müller.*
[2] *Some* MSS. *place* hominem . . . inquinatum *after* incendit. *Garatoni's transposition is followed.*

[a] Austin's note (*op. cit.* pp. 138-139) discusses the difficulties of reading and interpretation in this passage. For the use of *bonus* in a political sense (for Optimate or Conservative) see Cicero, *Epp. ad Att.* i. 13. 2 : " partium studiosus ac defensor bonarum " (a consul of 61 B.C., M. Valerius Messalla Niger). For *bonus vir* as meaning "an honest man " as opposed to " a good citizen " see Cicero, *Epp. ad Fam.* i. 9. 10.

[b] By his prosecutions of Antonius and Bestia.

[c] The henchman of P. Clodius known to scholars as Sex. Clodius was really called Sex. Cloelius. He drafted

citizen of honourable principles, a loyalist, an honest man.[a] I promise you this, and I pledge the State that, if I myself have served the State well, he will never swerve from my political principles. This I promise, relying upon the friendship between us, and also because he has already bound himself by the strictest of covenants.[b] For it is impossible that a man who has 78
summoned to trial a man of consular rank, because he declared that the State had been dishonoured by him, should himself be a turbulent citizen in the State ; it is impossible that a man who will not even allow one who has been acquitted of bribery to be acquitted, should ever himself go unpunished for bribery. The State, gentlemen, holds from Marcus Caelius two prosecutions, either as hostages against dangerous behaviour or pledges of his good will. And so, gentlemen, I beg and implore you, that in a city where a few days ago Sextus Cloelius [c] has been acquitted, whom for two years [d] you have seen either as an agent or a leader of sedition ; a man without money or credit, without hope or home or fortune, a man whose mouth, tongue, hand, and whole life are sullied with infamy ; who committed to the flames with his own hands a sacred temple,[e] the register of the Roman People and the archives of the State ; a man who

P. Clodius' laws, organized his riots and finally burned his body in the Senate House. This identification is due to Dr. D. R. Shackleton Bailey who has shown that manuscript evidence convincingly supports *Cloelius* (*C.R.* N.S. x, 1960, pp. 41 f.)

[d] 58–56 B.C.

[e] Nympharum Aedes, a temple in the Campus Martius, of unknown site, where documents relating to the census and other records were kept. Cicero, *Pro Milone*, 73, accuses Publius Clodius of this incendiarism.

monumentum adflixit, meam domum diruit, mei fratris incendit, qui in Palatio atque in urbis oculis servitia ad caedem et inflammandam urbem incitavit: in hac civitate ne patiamini illum absolutum muliebri gratia, M. Caelium libidini muliebri condonatum, ne eadem mulier cum suo coniuge et fratre et[1] turpissimum latronem eripuisse et honestissimum adulescentem
79 oppressisse videatur. Quod cum huius vobis adulescentiam proposueritis, constituitote ante oculos etiam huius miseri senectutem, qui hoc unico filio nititur, in huius spe requiescit, huius unius casum pertimescit; quem vos supplicem vestrae misericordiae, servum potestatis, abiectum non tam ad pedes quam ad mores sensusque vestros, vel recordatione parentum vestrorum vel liberorum iucunditate sustentate, ut in alterius dolore vel pietati vel indulgentiae vestrae serviatis. Nolite, iudices, aut hunc iam natura ipsa occidentem velle maturius exstingui vulnere vestro quam suo fato, aut hunc nunc primum florescentem firmata iam stirpe virtutis tamquam turbine aliquo aut subita
80 tempestate pervertere. Conservate parenti filium, parentem filio, ne aut senectutem iam prope despera-

[1] et *added by Bake.*

[a] Q. Lutatius Catulus (consul 102 B.C.) built on the Palatine a monument called the Porticus Catuli to commemorate the victory at Vercellae (101 B.C.); it was on the site of the confiscated house of M. Fulvius Flaccus, a partisan of C. Gracchus. Cicero's own house on the Palatine adjoined the Porticus Catuli. During Cicero's exile P. Clodius destroyed Cicero's house and pulled down the Porticus Catuli. In Nov. 57 B.C. P. Clodius burnt Q. Cicero's house in the same region and attempted to destroy the Porticus

wrecked the Monument of Catulus,[a] destroyed my own house, set fire to that of my brother; who, on the Palatine and before the eyes of the city, incited slaves to massacre and to set fire to the city—when, in this city, such a man has been acquitted by the favour of a woman, do not allow Marcus Caelius to be sacrificed to her lust; let it not be thought that this same woman with her brother and husband[b] has succeeded in rescuing an infamous robber, and in crushing a most honourable young man. But, when 79
you have contemplated the picture of this young man, I beg you to set also before your eyes this unhappy old man here[c]; whose stay is Caelius his only son, on whose promise depends his ease of mind; whose one dread is of disaster to him. And, entreating your compassion, submissive to your power, prostrate I will not say at your feet but before your hearts and minds, I entreat you to raise him up, either from your recollection of your parents or from the delight you take in your children, so that in assuaging another's grief you may obey the promptings of your affection or your compassion. Let it not be your will, gentlemen, that this old man, already declining to his end in the course of nature, should wish that death may come before its time because you rather than fate have dealt the blow, or that you should overthrow, as by some whirlwind or sudden tempest, this youth in the first flower of his prime, whose virtue has now taken so firm a root. Save a son for his 80
father, a father for his son. Do not let it be thought

Catuli which was being rebuilt. See Cicero, *Epp. ad Att.* iv. 3. 2.

[b] *Cf.* § 32: "cum istius mulieris *viro—fratre* volui dicere."

[c] Caelius' father was present in court.

tam contempsisse aut adulescentiam plenam spei maximae non modo non aluisse vos verum etiam perculisse atque adflixisse videamini. Quem si nobis, si suis, si rei publicae conservatis, addictum, deditum, obstrictum vobis ac liberis vestris habebitis omniumque huius nervorum ac laborum vos potissimum, iudices, fructus uberes diuturnosque capietis.

that you have treated with contempt an old man whose hopes are now almost ended or that you have not only failed to sustain a young man of the highest promise, but have even smitten him down and crushed him. If you restore Caelius in safety to me, to his own people, to the State, you will find in him one pledged, devoted and bound to you and to your children ; and, it is you above all, gentlemen, who will reap the rich and lasting fruits of all his exertions and labours.

IV. The Structure of the *Pro Caelio*

In his exordium (§§ 1-2), warmly praised by Quintilian, Cicero at once makes clear his plan of action. He sympathizes with the jury on their attendance in court on a day of public festival, and maintains that Caelius has committed no offence proper to the jurisdiction of the court before which he appears as a defendant arraigned under the *lex de vi*. Atratinus is the nominal prosecutor, but the real attack has been launched from the background by an evil woman.

In sections 3-50 Cicero presents his *praemunitio*, the consolidation (" building-up ") of his case, an unusual procedure because the *exordium* would normally be followed by the *narratio* or statement of the facts. The purpose of this *praemunitio* is to dispose of several insinuations made by the prosecution. This unorthodox procedure was, no doubt, made advisable by the fact that three of the five formal charges had already been dealt with by Crassus, and by Cicero's fear that a conventional *narratio* of matters connected with the two remaining charges might prejudice his client. In section 30 a *narratio* makes a brief appearance, only to disappear.

The prosecution's insinuations, intended to blacken Caelius' character, are thus refuted by Cicero in sections 3 to 24.

1. No discredit attaches to Caelius' father, who is an example to all members of the *ordo equester* and deserves the respect which his son has always paid him.

2. Caelius' alleged unpopularity with his fellow-townsmen is disproved by their sending a deputation to honour him.

3. Cicero regrets that Atratinus has been commissioned to attack Caelius' morals when he was a young man, for he can vouch for their excellence, since his father committed him to his care.

4. Caelius' connexion with Catiline has been cast in his teeth. This was pardonable, for his years of dependence were then over, and even Cicero himself once almost fell a victim to Catiline's sinister but remarkable spell.

5. Charges of complicity in the Catilinarian plot, and of bribery and corrupt practice, can be dismissed.

6. There is nothing to support the accusation that Caelius is in debt. It was with his father's full approval that he left home, and the prosecutor has quoted far too high a figure for the rent of Caelius' house on the Palatine where, unfortunately, he met his Medea (Clodia).

7. Cicero has no fear of the allegations which will be made by some mysterious witnesses, that Caelius laid violent hands on a senator at the pontifical elections and criminally assaulted certain married women after a dinner-party.

8. Cicero could wish that Crassus as one of Caelius' counsel, in his able treatment of the matters entrusted to him, had also replied to the point about Dio of Alexandria. But he asserts, and can prove, that the murder of Dio is a topic wholly irrelevant to the case.

In sections 25-30 Cicero turns from Atratinus to L. Herennius Balbus, one of the prosecutor's two *subscriptores* (junior counsel). Herennius' speech, the substance of which may be roughly deduced from Cicero's remarks, had made a great impression not only on the jury but also on Cicero. But the moral lecture which Herennius read to Caelius and certain allegations of little consequence were much less disturbing to Cicero than his quiet sermon against youthful excesses. The jurors, Cicero pleaded, must not allow Caelius to be made a scapegoat for the sins of others. In this connexion Herennius could hardly have avoided a reference to the relations between Caelius and Clodia.

The special purpose of the remainder of the *praemunitio* (§§ 30-50) was to clear Caelius' name of any discredit arising from Herennius' disclosures about Caelius' affair with Clodia. In paragraph 30 Cicero pretends to begin dealing with the two remaining charges, one about some gold, one about some poison. But they are introduced only to be dropped, for they served as a preliminary to Cicero's real attack on Clodia, whose name is now first mentioned. "Clodia, the source of both charges, is the real foe, but, so far as I can, I will spare her."

Cicero's case was won by his superb tactics and oratory in sections 33-38, a passage highly admired in ancient times. It contains two examples of the rhetorical figure *προσωποποιία*, "a speech in character," in which an orator impersonates individuals either long dead or still living. In sections 33-34 Cicero conjures up Appius Claudius Caecus, the Censor, Clodia's most famous ancestor, who, Cicero says, will be able to deal with her as she deserves.

In section 35 we have a transition to Cicero's second "speech in character." In this transition, after saying that later he will defend Caelius against any strictures from the austere Appius Claudius, Cicero turns to Clodia and demands that she shall explain her intimacy with Caelius. Cicero's second "speech in character" is found in section 36, where he impersonates P. Clodius, Clodia's profligate brother and his own enemy. Clodius' cynical questionings of his sister about her liaison with Caelius condemn her no less effectively than the stern interrogation of Appius Claudius.

As he had promised in section 35, Cicero passes in sections 37-38 to his defence of Caelius. He sets off his impersonations of Appius Claudius and Clodius by the device of introducing from Roman comedy two fathers of opposite temperaments (σύγκρισις). To the tirades of a crotchety old man from Caecilius, Caelius can reply that he never misconducted himself; to an indulgent father from Terence he can easily defend his gallant attentions to a lady of free and easy manners. The complaints of a *meretrix* like Clodia, now first openly called such, cannot substantiate any charge of misconduct against Caelius.

Cicero then passes to moral reflections in what may be called a *locus de indulgentia*. In sections 39-42 [a] he replies to any who may assert that his tutelage

[a] It has been observed that the *Pro Caelio* contains some parallel passages or "doublets"; (*a*) § 28 and §§ 41 and 43; (*b*) §§ 35, 38 and 48-50. In publications appearing between 1913 and 1944 foreign scholars investigated these sections and submitted varying explanations. In his edition of 1933 R. G. Austin summarized the opinions then available (Appendix viii, pp. 122-125) and offered a tentative solution: that Cicero, impressed by the speech of Herennius (§ 25),

of Caelius was nothing less than a schooling in profligacy, by classing complete abstinence from every kind of relaxation as inhuman and the strict morality of the past as out of date. Let youth by all means "sow its wild oats," but in moderation.

Cicero's moral lecture in defence of Caelius as a steady and industrious young man who knew where to draw the line is continued till the end of the *praemunitio* in paragraph 50. Many upright and distinguished Romans had their fling in youth. Caelius is young but not vicious : his own speech in his defence, his previous career proclaim his good character. The wild charges against him, for which Clodia is responsible, are without foundation. Liaisons with ladies of easy virtue have long been countenanced. "Who can blame the lovers of a gay widow who behaves so immodestly ? Do not imagine, Clodia, that anything I have said referred to you. But, as you are behind

---

decided to abbreviate, modify and even omit some of the material which he had already prepared for delivery; that we possess not only Cicero's original draft in its place, but also the actual arrangement which he followed in delivering his speech; and that the speech was published at once without careful revision. In his second edition (1952) Austin modifies his earlier solution in the light of the opinion of, among others, H. Drexler (" Zu Ciceros Rede pro Caelio," *Nachrichten von der Akademie der Wissenschaften in Göttingen*, Phil.-Hist. Kl., 1944, pp. 1-32). He considers that the difficulty of Cicero's case obliged him to repeat certain points vital for the defence; and that the first of each pair of "doublets" (in no sense awkward) serves a purpose different from the second. He rejects his earlier view that §§ 39-43 were never delivered, since he now regards the whole of the long passage in §§ 39-50 as vital for Cicero's purpose. A reasonable conclusion is that the *Pro Caelio* was published at once in the form in which it was delivered.

this charge, do you think that there is any disgrace in a young man's gallantries with a lady such as I have described? If you are modest, you will deny that Caelius has had any shameful dealings with you; if you are a wanton, there is clearly no case against Caelius."

Having thus dealt with various attempts to blacken Caelius' character and to prejudice his case, Cicero passes in sections 51-69 to his *argumentatio*. In the first part (§§ 51-55) Cicero gives in enigmatic language a *narratio* of the charge about some gold (*crimen auri*, § 30). Clodia, apparently, lent Caelius some gold ornaments to help him, as he said, to pay for some games which he was producing; she gave them with no witnesses, and did not ask for them back. Caelius' real purpose, however, in getting the ornaments was alleged to be their use as a bribe to induce the slaves of L. Lucceius to murder Dio of Alexandria, their master's guest. Cicero pleads that either Clodia gave Caelius the ornaments with full knowledge of his purpose, or, if he dared not tell her, she cannot have given them to him; and that his best course would be to call as a witness Lucceius himself, with whom Dio was lodging at the time of the alleged attack. If, as is not impossible, there is some truth behind this mystery, it must lie in an attempt by Caelius to ingratiate himself with Pompey who was suspected of authorizing or conniving at the murder of Dio. Lucceius' evidence, in documentary form, was deposed on oath and read out in court (§ 55).

Sections 56-58, in which the second part of the *argumentatio* begins, contain Cicero's general reflections on the inconsistency and improbability of the allegation that Caelius wanted to poison Clodia (*crimen veneni*, § 30). Then comes in sections 59-60 a skilful but malicious digression on the untimely death of Clodia's husband, Q. Metellus Celer (consul 60 B.C.), whom she was suspected of having poisoned. In a quick transition from gravity to clever frivolity Cicero, in sections 61-69, dwells on the details of Caelius' alleged attempt to poison Clodia. According to the prosecution, poison was given to a certain P. Licinius to be handed over to Clodia's slaves. But Clodia's slaves informed their mistress, who herself arranged a meeting that took place at the Senian Baths, so that Licinius could be caught actually handing over the poison. But Licinius was allowed to escape! No wonder Clodia manumitted her slaves! Since the detail is so circumstantial, this episode cannot have been entirely fictitious. Something must have happened at the Senian Baths which became the talk of Rome. The *obscenissima fabula* (§ 69) may well be the key to the mystery. Cicero's treatment of this episode is an outstanding example of his oratorical versatility and subtlety. The jury would be too entertained to give critical attention to an amusing but bewildering story.

Cicero's *peroratio* follows in sections 70-80. To have indicted Caelius under the *lex de vi* is monstrous treatment of a youth of such a creditable past and of such high promise. "Acquit him, and while earning the gratitude of his unhappy old father, you will also be serving the State." The detailed statement given in sections 72-77 of Caelius' public career, supplementing that of his earliest years (§§ 9-12), shows that Cicero felt it to be essential to present Caelius to the jury in a most favourable light.

Among Cicero's private orations the *Pro Caelio*

takes a very high, if not, as some scholars have held, the highest place, as an expression of his gifts of eloquence, audacity and brilliance. Invaluable as a social document, the speech also shows Cicero steering a course through dangerous waters with unerring skill. Just as the offence of *maiestas populi Romani* (high treason) was in the late Republic a weapon frequently used by politicians engaged in party struggles, so also was the *lex de vi* twisted into the service of those who sought to drive personal rivals or enemies from society. It may have been made clear that the prosecution's case was based on something more than allegation and insinuation. But it was where Cicero's case was on least firm ground that his tactics were most skilful: *gravitas* where appropriate, bold wit to entertain the jurors at awkward moments where their critical attention might have been fatal to Caelius. No wonder that on the very day (5 April) following this resounding triumph over Clodia an elated Cicero was displaying no less audacity in another place, but with less happy results: his proposal in the Senate for an attack on what he called the stronghold of the Triumvirate, the *lex Iulia de agro Campano*.[a]

V. The Later Career of Caelius

There is some reason to believe that Caelius was never quaestor, but that he became a senator by virtue of his curule aedileship or even of his tribunate.[b] In 52, when he was tribune, he vigorously championed the cause of Milo,[c] especially during the

[a] Cicero, *Epp. ad Fam.* i. 9. 8: "in arcem illius causae."
[b] Austin, *op. cit.* pp. 145-146.
[c] Cicero, *Pro Milone*, 91.

anarchy early in the year. Amid the rioting which followed the burning of the *curia* after Clodius' murder he convened a *contio* for an address by Milo, but the audience was dispersed by the Clodian faction. Later, he strenuously opposed the bills *de vi* and *de ambitu* which Pompey brought forward as sole consul, on the ground that they were almost *privilegia* to the disadvantage of Milo, and he was deterred only by Pompey's threat to pass his bills by force of arms. This marked a beginning of Caelius' estrangement from Pompey. After Milo's trial Caelius and Cicero secured the acquittal by one vote of M. Saufeius, leader of the band that had made an end of Clodius.

This year 52 also showed that Caelius had definite leanings towards Caesar, for he was one of those who carried the Law of the Ten Tribunes allowing Caesar to be a candidate for the consulship *in absentia*, Caelius' support for the law being secured by Cicero at the request of both Caesar and Pompey.[a]

At the beginning of 51 Caelius indicted, probably for *vis*, Q. Pompeius Rufus, one of his colleagues as tribune, and a grandson of Sulla. Rufus had been a most vigorous Clodian tribune; he vilified Milo as the murderer of Clodius and insinuated that he was plotting against Pompey's life. He was condemned and withdrew to a life of poverty at Bauli in Campania.[b] Later in the year Caelius was elected a curule aedile for 50 B.C. This same year 51 marked the beginning of the highly interesting correspondence between Caelius and Cicero. Before he left Rome towards the end of April for his governorship in Cilicia, Cicero commissioned Caelius to keep him

[a] Cicero, *Epp. ad Att.* vii. 1. 4; *Epp. ad Fam.* vi. 6. 5.
[b] Cicero, *Epp. ad Fam.* viii. 1. 5.

posted up not only in events on the political stage, but also in city news and gossip.[a] Caelius' letters to Cicero from June 51 to February 48 B.C. (*Epp. ad Fam.* viii), and Cicero's to him (*Epp. ad Fam.* ii), are an invaluable source for certain aspects of the history of the time, and vividly illuminate the differing personalities of the two men.

In his early letters to Cicero Caelius importuned him for a consignment of Cilician panthers and for donations from the province for the games which he would celebrate as aedile in 50 B.C. But Cicero was obdurate to both requests.[b] His aedileship was remarkable for an attack on an abuse connected with the public water supply. The managers (*aquarii*) had come to connive at the tapping of the mains by shopkeepers and others so that they could draw off private supplies. Caelius' strictures of this practice won, a century and a half later, the warm approval of the specialist Frontinus,[c] *curator aquarum* under Nerva and Trajan.

Caelius' leanings towards Caesar, already suggested by his association with the Law of the Ten Tribunes, became still clearer as the year 50 B.C. went its way. He quarrelled[d] with one of the censors, Appius Claudius Pulcher (consul 54 B.C.), a connexion of Pompey by marriage and Cicero's predecessor as governor of Cilicia. Hence he attached himself to the other censor, L. Calpurnius Piso (consul 58 B.C.), Caesar's father-in-law. Moreover, he was further estranged from the Pompeians by a quarrel with an

[a] Cicero, *Epp. ad Fam.* viii. 1. 1.
[b] Cicero, *Epp. ad Att.* vi. 1. 21.
[c] Frontinus, *De aquis*, 75.
[d] Cicero, *Epp. ad Fam.* viii. 12. 1.

extreme anti-Caesarian, L. Domitius Ahenobarbus (consul 54 B.C.), and by his support of M. Antonius, Caesar's quaestor and tribune-elect for 49 B.C., who defeated Domitius in an election to fill a vacancy in the College of Augurs caused in June of that year by the death of Hortensius.[a] In a letter to Cicero written early in August soon after Domitius' defeat at the augural election, Caelius' keen political insight and opportunism stand fully revealed[b]: his belief that within a year there would be open war between Pompey and Caesar unless one of them went to fight the Parthians; that in a civil crisis, so long as a peaceful solution was possible, the more respectable side should be followed, but, in the event of war, the stronger. Caelius clearly regarded the safer side as the better. Nor was he in any doubt about the superiority of Caesar's army.

In the final crisis of early January 49 B.C. Caelius proved himself a determined Caesarian. On 1 January he supported a proposal of M. Calidius[c] that Pompey should withdraw to his province of Spain and so do away with any pretext for war; and, when Q. Metellus Scipio (consul 52 B.C.) made his proposal that Caesar should be declared a public enemy if he refused to lay down his command by a date to be fixed,[d] he joined Curio in voting against it. On 7 January, after the passing of the *senatus consultum de re publica defendenda*, he fled to Caesar with Curio and the tribunes M. Antonius and Q. Cassius Longinus.[e]

[a] Cicero, *Epp. ad Fam.* viii. 14. 1.
[b] *Ibid.* viii. 14. 2-4.
[c] Caesar, *Bell. Civ.* i. 2.
[d] *C.A.H.* ix, p. 636.
[e] Caesar, *Bell. Civ.* i. 5; Dio Cassius, xli. 3.

Within two years Caelius' follies brought him to a miserable end. To his dissatisfaction [a] with a commission given him by Caesar in February 49 B.C. to suppress a revolt at Intimilium in Liguria was added disapproval of Caesar's clemency and financial policy. In April, however, he went with Caesar to Spain, after having vainly pressed Cicero not to leave Italy for the Pompeian camp but to remain neutral.[b] Of his fortunes in Spain nothing definite is known, but in some of Cicero's letters [c] of May 49 B.C. there are vague suggestions of intrigue. His end came in 48 B.C., after reckless and pathetic attempts at revolution.[d] Caesar had appointed him *praetor peregrinus* for that year, but had given the office of *praetor urbanus* to his loyal and competent follower C. Trebonius. From an attempt to obstruct Trebonius' administration of Caesar's wise law of debt and to substitute extremist measures, Caelius passed to rioting, until P. Servilius Isauricus, Caesar's colleague in the consulship, invoked the authority of the Senate and ended Caelius' activities in Rome by a force of Caesarian soldiers and a resolution divesting him of his praetorship. Thereupon, after a vain attempt to raise followers in Campania, he joined Milo, whom Caesar had not recalled from exile, in a

[a] Cicero, *Epp. ad Fam.* viii. 15. 2.

[b] Cicero, *Epp. ad Fam.* viii. 16. Caesar also, at Caelius' instance, urged Cicero to the same course (*Epp. ad Att.* viii. 6b).

[c] *Epp. ad Att.* x. 12a, 14, 15, 16.

[d] Caesar, *Bell. Civ.* iii. 20-22; Dio Cassius, xlii. 22-25. The final movements of Caelius and Milo in southern Italy are variously recorded by Caesar and Dio. Caelius' last letter to Cicero (*Epp. ad Fam.* viii. 17, of February 48 B.C.) suggests a loss of self-control.

wild enterprise in southern Italy. The two revolutionaries soon perished: Milo at Cosa, Caelius at Thurii, where he was cut down by a party of Caesar's Gallic and Spanish troopers.

Although M. Caelius Rufus [a] played but a secondary part on the stage of history, he is outstanding among contemporaries like Catullus, Licinius Calvus, Curio and Dolabella in helping us to learn something of those who may be styled in Cicero's phrase *barbatuli iuvenes*,[b] or the younger generation of the Caesarian Age. All of these, who lived in the decadence of the Republic, should be charitably judged by the spirit of their times and not by modern standards. Caelius, for all his faults, cannot be denied gifts of mind and heart and a compelling vitality. Opportunism, lack of principle and instability were his failings.

His accomplishments as an orator and as a letter-writer were considerable. Quintilian repeatedly testified to his great powers of speech. A few phrases preserved from his own defence at the trial in 56 B.C. reveal his command of pungent sarcasm and lampoon.[c] The well-known fragment [d] of the speech which he delivered against C. Antonius in

[a] Admirable accounts and appreciations of Caelius are to be found in: Boissier, *Cicéron et ses amis* (1895); Warde Fowler, *Social Life at Rome in the Age of Cicero* (1909), pp. 127-132; Tyrrell and Purser, *The Correspondence of Cicero*, iii (1914), pp. xxxvii-lx; Austin, *op. cit.* pp. v-xvi.

[b] *Epp. ad Att.* i. 14. 5.

[c] Clodia is nicknamed "a Clytaemnestra on hire for a farthing" (Quintilian, viii. 6. 53); an opponent (probably the prosecutor Atratinus) "a Pelias in ringlets" (Quintilian, i. 5. 61); and Atratinus' teacher, Plotius Gallus, "a barley-blown rhetorician" (Suetonius, *Rhet.* 2).

[d] Quintilian, iv. 2. 123.

59 B.C. reveals him as a dealer in merciless abuse. That he excelled at attack rather than at defence is clear from Cicero's observation that he had " a good right hand, but a weak left." [a] Ancient critics were not at one in appraising his oratorical style. Cicero [b] says that his brilliance, cleverness and wit made up for an old-fashioned delivery ; Tacitus [c] disapproved of his harshness, archaisms and vulgar expressions. His letters vividly reflect his character. They are informative, shrewd, racy. Two provide examples of his keen insight : an acute analysis (*Epp. ad Fam.* viii. 1. 3) of Pompey's tortuous disposition, " he often says one thing and thinks another, and has not the wit to conceal his real aims " ; his brief and clear statement (*Epp. ad Fam.* viii. 14. 2) of the crux of the antagonism between Pompey and Caesar. They were written in the language of ordinary life, in a light and almost conversational style, reminiscent of the phraseology of Roman comedy.[d] One letter [e] only can rank as literary : a studied appeal to Cicero to remain in Italy and not join the Pompeians in Greece.

That Caelius was attracted to two such opposites as Cicero and Clodia is proof of his power to impress and even to fascinate. Vivacity, glamour and other gifts of person and disposition won him entrance to Clodia's fashionable circle. Caelius' less ostentatious and more solid qualities, such as shrewd judgment and keen political sense, appealed strongly to Cicero. In an age which was inevitably drifting towards open

[a] Quintilian, vi. 3. 69.
[b] *Brutus*, 273. [c] *Dialogus*, 21.
[d] Tyrrell and Purser, *op. cit.* pp. cviii-cxvi.
[e] *Epp. ad Fam.* viii. 16.

war between armed dynasts, Caelius, after some temporary inclination towards Pompey, came to realize that it was Caesar who would dominate Roman politics. From his tribunate onwards, therefore, Caelius supported Caesar more and more actively. But no one can read the sorry story of the closing months of his life without realizing how his defects of character contributed to his tragic end. Out of sympathy with Caesar's far-sighted policy, he fell a victim to extreme impetuosity ; he " lost his head." There is justice in each of two ancient judgments on Caelius. Velleius Paterculus,[a] comparing him with Curio, calls him " quite as clever in his worthlessness " (*nec minus ingeniose nequam*) ; Quintilian [b] sums him up acutely and sympathetically as " a man who deserved both a wiser mind and a longer life " (*dignus vir cui et mens melior et vita longior contigisset*).

[a] ii. 68. 1. [b] x. 1. 115.

DE PROVINCIIS CONSULARIBUS

I. Introduction to the *De Provinciis Consularibus*

Cicero's successful defence of P. Sestius in the trial which ended on 11 March 56 B.C. was followed about three weeks later by a further notable victory in the courts. On 3 and 4 April (see p. 401), M. Caelius Rufus was prosecuted by L. Sempronius Atratinus on five charges, at the instigation of Clodia. On two of these charges he was defended by Cicero in masterly fashion on 4 April. The acquittal of Caelius, which left him free to follow his political career and caused Clodia to disappear from Roman society, was one of Cicero's greatest triumphs.

On the very next day, 5 April, Cicero, elated by these successes, took a leading part in a senatorial debate which was to prove one of the turning-points of his life. Encouraged, as has been said (see p. 31), by increasing signs of discord within the Triumvirate, he set about to repudiate the assertion that he had sought reconciliation with Caesar.[a] We hear of this debate from two of Cicero's letters. Writing before dawn on 8 April 56 B.C.[b] to his brother Quintus, who was a *legatus* in Sardinia on the staff of Pompey as corn-controller, Cicero briefly mentioned two items of business. First, the Senate approved a grant

[a] Cicero, *Epp. ad Fam.* i. 9. 7, a passage which has been deleted from the published edition of the *Pro Sestio*.
[b] *Epp. ad Quintum fratrem*, ii. 5.

of 40,000,000 sesterces to Pompey towards the cost of the corn-supply. Then there was "a heated debate on the Campanian land, the Senate being almost as uproarious as a public meeting. Discussion was embittered by financial straits and by the high price of food." But Cicero did not then disclose to his brother the leading part which he played in that debate. We first hear of it in the celebrated letter[a] written two years later, in 54 B.C., to P. Lentulus Spinther: that it was Cicero who proposed that the question of the Campanian land (which had already been raised in the Senate by a tribune, P. Rutilius Lupus, in December 57 B.C.)[b] should be referred to a full meeting of the Senate on 15 May. In the light of what followed Cicero admitted that by so doing he could not have made "a more direct assault on the stronghold of the Triumvirate," nor more fully disregarded the lessons of his recent past; and that his proposal made, he wrote, "a deep impression not only on those who, it seemed certain, would be disturbed (Caesar and Crassus), but on those also who, to my mind, would be unmoved (Pompey)."

Six[c] letters of Cicero are our chief source of information for the events which led from that point to the delivery of the speech *De provinciis consularibus*.

On 7 April Cicero, who was to leave Rome on 8 April for a visit to his places at Arpinum, Pompeii and Cumae, meaning to be back in Rome on 6 May in time for an adjournment of Milo's trial on 7 May,[d]

[a] *Epp. ad Fam.* i. 9. 8.

[b] *Epp. ad Quintum fratrem*, ii. 1. 1 (see p. 28).

[c] *Epp. ad Quintum fratrem*, ii. 5; ii. 6 (8 L.C.L.). *Epp. ad Att.* iv. 5; iv. 6. *Epp. ad Fam.* i. 7. 10; i. 9. 8-10. On their chronological order see Rice Holmes, *op. cit.* p. 297.

[d] See p. 31.

paid an after-dinner call on Pompey. Pompey told him that he was proposing to leave Rome on 11 April for corn-supply business in Sardinia, embarking at Labro (Leghorn ?) or Pisae, and, so far from showing any sign of annoyance at Cicero's proposal of 5 April, genially said that Quintus Cicero, his *legatus*, could rejoin his family in Rome immediately.

Caesar, meantime, was at Ravenna in his Cisalpine province, and received on 8 April or a day or two later a report from Crassus in person on what Cicero had done. He realized that a crisis had to be met : L. Domitius Ahenobarbus, who was a candidate for the consulship of 55 B.C., was bent on bringing about his recall ; Cicero must once more be reduced to submission ; a revolt of the Veneti demanded his own immediate return to Gaul. He therefore at once posted with Crassus across to Luca, the southernmost town in Cisalpine Gaul, and, if Pompey had no other intention than to sail straight to Sardinia, he requested him to confer first with him at Luca.[a] Pompey, full of the indignation which he had just concealed from Cicero, joined Caesar at Luca, after a journey from Rome of five days or so, say on 16 April, and the Conference was held immediately afterwards. The movements of the Triumvirate were an open secret, for, if we may believe Plutarch[b] and Appian,[c] more than two hundred senators found their way to Luca. Although the Triumvirate met in private, not a few must have known that Pompey and Crassus were to be the consuls of 55 B.C., and that they had no intention of interfering with Caesar's interests in Gaul.

[a] Suetonius, *Div. Iul.* 24. 1.
[b] *Pompey*, 51. 4 ; *Caesar*, 21. 5.
[c] *Bell. Civ.* ii. 17. 62.

Immediately after the Conference Caesar left for Transalpine Gaul, where he punished the rebellious Veneti with ruthless severity.[a] From Luca Pompey travelled to Sardinia where, a few days after the Conference, he met Quintus Cicero and pressed him to dissuade his brother from opposing Caesar even if he could not openly support him: "You are the very man I want to see. . . . Unless you remonstrate seriously with your brother, you will be held responsible for the pledge you gave me on his behalf."[b] Also, to make certain, Pompey sent to Italy L. Vibullius Rufus, who had been one of his officers in Asia, as the bearer of a request to Cicero not to commit himself on the Campanian land until he himself returned to Italy. It was early in May, probably, when Cicero heard from his brother and received Pompey's message from Vibullius. We do not know, however, whether, as he had intended, Cicero was back in Rome by 6 May, but, in any case, the debate on the Campanian land, arranged to open on 15 May, did not take place. Cicero absented himself from the meeting, and made a laconic reference to the matter in a letter written to his brother, who was on his way home from Sardinia, soon after 15 May[c]: "What, it has been alleged, was to be settled on the 15th and following day about the Campanian land, was never settled. I am in a fix about this business." But Cicero escaped from his "fix" by a rapid decision to abandon opposition to Caesar and Pompey and to

[a] Caesar, *Bell. Gall.* iii. 9. 2; 16. 4.

[b] Cicero, *Epp. ad Fam.* i. 9. 9. In return for Caesar's consent to Cicero's restoration from exile, his brother Quintus promised that Marcus would not attack the Triumvirate.

[c] Cicero, *Epp. ad Quintum fratrem*, ii. 6. (8 L.C.L.) 1 and 2.

give them his support. It is probable that soon after he had written the above letter to Quintus, that is, shortly after 15 May, he composed a letter to Pompey, who was then either in Sardinia or on his way to Africa, to make his peace. He called this letter his "palinode," and, as the matter pressed, he sent off the letter without, as he usually did, submitting a copy to Atticus.[a] He then retired to Antium, where he received a complaint from Atticus who, having heard in some way of the "palinode," expressed surprise at his friend's unusual action. Cicero defended himself in these words: "What's this? Do you really imagine that I prefer my things to be read and criticized by anyone but you? Then why did I send them to someone else first? The man I sent them to was very insistent, and I had no copy. Nothing else? Well, yes (I must swallow the pill and not keep mouthing it): I felt my 'palinode' just a shade discreditable." Cicero was then thinking of some public expression of his change of policy, and, in the same letter, hints at a speech: "I was, however, restrained in my theme, when I put pen to paper.[b] I will launch out more fully, if he (*i.e.* Pompey) shows that he is pleased with it." The same idea occurs in his next letter to Atticus from Antium [c] in which, at the same time, he bitterly laments the tyranny of the Triumvirate and his enforced submission to it: "What could be more degrading than our present life? . . . However, I am

[a] *Epp. ad Att.* iv. 5. 1. Alternatively, a speech composed by Cicero and circulated by the Triumvirs (T. A. Dorey, *J.R.S.* xlix (1959), p. 199).
[b] In his letter or speech.
[c] *Epp. ad Att.* iv. 6. 2.

spending my time here thinking out how to revoke my past." No doubt he was preparing his speech on the Consular Provinces.

It is possible that, while Cicero was preparing his contemplated speech, the Senate, at his instance, passed two decrees of a complimentary nature in favour of Caesar.[a] The first was a grant of money to provide pay for his Gallic army. To the four legions under his command early in 58 B.C. he had added four more, two in 58 and two in 57 B.C. This grant, however, was, according to Cicero,[b] not essential, as Caesar could support his army on the immense booty which he had captured. But Cicero says that there was much opposition [c] to this proposed grant and that the Treasury could ill afford it.[d]

The second decree sanctioned the appointment, in Cicero's words, of *decem legati*. This phrase is ambiguous and may be explained in one of two ways. Decision is difficult. The usual explanation [e] (for which the present writer feels a preference) is that by *legati* we are here to understand members of Caesar's military staff, officers of senatorial rank, normally appointed by the Senate, but, as a privilege under the *lex Vatinia*,[f] appointed by Caesar himself. As three *legati* were normally assigned to a consular command, Caesar, with a command covering two

[a] *De prov. cons.* 28; *Pro Balbo*, 61; *Epp. ad Fam.* i. 7. 10.

[b] *De prov. cons.* 28.

[c] *De prov. cons.* 28.

[d] *Pro Balbo*, 61. The difficulties of the Treasury were due, *inter alia*, to heavy expenditure on the corn-supply.

[e] H. E. Butler and M. Cary: *De provinciis consularibus*, p. 65; H. E. Butler and M. Cary, *Suetonius*, *Div. Iul.* p. 74; J. S. Reid, *Cicero*, *Pro Balbo*, p. 96.

[f] Cicero, *In Vatinium*, 35.

provinces (if Cisalpine Gaul and Illyricum may be regarded for this purpose as one province), would be entitled to six. The increase in Caesar's army called for an increase in his military staff. This second decree, therefore, may on one interpretation have sanctioned an increased establishment of *legati*.[a]

The following is a more recent explanation of the phrase. A case[b] has been made out for the view that *decem legati* in Latin was a technical phrase for a commission of senators sent by the Senate to co-operate with a general after a war in the organization of conquered territory. In view of Caesar's two defensive victories in 58 B.C., of the reduction of the Belgae in 57 B.C., and of the prospect of the subjugation of the maritime peoples in 56 B.C., it might well be claimed that Caesar's conquest of Gaul was completed.[c] Such an explanation would accord well with the difficulty[d] felt by Caesar's supporters at Rome in 56 B.C., not in achieving the appointment of *decem legati* (*qua* members of his military staff), but in securing almost simultaneously the dispatch of *decem legati* as a commission to organize the conquered Gallic territory,[e] and to allow Caesar to remain in Gaul for two years more.

In obedience to the terms of the *lex Sempronia de*

[a] From our various sources for the Gallic War it may be gathered that in all Caesar appointed as many as seventeen *legati*; and the status of six other officers is doubtful. See Rice Holmes, *Caesar's Conquest of Gaul*, pp. 563-565.

[b] By J. P. V. D. Balsdon, in "Consular Provinces under the Late Republic: II. Caesar's Gallic Command," in *J.R.S.* xxix, pt. 2, p. 171.

[c] Caesar, *Bell. Gall.* ii. 35; iii. 7.

[d] Cicero, *Epp. ad Fam.* i. 7. 10.

[e] Dio Cassius, xxxix. 25. 1. A vague phrase of Suetonius, *Div. Iul.* 24. 3, may point in the same direction.

provinciis consularibus of C. Gracchus,[a] under which before the consular elections the Senate had to choose the provinces to be governed by the new consuls after their year of office in Rome, the Senate met before the consular elections in 56 B.C. to select provinces for the consuls of the following year.

It is possible to fix roughly, but not precisely, the date of this meeting. Its *terminus post quem* is 15 May, when Cicero's submission to the Triumvirs was revealed by the dropping of the proposed debate on the Campanian land.[b] Its *terminus ante quem* is the consular elections usually held towards the end of July. It is reasonable to assume that the Senate met two or three weeks before the elections to assign the consular provinces. A date, therefore, late in June or early in July is possible, and finds support from two passages in Cicero. We are told in *Epp. ad Quintum fratrem*, ii. 6. (8 L.C.L.) 1, that on 15 May the Senate refused to vote Gabinius (then governor of Syria) a *supplicatio* in honour of his suppression in 57 B.C. of a revolt raised by Alexander, son of Aristobulus II, the unsuccessful claimant for the throne of Judaea whom Pompey had deported to Italy; and in *De prov. cons.* 15 we read that Cicero anticipated that within a few days from the time when he was speaking, Gabinius would receive news of the Senate's refusal. As a journey to Syria must have taken at least a month, even under the most favourable conditions, and might well have needed some seven or eight weeks, the meeting of the Senate when Cicero delivered the *De provinciis consularibus* cannot have

[a] This law may date to Gracchus' second (122) rather than to his first tribunate (123 B.C.).

[b] Cicero, *Epp. ad Quintum fratrem*, ii. 6. (8 L.C.L.) 2.

been earlier than the middle of June, and was, in all probability, at the end of June or early in July.[a]

Senior ex-consuls had made various proposals before Cicero rose to speak. Four provinces came under consideration: Cisalpine Gaul, governed by Caesar, Transalpine Gaul also governed by Caesar, Macedonia governed by L. Calpurnius Piso, Syria governed by A. Gabinius. Under one highly uncompromising proposal Caesar would have lost both his provinces, for it was suggested that both Cisalpine and Transalpine Gaul should be assigned to the consuls about to be elected. Others wished to select not both, but one of, the Gallic provinces. Cicero spoke strongly against disturbing Caesar in Gaul before his work was finished, and no less strongly in favour of speedily removing Piso from Macedonia and Gabinius from Syria. To deprive Caesar of both the Gauls would leave Piso and Gabinius at liberty to continue their misgovernment; to assign one of the Gallic provinces would still leave either Piso or Gabinius undisturbed. Cicero criticizes the author of the proposal that Transalpine Gaul should be made a consular province for lack of moral courage as a senator in failing to propose the Cisalpine province and thereby in failing to challenge the validity of the *lex Vatinia* of 59 B.C.[b] The proposal to deprive Caesar of Cisalpine Gaul would lead, Cicero claimed, to a constitutional difficulty, since Caesar's tenure of Cisalpine Gaul was guaranteed by the *lex Vatinia* till 1 March 54 B.C., so that, if Cisalpine Gaul were assigned to a consul of 55 B.C., the consul would be, constitutionally, in an anomalous position during January and February

[a] See Butler and Cary, *op. cit.* Appendix v, pp. 104-106.
[b] *De prov. cons.* 36.

54 B.C.: "He will have *imperium* as a proconsul and yet be legally debarred from entering his province, where alone he can exercise his *imperium*." [a]

Cicero eloquently supported the proposal made by a very senior and distinguished ex-consul, P. Servilius Vatia Isauricus (consul 79 B.C.), that Macedonia and Syria should be assigned to the consuls about to be elected. He added a supplementary proposal that Macedonia and Syria should be assigned to praetors for the coming year (55 B.C.), so that Piso and Gabinius might be superseded immediately. Although Cicero expected that tribunes would, as they were entitled to do under C. Gracchus' *lex Sempronia de provinciis consularibus*, veto his supplement which dealt with an assignment to praetors, the proposal itself that these two provinces be held by consuls in 54 B.C. could not be challenged by tribunes. Thus, at best, Piso and Gabinius might be superseded in the following year (55 B.C.); at worst, in the year after that (54 B.C.).

For Cicero the result of the debate was highly satisfactory: Caesar's two Gallic provinces were left untouched; Macedonia became a praetorian province and Piso was recalled in 55 B.C. [b]; but Gabinius was left in Syria, which was assigned to one of the consuls about to be elected.[c] We do not know which was the other consular province that was assigned. It may have been one of the two Spanish provinces, for Syria and the two Spains were to fall, as had surely been agreed at the Conference of Luca, to Pompey and Crassus after their second consulships in 55 B.C.

However bitterly Cicero lamented to Atticus his

[a] Balsdon, *op. cit.* p. 168. *De prov. cons.* 36 and 37.
[b] Cicero, *In Pisonem*, 88 sqq. Asconius, pp. 1 and 2 (Clark).
[c] Cicero, *In Pisonem*, 88.

enforced submission to the Triumvirate,[a] there can be no doubt of the tact and dexterity with which he gave expression in the Senate to his reconciliation with Caesar. His speech *De provinciis consularibus* was not only " a public demonstration of loyal acquiescence," [b] it was also " a brilliant piece of eloquence . . . containing one or two passages which Cicero rarely surpassed." [c]

The predominant note of the speech is struck in the opening sentences : " personal feelings must be subordinated to the good of the State." Since Piso and Gabinius had sold Cicero to Clodius, his hatred for them in no way " conflicted with the public good [d] ; " it rather intensified the vigour with which early in the speech (§§ 3-17) he urged their immediate recall from their provinces. They are mercilessly attacked, but Cicero's language is free from the coarse abuse which a year later disfigured the *In Pisonem* (55 B.C.). This speech has been called " a masterpiece of misrepresentation." [e] Many of Cicero's charges against Piso can be refuted, and there are clear signs of his ability as a governor. *Imperium infinitum*, with which Cicero alleged that both Gabinius and Piso were invested, was a term of rhetorical abuse not of constitutional theory.[f]

Much of Cicero's invective against Gabinius' rule in Syria must be discounted, as he is a not unbiased witness. Gabinius' vigorous repression in 57 B.C. of

[a] *Epp. ad Att.* iv. 5 and 6.
[b] Syme, *The Roman Revolution*, p. 37.
[c] Butler and Cary, *op. cit.* pp. 13 and 14.
[d] *De prov. cons.* 1.
[e] R. G. M. Nisbet, *In Pisonem*, p. xvi.
[f] Cicero, *De domo*, 55. J. Béranger, *Mélanges Marouzeau* (Paris, 1948), pp. 19 ff.

the revolt of Alexander, son of Aristobulus II, receives no recognition from Cicero save jubilation that the Senate refused his application for a *supplicatio* for this successful campaign.[a] Cicero's denunciation of Gabinius' treatment of the *publicani*[b] may be largely explained by his unfailing loyalty to the social order to which both he and the *publicani* alike belonged by birth, and by Gabinius' desire to relieve a suffering province from the deplorable exactions of Roman officials and money-makers.

Gabinius and Piso disposed of by a proposal for their immediate supersession, Cicero by an easy transition passes to cogent advocacy of reconciliation with Caesar and to eloquent praise of his victories in Gaul (§§ 18-39). Though admitting his differences of opinion with Caesar and Caesar's responsibility for his banishment, he supports by reference to many precedents from earlier days his plea that the welfare of the State should always override private feuds. In his relations with Caesar he had been at one with the Senate : he disapproved, as did the Senate, of Caesar's actions as consul, but he played a leading part in advocating the recent senatorial decrees so complimentary to Caesar. The Senate should retain Caesar in Gaul not so much as a compliment, but as a recognition that the interests of the State could best be served by allowing him to complete the great conquest that was so far advanced, and thereby to free Italy for ever from her old dread of invasion from beyond the Alps. In setting forth Caesar's claims to an extension of his command, Cicero found a theme worthy of his eloquence.[c]

[a] *De prov. cons.* 14. *Epp. ad Quintum fratrem*, ii. 6. (8 L.C.L.) 1. [b] *De prov. cons.* 11 and 12. [c] §§ 33-35.

The valuable summary of Cicero's relations with Caesar (§§ 40-44), in which Cicero now takes the blame for his exile, pleads for a truce to animosity. In the elaborately composed conclusion (§§ 45-47) Cicero argues that, if certain Optimates regard his banishment as legal, he is no less entitled to accept the validity of such of Caesar's laws as he may happen to approve, although by strict law the *obnuntiatio* of Bibulus made illegal not only Caesar's laws but also Clodius' tribunate and all his acts as tribune. Cicero is here clearly resentful of the jealousy of certain Optimates who petted Clodius and whom he blames for their perfidious encouragement of his plan *in arcem illius causae invadere.*[a]

[a] Cicero, *Epp. ad Att.* iv. 5. 1-2 ; *Epp. ad Fam.* i. 9. 8.

II. DE PROVINCIIS CONSULARIBUS

IN SENATU ORATIO

1 I. Si quis vestrum, patres conscripti, exspectat, quas sim provincias decreturus, consideret ipse secum, qui mihi homines ex provinciis potissimum detrahendi sint; non dubitabit, quid sentire me conveniat, cum, quid mihi sentire necesse sit, cogitarit. Ac si princeps eam sententiam dicerem, laudaretis profecto, si solus, certe ignosceretis; etiamsi paulo minus utilis vobis sententia videretur, veniam tamen aliquam dolori meo tribueretis. Nunc vero, patres conscripti, non parva adficior voluptate, vel quod hoc maxime rei publicae conducit, Syriam Macedoniamque decerni, ut dolor meus nihil a communi utilitate dissentiat, vel quod habeo auctorem P. Servilium, qui ante me sententiam dixit, virum clarissimum et cum in universam rem publicam, tum etiam erga meam salutem fide ac
2 benevolentia singulari. Quodsi ille et paulo ante, et

---

[a] See p. 534.

[b] When asked by the presiding magistrate "*quid censes?*" ("What is your opinion?"), the senator, whose opinion was asked first, was said *princeps sententiam dicere.*

[c] Against Piso and Gabinius, who had treated Cicero very badly during their consulship (58 B.C.), when Clodius forced him to withdraw from Rome.

[d] P. Servilius Vatia Isauricus (consul 79 B.C.), a senior ex-

II. A SPEECH CONCERNING THE CONSULAR PROVINCES

DELIVERED IN THE SENATE

I. If any one of you, Conscript Fathers, is waiting 1
to hear what I propose to do in regard to the assignation of provinces,[a] let him ask himself what persons in particular I think should be withdrawn from their governments; he will have no doubt what it is fitting my opinion should be, when he has reflected what it must be. And if I were the first to put forward this opinion,[b] you would assuredly praise me; if I were the only one to do so, you would no doubt excuse me; even if my proposal should appear to you to be of little value, you would yet make some allowance for my resentment.[c] But as it is, Conscript Fathers, I find no small satisfaction, either because it is specially advantageous to the State that Syria and Macedonia should be assigned, so that my resentment in no way conflicts with the public good, or because I am following the lead of Publius Servilius,[d] who gave his opinion before me, a man of the highest distinction, and one of singular loyalty and goodwill both to the State generally and to my own welfare in particular. But 2
if he, both just now and as often as he has had an

consul (p. 534), but probably not *princeps senatus*, for in the late Republic it is unlikely that there was any such title.

quotienscumque ei locus dicendi ac potestas fuit, Gabinium et Pisonem, duo rei publicae portenta ac paene funera, cum propter alias causas, tum maxime propter illud insigne scelus eorum et importunam in me crudelitatem non solum sententia sua, sed etiam verborum gravitate esse notandos putavit, quonam me animo in eos esse oportet, cuius illi salutem pro pignore tradiderunt ad explendas suas cupiditates? Sed ego in hac sententia dicenda non parebo dolori meo, non iracundiae serviam. Quo animo unus quisque vestrum debet esse in illos, hoc ero; praecipuum illum et proprium sensum doloris mei, quem tamen vos communem semper vobis mecum esse duxistis, a sententia dicenda amovebo, ad ulciscendi tempora reservabo.

3 II. Quattuor sunt provinciae, patres conscripti, de quibus adhuc intellego sententias esse dictas: Galliae duae, quas hoc tempore uno imperio videmus esse coniunctas, et Syria et Macedonia, quas vobis invitis et oppressis pestiferi illi consules pro perversae[1] rei publicae praemiis occupaverunt. Decernendae nobis sunt lege Sempronia duae. Quid est, quod possimus de Syria Macedoniaque dubitare? Mitto, quod eas ita partas habent ii, qui nunc optinent, ut non ante attigerint, quam hunc ordinem condemnarint, quam

[1] eversae *most MSS.*: perversae *Baiter.*

---

[a] They helped Clodius against Cicero in order that they might obtain the provinces which he had promised to secure for them.

[b] Cisalpine Gaul with Illyricum had been given to Caesar by the *lex Vatinia* in 59 B.C. Transalpine Gaul was later in the same year assigned to him by a decree of the Senate.

occasion and opportunity of speaking, not only expressed his opinion but did so in impressive language, that Gabinius and Piso, those two monsters of depravity who almost ruined the State, should be branded with infamy, both for other reasons, and particularly for their high crime and savage cruelty towards me, what ought to be my feelings towards them, who made my welfare a pawn for the satisfaction of their greedy passions ? [a] But, in giving my opinion here, I will not be a tool of resentment, I will not be a slave of anger. What ought to be the feelings of each one of you towards these men, those too shall be mine ; that special and personal feeling arising from my resentment, which however you have always held that you shared with me, will have no effect upon the opinion that I intend to give : I will reserve it for the moment of vengeance.

II. There are four provinces, Conscript Fathers, 3
about which I understand that so far opinions have been given : the two Gauls,[b] which we see at this moment united under a single command, and Syria and Macedonia, which, in defiance of your will, when you were under constraint, those accursed consuls seized as their reward for overthrowing the State.[c] Under the Sempronian Law we have to assign two provinces.[d] Can we have any doubt about how to deal with Syria and Macedonia ? I pass over the way in which those who now govern them acquired them,—not until they had condemned this Order,[e]

[c] For the bargain between Clodius and the two consuls see *Pro Sestio*, 24, 25, 53. [d] See p. 532.

[e] By banishing Cicero for the execution of Catiline's accomplices in Rome, which was approved by the Senate. His condemnation was thus a judgment against the Senate.

auctoritatem vestram e civitate exterminarint, quam fidem publicam, quam perpetuam populi Romani salutem, quam me ac meos omnes foedissime crude-
4 lissimeque vexarint. Omnia domestica atque urbana mitto, quae tanta sunt, ut numquam Hannibal huic urbi tantum mali optarit, quantum illi effecerint; ad ipsas venio provincias. Quarum Macedonia, quae erat antea munita plurimorum imperatorum non turribus, sed tropaeis, quae multis victoriis erat iam diu triumphisque pacata, sic a barbaris, quibus est propter avaritiam pax erepta, vexatur, ut Thessalonicenses positi in gremio imperii nostri relinquere oppidum et arcem munire cogantur, ut via illa nostra, quae per Macedoniam est usque ad Hellespontum militaris, non solum excursionibus barbarorum sit infesta, sed etiam castris Thraeciis distincta ac notata. Ita gentes eae, quae, ut pace uterentur, vim argenti dederant praeclaro nostro imperatori, ut exhaustas domos replere possent, pro empta pace bellum nobis prope iustum intulerunt.

5 III. Iam vero exercitus noster ille superbissimo dilectu et durissima conquisitione collectus omnis interiit. Magno hoc dico cum dolore. Miserandum

[a] The Senate gave Cicero moral authority for the execution of the conspirators. Moreover, on 3 Jan. 62 B.C., the Senate specially indemnified all who had acted against the Catilinarians.

[b] See *Pro Sestio*, 54.

[c] Notably by L. Aemilius Paullus, victor of Pydna (168 B.C.), Q. Caecilius Metellus, conqueror of Andriscus (148 B.C.), and T. Didius (at the end of the second century B.C., under whom the provincial frontier of Macedonia was extended; see *Supplementum Epigraphicum Graecum*, iii. 378, ll. 28-29).

not until they had driven your authority from the city, not until they had broken a pledge given by the State [a] and harassed the undisturbed security of the Roman People, not until they had most foully and mercilessly persecuted me and all my family.[b] I pass 4
over all their crimes among us here in Rome, which are so great that Hannibal never wished such misfortune for this city as they have inflicted upon it; I come to the provinces themselves. One of them, Macedonia, which was formerly protected, not by fortresses but by the trophies of many generals,[c] had for long enjoyed a peace, won at the cost of many victories and triumphs. This province is now so harassed by barbarians, whose greed had made them break the peace,[d] that the people of Thessalonica,[e] dwelling in the very heart of our power, are forced to abandon their city and fortify their citadel, that our great military road through Macedonia as far as the Hellespont is not only endangered by raiding barbarians, but even studded and dotted with Thracian encampments. Thus, these peoples who had paid a large sum of money to our illustrious victor as the price of peace, in order to replenish their exhausted households, instead of the peace they had paid for, brought almost regular war within our borders.

III. Moreover, our forces there, raised by the 5
strictest of levies and the most merciless of conscriptions, are a total loss. I say this with deep distress.

[d] Piso had attacked the Thracians and Dardani on the northern frontier; or, according to *Pro Sestio*, 94, he sold peace to them for a large sum, and then let them despoil Macedonia in order to repay themselves.

[e] The seat of the provincial government (now Salonica), on the Via Egnatia, the military road which ran from Dyrrhachium (now Durazzo) to Byzantium.

in modum milites populi Romani capti, necati, deserti, dissipati sunt, incuria, fame, morbo, vastitate consumpti, ut, quod est indignissimum, scelus imperatoris poena exercitus expiatum esse videatur.[1] Atque hanc Macedoniam domitis iam gentibus finitimis barbariaque compressa pacatam ipsam per se et quietam tenui praesidio atque exigua manu etiam sine imperio per legatos nomine ipso populi Romani tuebamur; quae nunc consulari imperio atque exercitu ita vexata est, vix ut se possit diuturna pace recreare; cum interea quis vestrum hoc non audivit, quis ignorat, Achaeos ingentem pecuniam pendere L. Pisoni quotannis, vectigal ac portorium Dyrrachinorum totum in huius unius quaestum esse conversum, urbem Byzantiorum vobis atque huic imperio fidelissimam hostilem in modum esse vexatam? quo ille, posteaquam nihil exprimere ab egentibus, nihil ulla vi a miseris extorquere potuit, cohortes in hiberna misit; iis praeposuit, quos putavit fore diligentissimos satellites
6 scelerum, ministros cupiditatum suarum. Omitto iuris dictionem in libera civitate contra leges senatus-

[1] in poenam exercitus expetitum *most MSS.*: exercitus expetisse videatur *Gulielmus*: in patriam exercitumque expiatum esse videatur *Butler-Cary*: poena exercitus expiatum *suggested by Reid.*

---

[a] The general meaning may be gathered from *In Pisonem*, 85: "tua scelera di immortales in nostros milites expiaverunt," with a slightly different construction.

[b] There is a strong presumption, but no conclusive evidence, that at that time Achaia (Greece) was included in the province of Macedonia. There was no separate province of Achaia till 27 B.C.

It is truly pitiable how soldiers of the Roman People have been captured, killed, abandoned, scattered; destroyed by neglect, famine, disease, and utter ruin, so that, most disgraceful of all, the crime of a general seems to have been expiated by the sufferings of his army.[a] And yet this Macedonia, after we had subdued the neighbouring peoples and crushed the barbarians, pacified and tranquil as it was in itself, we formerly secured with a small garrison and a handful of soldiers, through legates too with no supreme military authority, merely by the name of the Roman People; whereas now, in spite of consular authority and an army, it has been so devastated that even a long period of peace can hardly restore its strength. And meantime, which of you has not heard, who does not know that the Achaeans [b] pay a huge sum to Lucius Piso yearly? that the town- and customs-dues of the people of Dyrrhachium [c] have been wholly appropriated to the profit of Piso alone? that the city of Byzantium,[d] most devoted to you and this Empire, has been harassed as if it were an enemy? where Piso, finding that he could squeeze nothing from the poverty, extract nothing by any force from the misery of the inhabitants, sent cohorts into winter-quarters, putting at the head of them men who would be (he thought) most thorough as instruments of his crimes and as ministers to his desires.
I say nothing about his administration of justice in a 6
free state contrary to laws and decrees of the Senate;

[c] Since Dyrrhachium was a *civitas libera et immunis*, *vectigal* must refer, not to Roman provincial taxation, but to local customs dues.

[d] Byzantium, a *civitas foederata* since about 150 B.C., enjoyed complete autonomy and special privileges.

que consulta, caedes relinquo, libidines praetereo, quarum acerbissimum exstat indicium et ad insignem memoriam turpitudinis et paene ad iustum odium imperii nostri, quod constat nobilissimas virgines se in puteos abiecisse et morte voluntaria necessariam turpitudinem depulisse. Nec haec idcirco omitto, quod non gravissima sint, sed quia nunc sine teste dico.

IV. Ipsam vero urbem Byzantiorum fuisse refertissimam atque ornatissimam signis quis ignorat? quae illi, exhausti sumptibus bellisque maximis, cum omnes[1] Mithridaticos impetus totumque Pontum armatum effervescentem in Asiam atque erumpentem ore[2] repulsum et cervicibus interclusum suis sustinerent, tum, inquam, Byzantii et postea signa illa et reliqua urbis ornamenta sanctissime custodita tenue-
7 runt ; te imperatore infelicissimo et taeterrimo,
Caesonine Calventi, civitas libera et pro eximiis[3] suis beneficiis a senatu et a populo Romano liberata sic spoliata atque nudata est, ut, nisi C. Vergilius legatus, vir fortis et innocens, intervenisset, unum signum Byzantii ex maximo numero nullum haberent. Quod

[1] cumnis *P* : cum omnis *Halm.*

[2] aegre *some editors* : *Butler-Cary suggest* Bospori ore. *Nisbet proposes* corpore *for* ore. *This is adopted and translated.*

[3] *Madvig's correction of* proximis MSS.

---

[a] See *In Pisonem*, 83, 84.

[b] For the textual difficulty see R. G. M. Nisbet, *Classical Review* (lxxv), *N.S.* xi. 3, Dec. 1961, p. 201. He objects to Butler-Cary's *Bospori ore* and in proposing *corpore* he defends its use in the singular with reference to more than

I leave out murders [a]; I pass over deeds of lust, of which we have most pitiable proof, serving both as a notable record of his own disgrace and almost as a justification for hatred of our rule, in the admitted fact that maidens of most noble birth have thrown themselves into wells and of their own accord sought death as an escape from inevitable dishonour. If I omit these matters, it is not because they are not most serious, but because at the time of speaking I have no witnesses.

IV. But who does not know that the city of Byzantium itself was most profusely and beautifully decorated with statues? At the time when its inhabitants, crippled by expenditure and terrible wars, bore the brunt of all the attacks of Mithridates and of the whole of Pontus in arms, as it was seething into Asia and bursting out, damning its onset with their bodies and bearing it on their own shoulders [b]: then I say, and afterwards, the Byzantines kept those statues and other ornaments of their city most religiously guarded; but under your disastrous and 7
loathsome rule, Caesoninus Calventius,[c] a free city, whose liberty had been ratified by the Senate and People of Rome in return for its distinguished services, found itself so plundered and pillaged, that had not a courageous and upright officer, Gaius Vergilius, intervened, the Byzantines would no longer have possessed a single statue out of so many. What

one person and its conjunction with a plural *cervicibus*. There is no statement elsewhere that Mithridates attacked Byzantium.

[c] Piso's father was L. Calpurnius Piso Caesoninus, his mother a daughter of Calventius of Placentia, a Latin colony on the south side of the Po. Cicero pretends that Piso was a Gaul.

fanum in Achaia, qui locus aut lucus in Graecia tota tam sanctus fuit, in quo ullum simulacrum, ullum ornamentum reliquum sit? Emisti a foedissimo tribuno pl. tum in illo naufragio huius urbis, quam tu idem, qui gubernare debueras, everteras, tum, inquam, emisti grandi pecunia, ut tibi de pecuniis creditis ius in liberos populos contra senatus consulta et contra legem generi tui dicere liceret. Id emptum ita vendidisti, ut aut ius non diceres aut bonis cives
8 Romanos everteres. Quorum ego nihil dico, patres conscripti, nunc in hominem ipsum; de provincia disputo. Itaque omnia illa, quae et saepe audistis et tenetis animis, etiamsi non audiatis, praetermitto; nihil de hac eius urbana, quam ille praesens in mentibus vestris oculisque defixit, audacia loquor; nihil de superbia, nihil de contumacia, nihil de crudelitate disputo. Lateant libidines eius illae tenebricosae, quas fronte et supercilio, non pudore et temperantia contegebat; de provincia quod agitur, id disputo. Huic vos non summittetis, hunc diutius manere patiemini? cuius, ut provinciam tetigit, sic fortuna cum improbitate certavit, ut nemo posset, utrum posterior[1] an infelicior esset, iudicare.

[1] posterior MSS. (=" *worse* ") *should be retained*: protervior *Lambinus, followed by Baiter*: probrosior *suggested by Butler-Cary. C. Gracchus frag. 27* (*Malcovati, ORF*^{2}): omnium nationum postremissimum nequissimumque *supports* posterior. *See* Pro Roscio Amerino, *137* (*G. Landgraf, 1914*).

---

[a] *Graecia*, a general term. For *Achaia* see p. 544, note *b*.

[b] During the tribunate of Clodius, 58 B.C.

[c] Loans from citizens of free states to fellow-citizens or to Romans.

[d] Julius Caesar, husband of Calpurnia, the daughter of Piso. His law, the *lex Iulia de pecuniis repetundis*, confirmed the privileges of the free states and made regulations for the

temple was there in Achaia, what place or holy grove throughout all Greece [a] so sacred, that any image of the Gods or a single ornament remains in it? You bought from an infamous tribune of the commons, at a time when our city was made shipwreck,[b] ruined by you who should have been at the helm—then, I say, you bought from him for a large sum of money the right of administering justice over free states in matters of debt [c] contrary to decrees of the Senate and a law of your son-in-law.[d] The right you had bought you sold, either by denial of justice, or by ejecting Roman citizens from their property. How- 8
ever, when I mention these things, Conscript Fathers, I am not attacking the man himself; I am discussing the province. And so I pass over all those matters, which you have often heard and remember well even if you should not be reminded—I say nothing about his effrontery in the city,[e] which he imprinted deep in your minds and vision while he lived among you; I make no comment on his pride, his insolence, his cruelty. Close hidden be all those deeds of lust and darkness which he sought to conceal by a stern and lofty look,[f] not by modesty and self-control; what is being done about the province, that is my subject. Will you not supersede him? Will you allow him to remain there any longer, a man whose fortunes, from the moment he entered his province, were so well matched with his villainies that no one could decide whether his conduct or his misfortune was the worse?

better government of the provinces and for the checking of extortion.

[e] When consul in 58 B.C.

[f] See *Pro Sestio*, 19; *In Pisonem*, 13.

9 An vero in Syria diutius est Semiramis illa retinenda? cuius iter in provinciam fuit eius modi, ut rex Ariobarzanes consulem vestrum ad caedem faciendam tamquam aliquem Thraecem conduceret. Deinde adventus in Syriam primus equitatus habuit interitum, post concisae sunt optimae cohortes. Igitur in Syria imperatore illo nihil aliud neque gestum[1] neque actum est nisi pactiones pecuniarum cum tyrannis, decisiones, direptiones, latrocinia, caedes, cum palam populi Romani imperator instructo exercitu dexteram tendens non ad laudem milites hortaretur, sed omnia sibi et empta et emenda esse clamaret.

10 V. Iam vero publicanos miseros (me etiam miserum illorum ita de me meritorum miseriis ac dolore!) tradidit in servitutem Iudaeis et Syris, nationibus natis servituti. Statuit ab initio et in eo perseveravit, ius publicano non dicere; pactiones sine ulla iniuria factas rescidit, custodias sustulit; vectigales multos ac stipendiarios liberavit; quo in oppido ipse esset

[1] *A word has dropped out after* neque: gestum *Orelli*: cogitatum *Madvig*: nihil aliud umquam actum est *Butler-Cary, Peterson.*

---

[a] Cicero turns to Gabinius' governorship of Syria. He compares him with Semiramis (Sammuramat, wife of Shamshi-Adad V, king of Assyria 825–810 B.C.), because he combined effeminacy with warfare.

[b] Ariobarzanes II, king of Cappadocia, 62–51 B.C. Cicero's allusion is otherwise unknown.

[c] See *Pro Sestio*, 71; some unknown defeat.

[d] For example, with Hyrcanus II, of Judaea, whom he supported against his nephew Alexander son of Aristobulus II, whom Pompey had deported to Italy, and with other vassal princes.

[e] Cicero explains the extended hand not as an oratorical gesture, but as a sign that he was ready to receive payments for any favour.

Then again, Syria: is this new Semiramis [a] to be retained any longer there? As he marched to his province, it seemed as though King Ariobarzanes [b] was hiring your own consul to kill and slay like some Thracian cut-throat. Then no sooner had he arrived in Syria than his cavalry were lost, and afterwards some excellent cohorts were cut to pieces.[c] So, while he was conquering in Syria, nothing else has been done or settled except money bargains with princes,[d] settlements by compounding, robberies, brigandage, massacres, when, in open day, a general of the Roman People, with his troops drawn up in order of battle, as he held out his right hand,[e] was not exhorting his soldiers to glory, but proclaiming that he had bought or was ready to buy everything for money. 9

V. Then, too, there are those unhappy revenue-farmers [f]—and what misery to me were the miseries and troubles of those to whom I owed so much!—he handed them over as slaves to Jews and Syrians, themselves peoples born to be slaves. From the beginning he made it a rule, in which he persisted, not to hear any suits brought by revenue-farmers; he revoked agreements which had been made in which there was no unfairness; removed guards; released many from imposts or tribute,[g] forbade a revenue- 10

[f] Like Cicero, they chiefly belonged to the Equestrian Order. They had supported him in the Catilinarian Conspiracy and when he was a candidate for the consulship, and had interceded with Gabinius for him, when threatened with exile by Clodius. See *Pro Sestio*, 27-29.

[g] *Vectigales* may refer to people who paid taxes in kind, *stipendiarii* to those who paid in cash. In granting these exemptions, which would curtail the takings of the *publicani*, Gabinius was exceeding his authority, unless his *imperium infinitum* empowered him to do so.

aut quo veniret, ibi publicanum aut publicani servum esse vetuit. Quid multa? crudelis haberetur, si in hostes animo fuisset eo, quo fuit in cives Romanos, eius ordinis praesertim, qui est semper pro[1] dignitate
11 sua benignitate magistratus sustentatus. Itaque, patres conscripti, videtis non temeritate redemptionis aut negotii gerendi inscitia, sed avaritia, superbia, crudelitate Gabini paene adflictos iam atque eversos publicanos; quibus quidem vos in his angustiis aerarii tamen subveniatis necesse est; etsi iam multis non potestis, qui propter illum hostem senatus, inimicissimum ordinis equestris bonorumque omnium non solum bona, sed etiam honestatem miseri deperdiderunt, quos non parsimonia, non continentia, non virtus, non labor, non splendor tueri potuit contra
12 illius helluonis et praedonis audaciam. Quid? qui se etiam nunc subsidiis patrimonii aut amicorum liberalitate sustentant, hos perire patiemur? An, si qui frui publico non potuit per hostem, hic tegitur ipsa lege censoria; quem is frui non sinit, qui est, etiamsi non appellatur, hostis, huic ferri auxilium non oportet? Retinete igitur in provincia diutius eum,

[1] pro *inserted by Pluygers.*

---

[a] By bidding too high for the right to farm the revenues. See the scandal in 61 B.C. mentioned by Cicero, *Epp. ad Att.* i. 17. 9.

[b] Money had been wanted for Caesar's campaigns in Gaul, for the armies of Piso and Gabinius (the former receiving 18,000,000 sesterces), for the provision of free corn under Clodius' law of 58 B.C., and for Pompey's work as food-controller (40,000,000 sesterces granted on 5 April 56 B.C. *Epp. ad Quintum fratrem*, ii. 5).

[c] *Publico frui* is to have the enjoyment of something acquired from the State (in the case of the *publicani* a right to profit derived from the collection of public revenue), but if this

farmer or any of his slaves to remain in any town where he himself was or was on the point of going. In a word, he would be considered cruel, if he had shown the same feelings towards our enemies as he showed towards Roman citizens, and they too, members of an Order which has always been supported in a way befitting its position by the goodwill of our magistrates. And so, Conscript Fathers, you see 11
that the revenue-farmers have already been almost crushed and ruined, not by any rashness in making their contracts,[a] nor ignorance in conducting their business, but by the avarice, the arrogance, the cruelty of Gabinius; yet, in spite of the present exhaustion of the Treasury [b] it is your bounden duty to come to their assistance; although there are many past your aid, who, owing to that enemy of the Senate, that bitter foe of the Equestrian Order and of all good citizens, have not only lost their goods but also their honoured name in society—unfortunates whom neither economy nor self-restraint, neither integrity nor toil nor the highest personal character, has been able to defend against the effrontery of that glutton and robber. Again, are we to 12
suffer those to perish who even now support themselves on their patrimony or the generosity of their friends? If a man has been unable "by the action of an enemy" to enjoy a public right, his contract with the censors itself protects him; but when a man is prevented from such enjoyment by one who, though not called an enemy, is one, ought not such a man to receive assistance? [c] Very well, retain still longer in his province a man who makes compacts with enemies

enjoyment were prevented *per hostem*, there would be a legal remedy under the *lex censoria*, or contract with the censors.

qui de sociis cum hostibus, de civibus cum sociis faciat pactiones, qui hoc etiam se pluris esse quam collegam putet, quod ille vos tristitia vultuque deceperit, ipse numquam se minus, quam erat, nequam esse simularit. Piso autem alio quodam modo gloriatur se brevi tempore perfecisse, ne Gabinius unus omnium nequissimus existimaretur.

13 VI. Hos vos de provinciis, si non aliquando deducendi essent, deripiendos non putaretis et has duplices pestes sociorum, militum clades, publicanorum ruinas, provinciarum vastitates, imperii maculas teneretis? At idem vos anno superiore hos eosdem revocabatis, cum vix in provincias pervenissent. Quo tempore si liberum vestrum iudicium fuisset nec totiens dilata res nec ad extremum e manibus erepta, restituissetis, id quod cupiebatis, vestram auctoritatem iis, per quos erat amissa, revocatis et iis ipsis praemiis extortis, quae erant pro scelere atque eversione patriae con-
14 secuti. Qua e poena si tum aliorum opibus, non suis, invitissimis vobis evolarunt, at aliam multo maiorem gravioremque subierunt. Quae enim homini, in quo aliqui si non famae pudor, at supplicii timor est, gravior poena accidere potuit, quam non credi litteris iis, quae rem publicam bene gestam in bello nuntiarent? Hoc statuit senatus, cum frequens supplicationem Gabinio denegavit, primum homini

[a] In spring or early summer 57 B.C. This attempt (details unknown) was stopped by the Triumvirs and Clodius.

[b] Their provinces.

[c] Pompey, Caesar and Clodius.

[d] Over the son of Aristobulus II, Alexander, whe tried to recover Judaea after Pompey's settlement (63 B.C.).

[e] A public thanksgiving, usually for a military victory. The date of the refusal was 15 May 56 B.C. (*Epp. ad Quintum fratrem*, ii. 6. (8 L.C.L.) 1).

against allies, with allies against citizens, who even counts himself of more value than his colleague, just because his colleague has deceived you by his grim and gloomy looks, whereas he himself has never pretended to be less wicked than he was. Piso, on the other hand, parades a somewhat different claim to distinction, seeing that in a brief space he has deprived Gabinius of his reputation as the most villainous of men.

VI. Would you not think that such men, instead of 13
being at last called back, should be dragged back from their provinces? Would you keep there that couple to be scourges of our allies, murderers of our soldiers, destroyers of our revenue-farmers, devastators of our provinces, blots upon our Empire? You are the same men who endeavoured to recall them last year,[a] when they had hardly reached their provinces. At that time, if your votes had been free, and if the matter had not been so often adjourned and finally taken out of your hands, you would have done as you desired, and restored your authority by recalling those through whom you had lost it, and wresting from them the very rewards[b] which they had obtained in return for their crime and their destruction of our country. If then, very much against your will, they 14
escaped this penalty, not by their own resources but by those of others,[c] yet they have had to submit to one that was far greater and more severe. For what severer penalty could befall a man, in whom there is, if not any regard for reputation, at any rate some fear of punishment, than that no credit should be given to those dispatches which announced his military successes?[d] The Senate, when in large numbers it refused a public thanksgiving[e] to Gabinius, declared

sceleribus flagitiis[1] contaminatissimo nihil esse credendum, deinde a proditore atque eo, quem praesentem hostem rei publicae cognosset, bene rem publicam geri non potuisse, postremo ne deos quidem immortales velle aperiri sua templa et sibi supplicari hominis impurissimi et sceleratissimi nomine. Itaque ille alter aut ipse est homo doctus et a suis Graecis subtilius eruditus, quibuscum iam in exostra helluatur, antea post siparium solebat, aut amicos habet prudentiores quam Gabinius, cuius nullae litterae proferuntur.

VII. Hosce igitur imperatores habebimus? quorum alter non audet nos certiores facere, cur[2] imperator appelletur, alterum, si tabellarii non cessarint, necesse est paucis diebus paeniteat audere. Cuius amici si qui sunt, aut si beluae tam immani tamque taetrae possunt ulli esse amici, hac consolatione utuntur, etiam T. Albucio supplicationem hunc ordinem denegasse. Quod est primum dissimile, res in Sar-

[1] flagitiisque *edd. The addition of* -que *seems needless, as Cicero sometimes omits such a copula, especially in his Letters.* flagitiis MSS.

[2] ne *most* MSS. : cur *Ant. Augustinus* : qua re *Peterson.*

---

[a] Piso.

[b] A reference to Philodemus of Gadara, an Epicurean philosopher, elsewhere well spoken of by Cicero.

[c] *Exostra*: a movable platform, used to reveal to an audience something which had been happening behind the scenes.

[d] A light curtain concealing part of the stage.

[e] Piso either was clever enough to send no dispatches or

first, that no credit should be given to a man befouled with every sort of crime and outrage; next, that the State could not have been well served by a traitor, and one whom, when he was in Rome, it had recognized as a public enemy; and lastly, that not even the Immortal Gods desired their temples to be thrown open and prayers to be addressed to them in the name of the most vile and the most wicked of mankind. And so that colleague [a] of his is either himself well schooled and finely instructed by his Greek friends,[b] with whom he now revels in the open [c] though formerly he did so behind a curtain,[d] or he has friends more cautious than Gabinius, since no dispatches from him are produced.[e]

VII. Are these then the commanders we are to 15
have? One of whom does not dare to inform us why [f] he should be called *imperator*, while the other, unless the couriers [g] have been delayed, is bound within a few days to repent of daring to do so. If he has any friends, if so frightful and so foul a monster can have any, they may console themselves with the thought that the Senate refused a public thanksgiving to Titus Albucius also.[h] But, first, there is a distinction between a campaign waged in Sardinia with wretched

had friends who suppressed them; *cf. In Pisonem*, 39: "nihil enim mea iam refert, utrum tu conscientia oppressus scelerum tuorum nihil umquam ausus sis scribere . . . an amici tui tabellas abdiderint idemque silentio suo . . . condemnarint."

[f] *Cur* or *qua re* is preferable to the MSS. reading *ne*.

[g] The couriers who were to inform him that the Senate on 15 May 56 B.C. had refused him a *supplicatio* (*Epp. ad Quintum fratrem*, ii. 6. (8 L.C.L.) 1). These were probably the *tabellarii publicanorum*, as it is unlikely that a state postal service existed under the Republic, *pace J.R.S.* x, pp. 79-86.

[h] Propraetor of Sardinia, about 117 B.C.

dinia cum mastrucatis latrunculis a propraetore una cohorte auxiliaria gesta et bellum cum maximis Syriae gentibus et[1] tyrannis consulari exercitu imperioque confectum. Deinde Albucius, quod a senatu petebat, ipse sibi in Sardinia ante decreverat. Constabat enim Graecum hominem ac levem in ipsa provincia quasi triumphasse, itaque hanc eius temeritatem senatus
16 supplicatione denegata notavit. Sed fruatur sane hoc solacio atque hanc insignem ignominiam, quoniam uni praeter se inusta sit, putet esse leviorem, dum modo, cuius exemplo se consolatur, eius exitum exspectet, praesertim cum in Albucio nec Pisonis libidines nec audacia Gabini fuerit ac tamen hac una plaga conciderit, ignominia senatus.

17 Atqui duas Gallias qui decernit consulibus duobus, hos retinet ambo; qui autem alteram Galliam et aut Syriam aut Macedoniam, tamen alterum retinet et[2] in utriusque pari scelere disparem condicionem facit. "Faciam," inquit, "illas praetorias, ut Pisoni et Gabinio succedatur statim." Si hic sinat! Tum

[1] et *added by Baiter.*
[2] et *added in a first edition published in Rome in 1471.*

---

[a] *Mastrucatis*: *mastruca* was a jacket of undressed sheepskin. [b] The Jews, a rhetorical exaggeration.

[c] *Cf. Brutus*, 131: "doctus etiam Graecis T. Albucius vel potius paene Graecus." He was an Epicurean, and on return from Sardinia was condemned for extortion and retired to exile at Athens.

[d] The proposal of a senior consular to assign the two Gauls (Caesar's provinces) to the consuls to be elected would, if passed, have meant Caesar's supersession.

[e] A proposal made earlier in the debate.

[f] The answer to Cicero of the senator who proposed to assign the two Gauls to the two consuls.

[g] The praetorian provinces were assigned during the year of the praetors' magistracies in Rome, generally early.

bandits clad in sheepskins [a] by a propraetor with a single auxiliary cohort, and a war with the most powerful peoples and rulers in Syria [b] carried through by a consular army and a consular commander. In the next place, Albucius had already decreed for himself in Sardinia what he demanded from the Senate. For it was notorious that that good-for-nothing Greek [c] had had a sort of triumph actually in his province, and so the Senate stamped with the mark of its condemnation his presumption by refusing his demand for a public thanksgiving. But 16
let Gabinius really enjoy this consolation and regard this signal disgrace as somewhat trifling, since it has been branded upon one man besides himself; provided that he looks forward to the same end as the man by whose example he consoles himself, especially since Albucius had neither the depravity of Piso nor the effrontery of Gabinius, and yet was overthrown by this single blow—the disgrace brought upon him by the Senate.

And yet, the proposal to assign the two Gauls to 17
the two consuls to be elected means keeping both Piso and Gabinius in their provinces.[d] But, on the other hand, the proposal [e] to take one of the Gauls and either Syria or Macedonia retains, none the less, one of them in his province, and treats two men differently, although both are equally guilty. "I will make," says he,[f] "those two provinces praetorian, so that Piso and Gabinius can be immediately superseded." [g] Yes, if *he* should allow it ! [h] For a

Under C. Gracchus' *lex Sempronia de provinciis consularibus* tribunes could veto that assignment, but not that of the consular provinces.

[h] Cicero's rejoinder, as he pointed to some tribune present.

enim tribunus intercedere poterit, nunc non potest. Itaque ego idem, qui nunc consulibus iis, qui designati erunt, Syriam Macedoniamque decerno, decernam easdem praetorias, ut et praetores annuas provincias habeant et eos quam primum videamus, quos animo aequo videre non possumus.

VIII. Sed, mihi credite, numquam succedetur illis, nisi cum ea lege referetur, qua intercedi de provinciis non licebit. Itaque hoc tempore amisso annus est integer vobis exspectandus, quo interiecto civium calamitas, sociorum aerumna, sceleratissimorum hominum impunitas propagatur.

18 Quodsi essent illi optimi viri, tamen ego mea sententia C. Caesari succedendum nondum putarem. Qua de re dicam, patres conscripti, quae sentio, atque illam interpellationem mei familiarissimi, qua paulo ante interrupta est oratio mea, non pertimescam. Negat me vir optimus inimiciorem Gabinio debere esse quam Caesari; omnem illam tempestatem, cui cesserim, Caesare impulsore atque adiutore esse excitatam. Cui si primum sic respondeam, me communis utilitatis habere rationem, non doloris mei, possimne probare, cum id me facere dicam, quod exemplo fortissimorum et clarissimorum civium facere possim? An Ti. Gracchus (patrem dico, cuius utinam

[a] Since the consuls of 55 B.C. could not proceed to their provinces till the end of that year, Cicero intended to make a proposal (liable, of course, to be vetoed) that Syria and Macedonia should be assigned for a year as from the beginning of 55 B.C. to praetors of 56 B.C. Thus Gabinius and Piso might be expected back in Rome in 55 B.C.

[b] The *lex Sempronia de provinciis consularibus.*

[c] Should a tribune veto this proposal, a whole year would

tribune will then be able to interpose his veto, whereas he cannot do so now. And therefore, I also, who now propose to assign Syria and Macedonia to those consuls who are to be elected,[a] intend to propose that these same provinces shall be praetorian, so that praetors may govern them for a year and that we may at the earliest possible moment see amongst us those whom we cannot see without indignation.

VIII. But, believe me, they will never be superseded, unless a proposal is made under that law which forbids any veto in regard to the assignation of provinces.[b] And so, if this opportunity is lost,[c] you will have to wait for a whole year, a period during which the misfortunes of citizens and the afflictions of allies are prolonged, and villains continue to enjoy freedom from punishment.

But even if these two consuls were excellent men, 18
yet in my opinion I should still not think that a successor to Gaius Caesar ought to be appointed. And on this point, Conscript Fathers, I will say what I feel, I will not be intimidated by that remark of my intimate friend [d] who has just interrupted my speech. That excellent man says that I ought not to be a greater enemy of Gabinius than of Caesar, that that storm to which I yielded was wholly aroused at the instigation and with the assistance of Caesar. If I should first reply to him that I am taking account of the public welfare rather than my own grievances, could I not make good my case by saying that I am doing what I am justified in doing by the example of the bravest and most illustrious citizens? Did not Tiberius Gracchus—I mean the father, and would

have to pass before Piso and Gabinius were relieved by consuls in 54 B.C. [d] L. Marcius Philippus, consul 56 B.C.

filii ne degenerassent a gravitate patria!) tantam laudem est adeptus, quod tribunus pl. solus ex toto illo collegio L. Scipioni auxilio fuit, inimicissimus et ipsius et fratris eius Africani, iuravitque in contione se in gratiam non redisse, sed alienum sibi videri dignitate imperii, quo duces essent hostium Scipione triumphante ducti, eodem ipsum duci, qui trium-
19 phasset? Quis plenior inimicorum fuit C. Mario? L. Crassus, M. Scaurus alieni,[1] inimici omnes Metelli. At ii non modo illum inimicum ex Gallia sententiis suis non detrahebant, sed ei propter rationem Gallici belli provinciam extra ordinem decernebant. Bellum in Gallia maximum gestum est; domitae sunt a Caesare maximae nationes, sed nondum legibus, nondum iure certo, nondum satis firma pace devinctae.

[1] Alini, aliine MSS.: alieni *Madvig*.

---

[a] In 187 B.C. L. Scipio was protected by his brother P. Scipio Africanus and a tribune Ti. Sempronius Gracchus, father of the Gracchi, against attacks by the Petillii, tribunes in the employment of Cato. In 184 B.C. Africanus himself was accused, again at the instigation of Cato, by a tribune M. Naevius before the *comitia tributa* on a charge of relations, possibly treasonable, with Antiochus the Great. Africanus averted the charge, but was virtually driven from politics and withdrew to Liternum, where he died a year later. See H. H. Scullard's full investigation of "The Trials of the Scipios" in his *Roman Politics, 220–150 B.C.*, pp. 142-143, 151-152; and *ibid.* Appendix iv.

[b] To prison.

[c] A great *popularis*, he rose to power despite the opposition of the nobility.

[d] A great orator, consul 95 B.C. There is no other record of his enmity with Marius.

[e] Consul 115 B.C. and *princeps senatus*; the chief spokesman of the senatorial cause. See *Pro Sestio*, 101.

that, in weight of character, his sons had not fallen below their father !—did not he cover himself with glory, because when tribune of the commons,[a] he alone of the whole of that college of tribunes protected Lucius Scipio, although he was a most bitter enemy of Lucius himself and of his brother Africanus ? did he not solemnly declare at a meeting that he had not become reconciled to them, but that it seemed to him ill-befitting the dignity of our Empire, that Scipio, who had himself triumphed, should be led to the same place [b] to which our enemy's generals had been led on the day of his triumph ? Who ever had 19
more enemies than Gaius Marius ? [c] Were not Lucius Crassus [d] and Marcus Scaurus [e] ill-disposed towards him ? were not all the Metelli [f] his enemies ? Yet they not only did not urge the recall of that enemy of theirs from Gaul, but, in view of the importance of the war in that quarter, assigned Gaul to him as an extraordinary command.[g] A most important war has been fought in Gaul ; Caesar has subdued mighty peoples,[h] but the ties which bind them to us are not yet those of laws, nor of established rights, nor of a sufficiently consolidated peace. We see the

[f] Although after the death of Scipio Aemilianus Marius enjoyed the support of the Metelli, he actually when tribune in 119 B.C. ordered the arrest of L. Metellus (later Delmaticus), consul of the year, and when consul in 107 B.C. superseded Q. Metellus in command against Jugurtha.

[g] After the Roman defeat at Arausio (105 B.C.) Marius was re-elected consul in his absence and appointed to command in Gaul. His five successive re-elections to the consulship (for 104–100 B.C.) were contraventions of a statute, passed *c.* 150 B.C., forbidding re-election. But Scipio Aemilianus had been exempted from this in 135 B.C.

[h] The Helvetii, the Germans under Ariovistus, and most of the peoples of Belgic Gaul.

Bellum adfectum videmus et, vere ut dicam, paene confectum, sed ita, ut, si idem extrema persequitur, qui inchoavit, iam omnia perfecta videamus, si succeditur, periculum sit, ne instauratas maximi belli
20 reliquias ac renovatas audiamus. Ergo ego senator, inimicus, si ita vultis, homini, amicus esse, sicut semper fui, rei publicae debeo. Quid? si ipsas inimicitias depono rei publicae causa, quis me tandem iure reprehendet, praesertim cum ego omnium meorum consiliorum atque factorum exempla semper ex summorum hominum factis mihi censuerim petenda.

21 IX. An vero M. ille Lepidus, qui bis consul et pontifex maximus fuit, non solum memoriae testimonio, sed etiam annalium litteris et summi poetae voce laudatus est, quod cum M. Fulvio collega, quo die censor est factus, homine inimicissimo, in campo statim rediit in gratiam, ut commune officium censurae communi animo ac voluntate defenderent? Atque, ut vetera, quae sunt innumerabilia, mittam, tuus pater, Philippe, nonne uno tempore cum suis inimicissimis in gratiam rediit? quibus eum omnibus eadem res publica re-
22 conciliavit, quae alienarat. Multa praetereo, quod intueor coram haec lumina atque ornamenta rei

---

[a] Caesar's.

[b] M. Aemilius Lepidus, consul 187 and 175 B.C., Pontifex Maximus 180, censor 179, built the Via Aemilia from Ariminum to Placentia; founder (183) of Mutina and Parma.

[c] Ennius, who accompanied M. Fulvius Nobilior (consul 189 B.C.) into Aetolia, to describe the campaign (Gellius, xii. 8. 5). See *Remains of Old Latin* (L.C.L.), i, pp. xx, 142-145, 358-361.

[d] L. Marcius Philippus (consul 91 B.C.) quarrelled with the

war well carried on and, to tell the truth, almost brought to an end, but it is only on condition that he who began the operations follows them up to the last, that we may presently see a result that is final. But if he is superseded there may be reason to fear that we may hear of the embers of that great war being stirred anew and bursting out once more into flame. I, therefore, as a senator, the man's [a] personal 20
enemy if you like, am bound to be, as I have ever been, a friend of the State. Again, if I lay aside those very enmities for the sake of the State, who, pray, will have a right to blame me? especially as in every purpose and action of my own I have considered that I should always seek a precedent in the actions of our most illustrious citizens.

IX. Has not the great Marcus Lepidus, twice consul 21
and Pontifex Maximus,[b] been praised, not only by the voice of memory, but also in the pages of history and in the song of our greatest poet? [c] Has he not been praised, because on the day of his election to the censorship, before leaving the Campus Martius, he at once became reconciled to his colleague Marcus Fulvius, who was most hostile to him, in order that they might uphold their common responsibilities as censors with a common purpose and goodwill? And, to pass over innumerable examples from the past, did not your father, Philippus, become reconciled at one and the same time to his greatest enemies? One and all he was reconciled to them by the same public interests that had estranged them.[d] I pass over 22
many examples, since I see here present those bril-

Senate by opposing the tribune M. Livius Drusus, but was reconciled to the Senate when Drusus resorted to violence; father of L. Marcius Philippus, consul 56 B.C.

publicae, P. Servilium et M. Lucullum. Utinam etiam L. Lucullus illic adsideret![1] Quae fuerunt inimicitiae in civitate graviores quam Lucullorum atque Servili? quas in viris fortissimis non solum exstinxit rei publicae utilitas dignitasque[2] ipsorum, sed etiam ad amicitiam consuetudinemque traduxit. Quid? Q. Metellus Nepos nonne consul in templo Iovis optimi maximi permotus cum auctoritate vestra, tum illius P. Servili incredibili gravitate dicendi absens mecum summo suo beneficio rediit in gratiam? An ego possum huic esse inimicus, cuius litteris, fama, nuntiis celebrantur aures cotidie meae novis nomi-
23 nibus gentium, nationum, locorum? Ardeo, mihi credite, patres conscripti,—id quod vosmet de me existimatis et facitis ipsi,—incredibili quodam amore patriae, qui me amor et subvenire olim impendentibus periculis maximis cum dimicatione capitis, et rursum, cum omnia tela undique esse intenta in patriam viderem, subire coegit atque excipere unum pro universis. Hic me meus in rem publicam animus pristinus

[1] *Madvig's correction of* ille desideret *of most* MSS.; *an older reading is* ille viveret.

[2] rei publicae dignitasque MSS. *There is apparently a word omitted*: utilitas *inserted by Baiter. The ordinary reading is* res publica dignitasque.

---

[a] See § 1. He won the *cognomen* of Isauricus after campaigns in southern Asia Minor (78–75 B.C.). See H. A. Ormerod, "The Campaigns of Servilius Isauricus against the Pirates," *J.R.S.* xii, pp. 35-56.

[b] Consul 73 B.C. He fought successfully against the tribes menacing the frontier of Macedonia.

[c] Brother of Marcus, consul 74 B.C., and conqueror of Mithridates. This passage implies that he was dead.

[d] Servilius was prosecuted by the two Luculli, because he

liantly distinguished public men, Publius Servilius [a] and Marcus Lucullus.[b] Would that Lucius Lucullus [c] also were sitting there! What enmities in this state were ever more bitter than those between the Luculli and Servilius?[d] And yet, in those greatest of men, their regard for the public weal and their own honour not only extinguished those enmities, but even transformed them into friendship and intimacy. Again, did not Quintus Metellus Nepos [e] when consul, in the Temple of Juppiter Best and Greatest, deeply moved both by your authority and by the eloquence, impressive beyond belief, of Publius Servilius, did he not, though far away,[f] by doing me the greatest possible service, return to his place in my regard? Can I then be the enemy of this man,[g] whose dispatches, whose fame, whose envoys fill my ears every day with fresh names of races, peoples, places? I am con- 23
sumed, believe me, Conscript Fathers—as indeed you think of me and are yourselves consumed—with the fire of a surpassing love for my country; and this same love compelled me to come to its help in former times,[h] when terrible dangers were imminent, in a struggle for life and death, and once more,[i] when I saw violence of every sort menacing my country on every side, it impelled me to meet it and welcome it—alone on behalf of all. It is this old and unfailing

had prosecuted their father. No details of this reconciliation are known.

[e] See *Pro Sestio*, 129, 130. In July 57 B.C. Q. Metellus Nepos, when consul, a violent opponent of Cicero as tribune in 62 B.C., became reconciled to him and did not oppose his restoration.

[f] Metellus was in Rome, Cicero in exile.

[g] Caesar.

[h] At the time of the Catilinarian Conspiracy.

[i] When he quitted Rome in 58 B.C.

ac perennis cum C. Caesare reducit, reconciliat, restituit in gratiam.

24 Quod volent denique homines existiment, nemini ego possum esse bene merenti de re publica non amicus. X. Etenim, si iis, qui haec omnia flamma ac ferro delere voluerunt, non inimicitias solum, sed etiam bellum indixi atque intuli, cum partim mihi illorum familiares,[1] partim etiam me defendente capitis iudiciis essent liberati, cur eadem res publica, quae me in amicos inflammare potuit, inimicis placare non possit? Quod mihi odium cum P. Clodio fuit, nisi quod perniciosum patriae civem fore putabam, qui turpissima libidine incensus duas res sanctissimas, religionem et pudicitiam, uno scelere violasset? Num est igitur dubium ex iis rebus, quas is egit agitque cotidie, quin ego in illo oppugnando rei publicae plus quam otio meo, non nulli in eodem defendendo suo

25 plus otio quam communi prospexerint? Ego me a C. Caesare in re publica dissensisse fateor et sensisse vobiscum; sed nunc isdem vobis adsentior, cum quibus antea sentiebam. Vos enim, ad quos litteras L. Piso de suis rebus non audet mittere, qui Gabini litteras insigni quadam nota atque ignominia nova condem-

[1] *Halm inserts* essent *after* familiares.

[a] It is not clear to whom of the conspirators of 63 B.C. Cicero refers where he states that in his consulship he made war on some persons who had been his friends, and that he had defended some of them. Two alleged Catilinarians whom he defended later were: P. Cornelius Sulla in 62 B.C. and L. Calpurnius Bestia in 56 B.C.

loyalty of mine to the State which restores, reconciles, reinstates me in friendship with Gaius Caesar.

In fact, let men think what they will, for me it is 24
impossible not to be the friend of one who renders good service to the State. X. For if, against those who wished utterly to destroy this city with fire and sword, I declared and directed not merely personal enmity but open war, although some of them were my intimate friends, while others were even defended by me and acquitted on capital charges,[a] why should the same public interest which was able to rouse me against my friends, be unable to reconcile me with my enemies? For what reason had I to hate Publius Clodius, except that I accounted him one who would bring utter ruin upon his country, when, consumed with the most degraded lust, he had violated by one crime two of our most sacred possessions, sanctity and chastity?[b] Can there be any doubt then, according to what he has done and still does every day, that in attacking him I thought more of the public interest than of my own security, and that some,[c] in defending him, thought more of their own security than of that
of the State? I confess that I disagreed with Gaius 25
Caesar in politics[d] and was in agreement with you; but now I am in agreement with you just as I was in agreement before. For you, to whom Lucius Piso does not venture to send dispatches[e] concerning his achievements, you who condemned the dispatches[f] of Gabinius by stamping on them such a notable mark of unparalleled ignominy, you have voted to Gaius

[b] By his escapade at the mysteries of the Bona Dea early in December 62 B.C. [c] Such as Piso and Gabinius.

[d] Within the years 65–56 B.C.

[e] See § 14. [f] See § 14.

nastis, C. Caesari supplicationes decrevistis numero ut nemini uno ex bello, honore ut omnino nemini. Cur igitur exspectem hominem aliquem, qui me cum illo in gratiam reducat? Reduxit ordo amplissimus, et ordo is, qui est et publici consilii et meorum omnium consiliorum auctor et princeps. Vos sequor, patres conscripti, vobis obtempero, vobis adsentior, qui, quamdiu C. Caesaris consilia in re publica non maxime diligebatis, me quoque cum illo minus coniunctum videbatis; posteaquam rebus gestis mentes vestras voluntatesque mutastis, me non solum comitem esse sententiae vestrae, sed etiam laudatorem vidistis.

26 XI. Sed quid est, quod in hac causa maxime homines admirentur et reprehendant meum consilium, cum ego idem antea multa decrerim, quae magis ad hominis dignitatem quam ad rei publicae necessitatem pertinerent? Supplicationem quindecim dierum decrevi sententia mea. Rei publicae satis erat tot dierum quot C. Mario; dis immortalibus non erat exigua eadem gratulatio quae ex maximis bellis. Ergo ille cumulus dierum hominis est dignitati tributus.
27 In quo ego, quo consule referente primum decem dierum est supplicatio decreta Cn. Pompeio Mithridate interfecto et confecto Mithridatico bello, et cuius sententia primum duplicata est supplicatio con-

---

[a] One of fifteen days for the campaigns of 58 and 57 B.C. Caesar, *Bell. Gall.* ii. 35.

[b] See also *Pro Balbo*, 61; *Epp. ad Fam.* i. 9. 14.

[c] After the defeat of the Cimbri his *supplicatio* was five days. Previously no consular *supplicatio* was longer, but one of twenty days was awarded to Caesar for his work in 55 B.C. (*Bell. Gall.* iv. 38). For *supplicationes* see L. Halkin, *La Supplication d'Action de Grâces chez les Romains* (*Bibliothèque de la Faculté de Philosophie et Lettres de l'Université de Liège.* Fascicule cxxviii, Paris, 1953).

Caesar public thanksgivings for more days than were ever voted for a single war to one general,[a] and in more honourable terms than were ever voted to anyone. Why then should I wait for someone or other to reconcile me with Caesar? I have been reconciled, by the most distinguished of Orders, and by that Order in which both the policy of the State and all my own political conduct find their authority and guide. It is you I follow, Conscript Fathers, you I obey, with you I am in agreement, you who, as long as the policy of Gaius Caesar in public affairs did not meet with your hearty approval, found me also less united with him, you who, after his achievements had made you change your minds and inclinations, have found me not only sharing your opinions but even applauding them.

XI. But what is the reason why in this matter 26
especially men are astonished at my policy and blame me, seeing that before this also I have given many votes that had regard to the merits of an individual rather than to the necessities of the State? I gave my vote in favour of a public thanksgiving for fifteen days.[b] Public interest would have been satisfied by granting the same number of days as to Gaius Marius[c]; the Immortal Gods would have considered the same thanksgiving sufficient that had been offered them after our most important wars; so that increase in the number of days was a tribute to the merits of
the man. In regard to this, during my consulship 27
and on my proposal, a thanksgiving for ten days was for the first time voted to Gnaeus Pompeius after Mithridates had been slain and the Mithridatic War concluded. It was again on my proposal that a thanksgiving awarded to those of consular rank was

sularis (mihi enim estis adsensi, cum eiusdem Pompei litteris recitatis confectis omnibus maritimis terrestribusque bellis supplicationem dierum decem[1] decrevistis), sum Cn. Pompei virtutem et animi magnitudinem admiratus, quod, cum ipse ceteris omnibus esset omni honore antelatus, ampliorem honorem alteri tribuebat, quam ipse erat consecutus. Ergo in illa supplicatione, quam ego decrevi, res ipsa tributa est dis immortalibus et maiorum institutis et utilitati rei publicae, sed dignitas verborum, honos et novitas et numerus dierum
28 Caesaris ipsius laudi gloriaeque concessus est. Relatum est ad nos nuper de stipendio exercitus ; non decrevi solum, sed etiam, ut vos decerneretis, laboravi ; multa dissentientibus respondi ; scribendo adfui. Tum quoque homini plus tribui quam nescio cui necessitati. Illum enim arbitrabar etiam sine hoc subsidio pecuniae retinere exercitum praeda ante parta et bellum conficere posse ; sed decus illud et ornamentum triumphi minuendum nostra parsimonia non putavi. Actum est de decem legatis, quos alii omnino non dabant, alii

[1] duodecim *most* MSS., decem *Manutius*.

[a] It must, however, be remembered that he was the son-in-law of Caesar, and would naturally vote for the fifteen days.

[b] At the beginning of his Gallic command Caesar had taken over four legions. On his own authority he raised four more in 58 and 57 B.C., and pay was required for these. At some date that cannot be precisely determined but probably after the Conference of Luca, the Senate, thanks to Cicero's advocacy, approved this grant. See Cicero, *Epp. ad Fam.* i. 7. 10.

[c] Resolutions of the Senate were drafted by a committee of senators whose names formed a preamble. See Cicero, *Epp. ad Fam.* viii. 8. 5.

[d] Butler and Cary (*op. cit.* p. 65) follow the traditional view that Caesar began his Gallic command with a normal military staff of six legates which he found it necessary to increase to ten. On the other hand, it is held (most recently

for the first time doubled in length, for you sided with me, after dispatches from the same Pompeius had been read out, announcing the termination of all wars by land and sea, and awarded to him a thanksgiving for ten days. On this recent occasion, therefore, I admired the strength of mind and magnanimity of Gnaeus Pompeius,[a] because, while he had been himself preferred to distinctions beyond all other men, he was for granting greater distinction to another than he himself had obtained. So then, about that public thanksgiving for which I voted, the thanksgiving itself was something duly offered to the Immortal Gods, the customs of our ancestors, and the advantage of the State, but the dignified language, the unexampled distinction, and the number of days were concessions to the merit and glory of Caesar himself. We have 28
lately had referred to us the question of pay for his troops.[b] Not only did I vote for it, but I also did my utmost to make you do the same; I answered at length those who disagreed, I was one of those who were present to draft the resolution of the Senate.[c] Then also I thought more of the man than of any kind of necessity. For I believed, that even without this help in money, he could maintain his army with the booty which he had previously won, and finish the war; but I certainly did not think that the lustre and glory of his triumph ought to be lessened by meanness on our part. A resolution was passed concerning ten legates.[d] Some absolutely refused to approve

by Balsdon (*op. cit.* p. 171)) that *decem legati* was a technical phrase for a commission of senators dispatched by the Senate to co-operate with a general after a war concerning the organization of conquered territory. But may not §§ 19, 34 and 35 suggest that, in the present case, this provincial organization was still premature?

exempla quaerebant, alii tempus differebant, alii sine ullis verborum ornamentis dabant; in ea quoque re sic sum locutus, ut omnes intellegerent me id, quod rei publicae causa sentirem, facere uberius propter ipsius Caesaris dignitatem.

29 XII. At ego idem nunc in[1] provinciis decernendis, qui illas omnes res egi silentio, interpellor, cum in superioribus causis hominis ornamenta[2] fuerint, in hac me nihil aliud nisi ratio belli, nisi summa utilitas rei publicae moveat. Nam ipse Caesar quid est cur in provincia commorari velit, nisi ut ea, quae per eum adfecta sunt, perfecta rei publicae tradat? Amoenitas eum, credo, locorum, urbium pulchritudo, hominum nationumque illarum humanitas et lepos, victoriae cupiditas, finium imperii propagatio retinet. Quid illis terris asperius, quid incultius oppidis, quid nationibus immanius, quid porro tot victoriis praestabilius, quid Oceano longius inveniri potest? An reditus in patriam habet aliquam offensionem? utrum apud populum, a quo missus, an apud senatum, a quo ornatus est? an dies auget eius desiderium, an magis oblivionem, ac laurea illa magnis periculis parta amittit longo intervallo viriditatem? Quare, si qui hominem

[1] *Inserted by Lambinus.*
[2] *Peterson inserts* adiumento *after* ornamenta: *Müller suggests* apud me valuerint *for* fuerint.

them, others wanted precedents, others were for putting off the matter, and others were in favour of granting them without any complimentary expressions. On this matter also I spoke in such terms that every one could understand that I did what I felt was for the interest of the State with greater generosity owing to the merits of Caesar himself.

XII. Now, however, when it is a question of assigning provinces, whereas I was allowed to discuss all those matters [a] in silence, I find myself interrupted. Although these former proposals concerned honours to be conferred on Caesar nothing else now moves me except military considerations and the supreme interest of the State. For what reason is there why Caesar should himself wish to linger in his province, save that he should hand over to the State fully accomplished a work on which he is engaged? I suppose it is the pleasantness of the country, the beauty of the cities, the culture and refinement of the inhabitants and peoples, the desire for victory, the extension of the boundaries of our Empire, that detain him! What can be found more savage than those lands, more uncivilized than those towns, more ferocious than those peoples, what moreover more admirable than all those victories, what more distant than the Ocean? Will his return to his country be in any way unwelcome either to the People who sent him out, or to the Senate who honoured him? Does the passing of time whet our longing for him, or make us forget his existence more and more, and do those laurels won at the cost of great dangers lose their freshness after so long a time? And so, if there 29

[a] Pay for Caesar's new legions and *decem legati.*

non diligunt, nihil est, quod eum de provincia devocent; ad gloriam devocant, ad triumphum, ad gratulationem, ad summum honorem senatus, equestris
30 ordinis gratiam, populi caritatem. Sed si ille hac tam eximia fortuna propter utilitatem rei publicae frui non properat, ut omnia illa conficiat, quid ego senator facere debeo, quem, etiamsi ille aliud vellet, rei publicae consulere oporteret?

Ego vero sic intellego, patres conscripti, nos hoc tempore in provinciis decernendis perpetuae pacis habere oportere rationem. Nam quis hoc non sentit, omnia alia esse nobis vacua ab omni periculo atque
31 etiam suspicione belli? Iam diu mare videmus illud immensum, cuius fervore non solum maritimi cursus, sed urbes etiam et viae militares iam tenebantur, virtute Cn. Pompei sic a populo Romano ab Oceano usque ad ultimum Pontum tamquam unum aliquem portum tutum et clausum teneri; nationes eas, quae numero hominum ac multitudine ipsa poterant in provincias nostras redundare, ita ab eodem esse partim recisas, partim repressas, ut Asia, quae imperium antea nostrum terminabat, nunc tribus novis provinciis ipsa cingatur. Possum de omni regione, de omni genere hostium dicere. Nulla gens est, quae non aut ita sublata sit, ut vix exstet, aut ita domita, ut quiescat, aut ita pacata, ut victoria nostra imperioque laetetur.

---

[a] Owing to the scourge of piracy.

[b] The kingdom of Pergamum, bequeathed to Rome in 133 B.C., was constituted in 129 B.C. the province of Asia. To the east, client-kings were left in control.

[c] Bithynia, to which was annexed western Pontus; Cilicia,

some who do not love the man, there is no reason why they should recall him from his province; for that means to recall him to glory, to a triumph, to congratulations, to the highest honours the Senate can bestow, to the favour of the Equestrian Order, to
the affection of the People. But if he is in no hurry 30
to enjoy such brilliant fortune, simply for the advantage of the State, so that he may finish all the work he has begun, what ought I, a senator, to do, who, even if he wished otherwise, should be bound to consult the interests of the State?

But as for myself, Conscript Fathers, I feel that to-day our assignment of the provinces should aim at the maintenance of a lasting peace. For who does not see that in all other quarters we are free from
any danger and even from any suspicion of war? We 31
have long seen how those vast seas, whose unrest [a] endangered not only voyages but even cities and military roads, have become, thanks to the valour of Gnaeus Pompeius, from the Ocean to the farthest shores of Pontus, as it were one safe and closed harbour in the control of the Roman People; how, thanks also to Pompeius, of those peoples whose surging multitudes could sweep over our provinces, some have been cut off, others driven back; and how Asia,[b] once the frontier of our power, is now itself bounded by three new provinces.[c] I can speak of every region of the world, of every kind of enemies. There is no race which has not either been so utterly destroyed that it hardly exists, or so thoroughly subdued that it remains submissive, or so pacified [d] that it rejoices in our victory and rule.

enlarged to the N. and W.; Syria. *Cingatur* is an exaggeration.

[d] For a similar passage see *Pro Sestio*, 51.

32 XIII. Bellum Gallicum, patres conscripti, C. Caesare imperatore gestum est, antea tantum modo repulsum. Semper illas nationes nostri imperatores refutandas potius bello quam lacessendas putaverunt. Ipse ille C. Marius, cuius divina atque eximia virtus magnis populi Romani luctibus funeribusque subvenit, influentes in Italiam Gallorum maximas copias repressit, non ipse ad eorum urbes sedesque penetravit. Modo ille meorum laborum, periculorum, consiliorum socius, C. Pomptinus, fortissimus vir, ortum repente bellum Allobrogum atque hac scelerata coniuratione excitatum proeliis fregit eosque domuit, qui lacessierant, et ea victoria contentus re publica metu liberata quievit. C. Caesaris longe aliam video fuisse rationem. Non enim sibi solum cum iis, quos iam armatos contra populum Romanum videbat, bellandum esse duxit, sed totam Galliam in nostram
33 dicionem esse redigendam. Itaque cum acerrimis nationibus et maximis Germanorum et Helvetiorum proeliis felicissime decertavit, ceteras conterruit, compulit, domuit, imperio populi Romani parere adsuefecit

---

[a] The defence of the province of Gallia Narbonensis and of the northern frontier of Italy.

[b] The defeats of Cn. Papirius Carbo near Noreia in Noricum, between Klagenfurt and Ljubljana (113 B.C.), of M. Junius Silanus in the valley of the Rhône (109 B.C.), of L. Cassius Longinus in the valley of the Garonne (107 B.C.), and of Q. Servilius Caepio and Cn. Mallius Maximus at Arausio (105 B.C.).

[c] Marius' victories were in Gallia Narbonensis (Aquae Sextiae, 102 B.C.) and in the upper valley of the Po (Vercellae, 101 B.C.).

[d] Praetor 63 B.C. and a supporter of Cicero during the Catilinarian Conspiracy. As governor of Gallia Narbonensis he temporarily subdued the restless Allobroges in 61 B.C.

XIII. Under Gaius Caesar's command, Conscript 32
Fathers, we have fought a war in Gaul; before we merely repelled attacks.[a] Our commanders always thought that those peoples ought to be beaten back in war rather than attacked. The great Gaius Marius himself, whose divine and outstanding bravery was our stay after grievous disasters and losses suffered by the Roman People,[b] drove back vast hordes of Gauls that were streaming into Italy, but did not himself penetrate to their cities and dwelling-places.[c] Just recently that gallant man, who was associated with me in my labours, my dangers, and my counsels, I mean Gaius Pomptinus,[d] broke up by his battles a war that was begun on a sudden by the Allobroges and fomented by this wicked Conspiracy,[e] subdued those who had attacked us, and content with that victory, after the country had been freed from alarm, rested on his laurels. Gaius Caesar's plans, I observe, have been far different. For he did not think that he ought to fight only against those whom he saw already in arms against the Roman People, but that the whole of Gaul should be brought under our sway.[f]
And so he has, with brilliant success, crushed in battle 33
the fiercest and greatest tribes of Germania and Helvetia; the rest he has terrified, checked and subdued, and taught them to submit to the rule

His triumph, however, was delayed till 54 B.C. (*C.I.L.* i. 1², p. 50).

[e] *Hac* refers to the Conspiracy of 63 B.C., nearly seven years past. Cicero has in mind *mei labores, pericula, consilia* two lines before. These include the Conspiracy, which is thus very close, in this speech, to *hac*.

[f] There is no evidence for Caesar's original plans. But his establishment after 58 B.C. of winter quarters at Vesontio suggests an aggressive policy.

et, quas regiones quasque gentes nullae nobis antea litterae, nulla vox, nulla fama notas fecerat, has noster imperator nosterque exercitus et populi Romani arma peragrarunt. Semitam tantum Galliae tenebamus antea, patres conscripti ; ceterae partes a gentibus aut inimicis huic imperio aut infidis aut incognitis aut certe immanibus et barbaris et bellicosis tenebantur ; quas nationes nemo umquam fuit quin frangi domarique cuperet. Nemo sapienter de re publica nostra cogitavit iam inde a principio huius imperii, quin Galliam maxime timendam huic imperio putaret ; sed propter vim ac multitudinem gentium illarum numquam est antea cum omnibus dimicatum ; restitimus semper lacessiti. Nunc denique est perfectum, ut imperii nostri terrarumque illarum idem esset extremum.

34 XIV. Alpibus Italiam munierat antea natura non sine aliquo divino numine. Nam, si ille aditus Gallorum immanitati multitudinique patuisset, numquam haec urbs summo imperio domicilium ac sedem praebuisset. Quae iam licet considant. Nihil est enim ultra illam altitudinem montium usque ad Oceanum, quod sit Italiae pertimescendum. Sed tamen una atque altera aestas vel metu vel spe vel poena vel praemiis vel armis vel legibus potest totam Galliam sempiternis vinculis adstringere. Impolitae vero res et acerbae si erunt relictae, quamquam sunt accisae, tamen efferent se aliquando et ad renovandum bellum

---

[a] A summary of the campaigns of 58 and 57 B.C.

[b] Gallia Narbonensis (annexed 121 B.C.) was little more than a corridor between Italy and Spain.

[c] Gaul, in fact, was not definitely subdued until 50 B.C., six years later.

of the Roman People. Over these regions and races, which no writings, no spoken word, no report had before made known to us, over them have our general, our soldiers, and the arms of the Roman People made their way.[a] A mere path,[b] Conscript Fathers, was the only part of Gaul that we held before; the rest was peopled by tribes who were either enemies of our rule or rebels against it, or by men unknown to us or known only as wild, savage and warlike—tribes which no one who ever lived would not wish to see crushed and subdued. From the very beginning of our Empire we have had no wise statesman who did not regard Gaul as the greatest danger to our Empire. But, owing to the might and numbers of those peoples, never before have we engaged in conflict with them as a whole. We have always withstood them whenever we have been challenged. Now at length we have reached the consummation that the limits of our Empire and of those lands are one and the same.

XIV. The Alps, not without the favour of heaven, 34
were once raised high by nature as a rampart to Italy. For if that approach to our country had lain open to savage hordes of Gauls, never would this city have provided a home and chosen seat for sovereign rule. Let the Alps now sink in the earth! For there is nothing beyond those mountain peaks as far as the Ocean, of which Italy need stand in dread. Yet one or two summers,[c] and fear or hope, punishment or rewards, arms or laws can bind the whole of Gaul to us with eternal fetters. But if we leave this work not rounded-off and in the rough, the power of Gaul, cut back though it may have been, will some day revive and burst forth anew into war. Therefore let 35

35 revirescent. Quare sit in eius tutela Gallia, cuius fidei, virtuti, felicitati commendata est. Qui si Fortunae muneribus amplissimis ornatus saepius eius deae periculum facere nollet, si in patriam, si ad deos penates, si ad eam dignitatem, quam in civitate sibi propositam videt, si ad iucundissimos liberos, si ad clarissimum generum redire properaret, si in Capitolium invehi victor cum illa insigni laude[1] gestiret, si denique timeret casum aliquem, qui illi tantum addere iam non potest, quantum auferre, nos tamen oporteret ab eodem illa omnia, a quo profligata sunt, confici velle. Cum vero ille suae gloriae iam pridem, rei publicae nondum satis fecerit et malit tamen tardius ad suorum laborum fructus pervenire quam non explere susceptum rei publicae munus, nec imperatorem incensum ad rem publicam bene gerendam revocare nec totam Gallici belli rationem prope iam explicatam perturbare atque impedire debemus.

36 XV. Nam illae sententiae virorum clarissimorum minime probandae sunt, quorum alter ulteriorem Galliam decernit cum Syria, alter citeriorem. Qui ulteriorem, omnia illa, de quibus disserui paulo ante, perturbat; simul ostendit eam se tenere[2] legem,

[1] laude MSS. : laurea *Naugerius*.

[2] se tenere *Madvig* : sentire *most* MSS. : se sancire *Halm* : se tueri *Kayser*.

[a] Caesar had only one child, a daughter Julia, married to Pompey. But *liberi* is often used of single children.

[b] The laurel wreath of a *triumphator*.

[c] Senior consulars who had already spoken in the debate. See § 17.

[d] Cicero's somewhat sophisticated argument is this: the proposal to deprive Caesar of Transalpine Gaul is objectionable as interfering with his plans for the completion of the conquest of Gaul, shows respect for the unconstitutional

Gaul remain under the guardianship of him to whose honour, valour and good fortune it has been entrusted. For if Caesar, already distinguished with Fortune's fullest favours, were unwilling to take the risk of tempting that goddess too often, if he were impatient to return to his country, to the gods of his home, to that honour which he sees destined for him in Rome, to his delightful children,[a] to his illustrious son-in-law, if he were eager to ride up to the Capitol in triumph, graced with that signal mark of honour,[b] if, lastly, he feared some accident which cannot now add as much to his glory as it can take away, it would nevertheless be our duty to desire that all those tasks should be completed by the same man by whom they have been so far performed. But since Caesar, though he has by now achieved enough to glorify himself, has not yet satisfied the claims of the State, and since he prefers to enjoy the rewards of his labours at a later date rather than fail to complete the public service which he has undertaken, we ought neither to recall a commander who is so fired with devotion to the high service of the State, nor throw into confusion the whole of a policy for war in Gaul now so nearly unfolded.

XV. For we ought by no means to accept the pro- 36
posals of some distinguished men,[c] of whom one assigns to the consuls Transalpine Gaul [d] with Syria, the other Cisalpine Gaul. The assignment of Transalpine Gaul [e] upsets all the plans of which I have just spoken. At the same time it reveals the proposer as

lex Vatinia (see p. 540, note *b*), fear of the tribunician veto, and disrespect for the Senate which appointed Caesar to Transalpine Gaul.

[e] See §§ 34 and 35.

quam esse legem neget, et, quae pars provinciae sit, cui non possit intercedi, hanc se avellere, quae defensorem habeat, non tangere ; simul et illud facit, ut, quod illi a populo datum sit, id non violet, quod senatus 37 dederit, id senator properet auferre. Alter belli Gallici rationem habet, fungitur officio boni senatoris, legem quam non putat, eam quoque servat ; praefinit enim successori diem. Quamquam mihi nihil videtur alienius[1] a dignitate disciplinaque maiorum, quam ut, qui consul Kalendis Ianuariis habere provinciam debet, is ut eam desponsam, non decretam habere videatur. Fuerit toto in consulatu sine provincia, cui fuerit, antequam designatus est, decreta provincia. Sortietur an non ? Nam et non sortiri absurdum est et, quod sortitus sis, non habere. Proficiscetur paludatus ? Quo ? Quo pervenire ante certam diem

[1] Quae . . . minus *MSS.*; quo *Manutius, who also proposed* magis *for* minus ; alienius *is Madvig's alteration for* minus ; *Butler-Cary and Peterson substitute* quamquam *for* quo *or* quae. Quamquam *is adopted.*

---

[a] The *lex Vatinia* of 59 B.C., which conferred on Caesar the governorship of Cisalpine Gaul and of Illyricum for five years from 1 March 59 B.C., was regarded by the Optimates as unconstitutional because the intervention of the consul Bibulus, who tried to obstruct its passing by his action under the *leges Aelia et Fufia* (see § 46), had been disregarded.

[b] Caesar could have been deprived of Transalpine Gaul by the appointment of a consular successor under the *lex Sempronia* of C. Gracchus, under which a tribune's veto was barred. On the other hand, a tribune might veto a proposal to detach Cisalpine Gaul from Caesar's command on the ground that it contravened the *lex Vatinia* : for a consul of 55 B.C. appointed to succeed to the governorship of Cisalpine Gaul in 54 B.C. would normally arrive there early in 54 B.C., before Caesar's period of five years, fixed by the *lex Vatinia*, had expired on 1 March 54 B.C.

[c] The proposal to terminate Caesar's command in Cisalpine

upholding that law which he claims to be no law [a]; as depriving Caesar of that portion of his province the detachment of which is immune from veto, but disregarding that portion which has a champion to defend it [b]; with the result, too, that the proposer does not lay hands on what was given to Caesar by the People, but is eager, a senator though he be, to deprive him of what was given him by the Senate. The other 37
proposer [c] takes the Gallic War into consideration, performs the duty of a good senator, and respects a law which he does not regard as such, for he fixes a day for Caesar's successor. Yet nothing seems to me more at variance with the authority and practice of our ancestors than that a consul who ought to enter upon his province on the first day of January, should seem to have it promised only, not definitely assigned.[d] Assume that throughout his consulship he will have been without a province, although a province was assigned to him before he was elected consul. Will he draw lots for it or not? For to refrain from drawing lots and to be denied possession of what has been allotted are alike absurd. Is he to leave Rome wearing his general's cloak?[e] What is his destination? A place where he will not be allowed to present

Gaul would not interfere with his plans for the conquest of Transalpine Gaul and would respect the *lex Vatinia* by fixing 1 March, not 1 January 54 B.C., as the date of Caesar's relief by a consular successor.

[d] The proposal to relieve Caesar on 1 March 54 B.C. would involve a break of two months in the *imperium* of whichever consul of 55 B.C. should be allotted Cisalpine Gaul in succession to Caesar.

[e] The *paludamentum* was a scarlet cloak, symbolic of command in the field, assumed by a consul or proconsul on leaving Rome for a provincial command.

non licebit. Ianuario, Februario provinciam non habebit; Kalendis ei denique Martiis nascetur re-
38 pente provincia. Ac tamen his sententiis Piso in provincia permanebit. Quae cum gravia sunt, tum[1] nihil gravius illo, quod multari imperatorem deminutione provinciae contumeliosum est neque solum summo in viro, sed etiam mediocri in homine id ne[2] accidat providendum.

XVI. Ego vos intellego, patres conscripti, multos decrevisse eximios honores C. Caesari et prope singulares. Si,[3] quod ita meritus erat, grati, sin etiam, ut quam coniunctissimus huic ordini esset, sapientes ac divini fuistis. Neminem umquam est hic ordo complexus honoribus et beneficiis suis, qui ullam dignitatem praestabiliorem ea, quam per vos esset adeptus, putarit. Nemo umquam hic potuit esse princeps, qui maluerit esse popularis. Sed homines aut propter indignitatem suam diffisi ipsi sibi aut propter reliquorum obtrectationem ab huius ordinis coniunctione depulsi saepe ex hoc portu se in illos fluctus prope necessario contulerunt. Qui si ex illa iactatione cursuque populari bene gesta re publica referunt aspectum in curiam atque huic amplissimae dignitati esse commendati volunt, non modo non repellendi sunt, verum
39 etiam expetendi. Monemur a fortissimo viro atque optimo post hominum memoriam consule, ut providea-

[1] tum *inserted by Angelius.*
[2] id ne *inserted by Müller.* [3] Si *inserted by Gruter.*

[a] The date on which Caesar's command under the *lex Vatinia* expired, and likewise the date suggested for Caesar's supersession under the proposal criticized by Cicero.

himself before a fixed day. During January and February he will have no province ; all at once, on the first day of March, a province will be found for him.[a] And yet, by these proposals, Piso will remain 38
in his province. And however serious all this is, nothing is more serious than the fact that for a commander to be penalized by the loss of part of his province is an insult against which even an ordinary man, to say nothing of a distinguished personage, should be protected.

XVI. I see, Conscript Fathers, that you have conferred many exceptional and almost unexampled honours upon Gaius Caesar. If you did so because he deserved them, it was an act of gratitude ; but if also it were to attach him most closely to this Order, you therein showed more than mortal wisdom. No one has ever been welcomed by this Order with its own honours and favours who has considered any high position preferable to that which he had obtained from you. No one has ever here had it in his power to be a leading man in the State who has preferred to be a "Friend of the People"[b] ; but some men, either distrusting themselves on account of their own demerit, or, being driven from union with this Order because of disregard shown them by the others, have often, almost of necessity, left this harbour and dashed into those waves beyond. And if, after a tossing on the seas of a popular career, having rendered the State good service, they turn their gaze back upon the Senate House and seek to find favour with this most distinguished body, then, far from being spurned, they must even be courted. We are warned 39
by the bravest man and the best consul within the

[b] For *popularis* see *Pro Sestio*, 96, and p. 301.

mus, ne citerior Gallia nobis invitis alicui detur[1] post eos consules, qui nunc erunt designati, perpetuoque posthac ab iis, qui hunc ordinem oppugnent, populari ac turbulenta ratione teneatur. Quam ego plagam etsi non contemno, patres conscripti, praesertim monitus a sapientissimo consule et diligentissimo custode pacis atque otii, tamen vehementius arbitror pertimescendum, si hominum clarissimorum ac potentissimorum aut honorem minuero aut studium erga hunc ordinem repudiaro. Nam ut C. Iulius omnibus a senatu eximiis aut novis rebus ornatus per manus hanc provinciam tradat ei, cui minime vos velitis, per quem ordinem ipse amplissimam sit gloriam consecutus, ei ne libertatem quidem relinquat, adduci ad suspicandum nullo modo possum. Postremo, quo quisque animo futurus sit, nescio ; quid sperem, video ; praestare hoc senator debeo, quantum possum, ne quis vir clarus aut potens huic ordini iure irasci posse videatur. Atque haec, si inimicissimus essem C. Caesari, sentirem tamen rei publicae causa.

XVII. Sed non alienum esse arbitror, quo minus saepe aut interpeller a non nullis aut tacitorum existimatione reprendar, explicare breviter, quae mihi sit ratio et causa cum Caesare. Ac primum illud tempus

[1] decernatur *MSS.* : detur *Madvig.*

---

[a] Possibly Cn. Cornelius Lentulus Marcellinus, consul 56 B.C., of whom Cicero, when writing to his brother Quintus, speaks most warmly : " Consul est egregius Lentulus . . . sic, inquam, bonus, ut meliorem non viderim " (*Epp. ad Quintum fratrem*, ii. 4. 4).

[b] Lentulus was afraid that as the People had given Cisalpine Gaul to Caesar by the unconstitutional *lex Vatinia*, they might give it again to another *popularis* likely to cause unrest

memory of man,[a] to take care that, after the consuls who are about to be elected, Cisalpine Gaul is not given to anyone against our will, and that, in the future, it is not permanently controlled, through popular and seditious methods, by opponents of this Order.[b] For my part, Conscript Fathers, although I do not think lightly of such a disaster, especially after I have been warned by a consul of great wisdom, and a most vigilant guardian of peace and security, yet I think that there would be much greater reason for alarm, if I should slight the honour of most distinguished and powerful men, or disparage their loyalty to this Order. For that Gaius Julius, after the remarkable or unprecedented distinctions he has received from the Senate, should hand over this province to the last man whom you would wish to see there, and should leave not even a trace of liberty to that Order by whose favour he has obtained the highest distinction—such possibilities nothing can induce me to suspect. Lastly, what each man's future intentions are, I do not know: but I know what I hope. It is my duty as a senator to ensure that to the best of my power no eminent nor powerful man shall appear to have just cause for complaint against this House.
And even if I were Caesar's bitterest enemy, I should 40
yet maintain this for the good of the State.

XVII. But that I may not be frequently interrupted by some here nor silently condemned in their thoughts, I do not think it irrelevant briefly to explain the nature of my relations with Caesar. And in the first place, I say nothing about the time when

in the State. An opportunity, therefore, of making Cisalpine Gaul a consular province under the *lex Sempronia* should not be missed.

familiaritatis et consuetudinis, quae mihi cum illo, quae fratri meo, quae C. Varroni, consobrino nostro, ab omnium nostrum adulescentia fuit, praetermitto. Posteaquam sum penitus in rem publicam ingressus, ita dissensi ab illo, ut in disiunctione sententiae con-
41 iuncti tamen amicitia maneremus. Consul ille egit eas res, quarum me participem esse voluit; quibus ego si minus adsentiebar, tamen illius mihi iudicium gratum esse debebat. Me ille, ut quinqueviratum acciperem, rogavit, me in tribus sibi coniunctissimis consularibus esse voluit, mihi legationem, quam vellem, quanto cum honore vellem, detulit. Quae ego omnia non ingrato animo, sed obstinatione quadam sententiae repudiavi. Quam sapienter, non disputo; multis enim non probabo; constanter quidem et fortiter certe, qui cum me firmissimis opibus contra scelus inimicorum munire et populares impetus populari praesidio propulsare possem, quamvis excipere fortunam, subire vim atque iniuriam malui quam aut a vestris sanctissimis mentibus dissidere aut de meo statu declinare. Sed non is solum gratus debet esse,

---

[a] C. Visellius Varro, whose father married Helvia, sister of Cicero's mother.

[b] The execution of Caesar's first land law of 59 B.C. was entrusted to a Commission of Twenty, within which there was an inner Committee of Five, probably "figure-heads." That Cicero was invited to be a member of the Commission of Twenty is stated in *Epp. ad Att.* ix. 2a. 1 and in Vell. Pat. ii. 45. 2; but he was probably to be one of the "figure-heads." See also *Epp. ad Att.* ii. 19. 4.

we were young men together, when we associated on terms of the greatest intimacy with him—I, my brother, and Gaius Varro my cousin.[a] After I became deeply absorbed in public life, my relations with him were such, that although our opinions differed, we nevertheless remained united in friendship. As consul he engaged in measures in which he 41
wanted me to take a part, and although I did not approve of them, yet I was bound to be pleased with his opinion of me. He invited me to be one of the Commission of Five[b]; he desired me to be one of three men of consular rank most closely associated with him[c]; he offered me any titular embassy I pleased, with every privilege I could wish.[d] All these offers I rejected with firm adherence to my principles, but not without a feeling of gratitude. How far I acted wisely, I do not discuss, for there are many whom I shall not convince, but my conduct has been at least consistent and courageous. Although it was in my power to enlist a most powerful defender against the wickedness of my enemies and to repel popular attacks under the protection of a popular leader,[e] I preferred to hold my ground against all the blows of fortune, and to suffer violence and wrong, rather than to depart from your most sacred principles or to deviate from my own line of conduct. But it is not only the man who has received a favour who ought

[c] To join the coalition of Caesar, Pompey and Crassus, the First Triumvirate. See Cicero, *Epp. ad Att.* ii. 3. 3.

[d] Cicero (*Epp. ad Att.* ii. 18. 3) says that Caesar offered him a *legatio libera voti causa*, or a permit to travel abroad, nominally to fulfil a vow, with the status of an ambassador; also a post as *legatus* under him in Gaul, see § 42.

[e] The attacks are those of Clodius, the protection that of Caesar.

qui accepit beneficium, verum etiam is, cui potestas accipiendi fuit.[a] Ego illa ornamenta, quibus ille[b] me ornabat, decere me et convenire iis rebus, quas gesseram, non putabam; illum quidem amico animo me habere eodem loco quo principem civium, suum generum, sentiebam.

42 Traduxit ad plebem inimicum meum sive iratus mihi, quod me secum ne in beneficiis quidem videbat posse coniungi, sive exoratus.[c] Ne haec quidem fuit iniuria. Nam postea me, ut sibi essem legatus, non solum suasit, verum etiam rogavit.[d] Ne id quidem accepi; non quo alienum mea dignitate arbitrarer, sed quod tantum rei publicae sceleris impendere a consulibus proximis non suspicabar. XVIII. Ergo adhuc magis est mihi verendum, ne mea superbia in illius liberalitate quam ne illius iniuria in nostra amicitia reprendatur.

43 Ecce illa tempestas, caligo bonorum et subita atque improvisa formido, tenebrae rei publicae, ruina atque incendium civitatis, terror iniectus Caesari de eius actis, metus caedis bonis omnibus, consulum scelus, cupiditas, egestas, audacia! Si non sum adiutus, non

---

[a] This is well expressed in Cicero, *Epp. ad Att.* ii. 3. 4.

[b] Pompey.

[c] Caesar, in 59 B.C., consul and Pontifex Maximus, carried out Clodius' *traductio ad plebem* by the passing of a *lex curiata* on the afternoon of the day on which Cicero when defending C. Antonius had attacked the proceedings of Caesar, Pompey and Crassus. See Suetonius, *Div. Iul.* 20; Cicero, *De domo*, 41.

[d] An invitation to join his staff in Gaul (*Epp. ad Att.* ii. 18. 3; 19. 4) when Cicero would have been protected against Clodius. This invitation is different from the *legatio* offered in § 41.

to be grateful, but also the man who has had an opportunity of receiving one. I did not think that those distinctions with which he would have honoured me, became me or were in keeping with my previous career[a]; nevertheless, I felt that he was well disposed towards me, and that I held the same place in his regard as his son-in-law, the chief of our fellow-citizens.[b] He caused an enemy of mine to be invested 42
with plebeian status, whether through his anger at finding that even his favours could not attach me to him, or through his surrender to importunity.[c] Even that did me no harm; for afterwards he not only advised me, but begged me to join his staff.[d] Even this offer I did not accept; not that I considered it beneath my dignity, but because I had no suspicion of the criminal assault upon the State that was coming from the consuls of the following year.[e] XVIII. Up to the present, therefore, I have more reason to fear blame for my presumption in refusing his generous offers than he for the harm he did me notwithstanding our friendship.

Then came that storm![f]—black darkness for loyal 43
citizens, sudden and unforeseen panic, gloom over the State, ruin and conflagration for the country, Caesar terrified for his measures,[g] all loyalists fearful of massacre, the crime, the greed, the penury, the effrontery of the consuls! If I was not assisted by

[e] From Piso and Gabinius.

[f] The consulships of Piso and Gabinius and the tribunate of Clodius, 58 B.C. See *Pro Sestio*, 15-41.

[g] The reference is not to Clodius' attack on Caesar in 58 B.C., but to an earlier attack in the same year by two praetors, C. Memmius and L. Domitius Ahenobarbus who held consulships in 54 B.C. See *Pro Sestio*, 40; Suetonius, *Div. Iul.* 23.

debui[1]; si desertus, sibi fortasse providit; si etiam oppugnatus, ut quidam aut putant aut volunt, violata amicitia est, accepi iniuriam; inimicus esse debui, non nego; sed, si idem ille tum me salvum esse voluit, cum vos me ut carissimum filium desiderabatis, et si vos idem pertinere ad causam illam putabatis voluntatem Caesaris a salute mea non abhorrere, et si illius voluntatis generum eius habeo testem, qui idem Italiam in municipiis, populum Romanum in contione, vos mei semper cupidissimos in Capitolio ad meam salutem incitavit, si denique Cn. Pompeius idem mihi testis de voluntate Caesaris et sponsor est illi de mea, nonne vobis videor et ultimi temporis recordatione et proximi memoria medium illud tristissimum tempus debere, si ex rerum natura non possim evellere, ex animo quidem certe excidere?

44 Ego vero, si mihi non licet per aliquos ita gloriari, me dolorem atque inimicitias meas rei publicae concessisse, si hoc magni cuiusdam hominis et persapientis videtur, utar hoc, quod non tam ad laudem adipiscendam quam ad vitandam vituperationem valet, hominem me esse gratum et non modo tantis beneficiis, sed etiam mediocri hominum benevolentia commoveri.

XIX. A viris fortissimis et de me optime meritis

[1] *The common* MSS. *reading is* debuit, *i.e.* "*Caesar was under no obligation to assist me.*"

---

[a] By letters to the different communities. See Cicero, *Post red tum in senatu*, 29.

[b] Probably towards the close of July 57 B.C. See *Pro Sestio*, 107.

[c] In the Temple of Juppiter at the end of July 57 B.C. See *Pro Sestio*, 129-130.

[d] Shortly after the Conference of Luca, *c.* 17 April 56 B.C., Cicero had written to Pompey promising goodwill to the Triumvirate. See *Epp. ad Att.* iv. 5. 1.

Caesar, I did not deserve to be ; if I was abandoned by him, perhaps he was thinking of himself ; if I was even attacked, as some believe, or wish, then our friendship has been violated, then I have suffered a wrong, and I ought to have been his enemy, I do not deny it. But if Caesar indeed wished me to be recalled from exile at a time when you regretted my absence as if I were a beloved son ; if you also thought it was important for the good cause that Caesar's wishes should not be opposed to my recall ; and if I have as witness of those wishes his son-in-law, who indeed urged my recall upon Italy throughout her towns,[a] upon the Roman People in a public meeting,[b] and upon you yourselves, most eager for my presence, on the Capitol [c] ; if, lastly, Gnaeus Pompeius is at once my witness for Caesar's goodwill to me, and guarantor of my own to him,[d] does it not seem to you that, both recalling those days long past,[e] and keeping in mind these later ones,[f] I might, even if I cannot eradicate from existence that most unhappy time that intervened, at least wholly banish it from my heart ?

But as for myself, if some would forbid me to boast 44
that I have sacrificed my resentment and my enmities to the public interest, if such conduct is deemed possible only for some great man of outstanding wisdom, I will put forward this plea, which may avail me not so much to win praise as to escape invective, that I am a grateful man, and that I am deeply moved not only by special favours but also by any modest marks of general goodwill.

XIX. I ask certain gallant gentlemen who have

[e] Before Cicero had quarrelled with Caesar.
[f] After Cicero's return from exile.

quibusdam peto, ut, si ego illos meorum laborum atque incommodorum participes esse nolui, ne illi me suarum inimicitiarum socium velint esse, praesertim cum mihi idem illi concesserint, ut etiam acta illa Caesaris, quae neque oppugnavi antea neque defendi, meo iam iure
45 possim defendere. Nam summi civitatis viri, quorum ego consilio rem publicam conservavi et quorum auctoritate illam coniunctionem Caesaris defugi, Iulias leges et ceteras illo consule rogatas iure latas negant; idem illam proscriptionem capitis mei contra salutem rei publicae, sed salvis auspiciis rogatam esse dicebant. Itaque vir summa auctoritate, summa eloquentia dixit graviter casum illum meum funus esse rei publicae, sed funus iustum et indictum. Mihi ipsi omnino perhonorificum est discessum meum funus dici rei publicae; reliqua non reprendo, sed mihi ad id, quod sentio, adsumo. Nam, si illud iure rogatum dicere ausi sunt, quod nullo exemplo fieri potuit, nulla lege licuit, quia nemo de caelo servarat, oblitine erant tum, cum ille, qui id egerat, plebeius est lege curiata

---

[a] Certain violent opponents of the Triumvirate, such as Bibulus, Lentulus Spinther, and L. Domitius Ahenobarbus.

[b] Although Cicero's letters of 59 B.C. contain much personal criticism of Caesar's consulship, Cicero's public comments were restricted to an unfavourable reference to Caesar's coalition in his defence of C. Antonius.

[c] See note on § 41. Cicero is referring to leading Optimates, possibly including Bibulus himself.

[d] The whole of the legislation of 59 B.C., some passed by Caesar in person, some by his agent Vatinius, was illegal, according to strict constitutional theory, because Bibulus, assisted by several tribunes and by Cato, employed every device of political and religious obstruction.

[e] The Optimates' point was that no unfavourable omens had been announced when Clodius in 58 B.C. put forward his

rendered me the greatest services,[a] that, if I have not wished them to share my labours and misfortunes, they should not wish me to be associated with them in their enmities, especially since those very men have made it possible for me now to defend with good reason even those acts of Caesar, which hitherto I have neither attacked nor defended.[b] For some leading men of 45
the State, acting on whose advice I saved the country, and by whose authority I refused that partnership with Caesar,[c] say that the Julian Laws and others that were put before the People while he was consul were not legally passed[d]; but they also declared that the outlawry of myself, although it injured the interests of the State, was proposed without any infringement of the auspices.[e] And so a man,[f] whose authority is as great as his eloquence, said in weighty words that my downfall was the funeral of the State, but a regular funeral announced in all due form.[g] As for myself, I feel it is a great honour that my departure from Rome has been called a funeral of the State. I have no objection to the rest of what was said, but I adopt it to support my views. For, if they have ventured to say that a bill was legally passed (whereas in fact it could not be sanctioned by any precedent, nor be permitted by any law[h]), because no one had watched the sky for omens, had they forgotten that when the man, who proposed that bill, was made plebeian by

bill to exile Cicero. But such action had been forbidden by Clodius' repeal of the *leges Aelia et Fufia*.

[f] Probably Bibulus. [g] Cicero, *De domo*, 42.

[h] The main objections to the legality of Clodius' bill of outlawry against Cicero were (1) that it was a *privilegium*, (2) that it was a capital sentence passed not by the *comitia centuriata*, but by the *concilium plebis*, (3) that there had been no formal trial.

factus, dici de caelo esse servatum? Qui si plebeius omnino esse non potuit, qui tribunus pl. potuit esse? et, cuius tribunatus si ratus est, nihil est, quod inritum ex actis Caesaris possit esse, eius non solum tribunatus, sed etiam perniciosissimae res auspiciorum religione
46 conservata iure latae videbuntur? Quare aut vobis statuendum est legem Aeliam manere, legem Fufiam non esse abrogatam, non omnibus fastis legem ferri licere, cum lex feratur, de caelo servari, obnuntiari, intercedi licere, censorium iudicium ac notionem et illud morum severissimum magisterium non esse nefariis legibus de civitate sublatum, si patricius tribunus pl. fuerit, contra leges sacratas, si plebeius, contra auspicia fuisse, aut mihi concedant homines oportet in rebus bonis non exquirere ea iura, quae ipsi in perditis non exquirant, praesertim cum ab illis aliquotiens condicio C. Caesari lata sit, ut easdem res alio modo ferret, qua condicione auspicia requirebant,

---

[a] A *lex curiata*, passed by the *comitia curiata*, was required for the transference of a patrician to plebeian status. See note on § 42.

[b] The transfer of Clodius was rendered invalid by the *obnuntiatio* of Bibulus, see Cicero, *De domo*, 40. His tribunate, therefore, and all his *acta* were equally invalid.

[c] "If my exile is accepted as valid, then Caesar's *acta* also must be accepted as valid. But that must not imply that the auspices were not violated in 59 B.C."

[d] See "The *Lex Aelia Fufia* in the Late Republic," pp. 309-322.

[e] See *Pro Sestio*, 16, note. No patrician could be tribune. The power of the tribunes was not based on any statute, but on an oath of the plebeians to uphold their *sacrosanctitas*

a law of the *comitia curiata*,[a] it was said that the sky had been watched ?[b] If, then, he could not be a plebeian at all, how could he be a tribune of the commons ? If Clodius' tribunate is declared valid in law, there is nothing in the acts of Caesar that can be declared invalid. In that case, shall not only Clodius' tribunate but even his most scandalous measures be deemed to have been legally passed because the sanctity of the auspices has been duly respected ?[c]
You must, therefore, either decide that the Aelian 46
Law holds good and that the Fufian Law has not been repealed ; that a law cannot be passed on all days whereon public business is lawful ; that when a law is being proposed, the sky can still be watched, that announcement of evil omens and veto by intervention are still permissible[d] ; that the censors' verdict and power of investigation and their most strict supervision of morals have not been removed from the State by pernicious laws[d] ; that if Clodius was a patrician when he held the tribunate of the commons, the *leges sacratae* were defied, while, if he was a plebeian, the auspices were disregarded.[e] Or, if not, then my opponents must allow me,[f] when measures are good, not to examine too closely those points of law which they themselves do not examine when measures are bad ; especially since they more than once proposed to Gaius Caesar that he should put forward his same proposals in another way, thus showing that they

or inviolability. The violation of this oath rendered the transgressor accursed (*sacer*).

[f] Cicero's plea is that if the Optimates accept Clodius' legislation, which is bad, without looking closely into the question of the auspices, they must allow him to ignore the veto of Bibulus in the case of some of Caesar's laws, which he may approve.

leges comprobabant, in Clodio auspiciorum ratio sit eadem, leges omnes sint eversae ac perditae civitatis.

47 XX. Extremum illud est. Ego, si essent inimicitiae mihi cum C. Caesare, tamen hoc tempore rei publicae consulere, inimicitias in aliud tempus reservare deberem; possem etiam summorum virorum exemplo inimicitias rei publicae causa deponere. Sed cum inimicitiae fuerint numquam, opinio iniuriae beneficio sit exstincta, sententia mea, patres conscripti, si dignitas agitur Caesaris, homini tribuam, si honos quidam, senatus concordiae consulam, si auctoritas decretorum vestrorum, constantiam ordinis in eodem ornando imperatore servabo, si perpetua ratio Gallici belli, rei publicae providebo, si aliquod meum privatum officium, me non ingratum esse praestabo. Atque hoc velim probare omnibus, patres conscripti; sed levissime feram, si forte aut iis minus probaro, qui meum inimicum repugnante vestra auctoritate texerunt, aut iis,

---

[a] There is no further evidence concerning this offer. According to Pocock (*In Vatinium*, pp. 153 and 157) it was inspired by Pompey and was an invitation to Caesar to sever his connexion with the *populares*.

[b] Clodius' laws, like Caesar's, were carried in defiance of the auspices, but, unlike his, were utterly pernicious.

[c] See §§ 20-23.

[d] *i.e.* with the previous *supplicationes*.

[e] When, in the latter part of his tribunate (58 B.C.), Clodius turned against Pompey and Caesar, temporarily

approved his measures but insisted on the observance of the auspices [a]; and since all Clodius' laws,[b] implying the overthrow and ruin of the State, stand in the same relation (*as Caesar's*) to the auspices.

XX. Here follows my last word. If I were the 47 enemy of Gaius Caesar, nevertheless to-day I ought to consult the interests of the State and to adjourn my enmities for another occasion. I could even follow the example of distinguished men,[c] and lay them aside for the public welfare. But since I have never been his enemy, and since his favour has effaced an imaginary injury, in giving my vote, Conscript Fathers, if it is a question of rewarding the merits of Caesar, I will pay tribute to the man; if it is a question of some honourable distinction, I will have regard for harmony in the Senate; if it is a question of upholding the authority of your decrees, I will follow the firm practice of this House in conferring a distinction upon this same commander [d]; if it is a question of a consistent policy towards the war in Gaul, I will be true to the needs of the State; if it is a question of some personal obligation of my own, I will show that I am not ungrateful. Yes, I should be glad to persuade you all to accept this view, Conscript Fathers; but I shall not be greatly disturbed, either if perchance I shall not convince those who supported my enemy [e] against your authority, or those who

driving the former out of public life and attacking the latter's legislation (Cicero, *De domo*, 40; *De har. resp.* 48), Cicero says (*De har. resp.* 48) that he was supported by certain nobles. This same support may perhaps be seen in the encouragement given to Clodius in February 56 B.C. by "Curio, Bibulus and his (Pompey's) other detractors" to revile and harass Pompey (Cicero, *Epp. ad Quintum fratrem*, ii. 3. 4).

si qui meum cum inimico suo reditum in gratiam vituperabunt, cum ipsi et cum meo et cum suo inimico in gratiam non dubitarint redire.

---

[a] Caesar. [b] Clodius.

will inveigh against my reconciliation with their enemy,[a] although they have not hesitated to become reconciled themselves with one [b] who is as much their enemy as my own.

III. Summary of the *De provinciis consularibus*

§§ 1-2. The public interest so strongly demands the removal of the proconsuls Piso and Gabinius from their provinces of Macedonia and Syria that I can, without undue animosity, support the proposal of P. Servilius Isauricus (consul 79 B.C.) to assign their provinces to the consuls soon to be elected for 55 B.C.

§ 3. Four provinces come under consideration: the two Gallic provinces, now under one governor, Macedonia and Syria. I will first deal with the gross misgovernment of Piso and Gabinius in their provinces, disregarding the crimes which they committed as consuls in Rome.

§§ 4-8. In Macedonia Piso's rule has been such that that peaceful province has been overrun by Thracian invaders; our unusually strong army has melted away owing to defeat and losses arising from Piso's inefficiency and criminal negligence. The rights of the free towns of Macedonia and Achaia under their charters have been violated, and the towns themselves, Dyrrhachium and Byzantium in particular, have been shamefully treated. The interests of provincial debtors have been preferred to those of Roman citizens.

§§ 9-12. In Syria, Gabinius' horse and foot have been defeated in the field. His rule has been disgraced by plundering and extortion. The *publicani* in his province, a class bound to me by ties of loyalty, have been reduced to ruin by his avarice and cruelty. You must at once come to their aid.

§§ 13-16. Last year (57 B.C.) you tried in vain to recall them. You have recently refused Gabinius' demand for a *supplicatio*, and Piso has not yet dared to send any dispatches. Let Gabinius, however, console himself with the reflection how the Senate rebutted T. Albucius who, when propraetor in Sardinia (about 117 B.C.), demanded a *supplicatio*, and how Albucius never recovered from that disgrace.

§ 17. The proposal made in this debate to assign the provinces of Cisalpine and Transalpine Gaul to the consuls shortly to be elected leaves both Piso and Gabinius in their present commands; and the proposal to assign to them one of the two Gallic provinces and either Syria or Macedonia still leaves one or other of them in his command. "No," says the author of the former proposal, "for I shall assign Macedonia and Syria to praetors, so that Gabinius and Piso can be superseded at once." "That is all very well," I reply, "but your proposal will probably be vetoed by a tribune who could not, under the Sempronian Law, veto an assignment of Macedonia and Syria to consuls." I, however, am going to propose that Macedonia and Syria be assigned to praetors for the coming year (55 B.C.), but, as I expect that that will be vetoed, I am going to propose also that these provinces be assigned to consuls for the following year (54 B.C.). Thus, at best, Piso and Gabinius may be superseded next year (55 B.C.); at worst, they will be superseded in the following year (54 B.C.).

§§ 18-23. Even if Piso and Gabinius were the best of men, I could not agree to the appointment of successors to Caesar. The consul (L. Marcius Philippus) has just interrupted me by saying that I have more reason for animosity against Caesar than against Gabinius, who when consul merely carried out Caesar's orders in banishing me. But I am now guided by the welfare of the State rather than by private grievances, as was Ti. Gracchus, father of the tribunes, when he came to the help of P. and L. Cornelius Scipio, and as were M. Crassus, M. Scaurus and the Metelli in their support of Marius. Caesar has brought the war in Gaul almost to an end. He who began the war ought to be allowed to finish it. If Caesar is superseded, the smouldering embers of war may burst out into flame. Many precedents from our history urge me to lay aside personal enmity for the sake of the State: the reconciliations of M. Aemilius Lepidus and M. Fulvius Nobilior; of L. Marcius Philippus and the Senate; of the two brothers, M. and L. Lucullus with P. Servilius Vatia: and, most recently, of Q. Metellus Nepos and myself. My own old and unfailing loyalty to the State reinstates me as Caesar's friend.

§§ 24-28. Although Caesar and I have had differences of opinion, I can never be the enemy of one who has served the State so well. In fact I have followed the example of the Senate in my relations with Caesar: your disapproval of his policy found me also disapproving; your changed attitude towards him, induced by his great deeds, has evoked my own warm approval. In fact I have already been reconciled with him, for I proposed a *supplicatio* of fifteen days in honour of his victories in Gaul, and I have recently supported proposals for the appointment of *decem legati* and for pay for his troops.

§§ 29-35. You bore patiently with me when I spoke for these honours to Caesar, but you interrupt me now when I am seeking not so much to pay compliments to Caesar as to serve the public interest. Caesar is kept in Gaul not from any attachment to life there nor from fear of a return to Rome where, surely, he would be acclaimed, but from a sense of duty: he wishes to complete his great task. Now that Pompey has subdued the East, in Gaul alone within our Empire is war afoot. Whereas once we were content to defend the frontiers only of Transalpine Gaul, and held in it only " a mere path," the genius of Caesar is bringing the whole of Gaul into our possession. Italy no longer needs the Alps as a rampart. After one or two summers the whole of Gaul will be ours. But if Caesar's work is left unfinished, Gallic power will revive. Even if Caesar wished to return to Italy, it is our duty to retain him in Gaul.

§§ 36-38. I cannot therefore support the proposal to deprive Caesar of Transalpine Gaul, a province to which he was appointed by decree of the Senate. Moreover, such a proposal is objectionable because it respects the *lex Vatinia*, no law at all, which conferred Cisalpine Gaul upon him. The proposal, however, to take away from him Cisalpine Gaul is less objectionable. For, so far from conflicting with the Vatinian Law, it provides that Caesar shall not be superseded till 1 March 54 B.C., when his command under that law is due to expire. But it will cause a break in the consular *imperium*, for what will be the position during January and February 54 B.C. of the consul appointed to succeed Caesar in Cisalpine Gaul? Moreover, under either of these proposals Piso will remain proconsul in Macedonia.

§§ 38-40. You have shown not only gratitude but also wisdom in conferring exceptional honours on Caesar. They will make him loyal to the Senate. The Senate must not fail to court those who seek to return to allegiance after adventures as *populares*. Although I realize how disastrous it would be if Cisalpine Gaul came to be controlled by enemies of the Senate, yet I think that there would be much more reason for alarm if any distinguished and powerful man were to be alienated from the Senate. But we have surely nothing revolutionary to fear from Caesar, who would be the last man to hand over his province to a governor most unacceptable to you.

§§ 40-43. Now for the story of my relations with Caesar. As young men we were friends and continued to be so after our entry into public life, even though our views came to differ. Although I disapproved of his actions as consul, I was pleased by his attempt to win my support. But I refused all his generous offers : membership of his Land Commission ; the closest association with Pompey, Crassus and himself ; a *legatio libera*, with every privilege. Although by acceptance I could have won a powerful protector, I preferred to remain loyal to senatorial ideals. Although Caesar then made my enemy Clodius a plebeian, he yet invited me to join his staff in Gaul. I refused this offer also, not anticipating the disasters soon to come in the consulship of Piso and Gabinius. I was thus responsible for my own exile. But Caesar consented to my recall and Pompey is a guarantor both of Caesar's goodwill towards me and of mine towards him. I must forget and forgive.

§ 44. I must ask those who did not share my

troubles when I was exiled not to insist that I should share their enmities, especially as they have made it possible for me to defend Caesar's laws, which hitherto I have neither attacked nor defended.

§ 45. For those same men, through whose influence I refused to enter into partnership with Caesar, agree that all the laws passed in Caesar's consulship were made illegal by the *obnuntiatio* of Bibulus, but that the bill for my banishment, however deplorable and unconstitutional, was legal. If they assert that my banishment was legal because the sky was not watched for omens, have they not forgotten that the *lex curiata*, by which Clodius became a plebeian, was made illegal by the watching of the sky? Clodius, therefore, was by law neither a plebeian nor a tribune. If Clodius' tribunate is deemed legal, then not only the laws of Caesar but also the scandalous laws of Clodius must be legal.

§ 46. There is a choice between two alternatives. Either you must admit that Clodius was legally neither a plebeian nor a tribune and that all his legislation was illegal, or my opponents must allow me to accept Caesar's laws without examining too closely the question of the auspices, as they choose to do in the case of Clodius' criminal measures; especially as they have more than once offered to approve Caesar's laws if he would bring them forward in different fashion, with due regard for the auspices, and as the abominable legislation of Clodius stands in the same relation to the auspices as do Caesar's laws.

§ 47. My last word is that, if I were an enemy of Caesar, I would drop any resentment. But I have never been his enemy, and his favour has effaced an imaginary injury. Gratitude both public and private, political consistency, and patriotism all urge reconciliation. I am alike indifferent to the resentment of those who once scorned your authority by championing my enemy Clodius, and of those who inveigh against my reconciliation with Caesar.

PRO BALBO

I. The Early Career of L. Cornelius Balbus [a]

L. Cornelius Balbus Maior was born about 100 B.C., of good family, at Gades (Cadiz) in southern Spain, originally a Phoenician city which since 206 B.C. had been bound to Rome by treaty (*civitas foederata*). In the Hannibalic War, at the close of Scipio Africanus' victorious campaigns in Spain, Mago, the Carthaginian commander at Gades, was shut out from that city on his return from an unsuccessful attempt to surprise the Romans at Carthago Nova. Gades then surrendered,[b] probably to a Roman senior centurion, L. Marcius Septimus, who, after the defeats of P. and Cn. Scipio in 211 B.C., had been commanding in southern Spain. That was the end of Carthaginian domination in the peninsula. A treaty with Gades was then negotiated by L. Marcius [c]; it was informal, but was allowed validity. In 78 B.C. it was formally concluded or confirmed by a resolution of the Senate.[d] In 49 B.C., after the Pompeian defeat in Spain, Julius Caesar conferred Roman citizenship on the Gaditani,[e] and, later, Augustus gave the city the status of a *municipium civium Romanorum*.

[a] J. S. Reid, *Pro Balbo* (Cambridge, 1878 and 1908), pp. 5-9; Tyrrell and Purser, *The Correspondence of Cicero*, vol. iv, ed. 2, pp. lxxi-lxxix; P.-W. iv. 1260-1268 (Münzer).

[b] Livy, xxviii. 37. [c] *Pro Balbo*, 34. [d] *Pro Balbo*, 34.

[e] Livy, *Epitome*, cx; Dio Cassius, xli. 24. 1; Pliny, *N.H.* iv. 119.

During the Sertorian War (79–72 B.C.) Balbus served with the Roman forces, his participation in operations at Carthago Nova and on the rivers Sucro and Turia (in the plain of Valentia) being specially mentioned. He thereby won recognition from the Roman high commanders, Q. Metellus Pius and Pompey, and from a quaestor C. Memmius, brother-in-law of Pompey. Through the agency of Pompey, acting with the concurrence of his military staff (*consilium*), Balbus was rewarded for his services with Roman citizenship, an honour which was conferred at the same time on other members also of his family.[a] These grants of citizenship to individuals, together with other similar grants made by Pompey, were ratified by a law of 72 B.C., the *lex Gellia Cornelia*,[b] "ut cives Romani sint ii quos Cn. Pompeius de consilii sententia singillatim civitate donaverit." The fairly common cognomen of Balbus ("Stammerer") was possibly a near equivalent of a Punic name, or may have been given to foreigners from their imperfect pronunciation of Latin.[c] His praenomen and gentile name, L. Cornelius, he probably derived from L. Cornelius Lentulus Crus[d] (consul 49 B.C.), who must

[a] Pliny, *N.H.* v. 36; vii. 136, for his brother and his nephew (L. Balbus Minor). Since his father is called Lucius in the Fasti (*C.I.L.* (ed. 2), i, p. 158) he also must have been enfranchised. [b] *Pro Balbo*, 19.

[c] Tyrrell and Purser, *The Correspondence of Cicero*, vol. iv, p. lxxi.

[d] For Balbus' close tie of loyalty to L. Cornelius Lentulus Crus see Cicero, *Epp. ad Att.* viii. 15a. 2; ix. 7b. 2. This is more satisfactory than to suppose that Balbus took his names from L. Cornelius Lentulus, a Roman commander in Spain who had rendered services to Gades (Livy, xxviii. 38); or from the consuls of 72 B.C., L. Gellius Poplicola and Cn. Cornelius Lentulus.

have served in the Sertorian War and recommended him for citizenship.

When the censorship was restored in 70 B.C. Balbus was enrolled as a citizen in one of the four city tribes (*tribus urbanae*), and his wealth would qualify him for membership of the *equester ordo*. But he soon improved his social status by a successful prosecution : he impeached on a charge of *ambitus* a member of the fashionable *tribus Clustumina*, of which Pompey [a] was a member, and, having won his case, was rewarded, under a provision of Roman criminal law, with the convicted man's place in the tribe.[b]

At some time, probably early in his career, Balbus received, by gift from Pompey, a site for a suburban property (*horti*) ; his country house at Tusculum (*Tusculanum*) he acquired, before 56 B.C., by purchase.[c] But Caesar also was not slow to discern the merits of this Spaniard, having probably come to know him when quaestor in Further Spain (perhaps 68 B.C.). This bond was strengthened when Balbus was taken to Further Spain by Caesar (propraetor 61 B.C.), and was made *praefectus fabrum*, or "Chief Engineer." [d] By then the Gaditani had appointed Balbus their *hospes publicus* or *patronus* in Rome, and at the instance of Balbus Caesar rendered many services to Gades when propraetor.[e]

The immediate prelude to the formation of the First Triumvirate shows that Balbus had come to rank high in the confidence of Caesar, having gradu-

[a] Dessau, 8888. Cn. Pompeius Cn. f. Clu. See note *a*, p. 706.

[b] *Pro Balbo*, 57.

[c] Cicero, *Epp. ad Att.* vii. 7. 6 ; ix. 13. 8. *Pro Balbo*, 56.

[d] A subordinate of high rank, with duties unrelated to his title. See Tyrrell and Purser, *op. cit.* vol. iii (ed. 2), p. 336.

[e] *Pro Balbo*, 43.

ally edged away from his earlier patron, Pompey, towards a more powerful personality. Towards the end of 60 B.C., a few months after his return to Rome from Spain, Balbus was entrusted by Caesar with some of the delicate negotiations which led to the coalition of Pompey, Caesar and Crassus, known as the First Triumvirate. Balbus sought, in vain, to bring Cicero into it.[a]

If Caesar had brought an able Spaniard into his counsels, Pompey had by that time taken into confidential employment a talented Asiatic Greek, Theophanes [b] of Mitylene. He accompanied Pompey in the Third Mithridatic War as his secretary and historian, and wrote an account of Pompey's campaigns which he compared with those of Alexander. This was written in 63–62 B.C., to further Pompey's cause in Rome. Pompey, before returning from the Near East to Italy, conferred Roman citizenship upon Theophanes in the presence of his army.[c] Theophanes, who took Pompey's [d] name as a compliment to his benefactor, soon exchanged the role of historian for that of a leading adviser and agent.[e] He was, in fact, Pompey's reply to Caesar's Balbus. And, just as the partnership between Pompey and Caesar was confirmed by the marriage of Julia, so also were their two agents drawn into relationship by the bond of adoption. Balbus was adopted by Theophanes: nothing illegal, but, as Cicero complained when civil

[a] Cicero, *Epp. ad Att.* ii. 3. 3.

[b] See R. Laqueur in P.-W. v. 2090-2127.

[c] *Pro Archia*, 24. By 62 B.C., when this speech was delivered.

[d] Dittenberger (ed. 3), 753. Cn. Pompeius Theophanes.

[e] Cicero, *Epp. ad Att.* vii. 11. 3; Caesar, *Bell. Civ.* iii. 18. 3.

war seemed near, an irregularity and even a monstrosity.[a]

Balbus has been thought to have played a part in a political trial of 59 B.C. Late in that year L. Valerius Flaccus (praetor 63 B.C.) was impeached by D. Laelius for *repetundae* arising from his propraetorship in Asia (62 B.C.). Flaccus was acquitted on the defence of Hortensius and Cicero. On one interpretation,[b] Balbus supported Laelius in the prosecution; on another, Laelius was supported not by L. Cornelius Balbus but by L. Herennius Balbus who, in 56 B.C., joined L. Sempronius Atratinus in the prosecution of Caelius.[c]

In 58 B.C. Balbus was reappointed to his former post of *praefectus fabrum* under Caesar, but during Caesar's Gallic campaigns he spent much time as his agent in Rome. Favoured by both Pompey and Caesar, wealthy, and no doubt something of a figure in society, this naturalized foreigner could not avoid the dislike and the enmity of Roman nobles, especially of those hostile to Caesar's coalition. The more he became valued to his employers, the more he became obnoxious to their opponents. Balbus' unpopularity is revealed by Cicero's studied excuses.[d] Early in 56 B.C. the partnership of Pompey, Caesar and Crassus seemed about to dissolve. At such a favourable moment a fellow-townsman from Gades was incited by enemies of the Triumvirate to attack Balbus' title to his Roman citizenship. But the Con-

[a] Cicero, *Epp. ad Att.* vii. 7. 6; *Pro Balbo*, 57.
[b] Münzer, in P.-W. iv. 1262-1263; Tyrrell and Purser, *op. cit.* pp. xxii-xxiii.
[c] T. B. L. Webster, *Cicero, Pro L. Flacco* (Oxford, 1931), Introduction, p. v. See p. 404.
[d] *Pro Balbo*, 18; 56-59.

ference at Luca reunited the three partners and saved Balbus. "But for the failure of certain political intrigues, the fate of Balbus and the role of Cicero would have been very different." [a]

II. The Trial of L. Cornelius Balbus

For sixteen years after the passing of the *lex Gellia Cornelia* (72 B.C.) Balbus had enjoyed the privileges of the Roman citizenship conferred on him by Pompey. But in 56 B.C. his claim to this citizenship was challenged in a prosecution, prompted for political motives and instigated by enemies of the Triumvirate. In the absence of contemporary evidence for events in Rome between the Conference of Luca (about 17 April) and the end of the year 56 B.C., the date of Balbus' trial cannot be precisely fixed. But, as internal evidence [b] from Cicero's speech shows that it was delivered after the *De provinciis consularibus* (late in June or early in July), it may perhaps be dated to the late summer or early autumn of 56 B.C.

The prosecution used as an offensive weapon against Balbus the *lex Papia*,[c] of 64 B.C., a kind of "Alien Act." This law had already been invoked in 62 B.C. to indict a poet, A. Licinius Archias, as a political manœuvre against L. Lucullus. The claim of Archias, a Greek born at Antioch, to Roman citizenship under the *lex Plautia Papiria* (89 B.C.) was

[a] R. Syme, *The Roman Revolution*, p. 72.

[b] *Pro Balbo*, 61.

[c] E. G. Hardy, "The Transpadane Question and the Alien Act of 65 or 64 B.C.," *J.R.S.* vi, pp. 77-82. T. Rice Holmes, *The Roman Republic*, i, p. 237; *C.A.H.* ix, p. 481. The ancient sources are: Cicero, *De lege agraria*, i. 13; *Pro Archia*, 10; *De officiis*, iii. 47. Dio Cassius, xxxvii. 9. 5.

vindicated by Cicero in a brilliant literary speech[a] before a court presided over by his brother Quintus, a praetor of the year. The *lex Papia* was a tribunician law sponsored by the Senate as a precaution against an attempt by Crassus to win for his intrigues against Pompey, then engaged in the Third Mithridatic War, the support of the unenfranchised Transpadane Gauls. The law made liable to eviction from Rome all non-citizens then resident there, but was mainly directed at the residue of dwellers in the Italian peninsula, mostly Transpadanes, who had not been enfranchised after the Social War. As, however, the exact provisions of the *lex Papia* are unknown, we cannot be certain of the constitution of the court before which Balbus appeared. As it is improbable that the *lex Papia* set up a special court for trying aliens, Balbus' case must have been brought up before one of the *quaestiones perpetuae*. The most likely one is the *quaestio de maiestate*, a new standing court possibly set up by L. Appuleius Saturninus in his first tribunate (103 B.C.) with a view, in part at least, to overcoming resistance to his own position in Rome. But in later years this court, as part of Sulla's system of criminal jurisdiction, was the scene of many prosecutions in the bitter political warfare of the Republic's close : a charge of wanton injury to the *maiestas populi Romani* was a weapon frequently used in personal or party feuds, and was a conveniently indefinite term covering all varieties of constitutional irregularity, sedition and treason. The indictment, therefore, against Balbus was based on the *lex*

[a] J. S. Reid's introduction to his edition of the *Pro Archia* (Cambridge, 1877, revised 1886) is a valuable aid to a study of the *Pro Balbo* also.

Papia, and the case has thus something in common with that of Archias. We are alike ignorant both of the name of the prosecutor and of the president of the *quaestio*. The prosecutor was a Gaditane who had somehow acquired Roman citizenship, but who, owing to a condemnation on a criminal charge, had suffered deprivation of civil rights.[a] The prospect of a successful prosecution which would restore his lost privileges would thus make him a willing tool in the service of employers hostile to Pompey, Caesar and Crassus.

The defence of Balbus was entrusted to Pompey, Crassus and Cicero. Cicero, who had lost his political independence as a result of the Conference of Luca, had already in the *De provinciis consularibus* begun to use his eloquence in the Senate on behalf of the Triumvirate, and was to use it still further in the courts. His defence of Balbus was followed in 55 B.C. by that of L. Caninius Gallus, a protégé of Pompey, and by those of C. Messius, P. Vatinius, A. Gabinius and C. Rabirius Postumus in 54 B.C. Cicero, who, when engaged with other advocates in a defence, always, by arrangement, spoke last, because of his unrivalled power of addressing a moving appeal to a jury, made, as one would expect, most complimentary references to the speeches of Crassus and Pompey. There remained, he asserted, little left for him to say. Balbus was acquitted.

To this account of the prosecution of Balbus it may be appropriate to add a brief supplement on Rome's attitude in the later Republic towards the enfranchisement of non-citizens. According to Roman constitutional theory the power to confer *civitas*, whether on

[a] *Pro Balbo*, 32.

Italians or on non-Italians, lay with the citizen body itself.[a] Although, in some recorded instances,[b] we are told that the Senate took the initiative by passing a resolution and instructing a magistrate to put a *rogatio* to the vote, such senatorial action was, strictly speaking, unnecessary. When, for example, it was proposed in 188 B.C. to grant full citizenship to the *municipia* of Fundi, Formiae and Arpinum, which had held the " half-citizenship " or *civitas sine suffragio* since the latter part of the fourth century, a *plebiscitum* was brought forward without any previous consultation of the Senate, and some tribunes who demurred were informed " populi esse non senatus ius suffragii quibus velit impertire." [c]

Down to the end of the second century recorded examples of the enfranchisement of non-citizens are extremely rare. In 211 B.C. Sosis, a Syracusan, and Moericus, a Spaniard, were awarded Roman citizenship for valuable services rendered at the siege of Syracuse[d]; and in the following year (210 B.C.) Muttines,[e] a Carthaginian, was similarly honoured for gallantry at the capture of Agrigentum. In 186 B.C., as a reward for information given concerning the Bacchanalian disturbances, Faecenia Hispala, a

[a] *Cf.* Polybius, vi. 14.

[b] *e.g.* in the settlement following the Social War the method of implementing the franchise legislation of 90 and 89 B.C. is recorded by Sisenna: "Tudertibus senati consulto et populi iussu dat civitatem." Sisenna, fr. 17. 119.

[c] Livy, xxxviii. 36. 7-8.

[d] Livy, xxvi. 21. 9-11.

[e] Livy, xxvii. 5. 6-7. Muttines took the praenomen and nomen of M. Valerius Laevinus, consul in the year of his enfranchisement. He appears in a Greek inscription as Μάαρκος Οὐαλέριος ὁ Μοττόνης: see Dittenberger (ed. 3), 585, line 32 (vol. ii, p. 93).

freedwoman, was given the rights of an *ingenua.*[a] Three names in all: a short list. But others no doubt have not been recorded. Moreover, by Gracchan times the local magistrates (dictator, praetor or aedile) in towns of Latin status could claim Roman citizenship by virtue of their office; and the movement towards allied enfranchisement which began under the Gracchi found expression in the *lex Acilia* (122 B.C.), which offered to any non-Roman the reward of citizenship for a successful prosecution in the *quaestio repetundarum.*[b]

But, from the beginning of the period marked by the Social, Sertorian, and Mithridatic Wars, there is much evidence for the conferment by Roman commanders of *civitas* for military merit, both on Italians and on non-Italians. Although, in theory, such grants required either authorization or confirmation by the Assembly, the formality of a law seems in practice to have been often neglected, and it may have come to be recognized that such enfranchisements did not require statutory confirmation. In any case, Marius' enfranchisement on the field of Vercellae [c] (101 B.C.) of two cohorts of the Umbrian Camertes, members of a *civitas foederata* (Camerinum), for which no confirmation by the Assembly has been recorded, was severely

[a] Livy, xxxix. 19. 5.

[b] *Lex Acilia*, 76, 77, 78 in L.C.L. *Remains of Old Latin*, iv, pp. 366-371.

[c] *Pro Balbo*, 46, 47; Plutarch, *Marius*, 28. 2 (1000 men); Valerius Maximus, v. 2. 8. Cicero, *pace* Valerius Maximus, denies that the Camertes' treaty with Rome forbade the enfranchisement of any of their citizens. Other known enfranchisements by Marius were of individuals: M. Annius Appius of Iguvium (*Pro Balbo*, 46) and T. Matrinius of Spoletium (*ibid.* 48).

criticized, and Marius himself was evidently uneasy about the legality of his action.

An enfranchisement for a special purpose may be dated to about 98 B.C.[a]: that of Calliphana, a Greek priestess of Ceres, born at Velia, a *civitas foederata* in Lucania, to enable the rites of Ceres to be administered to Romans by a celebrant who was herself a Roman citizen. Cicero, the source of this fact, adds that this was one of many similar earlier enactments.

The early first century provides two examples only of laws passed to legalize the conferment of citizenship for services in war. The first was the *lex Iulia* of 90 B.C. under which, as we learn from an inscription,[b] Cn. Pompeius Strabo, consul 89 B.C., conferred Roman citizenship on a squadron of Spanish auxiliary cavalry: "Cn. Pompeius . . . imperator virtutis caussa equites Hispanos ceives Romanos fecit in castreis apud Asculum . . . ex lege Iulia." Thus the devotion of allies on the field could be rewarded by Roman citizenship. This squadron of Spanish horse, thirty strong, the *Turma Salluitana* (perhaps "Salvitto's Horse," from the name of its commander), serving in the Social War, was enfranchised in 89 B.C. by Cn. Pompeius Strabo, father of Pompey the Great, under the authority of the *lex Iulia*. There is no earlier parallel for the enfranchisement of non-Italian *socii* on so large a scale. Also Strabo's enfranchisement

[a] *Pro Balbo*, 55.

[b] *C.I.L.* (ed. 2), i. 709 and p. 714; Dessau, 8888. See C. Cichorius, *Das Offiziercorps eines römischen Heeres aus dem Bundesgenossenkriege. Römische Studien*, Leipzig-Berlin, 1922, pp. 130-185. G. H. Stevenson, "Cn. Pompeius Strabo and the Franchise Question," *J.R.S.* ix (1919), pp. 95-101. L.C.L. *Remains of Old Latin*, iv, pp. 272-277.

of an individual, P. Caesius [a] of Ravenna, was perhaps carried out under the authority of the *lex Iulia.* The enfranchisement, however, of Minatus Magius, of Aeclanum,[b] great-grandfather of the historian Velleius Paterculus, for services rendered to the Romans in 89 B.C. in Campania and Samnium, was almost certainly due to a special act of the Assembly. The second example of a law legalizing the conferment of citizenship was the *lex Gellia Cornelia* [c] (72 B.C.), which, as has been stated, confirmed Pompey's action in enfranchising Balbus and other individuals.

Two paragraphs in the *Pro Balbo* [d] record isolated enfranchisements of individual non-Italians performed early in the first century by five Roman commanders: P. Licinius Crassus (consul 97 B.C. and proconsul in Further Spain 96–93 B.C.), L. Sulla, Q. Metellus Pius, M. Licinius Crassus and Pompey.[e] Their beneficiaries came from Avennio (now Avignon), Massilia, Gades, Saguntum, Heraclea (Lucania), Messana and Utica. A passage in Caesar's *de Bello Gallico* [f] tells of the enfranchisement by C. Valerius Flaccus, consul in 93 B.C. and governor in Transalpine Gaul about 83 B.C.,[g] of a Gaul, tribal chieftain of the Helvii, who took the name of C. Valerius Caburus, and whose son, C. Valerius Troucillus, became an important agent of Caesar in Gaul. These

[a] *Pro Balbo*, 50. [b] Velleius Paterculus, ii. 16. 3.

[c] *Pro Balbo*, 19. [d] 50 and 51.

[e] In the *Pro Balbo* Cicero refrains from any reference to Pompey's enfranchisement of Theophanes of Mitylene (by 62 B.C.). *Pro Archia*, 24.

[f] i. 47. 4. For an example of Troucillus' services see *ibid.* i. 19. 3.

[g] Broughton, *op. cit.* p. 628, says "85 ?–81." See *Pro Balbo*, note to § 40; also note to § 55.

are specific examples illustrating Cicero's general statements [a] that Roman citizenship had already been given to many Africans, Sardinians, Sicilians and Spaniards.[b] When these enfranchisements, however authorized or confirmed, are considered in the light of Cicero's declaration [c] that " no one has ever been condemned, when it was clear that citizenship had been conferred upon him by one of our commanders," it must be evident that Cicero had a good case.

[a] *Pro Balbo*, 24 and 41.

[b] E. Badian, *Foreign Clientelae*, 1958, gives a list aiming to include all those who, during the last few generations of the Republic, are attested as having received the Roman citizenship otherwise than through the incorporation of their communities.

[c] *Pro Balbo*, 53.

III. PRO L. CORNELIO BALBO ORATIO

1 I. Si auctoritates patronorum in iudiciis valent,[1] ab amplissimis viris L. Corneli causa defensa est, si usus, a peritissimis, si ingenia, ab eloquentissimis, si studia, ab amicissimis et cum beneficiis cum L. Cornelio, tum maxima familiaritate coniunctis. Quae sunt igitur meae partes? Auctoritatis tantae, quantam vos in me esse voluistis, usus mediocris, ingenii minime voluntati paris; nam ceteris, a quibus est defensus, hunc debere plurimum video; ego quantum ei de-
2 beam, alio loco. Principio orationis hoc pono, me omnibus, qui amici fuerint saluti et dignitati meae, si minus referenda gratia satis facere potuerim, praedicanda et habenda certe satis esse facturum. Quae fuerit hesterno die Cn. Pompei gravitas in dicendo, iudices, quae facultas, quae copia, non opinione tacita vestrorum animorum, sed perspicua admiratione declarari videbatur. Nihil enim umquam audivi, quod mihi de iure subtilius dici videretur, nihil memoria

[1] valerent *MSS.* valent *Ernesti.*

---

[a] See § 58 for Balbus' services to Cicero's family during his exile. Balbus also may have helped to secure Caesar's approval of Cicero's recall from exile. *Alio loco* is a conversational touch inserted to relieve the formality of his opening.

III. A SPEECH IN DEFENCE OF LUCIUS CORNELIUS BALBUS

I. If in judicial proceedings the position of those 1
who support a case carries any weight, the case of Lucius Cornelius has been defended by counsel of the greatest distinction; if experience, by the most practised; if talent, by the most eloquent; if devotion, by the nearest of friends, and by men bound to Lucius Cornelius by services rendered and the closest intimacy. What then have I to offer? A position such as it has been your pleasure to allow me, some modest experience, a talent by no means equal to my goodwill. For I observe that my client's debt to those others who have defended him is of the greatest, but how great my own debt to him—of that I will speak elsewhere.[a] Here at the opening of my speech 2
I state this: that in regard to all those who have favoured my welfare and position,[b] if I have been unable fully to repay their claims upon my gratitude, I will at least seek to satisfy them by proclaiming and acknowledging it. What weight of words was shown by Gnaeus Pompeius in his speech of yesterday, gentlemen, what eloquence, what fluency, was clearly manifested, not by your tacit approval, but by your evident admiration. For I have never heard what seemed to me a more acute exposition of a point of law, nothing that

[b] With special reference to his recall from exile.

maiore de exemplis, nihil peritius de foederibus, nihil illustriore auctoritate de bellis, nihil de re publica gravius, nihil de ipso modestius, nihil de causa et
3 crimine ornatius, ut mihi iam verum videatur illud esse, quod non nulli litteris ac studiis doctrinae dediti quasi quiddam incredibile dicere putabantur, ei, qui omnes animo virtutes penitus comprehendisset, omnia, quae faceret, recte se dare.[1] Quae enim in L. Crasso potuit, homine nato ad dicendi singularem quandam facultatem, si hanc causam ageret, maior esse ubertas, varietas, copia, quam fuit in eo, qui tantum potuit impertire huic studio temporis, quantum ipse a pueritia usque ad hanc aetatem a continuis
4 bellis et victoriis conquievit? Quo mihi difficilior est hic extremus perorandi locus. Etenim ei succedo orationi, quae non praetervecta sit aures vestras, sed in animis omnium penitus insederit, ut plus voluptatis ex recordatione illius orationis quam non modo ex mea, sed ex cuiusquam oratione capere possitis.

II. Sed mos est gerundus non modo Cornelio, cuius ego voluntati in eius periculis nullo modo deesse possum, sed etiam Cn. Pompeio, qui sui facti, sui iudicii, sui beneficii voluit me esse, ut apud eosdem vos, iudices, nuper in alia causa fuerim, et praedicatorem et actorem.

[1] tractare MSS.; se dare *Madvig*, cadere *Reid*; evadere *is suggested by Warmington.*

---

[a] The reference is to the Stoic paradox that the ideal wise man could do everything well.

[b] Lucius Licinius Crassus began soon after 120 B.C. a career as an orator unsurpassed save by Hortensius and Cicero. Consul in 95 and censor in 92, he died in 91 B.C. For his oratory see Cicero, *Brutus*, 143 and 148.

[c] It is not known what case is referred to; the *Pro Sestio* is possible.

showed a fuller recollection of precedents, nothing more learned in regard to treaties, nothing more brilliant and authoritative concerning warfare, nothing more weighty concerning state affairs, nothing more modest as to the speaker himself, nothing more eloquent about the case and the charge. So that I am 3
now convinced of the truth of the saying, which when put forward by some of those who are devoted to literature and the study of philosophy seemed to be incredible,[a] that, for a man who has in his soul got a firm grasp of all the virtues, everything that he does turns out well. For could even Lucius Crassus,[b] though he was a man born to show quite outstanding quality as an orator, had he been pleading this case, have shown greater richness, variety, and fluency, than was shown by him who has only been able to devote to the study of oratory just so much time as he could spare from the continuous wars and victories in which he has passed his life from boyhood to the present time? For me, on this account, my present task of 4
speaking last is made more difficult. For I have to follow a speech of such a nature that it has not passed over your ears, but has sunk deeply into the minds of all, so that from your recollection of that speech you can derive more pleasure not only than from my own, but from anyone's speech.

II. But I must fall in with the views not only of Cornelius, whose wishes in the hour of danger I can on no account fail to serve, but also with those of Gnaeus Pompeius, who has desired that, as I lately did in another case [c] before you, gentlemen, I should now also eulogize and defend [d] his action, his judgment, and his rendering of service.

[d] A variant *auctorem*, "approver," is less suitable.

5 Ac mihi quidem hoc dignum re publica[1] videtur, hoc deberi huius excellentis viri praestantissimae gloriae, hoc proprium esse vestri officii, hoc satis esse causae, ut, quod fecisse Cn. Pompeium constet, id omnes ei licuisse concedant. Nam verius nihil est, quam quod hesterno die dixit ipse, ita L. Cornelium de fortunis omnibus dimicare, ut nullius in delicti crimen vocaretur. Non enim furatus esse civitatem, non genus suum ementitus, non in aliquo impudenti mendacio delituisse, non irrepsisse in censum dicitur; unum obicitur, natum esse Gadibus; quod negat nemo. Cetera accusator fatetur, hunc in Hispania durissimo bello cum Q. Metello, cum C. Memmio et in classe et in exercitu fuisse, ut Pompeius in Hispaniam venerit Memmiumque habere quaestorem coeperit, numquam a Memmio discessisse, Carthagine esse obsessum,[2] acerrimis illis proeliis et maximis, Sucronensi et Turiensi, interfuisse, cum Pompeio ad extremum
6 belli tempus fuisse. Haec sunt propria[3] Corneli, pietas in rem publicam nostram, labor, assiduitas,

[1] rei *and* re (MSS. *without* p. *or* publica), reo *some edd.* re publica *Garatoni-Baiter.*

[2] isse *or* esse possessum MSS. *The correction in the text is by Madvig.*

[3] proelia *one* MS.; propria *Klotz-Baiter.*

---

[a] Quintus Caecilius Metellus Pius, son of Metellus Numidicus and consul with Sulla in 80 B.C., took the field against Sertorius in 79 B.C. as governor of Further Spain. From 76 B.C. till the end of the war he shared command with Pompey. Gaius Memmius was a brother-in-law of Pompey; he was killed under the walls of Saguntum (75 B.C.).

[b] In 77 B.C. the Senate was forced by Sertorius' victories to commission Pompey to Spain, *non pro consule sed pro consulibus* (Cicero, *Phil.* xi. 8. 18).

[c] In 76 B.C. Memmius was besieged by Sertorius at

Now I am convinced that it is befitting to the dignity of the State, a debt owed to the outstanding renown of this eminent man, a matter which is essential to your duty, and a sufficient plea, that what is known to have been done by Gnaeus Pompeius should be admitted by all to have been lawfully done. For nothing is more true than what he himself said yesterday—that Lucius Cornelius was fighting for his very existence, but was not charged with any offence. For he is accused neither of having stolen the citizenship, nor of having given a false account of his family, nor of having skulked behind some shameless lie, nor of having sneaked into the censors' list. One reproach is made—that he was born at Gades; and that nobody denies. As for the rest, the accuser admits that when a most arduous war was being fought in Spain, Balbus served under Quintus Metellus [a] and Gaius Memmius [a] on both sea and land; that from the time when Pompeius came to Spain [b] and chose Memmius as his quaestor, Balbus never left Memmius; that he was besieged in Carthage [c]; that he fought in those fierce and desperate battles on the Sucro [d] and the Turia [e]; that he was with Pompeius till the very end of the war. 5

6 This is what Cornelius claims as his own: affection for our State, toil, industry, hard fighting, valour

Carthago Nova, which since 209 B.C. had been a Roman stronghold in southern Spain.

[d] In 75 B.C. on the river Sucro (now Jucar), at the south of the plain of Valentia, Pompey, after an indecisive battle with Sertorius and Perperna, was saved by Metellus Pius from defeat by them.

[e] In the same year (75 B.C.) the Sertorians were defeated on the Turia, a river running through the plain of Valentia, with Valentia at its mouth.

dimicatio, virtus digna summo imperatore, spes pro periculis praemiorum ; praemia quidem ipsa non sunt in eius facto, qui adeptus est, sed in eius, qui dedit.

III. Donatus est igitur ob eas causas a Cn. Pompeio civitate. Id accusator non negat, sed reprehendit, ut in Cornelio causa ipsius probetur, poena quaeratur, in Pompeio causa laedatur, poena sit nulla nisi famae. Sic innocentissimi hominis fortunas, praestantissimi imperatoris factum condemnari volunt. Ergo in iudicium caput Corneli, factum Pompei vocatur. Hunc enim in ea civitate, in qua sit natus, honestissimo loco natum esse concedis et ab ineunte aetate relictis rebus suis omnibus in nostris bellis nostris cum imperatoribus esse versatum, nullius laboris, nullius obsessionis, nullius proelii expertem fuisse. Haec sunt omnia cum plena laudis, tum propria Corneli, nec in iis rebus
7 crimen est ullum. Ubi igitur est crimen ? Quod eum Pompeius civitate donavit. Huius crimen ? Minime, nisi honos ignominia putanda est. Cuius igitur ? Re vera nullius, actione accusatoris eius unius, qui donavit. Qui si adductus gratia minus idoneum hominem praemio adfecisset, quin etiam si virum bonum, sed non ita meritum, si denique aliquid non contra, ac

[a] Rhetorical exaggeration.

such as a great general expects, hope of rewards in return for dangers. As for rewards themselves, they depend on the act, not of him who won them, but of him who conferred them.

III. For these reasons, therefore, citizenship was granted to him by Pompeius. That fact the prosecutor does not dispute. But he so attacks the grant of citizenship that, with regard to Cornelius, he accepts my client's defence but demands a penalty, while, with regard to Pompeius, he rejects the defence, without penalty, however, save for Pompeius' reputation. Thus what the prosecution desire is that the fortunes of a man wholly innocent, and the act of a most distinguished commander, should be condemned. It is therefore Cornelius' rights as a citizen, and an act of Pompeius that are now on their trial. For you agree that my client, in the city in which he was born, belongs to one of its most distinguished families, and that from his earliest youth, renouncing all personal interests, he has accompanied our generals in our wars, that there is no toil, no siege, no battle in which he has not taken part.[a] All this is not only most praiseworthy, but is Cornelius' own, nor is there in it any ground for accusation. Wherein then 7
does the accusation consist? In this: that Pompeius has honoured him with citizenship. A charge against my client? By no means, unless an honour is to be thought a disgrace. Whose then? In reality, nobody's; but as the prosecutor handles the case, it concerns the one man who granted him citizenship. But if he had been moved by interest, and if he had rewarded someone who was hardly suitable, nay more, someone who, although a worthy man, had not deserved it; if, in fact, it were asserted that

liceret, factum diceretur, sed contra, atque oporteret, tamen esset omnis eius modi reprehensio a vobis,
8 iudices, repudianda. Nunc vero quid dicitur? Quid ait accusator? Fecisse Pompeium, quod ei facere non licuerit; quod gravius est, quam si id factum ab eo diceret, quod non oportuisset. Est enim aliquid, quod non oporteat, etiamsi licet; quicquid vero non licet, certe non oportet.

IV. Hic ego nunc cuncter [sic agere, iudices, non esse fas dubitari, quin, quod Cn. Pompeium fecisse constet, id non solum licuisse, sed etiam decuisse fa-
9 teamur][1]? Quid enim abest huic homini, quod si adesset, iure haec ei tribui et concedi putaremus? Ususne rerum? Qui pueritiae tempus extremum principium habuit bellorum atque imperiorum maximorum, cuius plerique aequales minus saepe castra viderunt, quam hic triumphavit, qui tot habet triumphos, quot orae sunt partesque terrarum, tot victorias bellicas, quot sunt in rerum natura genera bellorum. An ingenium? Cui etiam ipsi casus eventusque rerum non duces, sed comites consiliorum fuerunt, in quo uno ita summa fortuna cum summa virtute certavit, ut omnium iudicio plus homini quam deae tribueretur. An pudor, an integritas, an religio in eo, an diligentia umquam requisita est? Quem provinciae nostrae, quem liberi populi, quem reges, quem ultimae gentes castiorem,

[1] *There is a gap of four lines in the* MS., *which has been filled up by conjecture.*

---

[a] Of granting citizenship where he thinks fit.

[b] A similar passage is found in Cicero, *De imperio Cn. Pompei*, 28.

[c] *i.e.* events have not directed his plans but happened exactly in accordance with them.

something had been done not contrary to what was legal, but to what was befitting, nevertheless, gentlemen, every such objection ought to be over-ruled by you. But, as things are, what is alleged? What 8
does the prosecutor claim? That Pompeius has done what it was not lawful for him to do; and that is more serious than if he claimed that what was done by him was not befitting. For there are certain things which are unbefitting, even though lawful; but whatever is unlawful is certainly unbefitting.

IV. Am I now to hesitate, gentlemen, [to maintain that it is monstrous to doubt that, in what it is agreed that Gnaeus Pompeius did, he did not only what was lawful, but also what was befitting]? For what does 9
he lack, the possession of which would make us hold that this privilege [a] is rightly given and allowed to him? Is it experience of affairs,[b] when the end of his youth was the beginning of his warlike career and his most important commands; when most of his equals in age have seen fewer camps than he has gained triumphs; when he can count as many triumphs as there are countries and parts of the earth; when he has won as many victories in war as there are kinds of war in the world? Or is it ability, when even the chances and issues of events have been not the leaders but the associates of his policy [c]; when in him alone there has been such rivalry between Fortune and valour at their highest, that in the judgment of all men more credit was attributed to the man than to the divinity? Has honour, has integrity, has piety, has application ever been found wanting in him? Is there a man whom our provinces, whom free peoples, whom kings, whom most distant races, have ever, I do not say seen, but

moderatiorem, sanctiorem non modo viderunt, sed aut
10 sperando umquam aut optando cogitaverunt? Quid dicam de auctoritate? Quae tanta est, quanta in his tantis virtutibus ac laudibus esse debet. Cui senatus populusque Romanus amplissimae dignitatis praemia dedit non postulanti, imperia vero etiam recusanti, huius de facto, iudices, ita quaeri, ut id agatur, licueritne ei facere, quod fecit, an vero non dicam non licuerit, sed nefas fuerit (contra foedus enim, id est contra populi Romani religionem et fidem, fecisse dicitur), non turpe populo Romano, nonne vobis?

11 V. Audivi hoc de parente meo puer, cum Q. Metellus L. f. causam de pecuniis repetundis diceret, ille vir, cui patriae salus dulcior quam conspectus fuit, qui de civitate decedere quam de sententia maluit—hoc igitur causam dicente cum ipsius tabulae circumferrentur inspiciendi nominis causa, fuisse iudicem ex illis equitibus Romanis gravissimis viris neminem, quin removeret oculos et se totum averteret, ne forte, quod ille in tabulas publicas rettulisset, dubitasse quisquam, verumne an falsum esset, videretur; nos Cn. Pompei decretum de consilii sententia pronuntiatum recog-

---

[a] Pompey is said (Dio Cassius, xxxvi. 8) to have disliked the proposal for his appointment to command against the pirates in 67 B.C. See also Cicero, *Epp. ad Att.* iv. 9. 1, for an example of Pompey's pretended indifference to commands ("Syriam spernens, Hispaniam iactans").

[b] From the *lex Acilia* (122 B.C.) down to Sulla, save for a short period probably from 106 to 104 B.C., the *iudicia* were in the hands of *equites Romani.* See Balsdon, "The History of the Extortion Court at Rome, 123–70 B.C.," in *P.B.S.R.* xiv, pp. 98-114.

[c] See also *Epp. ad Att.* i. 16. 4. The trial of Q. Metellus (Numidicus) for misappropriating public money took place

ever imagined in their hopes or dreams, more upright,
more self-controlled, more righteous? What shall 10
I say of his influence, which is as great as it is bound
to be in view of his virtues and his renown? And this
man, upon whom the Senate and People of Rome
bestowed rewards of the highest distinction though
he never claimed them, but even refused great commands [a]—is it not disgraceful for the Roman People
and for you, that an act of such a man should be
so discussed, gentlemen, that the point at issue is
whether it was lawful for him to do what he did, or
whether indeed it was—I will not say unlawful, but
even impious—since it is alleged that he acted contrary to a treaty, that is, against the sacred obligations and good faith of the Roman People?

V. In my boyhood, I heard this from my father. 11
When Quintus Metellus, son of Lucius, was defending himself against a charge of embezzlement, that great man, to whom the welfare of his country was dearer than the sight of it, who preferred to abandon his country rather than his principles—well, when he was pleading his cause, and his accounts were being handed round for the purpose of examining some entry, there was not a single one of the jurors amongst those most estimable Roman Knights,[b] who did not avert his gaze and turn completely away, for fear that anyone might seem to have any doubt as to the truth or falsehood of what he had entered in his books [c]; and shall *we* subject to our revision a decree of Gnaeus Pompeius

more probably after his praetorship (112 B.C.), when he may have governed Sicily, than after his two years' command against Jugurtha in Africa, as consul (109 B.C.) and proconsul (108 B.C.). In 100 B.C. his refusal to swear an oath of obedience to a bill of Saturninus for the foundation of colonies led to his exile.

noscemus, cum legibus conferemus, cum foederibus,
12 omnia acerbissima diligentia perpendemus? Athenis aiunt cum quidam, apud eos qui sancte graviterque vixisset, testimonium publice dixisset et, ut mos Graecorum est, iurandi causa ad aras accederet, una voce omnes iudices, ne is iuraret, reclamasse. Cum Graeci homines spectati viri noluerint religione videri potius quam veritate fidem esse constrictam, nos, etiam in ipsa religione et legum et foederum conservanda qualis fuerit Cn. Pompeius, dubitabimus?
13 Utrum enim scientem vultis contra foedera fecisse an inscientem? Si scientem, o nomen nostri imperii! O populi Romani excellens dignitas! O Cn. Pompei sic late longeque diffusa laus, ut eius gloriae domicilium communis imperii finibus terminetur! O nationes, urbes, populi, reges, tetrarchae, tyranni testes Cn. Pompei non solum virtutis in bello, sed etiam religionis in pace! Vos denique, mutae regiones, imploro, et sola terrarum ultimarum, vos, maria, portus, insulae, litora! Quae est enim ora, quae sedes, qui locus, in quo non exstent huius cum fortitudinis, tum vero humanitatis, cum animi, tum consilii impressa vestigia? Hunc quisquam incredibili quadam atque in-

---

[a] For example, Pompey's father, Gnaeus Pompeius Strabo (consul 89 B.C.), conferred, under the *lex Iulia*, Roman citizenship on a squadron of auxiliary Spaniards, *de consilii sententia* (Dessau, 8888). See p. 623.

[b] The same story is told in *Epp. ad Att.* i. 16. 4; he was Xenocrates (a pupil of Plato), who was head of the Academy from 338 to 313 B.C. and is frequently quoted by Cicero.

issued with the concurrence of his advisers,[a] compare it with laws and with treaties, and examine everything with the harshest minuteness? At Athens they 12 say that when a certain man [b] who had lived among them a life of piety and worth had given evidence in court, and, according to the Greek [c] custom, was moving up to the altar, to take an oath, all the jurors with one voice cried out aloud in protest. Seeing then that Greeks did not wish it to be thought that the credibility of a man of proved honesty was more strictly secured by a ritual observance than by truthfulness of character, have we any reason to doubt what kind of a man Pompeius was, in his observance also of the sanctity both of laws and of treaties? For do you wish to maintain that he acted against 13 treaties wittingly, or unwittingly? If wittingly—I invoke the name of our Empire! I invoke the surpassing greatness of the Roman People! I invoke the renown of Gnaeus Pompeius, spread so far and wide that the home of his glory is bounded only by the limits of our common Empire! I invoke the tribes, cities, peoples, kings, tetrarchs, rulers, who have witnessed not only the valour of Gnaeus Pompeius in war, but also his piety in peace! Lastly, I appeal to you, ye voiceless tracts, remotest lands, ye seas, harbours, islands, coasts! For where is the region, where is the country, where is the spot on which the marks at once of his bravery and his quality as a man, of his spirit and his wisdom do not remain stamped? Will anyone dare to say that such a man

Xenocrates is here referred to as *quidam*, since Roman juries disliked a display of Greek learning.

[c] Before an Athenian trial all evidence was reduced to writing and affirmed by oath during the trial.

audita gravitate, virtute, constantia praeditum foedera scientem neglexisse, violasse, rupisse dicere audebit?

14 VI. Gratificatur mihi gestu accusator, inscientem Cn. Pompeium fecisse significat. Quasi vero levius[1] sit, cum in tanta re publica versere et maximis negotiis praesis, facere aliquid, quod scias non licere, quam omnino non scire, quid liceat. Etenim utrum qui in Hispania[2] bellum acerrimum et maximum gesserat, quo iure Gaditana civitas esset, nesciebat an, cum ius illius populi nosset, interpretationem foederis non tenebat? Id igitur quisquam Cn. Pompeium ignorasse dicere audebit, quod mediocres homines, quod nullo usu, nullo studio praediti militari, quod
15 librarioli denique se scire profiteantur? Equidem contra existimo, iudices, cum in omni genere ac varietate artium, etiam illarum, quae sine summo otio non facile discuntur, Cn. Pompeius excellat, singularem quandam laudem eius praestabilem esse scientiam in foederibus, pactionibus, condicionibus populorum, regum, exterarum nationum, in universo denique belli

[1] levius *MS.*; levioris *Reid.*

[2] Etenim quum in Hispania *most texts*: utrum qui in Hispania *Baiter.*

---

[a] As though he agreed with my last words.

[b] Pompey is charged with having acted illegally. The question is whether he acted *sciens* or *insciens*. In § 13 the former alternative is dismissed as incredible. In § 14 the prosecutor suggests *insciens*. Cicero replies ("quasi vero levius sit . . .") that the prosecutor should have stuck to *sciens*: "just as though it were less heinous to do an illegal act knowingly than not to know what is legal! In fact, it is more heinous. You will not make it worse for Pompey by saying *insciens*" (Peterson, *Class. Quart.* iv. p. 176). Cicero, however, offers no argument beyond proba-

as this, endowed with quite incredible and unexampled force of character, virtue, and stedfastness, has knowingly set at naught, violated, broken treaties?

VI. The accuser favours me with a gesture [a]: he suggests that Gnaeus Pompeius acted unwittingly. As if indeed it were less [b] heinous for a man, when engaged in such important public affairs and conducting business of the greatest consequence, to do something which he knows to be illegal than to be wholly ignorant of what is legal. For was the man who waged a desperate and most important war in Spain ignorant of the nature of the rights of the people of Gades, or, although he knew what were the rights of that people, had he not grasped the meaning of the treaty? Will then anyone dare to say that Gnaeus Pompeius was ignorant of what ordinary men, without any experience, without any interest in military matters, what even mere copyists claim to know? For my part, gentlemen, I think on the contrary, that while Gnaeus Pompeius excels in every sort and variety of accomplishments, even those which it is not easy to acquire without much leisure, his quite outstanding merit is his most remarkable knowledge of treaties, of agreements, of terms [c] imposed upon peoples, kings, and foreign races, and, in fact, of the whole code of law that deals with war and peace [d];

bility that Pompey must have been familiar with the treaty between Rome and Gades.

[c] *Foedus* was concluded with religious formalities, *pactio* was a simple agreement (oral or written), *condicio* the terms of an agreement.

[d] Also called *ius fetiale*, as superintended by the *fetiales* who are called *interpretes iuris belli et pacis* (*De officiis*, iii. 29), which was equivalent to "International Law" as understood by the Romans.

iure atque pacis; nisi forte ea, quae nos libri docent in umbra atque otio, ea Cn. Pompeium neque, cum requiesceret, litterae neque, cum rem gereret, regiones ipsae docere potuerunt.

Atque, ut ego sentio, iudices, causa dicta est. Temporum magis ego nunc vitiis quam genere iudicii plura dicam.

Est enim haec saeculi quaedam macula atque labes, virtuti invidere, velle ipsum florem dignitatis
16 infringere. Etenim, si Pompeius abhinc annos quingentos fuisset, is vir, a quo senatus adulescentulo atque equite Romano saepe communi saluti auxilium expetisset, cuius res gestae omnes gentes cum clarissima victoria terra marique peragrassent, cuius tres triumphi testes essent totum orbem terrarum nostro imperio teneri, quem populus Romanus inauditis honoribus[1] singularibusque decorasset, si nunc apud nos id, quod is fecisset, contra foedus factum diceretur, quis audiret? Nemo profecto. Mors enim cum exstinxisset invidiam, res eius gestae sempiterni nominis gloria niterent.[2] Cuius igitur audita virtus dubitationi locum non daret, huius visa atque[3] perspecta obtrectatorum voce laedatur?

[1] *A gap between* Romanus in . . . *and* singularibusque *is filled up by Madvig.*
[2] niterentur *MSS.*; niterent *Reid.*
[3] huius atque *MS.*; huius visa atque *Halm.*

[a] When he held no office that entitled him to a seat in the Senate.
[b] These triumphs were: (1) on his victory in Africa over a Marian refugee Cn. Domitius Ahenobarbus and a Numidian leader Iarbas, celebrated on 12 March 79 (or 80) B.C.; (2) "ex Hispaniis," on the last day of 71 B.C., after the Sertorian War;

unless perhaps, what books teach us in the quiet of a sheltered life is something which neither books could teach Gnaeus Pompeius when he had leisure, nor foreign countries themselves when he was in the field.

And now, gentlemen, in my opinion my case is finished. But owing to the faults of our times rather than the nature of this trial, I shall have more to say.

Now it is a sort of blot and blemish of this age to be envious of virtue, to seek to crush merit in its very bloom. For if Pompeius had lived five hundred years 16
ago, a man from whom the Senate, when he was a mere youth and a Roman Knight,[a] had often sought help for the safety of the State, whose exploits, crowned by glorious victory on land and sea had compassed all peoples, whose three triumphs [b] were a witness that the whole world was subject to our Empire, whom the Roman People had invested with unexampled and outstanding honours,[c]—if to-day it should be said among us that what such a man had done was done contrary to a treaty, who would listen? In my opinion, no one. For when death had hushed the voice of envy, his exploits would shine [d] by the glory of his immortal name. If a mere report of a man's merit could leave no room for hesitation—is such merit when actually seen and experienced to be attacked by the voice of traducers?

(3) over the pirates and Mithridates, on 28 and 29 September 61 B.C.

[c] He celebrated his first triumph, and was also elected consul, before he had held any regular magistracy and while still an *eques Romanus* (Velleius Paterculus, ii. 30).

[d] The MSS. reading *niterentur* (from *niti* "to lean upon") may be translated "his exploits would remain, supported by the glory of his immortal name."

17 VII. Omittam igitur Pompeium iam oratione mea reliqua, sed vos, iudices, animis ac memoria tenetote. De lege, de foedere, de exemplis, de perpetua consuetudine civitatis nostrae renovabo ea, quae dicta sunt. Nihil enim mihi novi, nihil integri neque M. Crassus, qui totam causam et pro facultate et pro fide sua diligentissime vobis explicavit, neque Cn. Pompeius, cuius oratio omnibus ornamentis abundavit, ad dicendum reliquit. Sed quoniam me recusante placuit ambobus adhiberi hunc a me quasi perpoliendi quendam operis extremum laborem, peto a vobis, ut me officii potius quam dicendi studio hanc suscepisse operam ac
18 munus putetis. Ac, priusquam adgrediar ad ius causamque Corneli, quiddam de communi condicione omnium nostrum deprecandae malevolentiae causa breviter commemorandum videtur. Si, quo quisque loco nostrum est, iudices, natus, aut si, in qua fortuna est nascendi initio constitutus, hunc vitae statum usque ad senectutem optinere deberet, et si omnes, quos aut fortuna extulit aut ipsorum inlustravit labor et industria, poena essent adficiendi, non gravior L. Cornelio quam multis viris bonis atque fortibus constitui lex vitae et condicio videretur. Sin autem multorum virtus, ingenium, humanitas ex infimo genere et fortunae gradu non modo amicitias et rei familiaris copias consecuta est, sed summam laudem, honores, gloriam, dignitatem, non intellego, cur potius invidia

---

[a] Reid suggests *honorem* " public esteem," since Balbus had not yet obtained any magistracy.

VII. I will therefore say no more of Pompeius in 17
the rest of my speech, but do you, gentlemen, keep a recollection of him in your minds and memory. As for the law, the treaty, precedents, and the unchanging custom of our State, I will recall to your minds what you have already heard. For nothing new, nothing fresh has been left me to say, either by Marcus Crassus, who has most minutely set forth to you the whole case in a manner worthy of his ability and sincerity, or by Gnaeus Pompeius, whose speech was enriched by every grace of eloquence. But since, although I protested, both of them desired that the task of putting a sort of finishing touch upon their work should be undertaken by me, I beg you to believe that I have entered upon this responsible task more from a sense of duty than from any desire of playing the orator. And, before I deal with the legal 18
aspect and the facts of the case of Cornelius, it seems to me that there is something affecting us all in common, about which I ought to make some brief statement with a view to deprecating spite. If each of us, gentlemen, were bound to remain in the position in which he was born, or, in whatever station of life he was established by fortune at his birth, to maintain it until old age; if all those whom good luck has advanced, or their own labour and the spirit of industry have rendered illustrious, were to be punished for it; the law and condition of existence would not seem harder for Lucius Cornelius than for many good men and true. But if in many cases, virtue, talent, and quality as a man, starting from the humblest origin and state of life, have procured not only friendships and abundant means, but also the highest praise, positions,[a] glory, and rank, I do not

violatura virtutem L. Corneli quam aequitas vestra
19 pudorem eius adiutura videatur. Itaque, quod maxime petendum est, a vobis idcirco non peto, iudices, ne de vestra sapientia atque de vestra humanitate dubitare videar. Est autem petendum, ne oderitis ingenium, ne inimici sitis industriae, ne humanitatem opprimendam, ne virtutem puniendam putetis. Illud peto, ut, si causam ipsam per se firmam esse et stabilem videritis, hominis ipsius ornamenta adiumento causae potius quam impedimento esse malitis.

VIII. Nascitur, iudices, causa Corneli ex ea lege, quam L. Gellius Cn. Cornelius ex senatus sententia tulerunt; qua lege videmus ita esse sanctum,[1] ut cives Romani sint ii, quos Cn. Pompeius de consilii sententia singillatim civitate donaverit. Donatum esse L. Cornelium praesens Pompeius dicit, indicant publicae tabulae, accusator fatetur, sed negat ex foederato populo quemquam potuisse, nisi is populus fundus
20 factus esset, in hanc civitatem venire. O praeclarum interpretem iuris, auctorem antiquitatis, correctorem atque emendatorem nostrae civitatis, qui hanc poenam foederibus adscribat, ut omnium praemiorum beneficiorumque nostrorum expertes faciat foederatos!

[1] satis esse sancti *MS.*; satis esse sanctum *edd.*; ita esse sanctum *Reid*; rite esse sanctum *Peterson.*

---

[a] See p. 614.

[b] *Satis esse sancti* is the MS. reading, in which *sancti* must be a genitive after *satis*; Reid conjectures *ita esse sanctum*, which is followed in the translation.

[c] See note on § 11.

[d] This word *fundus* seems totally distinct from *fundus* "a farm" and to be connected with our "bond" and "bound"; and *fundus fieri* (literally "to become bound") is used of formally accepting an offer or obligation. The

understand why it seems more likely that jealousy will injure the merit of L. Cornelius than that your sense of justice will help a man of such modesty. There- 19 fore, gentlemen, the request above all which I ought to make to you, I do not make for fear of appearing to doubt your wisdom and your human feelings. But I must ask you not to hate talent, not to show yourselves enemies of industry, not to think that human feelings should be crushed and that virtue should be penalized. And I do ask that, if you see that my client's case is in itself sound and unshakable, you should prefer his own personal distinctions to be a help rather than a hindrance to his case.

VIII. What has given rise to the case of Cornelius, gentlemen, is a law which Lucius Gellius and Gnaeus Cornelius [a] carried, in accordance with a resolution of the Senate; and we see that by this law it was enacted [b] that those on whom Gnaeus Pompeius, with the concurrence of his advisers,[c] conferred Roman citizenship individually, should be Roman citizens. That Roman citizenship was conferred upon Lucius Cornelius, Pompeius states in this court, public records attest, the prosecutor acknowledges, but claims that no member of a state bound to us by treaty could have become a Roman citizen, unless that state had "given its consent." [d] What a 20 brilliant lawyer and antiquarian, what a marvellous reformer and improver of our constitution, since he appends to treaties a penal clause excluding members of states bound to us by treaty from any share in our

phrase hardly occurs except in this speech and Plautus, *Trin.* 1123: "ei rei fundus pater sit potior," "a better security or guarantor for a debt," and in Gellius, xvi. 13. 6; xix. 8. 12. See *Thes. Ling. Lat. s.v.*, vol. vi. i, col. 1580.

Quid enim potuit dici imperitius quam foederatos populos fieri fundos oportere? Nam id non magis est proprium foederatorum quam omnium liberorum. Sed totum hoc, iudices, in ea fuit positum semper ratione atque sententia, ut, cum iussisset populus Romanus aliquid, si id adscivissent socii populi ac Latini, et si ea lex, quam nos haberemus, eadem in populo aliquo tamquam in fundo resedisset, ut tum lege eadem is populus teneretur, non ut de nostro iure aliquid deminueretur, sed ut illi populi aut iure eo, quod a nobis esset constitutum, aut aliquo commodo aut beneficio uterentur.

21 Tulit apud maiores nostros legem C. Furius de testamentis, tulit Q. Voconius de mulierum hereditatibus, innumerabiles aliae leges de civili iure sunt latae; quas Latini voluerunt, adsciverunt; ipsa denique Iulia, qua lege civitas est sociis et Latinis data, qui fundi populi facti non essent, civitatem non haberent. In quo magna contentio Heracliensium et Neapolitanorum fuit, cum magna pars in iis civitatibus

---

[a] Whereby a state *fiebat fundus*.

[b] Cicero here seems mistaken in his etymology.

[c] By a *lex Furia*, assigned to 183 B.C., a testator was prevented from bequeathing more than 1000 *asses* to any persons other than his *heres* or *heredes*. This law did not invalidate such legacies, but gave an action for a fourfold penalty against the person who had received such a legacy.

[d] The *lex Voconia* (169 B.C.) forbade the institution of women as heirs by persons rated in the wealthiest class at the *census* (Gaius, ii. 274). It also forbade any legacies to be greater than the amount which remained for the heir. The combined result of these provisions was that no person rated in the first class of the *census* could leave a woman more than half his property.

rewards and favours! How could greater ignorance be shown than by saying that states bound to us by treaty must "give consent"? For this is a condition which does not apply to states bound to us by treaty any more than to free states in general. In fact, gentlemen, this whole practice [a] was always based upon this principle and intention that, when the Roman People had made any law, if the allied states and the Latins adopted it, and if that same law, which we observed, had, as it were, settled down "on solid ground" [b] in some state, then that state should be bound by the same law. The purpose was, not that our own legal system should be in any way weakened, but that those states either might make use of that legal principle which had been established by us, or might enjoy some advantage or privilege.

In the days of our forefathers Gaius Furius [c] passed 21
a law concerning wills, Quintus Voconius [d] one concerning women's inheritances, and countless other laws were passed dealing with civil law [e]; of these the Latins adopted what they pleased. Last of all came the Julian Law [f] itself under which citizenship was offered to the Allies and the Latins on condition that those states which had not "given consent," should not hold the citizenship. This was the cause of a lively dispute among the citizens of Heraclea and of Neapolis, since a great part of the inhabitants of those states preferred to our citizenship the freedom en-

[e] *Ius civile* regulated ordinary affairs of life and had no concern with forms of government.

[f] The *lex Iulia* of 90 B.C. offered full Roman citizenship to all Latins and to all allied communities in Italy which had not revolted; this offer was made to communities, not to individuals, and a decree accepting citizenship had to be passed by each community before the law could take effect.

foederis sui libertatem civitati anteferret. Postremo haec vis est istius et iuris et verbi, ut fundi populi bene-
22 ficio nostro, non suo iure fiant. Cum aliquid populus Romanus iussit, id si est eius modi, ut quibusdam populis sive foederatis sive liberis permittendum esse videatur, ut statuant ipsi non de nostris, sed de suis rebus, quo iure uti velint, tum, utrum fundi facti sint an non, quaerendum esse videtur; de nostra vero re publica, de nostro imperio, de nostris bellis, de victoria, de salute fundos populos fieri noluerunt.

IX. Atqui, si imperatoribus nostris, si senatui, si populo Romano non licebit propositis praemiis elicere ex civitatibus sociorum atque amicorum fortissimum atque optimum quemque ad subeunda pro salute nostra pericula, summa utilitate ac maximo saepe praesidio periculosis atque asperis temporibus carendum nobis erit.

23 Sed per deos immortales! Quae est ista societas, quae amicitia, quod foedus, ut aut nostra civitas careat in suis periculis Massiliensi propugnatore,

[a] The treaty between Rome and Heraclea, made in 278 B.C. during the Pyrrhic War, when Rome was fighting hard in southern Italy, was most favourable in character for Heraclea, a *civitas aequissimo iure ac foedere* (Cicero, *Pro Archia*, 6). It is possible that by an exemption from the furnishing of ships to the Roman government (a duty imposed on other Graeco-Italian states) Heraclea would be free from all service in time of war, as troops were never required from coast towns.

The treaty between Rome and Neapolis was made in 326 B.C. and was so favourable that the Neapolitans rejected all offers from Hannibal. All privileges under their treaties would be lost by Heraclea and Neapolis if they became Roman. We know from Cicero, *Epp. ad Fam.* xiii. 30 that Neapolis accepted the *lex Iulia.*

joyed under their own treaty.[a] Finally, the force both of that principle of law and of its terms is that states become " consenting," not of their own legal right but by our favour.[b] When the Roman People 22 have made any law, and if this law is of such a kind that it seems likely to give certain states, whether bound to us by treaty or free, an option to decide themselves, not with reference to our but to their own concerns, what legal principle they desire to adopt, in that case we clearly ought to ask whether these states have, or have not, " given consent." But when it is a question of our own State, of our Empire, of our wars, of our victory or of our welfare, our forefathers did not desire that states should " give consent."

IX. And yet, if neither our commanders, nor the Senate, nor the Roman People, are to be permitted, by offering rewards, to attract the bravest and best of our allies and friends from states bound to us by treaty to expose themselves to dangers for our welfare, then, in dangerous and stormy times, we shall be deprived of a most valuable advantage and often of a most powerful aid.

But, in the name of heaven, what sort of alliance 23
is it, what sort of friendship, what sort of treaty, under which our State, in times of danger, is to be deprived of the championship of a citizen of Massilia,[c] of

[b] That is, their original right to become *fundi populi* is derived from us.

[c] Friendship between Rome and Massilia, a Greek colony founded about 600 B.C., existed at least as early as the end of the fifth century. The base of a gold *krater* vowed by Camillus to Delphi in 396 B.C., the year of the capture of Veii, long survived in the Treasury of Massilia at Delphi. In 49 B.C. the city declared for Pompey, but after a short siege capitulated to Caesar's officers D. Brutus and C. Trebonius.

careat Gaditano, careat Saguntino, aut, si quis ex his populis sit exortus, qui nostros duces auxilio laboris, commeatus periculo suo iuverit, qui cum hoste nostro comminus in acie saepe pugnarit, qui se saepe telis hostium, qui dimicationi capitis, qui morti obiecerit, nulla condicione huius civitatis praemiis adfici possit?

24 Etenim in populum Romanum grave est non posse uti sociis excellenti virtute praeditis, qui velint cum periculis nostris sua communicare; in socios vero ipsos et in eos, de quibus agimus, foederatos iniuriosum et contumeliosum est iis praemiis et iis honoribus exclusos esse fidelissimos et coniunctissimos socios, quae pateant stipendiariis, pateant hostibus, pateant saepe servis. Nam stipendiarios ex Africa, Sicilia, Sardinia, ceteris provinciis multos civitate donatos videmus, et, qui hostes ad nostros imperatores perfugissent et magno usui rei publicae nostrae fuissent, scimus civitate esse donatos; servos denique, quorum ius, fortuna, condicio infima est, bene de re publica

---

[a] See p. 613.

[b] Saguntum, a hundred miles south of the Ebro, was a small and unimportant Iberian town with which Massilia had close trade relations. It is possible that Massilia's alarm at Punic activity in Spain caused Rome to make something like an alliance with Saguntum as early as about 231 B.C. Polybius (iii. 30. 1) says "several years before the time of Hannibal." See also p. 694, note *a*.

[c] A state which permanently paid tribute to Rome, in money or kind, was called *stipendiaria*, and its inhabitants *stipendiarii*.

Gades,[a] or of Saguntum ?[b] or, if from these states a man has arisen who at his own risk has helped our generals by his efforts or aided our supplies, who has often fought against an enemy of ours hand to hand in battle, who has often braved the weapons of our foes, risked a struggle for his life, or faced death, is he never on any condition to be honoured with the prize of Roman citizenship ?

The fact is that, for the Roman People, it is a 24
grievous matter to be unable to make use of allies of outstanding merit, such as are prepared to share their perils with ours ; but, for our allies themselves and for those states bound to us by treaty, with whom we are now concerned, it is an injury and an insult that most loyal and devoted allies should be excluded from those rewards and those honours which are open to those who pay tribute,[c] open to enemies, and often open to slaves. For we are aware that citizenship has been conferred upon many members of tributary states in Africa, Sicily, Sardinia and the other provinces, and we know that enemies who have gone over to our commanders and rendered our State great services have been honoured with citizenship[d] ; and, lastly, we are aware that slaves, whose legal rights, fortune, and status are of the lowest, are very often,

[d] The following examples may be quoted : L. Mamilius, dictator of Tusculum, in 458 B.C. (Livy, iii. 29. 6) ; three hundred *equites Campani*, for services in Sicily, in 215 B.C. (Livy, xxiii. 31. 10) ; in 211 B.C. Sosis, a Syracusan, and Moericus, a Spaniard, for gallantry at the siege of Syracuse (Livy, xxvi. 21. 10) ; in 210 B.C. Muttines, a Carthaginian (Livy, xxvii. 5. 7). In 89 B.C. a squadron of thirty Spanish auxiliary cavalry, called *Turma Salluitana*, was enfranchised under the *lex Iulia* by Cn. Pompeius Strabo, consul, for gallantry at the siege of Asculum in the Social War. *C.I.L.* i. 2, p. 709 (and p. 714) (Dessau, 8888). See pp. 622-623 ; 625, note *b*.

meritos persaepe libertate, id est civitate, publice donari videmus.

25 X. Hanc tu igitur, patrone foederum ac foederatorum condicionem statuis Gaditanis, tuis civibus, ut, quod iis, quos magnis adiuti opibus a maioribus tuis armis [1] subegimus atque in dicionem nostram redegimus, liceat, si populus Romanus permiserit, ut ab senatu et ab imperatoribus nostris civitate donentur, id ne liceat ipsis? Qui si suis decretis legibusve sanxissent, ne quis suorum civium castra imperatorum populi Romani iniret, ne quis se pro nostro imperio in periculum capitis atque in vitae discrimen inferret, Gaditanorum auxiliis, cum vellemus, uti nobis ut liceret,[2] privatus vero ne quis vir et animo et virtute praecellens pro nostro imperio periculo suo dimicaret, graviter id iure ferremus, minui auxilia populi Romani, debilitari animos fortissimorum virorum, alienigenarum nos hominum studiis atque externa virtute privari.

26 Atqui nihil interest, iudices, utrum haec foederati iura constituant, ut ne cui liceat ex iis civitatibus ad nostrorum bellorum pericula accedere, an, quae nos

[1] magnis adiutoribus tuis armis *MSS.* *The reading in the text is Madvig's.* *Reid suggests* Magni armis adiutoribus tuis: "*by the arms of Magnus* (i.e. *Pompeius*), *with the aid of your citizens.*"

[2] ut non liceret *MSS.*; *Madvig omits* non.

---

[a] A slave had neither property (*fortuna*) nor rights (*Digest*, IV. v. 3), but was an object of law because he had a value. After Cannae (216 B.C.) the freedom was purchased of 8000 slaves ready to volunteer (Livy, xxvii. 57. 11). Livy (xxiv. 16. 9) records the freeing of 4000 slave volunteers for gallantry near Beneventum (214 B.C.). In 210 B.C. thirteen

for having deserved well of the State, publicly presented with freedom, that is, with citizenship.[a]

X. Is this the condition, then, you patron of treaties and states under treaty, to which you reduce the people of Gades, your fellow-citizens—that, although those whom, with much assistance from your own ancestors, we have subdued by force of arms and brought under our sway, have a right to be admitted into our citizenship by the Senate and our commanders, with the approval of the Roman People, yet such a right is denied to the people of Gades themselves? If by their decrees or laws they had enacted that none of their citizens should enter a camp of the commanders of the Roman People; that no one should expose his life to danger nor risk death on behalf of our Empire; that we should have the right, when we wished, to employ auxiliary forces from the people of Gades, but that no private individual, distinguished for courage and for merit, should fight for our Empire at his own risk, then we should rightly be indignant at a diminution in number of the auxiliary forces of the Roman People, at a discouragement to the spirit of gallant men, at our own loss of loyal service from foreigners and of valour from abroad.[b] 25

And yet, gentlemen, it makes no difference whether peoples under treaty make laws forbidding anyone from their states to share the perils of our wars, nor whether those privileges which we have conferred 26

slaves who saved the Temple of Vesta from fire were bought and freed. Roman policy herein impressed Philip V of Macedon; see Dittenberger (ed. 3), 543 (214 B.C.).

[b] The MSS. have various readings here: *externa*, *patria*, *paterna*. Halm suggests *privata*.

eorum civibus virtutis causa tribuerimus, ea rata esse non possint. Nihilo enim magis uteremur iis adiutoribus sublatis virtutis praemiis, quam si omnino iis versari in nostris bellis non liceret. Etenim, cum pro sua patria pauci post genus hominum natum reperti sint qui nullis praemiis propositis vitam suam hostium telis obiecerint, pro aliena re publica quemquam fore putatis qui se opponat periculis non modo nullo proposito praemio, sed etiam interdicto?

27 XI. Sed cum est illud imperitissime dictum de populis fundis, quod commune liberorum est populorum, non proprium foederatorum, ex quo intellegi necesse est aut neminem ex sociis civem fieri posse aut etiam posse ex foederatis, tum vero ius omne nostrum iste magister mutandae civitatis ignorat, quod est, iudices, non solum in legibus publicis positum, sed etiam in privatorum voluntate. Iure enim nostro neque mutare civitatem quisquam invitus potest neque, si velit, mutare non potest, modo adsciscatur ab ea civitate, cuius esse se civitatis velit. Ut, si Gaditani sciverint nominatim de aliquo cive Romano, ut sit is civis Gaditanus, magna potestas sit nostro civi mutandae civitatis, nec foedere impediatur, quo minus ex cive Romano civis Gaditanus possit esse.

---

[a] See § 20.
[b] The prosecutor.
[c] For the thesis that no one can lose his Roman citizenship without his own consent see Cicero, *Pro Caecina*, 95-100, and *De domo*, 77.

upon their citizens as a reward of courage can have no validity. For, if rewards for valour were abolished, we should not enjoy their services to any greater degree than if they were totally forbidden to take part in our wars. Since, in fact, even for the sake of their own country, few men, within human history, have been found who have actually risked their lives before the weapons of an enemy when no rewards are offered, do you think that, for the sake of a foreign state, there will be anyone prepared to expose himself to dangers, not merely when no reward is offered but even when it is definitely forbidden?

XI. But, not only did the prosecutor show gross 27
ignorance by saying,[a] with reference to peoples "giving consent," that this was a principle which applied to free peoples and was not restricted to those bound to us by treaty—the deduction which must be drawn from this statement being that no one from our allies nor even from states under treaty can become a Roman citizen—, but he also, this mentor of ours,[b] knows nothing whatever about our legal principle governing change of citizenship, which depends not merely upon the laws of the State but also upon the wishes of individuals. For, by our law, a man cannot change his citizenship against his will,[c] and, if he should wish to change it, he cannot be prevented from doing so, provided he be adopted by that state of which he should desire to become a citizen. For example, if the people of Gades were to pass a decree expressly about some Roman citizen, that he should become a citizen of Gades, our fellow-citizen would have full power to change his citizenship, nor would he be debarred by treaty from being able to become a citizen of Gades instead of a citizen of Rome.

28 Duarum civitatum civis noster esse iure civili nemo potest; non esse huius civitatis, qui se alii civitati dicarit, potest. Neque solum dicatione, quod in calamitate clarissimis viris Q. Maximo, C. Laenati, Q. Philippo Nuceriae, C. Catoni Tarracone, Q. Caepioni, P. Rutilio Smyrnae videmus[1] accidisse, ut earum civitatum fierent cives, cum[2] hanc ante amittere non potuissent, quam hoc solum civitatis mutatione vertissent, sed etiam postliminio potest civitatis fieri mutatio. Neque enim sine causa de Cn. Publicio

[1] vidimus MS., *which would imply that Cicero had personal knowledge of the facts*: videmus *Madvig*.
[2] cum *inserted by Madvig*; *Halm suggests* nam.

---

[a] Probably Q. Fabius Maximus Eburnus (praetor 120, consul 116), who about 105 B.C. stretched the theory of *patria potestas* so far as to put to death a disobedient son. He was condemned after prosecution by Cn. Pompeius Strabo, father of Pompeius Magnus.

[b] In 107 B.C. C. Popillius Laenas a *legatus* rescued the remnants of a Roman army from the Tigurini by accepting humiliating terms; he was exiled probably as the result of a trial under a treason-law carried by Saturninus when tribune in 103 B.C.

[c] Possibly a son of Q. Marcius Philippus, consul 169 B.C., who commanded against Perseus of Macedon: nothing is known of his condemnation and exile at Nuceria, a *civitas foederata* in Campania.

[d] C. Porcius Cato, consul 114 B.C., was as governor of Macedonia routed by the Scordisci in Thrace and was subsequently condemned to pay heavy damages for illegal exactions in his province. In 110 B.C. he was condemned by the *Quaestio Mamilia* set up to try those accused of complicity with Jugurtha. He withdrew to exile at Tarraco.

Our civil law does not allow any Roman citizen to 28
hold the franchise of two states ; but to cease to be a citizen of our state is possible for anyone who has attached himself to another. Nor is it merely by such "attachment" (and we know that this happened in their misfortunes to such distinguished persons as Quintus Maximus,[a] Gaius Laenas[b] and Quintus Philippus at Nuceria,[c] Gaius Cato at Tarraco,[d] Quintus Caepio[e] and Publius Rutilius[f] at Smyrna, all of whom became citizens of those states, although they could not have ceased to become citizens of Rome before they had changed their place of abode by a change of citizenship), but also by the "right of subsequent return"[g] that a change of citizenship can be made. For it was not without reason that,

[e] Q. Servilius Caepio, consul 106 B.C., was suspected of appropriating a great treasure from the temples of Tolosa, a Gallic town which he recovered after a campaign against the Volcae Tectosages in S. Gaul. He was, with the consul Cn. Mallius Maximus, responsible for the destruction of two Roman armies at Arausio on 6 Oct. 105 B.C. After being deprived of his proconsular *imperium* and his seat in the Senate he was condemned (probably in 103 B.C.) by a special court set up by Saturninus.

[f] P. Rutilius Rufus, consul 105 B.C., a man of great versatility, was prosecuted and condemned in 92 B.C. on a charge of misgovernment in the province of Asia, a political manœuvre because of his repression of the rapacity of the *publicani*.

[g] *Postliminium*. A Roman citizen who became a prisoner of war suffered *capitis deminutio maxima*, that is loss of all his civil rights, and ceased to be a citizen. But on recovery of his freedom he regained his former rights and citizenship, *iure postliminii*, "by right of subsequent return." Cicero here uses this legal term of a man who had voluntarily ceased to be a citizen of a state, but who returned and resumed his former status. It is the corollary of *exsilium* : the right of a voluntary exile and of a prisoner of war to recover his original *civitas*. See P.-W. xxii. 1, cols. 863-873.

Menandro, libertino homine, quem apud maiores legati nostri in Graeciam proficiscentes interpretem[a] secum habere voluerunt, ad populum latum est, ut is Publicius, si domum revenisset et inde Romam redisset, ne minus civis esset.[b] Multi etiam superiore memoria cives Romani sua voluntate indemnati et incolumes his rebus relictis alias se in civitates contulerunt.

29 XII. Quodsi civi Romano licet esse Gaditanum sive exsilio[c] sive postliminio sive reiectione huius civitatis (ut iam ad foedus veniam, quod ad causam nihil pertinet : de civitatis enim iure, non de foederibus disceptamus), quid est, quam ob rem civi Gaditano in hanc civitatem venire non liceat ? Equidem longe secus sentio. Nam cum ex omnibus civitatibus via sit in nostram, cumque nostris civibus pateat ad ceteras iter civitates, tum vero, ut quaeque nobiscum maxime societate, amicitia, sponsione, pactione, foedere est coniuncta, ita mihi maxime communione bene-

---

[a] Cn. Publicius Menander. This freedman, no doubt a war captive from Greece, was chosen to act as interpreter to a senatorial commission sent out to Greece to arrange a political settlement, possibly either after the defeat of Perseus of Macedon at Pydna (168 B.C.) or after the capture of Corinth by Mummius (146 B.C.).

[b] The *Digest* XLIX. XV. 15 ; 3, quotes the case of Menander as from Q. Mucius Scaevola, but regards the law passed in his favour as unnecessary. But it was no doubt a precaution against a contention at some future time that by returning to his native town in Greece he had forfeited his Roman citizenship.

[c] This is the *ius exsilii*, primitive in origin, which remained a voluntary act down to the age of Cicero ; a means of avoiding punishment for an offence, it was not under the Republic a penalty assigned by law (Cicero, *Pro Caecina*, 100). In the earlier period an *exsul* acquired the citizenship of the community to which he went, *e.g.* Camillus became a

with respect to Gnaeus Publicius Menander,[a] a freedman, whom in the time of our forefathers commissioners of ours, when leaving for Greece, desired to have with them as interpreter, a proposal was made before the People that, if the man Publicius went back to his home and then returned to Rome, he should nevertheless remain a Roman citizen.[b] Many Roman citizens also, in the course of former times, of their own accord, without being condemned or affected by the law, left this country and betook themselves to other states.[c]

XII. But if a Roman citizen may become a citizen 29
of Gades either by exile or " by right of subsequent return " or by surrendering his Roman citizenship (to come now to the treaty, which has no connexion with the case ; for our subject is not treaties but the law of citizenship), what reason is there why a citizen of Gades should not be allowed to become a citizen of Rome? For my part, I think none at all. For since from every state there is a road open to ours, and since a way is open for our citizens to other states, then indeed the more closely each state is bound to us by alliance, friendship, contract, agreement, treaty,[d] the more closely I think it is associated with us by sharing our

citizen of Ardea (Livy, v. 1). The Roman *tibicines* who in 311 B.C. went on strike, and retired to Tibur, exercised the *ius exsilii* (Livy, ix. 30. 5-10).

[d] A *foedus* was concluded by the *fetiales* with elaborate religious formalities. Both a *sponsio* and a *pactio* were agreements concluded with an enemy by a Roman commander without special authorization from the government, with the distinction that whereas a *pactio* was a simple verbal or written agreement, a *sponsio* was concluded by the use of the solemn phrases " *spondesne?* " and " *spondeo.*" The Senate refused to ratify a *sponsio* entered into at Numantia in 137 B.C. by the Roman commander, C. Hostilius Mancinus.

ficiorum, praemiorum, civitatis contineri videtur. Atqui ceterae civitates omnes non dubitarent nostros homines recipere in suas civitates, si idem nos iuris haberemus quod ceteri. Sed nos non possumus et huius esse civitatis et cuiusvis praeterea; ceteris concessum est.

30 Itaque in Graecis civitatibus videmus Athenienses, Rhodios, Lacedaemonios, ceteros undique adscribi multarumque esse eosdem homines civitatum. Quo errore ductos vidi egomet non nullos imperitos homines nostros cives Athenis in numero iudicum atque Areopagitarum certa tribu, certo numero, cum ignorarent, si illam civitatem essent adepti, hanc se perdidisse, nisi postliminio reciperassent. Peritus vero nostri moris ac iuris nemo umquam, qui hanc civitatem retinere vellet, in aliam se civitatem dicavit.

XIII. Sed hic totus locus disputationis atque orationis meae, iudices, pertinet ad commune ius mutandarum civitatum; nihil habet, quod sit proprium religionis ac foederum. Defendo enim rem universam, nullam esse gentem ex omni regione terrarum neque tam dissidentem a populo Romano odio quodam atque

---

[a] Strictly speaking, an inaccuracy; *errore = errore ex ea re nato*, and the real meaning is "misled by this": the Romans referred to thought that, since they saw foreigners as citizens of more than one state at the same time, they themselves could be citizens of Athens as well as of Rome.

[b] At Athens there were ten Courts of Justice, the jurors being assigned by lot to each Court from a panel of 6000, chosen 600 from each tribe (hence *certa tribu*). Each juror assigned to a court was given a ticket which bore a letter (denoting a number, hence *certo numero*) to indicate the court where he was to serve.

[c] Since the Areopagus, which had existed at Athens in

privileges, rewards, and citizenship. Now all other states would, without hesitation, bestow their citizenship upon our citizens, if we had the same rights as themselves. But we cannot be citizens of Rome and of any other state as well, whereas to the rest this privilege has been conceded.

Thus we see that citizens of Athens, Rhodes, Sparta, 30
and of other states are enrolled from far and wide as citizens of Greek states, and that the same persons are citizens of many states. And I myself have seen certain ignorant men, citizens of ours, misled by this,[a] sitting at Athens amongst jurymen[b] and members of the Areopagus,[c] in a definite tribe, under a definite number, since they did not know that if they had acquired citizenship there, they had forfeited it here, unless they should recover it " by right of subsequent return."[d] But no one who understands our custom and our law has ever, if he wished to retain the citizenship of Rome, formally attached himself to another state.

XIII. But the whole of this argument and of this part of my speech, gentlemen, is concerned with the general rules that have to do with change of state ; it contains nothing which specially concerns the sanctity of treaties. For what I am maintaining is the general proposition that there is no people in any quarter of the world (whether it be at variance with the Roman People owing to some sort of hatred and natural

pre-Solonian times, was composed of ex-archons and had no fixed number of members, the words *certa tribu* and *certo numero* refer only to the ten Courts of Justice.

[d] Cicero shows that the principle of *postliminium* applied not only to Romans who had been prisoners of war but also to those who returned to Rome after having been citizens of other towns.

discidio neque tam fide benevolentiaque coniunctam, ex qua nobis interdictum sit ne quem adsciscere civem aut civitate donare possimus.

31 O iura praeclara atque divinitus iam inde a principio Romani nominis a maioribus nostris comparata, ne quis nostrum plus quam unius civitatis esse possit (dissimilitudo enim civitatum varietatem iuris habeat necesse est), ne quis invitus civitate mutetur neve in civitate maneat invitus! Haec sunt enim fundamenta firmissima nostrae libertatis, sui quemque iuris et retinendi et dimittendi esse dominum. Illud vero sine ulla dubitatione maxime nostrum fundavit imperium et populi Romani nomen auxit, quod princeps ille creator huius urbis, Romulus, foedere Sabino docuit etiam hostibus recipiendis augeri hanc civitatem oportere. Cuius auctoritate et exemplo numquam est intermissa a maioribus nostris largitio et communicatio civitatis. Itaque et ex Latio multi, ut Tusculani, ut Lanuvini, et ex ceteris generibus[1] gentes universae in civitatem sunt receptae, ut Sabinorum, Volscorum,

[1] generibus *MSS.*; regionibus *Baiter.*

[a] See Cicero, *De Republica*, ii. 7. 13: "quo foedere . . . Sabinos in civitatem adscivit [Romulus]." Sabines settled in and were absorbed by Rome from the early coalescence of the inhuming Sabines of the Quirinal and Esquiline with the cremating peoples of the Palatine down to about 450 B.C.: witness Titus Tatius, Numa, and Attius Clausus (505 B.C.).

[b] This statement is inaccurate since, from 188 B.C., when Fundi, Formiae and Arpinum, after a century and a half, or less, with *civitas sine suffragio*, received the *ius suffragii*, down to 90 B.C., no Italian communities, so far as we know, were enfranchised.

[c] In 338 B.C. after the Latin War (340–338 B.C.) the Latin League which had contracted the *foedus Cassianum* with

disagreement or united to it by loyalty and affection) so constituted that we are forbidden to adopt any one of its citizens, or to present him with the citizenship of Rome.

How admirable that legal system which by divine 31
guidance our forefathers have built up right from the beginnings of the name of Rome! That none of us can be a citizen of more than one state (for a difference of state must needs entail a difference in legal system), that no one should be removed from his citizen-roll against his will, nor be forced to remain on it against his will! For the unshakable foundations of our liberty are that each one of us has the absolute power of retaining or of renouncing his right of citizenship. But what undoubtedly has done most to establish our Empire and to increase the renown of the Roman People, is that Romulus, that first founder of this city, taught us by the treaty which he made with the Sabines,[a] that this State ought to be enlarged by the admission even of enemies as citizens. Through his authority and example our forefathers never ceased to grant and to bestow citizenship.[b] And so, many members of Latin[c] towns, the inhabitants of Tusculum[d] and of Lanuvium[e] for instance, and from other stocks whole peoples, such as the Sabines,[f] the Volscians and the

Rome in 493 B.C. was dissolved. Originally composed of thirty peoples it had shrunk by 338 B.C. to thirteen.

[d] Tusculum was incorporated in the Roman state, first, in 381 B.C., and later, perhaps after revolt, in 338 B.C.

[e] Lanuvium, Aricia, Pedum and Nomentum were enfranchised in 338 B.C. in the settlement after the Latin War.

[f] The Sabines, after conquest by M'. Curius Dentatus, received the *civitas sine suffragio* in 290 B.C., full citizenship in 268 B.C.

Hernicorum; quibus ex civitatibus nec coacti essent civitate mutari, si qui noluissent, nec, si qui essent civitatem nostram beneficio populi Romani consecuti, violatum foedus eorum videretur.

32 XIV. At enim[1] quaedam foedera exstant, ut Cenomanorum,[2] Insubrium, Helvetiorum, Iapudum, non nullorum item ex Gallia barbarorum, quorum in foederibus exceptum est, ne quis eorum a nobis civis recipiatur. Quod si exceptio facit ne liceat, ubi non sit exceptum, ibi[3] necesse est licere. Ubi est igitur in foedere Gaditano exceptum, ne quem populus Romanus Gaditanum recipiat civitate? Nusquam. Ac sicubi esset, lex id Gellia et Cornelia, quae definite potestatem Pompeio civitatem donandi dederat, sustulisset. "Ex-

[1] etenim *MSS.*, *but* at enim *is the usual form in introducing an opponent's objection.*

[2] genum horum *MSS.*, Germanorum *earlier edd.*, Cenomanorum *Madvig.*

[3] *The words* non sit exceptum, ibi, *not in the MSS.*, *are added by edd.*

---

[a] Much Volscian territory was annexed for the foundation of *coloniae civium Romanorum* and *coloniae Latinae* and five tribe districts were formed there. Some of the Hernican towns received *civitas sine suffragio* at an early date (*e.g.* Anagnia in 306 B.C.), but Ferentinum, Aletrium and Verulae remained *civitates foederatae* till the Social War.

[b] Before the Second Punic War Rome had imposed her suzerainty on the Gauls of the Po Valley, but during the war the loyalty of the Cenomani, round Verona and Mantua, was shaken, and the Insubres, N.W. of Placentia, revolted on the approach of Hannibal. When Carthage surrendered in 202 B.C. Hamilcar, Hannibal's agent, was still in N. Italy and roused the Cenomani and Insubres to active revolt. In 197 B.C. the Cenomani were recalled to allegiance and in 197 and 196 B.C. the Insubres were decisively defeated.

Hernicans,[a] were admitted to citizenship; and the members of those communities would neither have been forced to change their status, had they been unwilling to do so, nor, had any of them acquired our citizenship by favour of the Roman People, would that have been regarded as an infringement of any treaty concluded with them.

XIV. But, the prosecutor contends, there are in 32
existence certain treaties, such as those concluded with the Cenomani, the Insubres,[b] the Helvetii[c] and the Iapudes,[d] and also with some of the barbarians in Gaul, and in these treaties there is a saving clause that none of their people may be admitted by us to citizenship.[e] But if a saving clause makes admission to citizenship unlawful, then, where there is no saving clause, admission must be lawful. Where, then, is there any saving clause in the treaty with Gades, under which the Roman People may not admit to citizenship any citizen of Gades?[f] Nowhere; and even if it did occur anywhere, the Gellian and Cornelian Law,[g] which expressly gave to Pompeius the power of granting citizenship, would have overridden

[c] The Helvetii first appear in Roman history as allies of the Cimbri and Teutoni between their victories at Noreia (113 B.C.) and Arausio (105 B.C.). Their plan to move into W. Gaul led to their defeat by Julius Caesar in 58 B.C.

[d] The Iapudes, an Illyrian people of the Carso at the N.E. extremity of the Adriatic, were defeated in 129 B.C. by a consul C. Sempronius Tuditanus, but later gave continual trouble and were finally conquered by Augustus.

[e] Possibly to disqualify them from receiving allotments of land in Cisalpine Gaul.

[f] In the difficult sections, part of 32 and 33, Reid's text, commentary and interpretation are generally followed (*op. cit.* pp. 18-19; 32-33; 76-77; 105-106).

[g] See p. 614.

ceptum," inquit, " est foedus, SI QUID SACROSANCTUM EST." Ignosco tibi, si neque Poenorum iura calles (reliqueras enim civitatem tuam) neque nostras potuisti leges inspicere ; ipsae enim te a cognitione sua
33 iudicio publico reppulerunt. Quid fuit in rogatione ea, quae de Pompeio a Gellio et a Lentulo consulibus lata est, in quo aliquid sacrosanctum exceptum videretur ? Primum enim sacrosanctum esse nihil potest, nisi quod populus plebesve sanxit ; deinde sanctiones sacrandae sunt aut genere ipso poenae aut cum obtestatione et consecratione legis, caput eius, qui contra fecerit, consecratur. Quid habes igitur dicere de Gaditano foedere eius modi ? Utrum capitis consecratione an obtestatione legis sacrosanctum esse confirmas ? Nihil omnino umquam de isto foedere

---

[a] At the end of some *leges* there was a clause called *sanctio* which fixed penalties for transgression, but it is not known whether such a *sanctio* was always added (H. F. Jolowicz, *Historical Introduction to the Study of Roman Law* (Cambridge, 1952), p. 85). *Sanctio* and *poena* are almost equivalent terms. A *sanctio* might prescribe a penalty inflicted by the gods or by man (Cicero, *De legibus*, ii. 22). The application of the term *sacrosancta* to a *lex* meant that the penalty for transgression was punishment by the gods.

[b] *i.e.* of Gades, which, however, was of Phoenician rather than of Carthaginian origin.

[c] The prosecutor, who had somehow attained the Roman franchise, had suffered deprivation of civil rights through a conviction in a criminal trial.

[d] *i.e.* " What clause is there in the *lex Gellia Cornelia* which makes it invalid against an enactment by nature *sacrosanctum* such as the treaty with Gades ? "

[e] *i.e.* the *comitia populi* or the *concilium plebis.* The

it. "But," says the prosecutor, "the treaty has been made subject to a saving clause by the words, 'If there is anything sacrosanct.'"[a] I pardon you, if you are not well acquainted with Carthaginian[b] jurisprudence—for you had left your city—and if you have not been able to examine our own laws, which by a public trial have themselves prevented you from making their acquaintance.[c] What words 33
were there in the law passed in respect of Pompeius by the consuls Gellius and Lentulus, which would seem to be a saving clause applicable to something sacrosanct?[d] (*None*;) for, in the first place, nothing can be sacrosanct save what has been enacted by the People or by the Commons.[e] In the second place, penal clauses must be placed under divine sanction,[f] either merely by the class of punishment which they prescribe, or when, by an invocation of the gods or by a clause of consecration contained in a law, the civil rights[g] of a man who has transgressed that law are forfeited. Have you therefore anything of this kind to say concerning the treaty with Gades? Do you assert that it is sacrosanct by reason of a clause of consecration or of an invocation of the gods contained in a law?[h] I maintain that no proposal of any kind

treaty with Gades was informal and was not ratified by the *comitia* or the *concilium plebis*, in 206 or 78 B.C.

[f] The phrase *sacrare sanctionem* does not occur elsewhere. It may be explained on the analogy of the phrase *sacrare legem*, "to attach a religious sanction to a law, so that a person violating it becomes *sacer*" (R. G. Nisbet, *Cicero, De domo*, p. 108).

[g] "The *caput* of a Roman citizen was the sum of the rights which he enjoyed in virtue of his birth." *C.A.H.* vii, p. 415.

[h] Cicero asks: "Can you point out any *lex* relating to this so-called *foedus*, and containing either an *obtestatio* or a *consecratio*?" (Reid, *op. cit.* p. 77).

ad populum, nihil ad plebem latum esse dico: de quibus etiam si latum esset ne quem civem reciperemus, tamen id esset, quod postea populus iussisset, ratum, nec quicquam illis verbis SI QUID SACROSANCTUM EST, esse exceptum videretur, de iis, cum populus Romanus nihil umquam iusserit, quicquam audes dicere sacrosanctum fuisse?

34 XV. Nec vero oratio mea ad infirmandum foedus Gaditanorum, iudices, pertinet. Neque enim est meum contra ius optime meritae civitatis, contra opinionem vetustatis, contra auctoritatem senatus dicere. Duris enim quondam temporibus rei publicae nostrae, cum praepotens terra marique Carthago nixa duabus Hispaniis huic imperio immineret, et cum duo fulmina[1] nostri imperii subito in Hispania, Cn. et P. Scipiones, exstincti occidissent, L. Marcius, primi pili

[1] fulmina *MSS.*, lumina *Ernesti followed by Reid.*

---

[a] See note *e* on pp. 668-669.

[b] The Gaditanes.

[c] Cicero is referring to a clause in the Twelve Tables given in Livy, vii. 17. 12: "ut quodcumque postremum populus iussisset, id ius ratumque esset." Cicero argues that the *lex Gellia Cornelia* would override any stipulation in the treaty with Gades, a dangerous assumption that resolutions of the Assembly could override all treaty obligations.

[d] See § 33, p. 669: "What words were there in the law passed in respect of Pompeius by the consuls Gellius and Lentulus, which would seem to be a saving clause applicable to something sacrosanct? (*None*)"

[e] A resolution of the Senate, when deprived of its binding force by the veto of a tribune or some legal defect, was called an *auctoritas*, not a *consultum*, but might, if the Senate so resolved, be regularly drawn up (*perscripta*) and recorded in the minutes, like a formal decree. For examples see Cicero, *Epp. ad Fam.* viii. 8. 5-8, of a debate in the Senate on 29

concerning this treaty was ever submitted, either to the People or to the Commons.[a] Even if a proposal had been made concerning some persons [b] that we should not admit any of them to citizenship, and if nevertheless a subsequent enactment of the People would be valid[c] and no saving clause would seem to to be made by those words, " If there is anything sacrosanct . . .",[d] do you dare to talk of something sacrosanct applicable to those persons, although the Roman People never made any enactment concerning them?

XV. Nor is there anything, gentlemen, in what I say which tends to invalidate the treaty with Gades. 34
For indeed it is not for me to say a word against the rights of a most deserving state, against the judgment of the past, against a resolution of the Senate.[e] For at a dark hour in the life of our country, when Carthage, all-powerful on land and sea, and supported by the two Spains, was threatening this Empire, and when those two thunderbolts of our Empire, Gnaeus and Publius Scipio, had on a sudden been destroyed in Spain,[f] Lucius Marcius, a senior centurion,[g] is

September 51 B.C. The subject of this *auctoritas* was the renewal or conclusion of the treaty with Gades, mentioned later in this section (34).

[f] P. Cornelius Scipio, consul 218 B.C., and father of the elder Africanus, and his brother Cn. Scipio, after successful warfare against Carthage in Spain from 218 B.C., were defeated and slain in 211 B.C. The word *fulmina*, used of the elder and of the younger Africanus (Scipio Aemilianus) by Virgil, *Aeneid*, vi. 842, and of the elder Africanus by Lucretius, iii. 1034, is surely right, despite the disaster to the two Scipiones in 211 B.C. *Cf.* O. Skutch, *Studi Italiani di Filologia Classica*, xxvii-xxviii (1956), pp. 536 ff. Reid prefers Ernesti's *lumina*.

[g] In 211 B.C. L. Marcius Septimus, an able soldier, prevented the Carthaginians from further exploiting their defeat

centurio, cum Gaditanis foedus icisse dicitur. Quod cum magis fide illius populi, iustitia nostra, vetustate denique ipsa quam aliquo publico vinculo religionis teneretur, sapientes homines et publici iuris periti, Gaditani, M. Lepido Q. Catulo consulibus a senatu de foedere postulaverunt. Tum est cum Gaditanis foedus vel renovatum vel ictum ; de quo foedere populus Romanus sententiam non tulit, qui iniussu suo nullo pacto potest religione obligari.

35 Ita Gaditana civitas, quod beneficiis suis erga rem publicam nostram consequi potuit, quod imperatorum testimoniis, quod vetustate, quod Q. Catuli, summi viri, auctoritate, quod iudicio senatus, quod foedere, consecuta est ; quod publica religione sanciri potuit, id abest ; populus enim se nusquam obligavit. Neque ideo est Gaditanorum causa deterior ; gravissimis enim et plurimis rebus est fulta. Sed isti disputationi hic[1] certe nihil est loci. Sacrosanctum enim nihil potest esse, nisi quod per populum plebemve sanctum est. XVI. Quodsi hoc foedus, quod populus Romanus auctore senatu, commendatione et iudicio vetustatis, voluntate et sententiis suis comprobat, idem suffragiis comprobasset, quid erat, cur ex ipso foedere Gaditanum in civitatem nostram recipi non liceret ? Nihil est enim aliud in foedere, nisi ut " PIA ET AETERNA

[1] *Inserted by Cobet.*

---

of the Scipios by concentrating the remnants of the Roman forces in Spain at a base north of the Ebro. Gades surrendered to him in 206 B.C., when the treaty was probably concluded (Livy, xxviii. 23, 30, 36, 37). On Marcius' rank as a senior centurion see the article " Centurio " by H. M. D. Parker in *The Oxford Classical Dictionary*, p. 180.

[a] 78 B.C.

[b] The renewal or the conclusion of the treaty was treated purely as a piece of senatorial business.

said to have struck a treaty with the people of Gades. And since this treaty was upheld more by the good faith of that people, by our own sense of justice, and, finally, by its great age, than by any public bond of sacred obligation, the people of Gades, being prudent men and skilled in law relating to affairs of state, in the consulship of Marcus Lepidus and Quintus Catulus,[a] submitted a request to the Senate concerning their treaty. At that time the treaty with the people of Gades was either renewed or struck. Upon this treaty the Roman People passed no vote, and, since they made no enactment, they cannot in any way be bound by a sacred obligation.[b]

And so the state of Gades gained what it could gain 35
through its services to our country, by the testimony of our commanders, by the passing of time, by the influence of that distinguished man Quintus Catulus, by a decision of the Senate, by a treaty; but any enactment based on a sacred public obligation is not there; for the People nowhere laid themselves under any obligation. Nor is the case of the people of Gades made thereby any weaker, for it is based upon numerous and most impressive considerations. But here there is certainly no room for this argument of yours. For nothing can be sacrosanct unless it has been enacted through the People or the Commons. XVI. But even if this treaty, which the Roman People approve by the authority of the Senate, by the commendation and judgment of the past, by their own wishes and feelings, had also been approved by their votes, what would there be in the treaty itself to make it unlawful for a citizen of Gades to be admitted into our citizenship? For there is nothing else in the treaty save that "There shall be a holy and ever-

PAX" sit. Quid id ad civitatem? Adiunctum illud etiam est, quod non est in omnibus foederibus: "MAIESTATEM POPULI ROMANI COMITER CONSERVANTO." Id habet hanc vim, ut sint illi in foedere inferiores.

36 Primum verbi genus hoc "conservanto," quo magis in legibus quam in foederibus uti solemus, imperantis est, non precantis. Deinde, cum alterius populi maiestas conservari iubetur, de altero siletur, certe ille populus in superiore condicione causaque ponitur, cuius maiestas foederis sanctione defenditur. In quo erat accusatoris interpretatio indigna responsione, qui ita dicebat, "comiter" esse "communiter," quasi vero priscum aliquod aut insolitum verbum interpretaretur. Comes benigni, faciles, suaves homines esse dicuntur; "qui erranti comiter monstrat viam," benigne, non gravate; "communiter" quidem certe non convenit.

37 Et simul absurda res est caveri foedere, ut maiestatem populi Romani "communiter" conservent,

[a] A loose statement, for Livy, xxxii. 2. 5 says that the original treaty stipulated that Rome should not send a *praefectus* to govern the city.

[b] The insertion of this clause was characteristic of a *foedus iniquum*, in which Gades was subordinated to Rome and was bound to assist Rome not only in defensive wars but in offensive wars also. The Aetolian League, the first of Rome's allies to quarrel with her, was in 189 B.C. subjected to a *foedus iniquum* (Livy, xxxviii. 2. 2). A *foedus aequum* was a defensive alliance of equal partners, *e.g.* that of the

lasting peace."[a] What has that to do with the right of citizenship? This clause also was added, which is not found in all treaties, "Let them uphold the greatness of the Roman People in a friendly way."[b] The force of this is that the people of Gades are less favoured in the treaty than ourselves.[c]

In the first place, this form of words, "Let them uphold," which we are in the habit of using in laws rather than in treaties, implies a command, not an entreaty. Secondly, when an order is given that the greatness of one people be upheld, while nothing is said about that of the other, undoubtedly that people is placed in a superior position and circumstances whose greatness is upheld by the sanction of a treaty. On this point the prosecutor's explanation does not deserve an answer, for, said he, *comiter* (in a friendly way) is the same as *communiter* (mutually), as if indeed he were giving an interpretation of an old or uncommon word.[d] Men are said to be friendly and generous, good-natured and agreeable: "One who in friendly fashion shows the way to one who is lost,"[e] does so generously, not grudgingly; the meaning "mutually" is assuredly unsuitable. 36

At the same time, it is absurd that a treaty should contain a stipulation that the parties should "mutually" uphold the greatness of the Roman People, that 37

Umbrian Camertes (Livy, xxviii. 45. 20; *Pro Balbo*, 46). See Sherwin-White, *The Roman Citizenship*, pp. 43-44.

[c] Reid prefers *ut sit ille* (sc. *populus Romanus*) *in foedere inferior* and queries, "Does this clause infringe the right of Rome to grant the *civitas* to whom she pleases?"

[d] The prosecutor tried to show that the clause bound Rome as well as Gades.

[e] The end of a line in Ennius (quoted in Cicero, *De officiis*, i. 51): "Ut homo qui erranti comiter monstret viam."

id est ut populus Romanus suam maiestatem esse salvam velit. Quodsi iam ita esset, ut esse non potest, tamen de nostra maiestate, nihil de illorum caveretur. Potestne igitur nostra maiestas a Gaditanis benigne conservari, si ad eam retinendam Gaditanos praemiis elicere non possumus? Potest esse ulla denique maiestas, si impedimur, quo minus per populum Romanum beneficiorum virtutis causa tribuendorum potestatem imperatoribus nostris deferamus?

38 XVII. Sed quid ego disputo, quae mihi tum, si Gaditani contra me dicerent, vere posse dici viderentur? Illis enim repetentibus L. Cornelium responderem legem populum Romanum iussisse de civitate tribuenda; huic generi legum fundos populos fieri non solere; Cn. Pompeium de consilii sententia civitatem huic dedisse, nullum populi nostri iussum Gaditanos habere; itaque nihil esse sacrosanctum, quod lege exceptum videretur; si esset, tamen in foedere nihil esse cautum praeter pacem; additum esse etiam illud, ut maiestatem illi nostram conservare deberent, quae certe minueretur, si aut adiutoribus illorum civibus uti in bellis nobis non liceret aut praemii tribuendi potestatem nullam haberemus.

39 Nunc vero quid ego contra Gaditanos loquar, cum id, quod defendo, voluntate eorum, auctoritate, legatione ipsa comprobetur? Qui a principio sui generis

---

[a] An inaccurate statement (see p. 674, note *a*).

[b] A deputation from Gades had come to Rome to present a *laudatio* on behalf of Balbus. Similarly, P. Sestius was supported by a deputation from Capua (*Pro Sestio*, 9), and M. Caelius Rufus by one from Interamnia (*Pro Caelio*, 5).

is to say, that the Roman People should wish to have their own greatness upheld. But, supposing for a moment that this were so—impossible as it is—, none the less a stipulation would be made about our own greatness, not about theirs. Can our own greatness, then, be upheld "in a friendly way" by the people of Gades, if we are unable to attract them by rewards to preserve it? Lastly, can there be any greatness at all, if we are prevented from conferring upon our commanders, through the Roman People, the power of bestowing favours as a reward of courage?

XVII. But why am I making use of arguments which, 38
if the people of Gades were my opponents, might then, I think, be justly employed by me? For if *they* claimed the return of Lucius Cornelius, I should answer that the Roman People had passed a law dealing with the bestowal of citizenship; that it was not usual for peoples to "give consent" to this kind of law; that Gnaeus Pompeius, with the approval of his advisers, conferred citizenship upon my client, that the people of Gades cannot point to any enactment of our People; and that there is therefore nothing sacrosanct, to which a saving clause in the law might seem to apply; even if there were, there is no stipulation in the treaty except in regard to peace [a]; to this a clause also is added, under which they are under an obligation to uphold our greatness, which would certainly be impaired, either if we were not entitled to employ their citizens to help us in our wars, or if we had no power of bestowing a reward.

But now why need I argue against the people of 39
Gades, when the very point which I am maintaining is approved by their goodwill, their expressed opinion, and even by a deputation from them? [b] Men who,

ac rei publicae, id est,[1] ab omni studio sensuque Poenorum mentes suas ad nostrum imperium nomenque flexerunt; qui, cum maxima bella nobis inferrentur, eos, a quibus inferrentur,[2] moenibus excluserunt, classibus insecuti sunt, corporibus, opibus, copiis depulerunt; qui et veterem illam speciem foederis Marciani semper omni sanctiorem arce[3] duxerunt et hoc foedere Catuli senatusque auctoritate se nobiscum coniunctissimos esse arbitrati sunt; quorum moenia, delubra, agros ut Hercules itinerum ac laborum suorum, sic maiores nostri imperii ac nominis populi Romani terminos esse voluerunt.

40 Testantur et mortuos nostros imperatores, quorum vivit immortalis memoria et gloria, Scipiones, Brutos, Horatios, Cassios, Metellos, et hunc praesentem Cn. Pompeium, quem procul ab illorum moenibus acre et magnum bellum gerentem commeatu pe-

[1] aut studio rei publicae ii MSS.; *the text given*, ac rei publicae, id est, *is Reid's adoption of a correction by Klotz.*

[2] eos, a quibus inferrentur, *inserted by Madvig.*

[3] *Edd. vary between* ara *and* arce (" *a stronghold, citadel* "). arce (*Reid*) *is adopted.*

---

[a] This seems to be the sense of a very uncertain text: Gades was a Phoenician, not specially a Carthaginian colony, and had once been independent; it was treated very cruelly by the Carthaginian commander Mago in 206 B.C. before he finally abandoned the city to the Romans. Livy, xxviii. 30 and 36.

[b] Services rendered by Gades to Rome during the last years of the Second and during the Third Punic War.

[c] In 78 B.C. See §§ 34 and 35.

[d] Scipio Africanus Maior (236–184 B.C.) and Scipio Aemilianus Africanus Numantinus (185/4–129 B.C.).

[e] Possibly a reference (plural for singular) to D. Iunius Brutus Gallaecus, consul 138 B.C., governor of Further Spain, who triumphed over the Gallaeci in 132 B.C.

[f] The readings are doubtful. Reid regards *Horatios*

disregarding the source of their race and commonwealth, putting aside, that is, all sympathy and fellow-feeling for the Carthaginians, have directed their minds towards our Empire and the name of Rome [a]; who, when terrible wars were being waged against us, shut out from their walls those by whom they were being waged, harassed them with their fleets, and repulsed them with their own bodies, their resources, their troops [b]; who always considered that ancient semblance of a treaty of which Marcius was the author to be more inviolable than any stronghold, and deemed themselves most closely united to us by this present treaty concluded by Catulus and ratified by a resolution of the Senate [c]; whose walls, shrines and territories our fathers desired to be the limits of our Empire and of the name of the Roman People, even as Hercules made them to mark the end of his journeyings and toils.

They call as witnesses not only our dead comman- 40
ders, whose glorious memory lives and will never die —the Scipiones,[d] the Bruti,[e] the Horatii,[f] the Cassii,[f] and Metelli [g]—but also Gnaeus Pompeius, here present, whom they assisted with supplies and money when he was waging a bitter and important war

as corrupt, by association with *Brutos*, a name similarly associated with early Republican history. He prefers *Flaccos*, a possible allusion to C. Valerius Flaccus, consul 93 B.C., who fought against the Celtiberi. For *Cassios* Reid prefers *Crassos*, perhaps alluding to P. Licinius Crassus Dives, consul 97 B.C., who commanded in Spain and triumphed in 93 B.C. E. H. Warmington suggests *Porcios*, ⟨*Gracchos*⟩, in reference to the achievements in Spain of Cato (the Censor) and Ti. Sempronius Gracchus (the elder).

[g] Q. Caecilius Metellus Pius is meant: consul in 80 B.C., he commanded in Spain from 79 to 72 B.C. during the Sertorian War. Pontifex Maximus, he died about 64 B.C.

cuniaque iuverunt, et hoc tempore ipsum populum Romanum, quem in caritate annonae, ut saepe ante fecerant, frumento suppeditato levarunt, se hoc ius esse velle, ut sibi et liberis, si qui eximia virtute fuerit, sit in nostris castris, sit in imperatorum praetoriis, sit denique inter signa atque in acie locus, sit his gradibus ascensus etiam ad civitatem.

41 XVIII. Quodsi Afris, si Sardis, si Hispanis agris stipendioque multatis virtute adipisci licet civitatem, Gaditanis autem officiis, vetustate, fide, periculis, foedere coniunctis hoc idem non licebit, non foedus sibi nobiscum, sed iniquissimas leges impositas a nobis esse arbitrabuntur. Atque hanc, iudices, non a me fingi orationem, sed me dicere, quae Gaditani iudicarint, res ipsa declarat. Hospitium multis annis ante hoc tempus cum L. Cornelio Gaditanos fecisse publice dico. Proferam tesseram ; legatos excito ; laudatores ad hoc iudicium summos homines ac nobilissimos deprecatores huius periculi missos videtis ; re denique multo ante Gadibus audita, ne forte huic ab illo

---

[a] Either the Sertorian War is meant or Pompey's campaigns against the pirates or the later phase of the Third Mithridatic War.

[b] The reference is possibly to an unforeseen famine in September 57 B.C. (Cicero, *Epp. ad Att.* iv. i. 6 : " cum esset annonae summa caritas ") which led to the appointment of Cn. Pompeius as food-controller for five years.

[c] They appointed him their *hospes publicus* or *patronus* at Rome.

[d] This is a *tessera hospitalis*, a tally or token, divided between two friends, by which they or their descendants

far from their walls [a]; and at this present time they call the Roman People themselves, whom they relieved, when corn was dear,[b] by a supply of grain, as they have often done before, to bear witness that they desire it to be established as their right, that for themselves and for their children, should anyone be distinguished for his valour, he should find a place in our camps, at the headquarters of our commanders, and finally amid our standards and in the ranks of battle, and that by these steps he should rise even to citizenship.

XVIII. But if the people of Africa, Sardinia and 41
Spain, mulcted in land and tribute, are entitled to win citizenship for gallantry, while the people of Gades, who are united to us by services, by ancient bond, by loyalty, by dangers and by treaty, are not entitled to enjoy this same privilege, they will consider that it is not a treaty that they have made with us, but that most unjust laws have been imposed on them by us. And the facts of the case show, gentlemen, that my statements are not my own invention, but that I am expressing the view held by the people of Gades. I assert that many years before this the people of Gades publicly appointed Lucius Cornelius as their guest-friend at Rome.[c] I will produce the token [d]; I summon their envoys; you see men of the highest rank and distinction sent to give evidence of character at this trial and by their prayers to guard my client against the danger now facing him; in fact, when news of this had long ago been heard of at Gades, the people of Gades in their Senate most

could always recognize each other. Cicero offers to produce the *tessera hospitalis* to show what Gades had done for Balbus.

periculum crearetur, gravissima in istum civem suum Gaditani in senatu convicia[1] fecerunt.

42 Potuit magis fundus populus Gaditanus fieri, quoniam hoc magnopere delectare verbo, si tum fit fundus, cum scita ac iussa nostra sua sententia comprobat, quam cum hospitium fecit, ut et civitate illum mutatum esse fateretur et huius civitatis honore dignissimum iudicaret? Potuit certius interponere iudicium[2] voluntatis suae, quam cum etiam accusatorem huius multa et poena notavit? Potuit magis de re iudicare, quam cum ad vestrum iudicium cives amplissimos legavit testes huius iuris, vitae laudatores, periculi deprecatores?

43 Etenim quis est tam demens, quin sentiat ius hoc Gaditanis esse retinendum, ne saeptum sit iis iter in perpetuum ad hoc amplissimum praemium civitatis, et magnopere iis esse laetandum huius L. Corneli benevolentiam erga suos remanere Gadibus, gratiam et facultatem commendandi in hac civitate versari? Quis est enim nostrum, cui non illa civitas sit huius studio, cura, diligentia commendatior? XIX. Omitto, quantis ornamentis populum istum C. Caesar, cum esset in Hispania praetor, adfecerit, controversias

[1] convicia *Reid*; *Klotz-Schöll retain* consulta.
[2] indicium *Madvig*.

---

[a] A criminal charge, see § 64.

[b] For this rendering of *iudicium* see Reid's note *ad loc.* (*op. cit.* p. 83), where he objects to Madvig's proposal of *indicium*.

[c] He had been convicted in a criminal trial. See note on § 32.

[d] Caesar, who was praetor in 62 B.C., left Rome as governor

violently abused the prosecutor, their own fellow-citizen, with a view to safeguarding my client against any risk of danger [a] from him.

Could the people of Gades have given a more formal "consent," since you are highly delighted with this word, if "consent" is given by approval through their vote of our resolutions and orders, than by appointing Balbus as their guest-friend, thereby admitting that he had exchanged citizenship and pronouncing him most worthy of the honour of our citizenship? Could they express their feelings [b] more decisively than by stigmatizing also my client's prosecutor by a fine and a penalty? [c] Could they give a more decided judgment on the matter than by sending a deputation of their most eminent citizens to your Court to bear witness to my client's right, to express their admiration of his character, to guard him from danger by their intercessions? 42

In fact, is there anyone so demented as not to see that this is a right which the people of Gades must retain, in order that a way to the reward of citizenship, that supreme distinction, may not be absolutely closed to them for ever, and that they have great reason to rejoice that Gades still retains the affection of my client Lucius Cornelius towards his fellow-townsmen, and that his influence and power of favouring their interests find employment here in Rome? For who is there among us who has not a livelier interest in Gades thanks to the zeal, the care, the devotion of Balbus? XIX. I say nothing about the great distinctions which Gaius Caesar, when he was governor in Spain,[d] conferred upon that people, how 43

of Further Spain early in 61 B.C., after he had directed action against P. Clodius, and returned to Rome in June 60 B.C.

sedarit, iura ipsorum permissu statuerit, inveteratam quandam barbariam[a] ex Gaditanorum moribus disciplinaque delerit, summa in eam civitatem huius rogatu studia et beneficia contulerit. Multa praetereo, quae cotidie labore huius et studio aut omnino aut certe facilius consequantur. Itaque et adsunt principes civitatis et defendunt amore ut suum civem, testimonio ut nostrum, officio ut ex nobilissimo civi sanctissimum hospitem, studio ut diligentissimum defensorem commodorum suorum.

44 Ac ne ipsi Gaditani arbitrentur, quamquam nullo incommodo adficiantur, si liceat eorum cives virtutis causa in nostram civitatem venire, tamen hoc ipso inferius esse suum foedus quam ceterorum, consolabor et hos praesentes viros optimos et illam fidelissimam atque amicissimam nobis civitatem simul et vos non ignorantes, iudices, admonebo, quo de iure hoc iudicium constitutum sit, de eo numquam omnino esse dubitatum.

45 Quos igitur prudentissimos interpretes foederum, quos peritissimos bellici iuris, quos diligentissimos in exquirendis condicionibus civitatum atque causis esse arbitramur? Eos profecto, qui iam imperia ac bella gesserunt. XX. Etenim, si Q. Scaevola[b] ille augur, cum de iure praediatorio consuleretur, homo iuris

[a] Rice Holmes, *The Roman Republic*, I, p. 303, says: "an old barbarous usage, which we may perhaps suppose to have been human sacrifice."

[b] Q. Mucius Scaevola, consul 117 B.C. and "Augur," a name by which he was distinguished from his cousin who was consul in 95 B.C., usually called "Pontifex." He was a great jurist. Cicero as a youth attended his legal consultations (*De amicitia*, 1).

he settled disputes, by their own consent established codes of law, extirpated a kind of ingrained barbarity[a] from the customs and institutions of the people of Gades, and, at Balbus' request, bestowed upon that state the greatest interest and the greatest favours. I say nothing about many favours which they may obtain every day, either wholly or certainly more easily, by the efforts and devotion of my client. Accordingly, the chief men of his state are both present here and defend him by their affection as a citizen of their own, by their testimony as a citizen of our own, by their kindly offices as one who from a most distinguished citizen has become a revered guest-friend, and by their zeal as a most painstaking champion of their interests.

And lest the people of Gades themselves should 44
imagine that, although they have no inconvenience put upon them, should their citizens be entitled to earn our citizenship by gallantry, yet their treaty becomes for this very reason less favourable than that of other peoples, I will reassure both these excellent gentlemen here present, and that city, most loyal and devoted to us, and I will also remind you, gentlemen, although you well know it already, that the legal point which this Court has to decide never has been in any possible doubt.

Who, then, are those whom we consider to be the 45
most skilled interpreters of treaties, the most learned in military law, the most scrupulous in investigating the relations of states to ourselves and their legal position? Undoubtedly those who have already commanded armies and waged wars. XX. In fact, if Quintus Scaevola,[b] that famous augur, on being consulted about the law of mortgaged properties, some-

peritissimus consultores suos non numquam ad Furium et Cascellium praediatores reiciebat; si nos de aqua nostra Tusculana M. Tugionem potius quam C. Aquilium consulebamus, quod adsiduus usus uni rei deditus et ingenium et artem saepe vincit, quis dubitet de foederibus et de toto iure pacis et belli omnibus iuris peritissimis imperatores nostros anteferre?

46 Possumusne igitur tibi probare auctorem exempli atque facti illius, quod a te reprenditur, C. Marium? Quaeris aliquem graviorem, constantiorem, praestantiorem virtute, prudentia, religione? Is igitur Iguvinatem[1] M. Annium Appium, fortissimum virum summa[2] virtute praeditum, civitate donavit, idem cohortes duas universas Camertium civitate donavit[3] cum Camertinum foedus omnium[4] foederum sanctissimum atque aequissimum sciret esse. Potest igitur,

[1] religionis igitur aequitate *MSS.*; religione? Is igitur Iguvinatem *Halm.* [2] *Added by Gryphaeus.*
[3] idem . . . donavit *supplied by Madvig.*
[4] foedus omnium *added by Müller.*

---

[a] A *praediator* was a broker or speculator who bought up at public auctions the property of sureties which had been distrained for the non-performance of duties to the State. A *lex praediatoria* is mentioned in Suetonius, *Claudius*, 9. Furius and Cascellius are mentioned elsewhere only by Valerius Maximus, viii. 12. 1, who quotes Cicero's words and wrongly supposes that the men were lawyers, not brokers.

[b] A specialist in the law of water rights.

[c] The most brilliant lawyer of his time, he was a colleague of Cicero in the praetorship of 66 B.C. Cicero (*Epp. ad Att.* i. 1. 1) says that owing to illness and *illud suum regnum iudiciale* Aquilius was not to be a candidate for the consulship of 64 B.C. See also Cicero, *Pro Caecina*, 77-79.

[d] Cicero's fellow-townsman from Arpinum and his hero among the early *populares*.

times, most able lawyer though he was, referred his clients to the brokers Furius and Cascellius [a]; if, with reference to water-rights on my land at Tusculum, I consulted Marcus Tugio [b] rather than Gaius Aquilius,[c] because continued practice and application to a single subject are often superior to natural ability and skill; who would hesitate to prefer our commanders to all the most skilful lawyers with reference to treaties and to the whole law of peace and war?

Can we then submit for your approval, as an 46 authority for a precedent and for that course of action which you blame, the name of Gaius Marius? [d] Do you want anyone of greater authority or stedfastness, one more distinguished for courage, wisdom or conscience? Well and good: he conferred citizenship upon Marcus Annius Appius, of Iguvium, a man of outstanding courage and excellence; he also conferred citizenship upon two whole cohorts from Camerinum, although he knew that the treaty with Camerinum was of all treaties one of the most solemn character and on the most equitable terms.[e] Can then Lucius

[e] In the second phase of the Great Samnite War Rome concluded *foedera* in 310 B.C. with Camerinum, whose people were called Camertes (Livy, ix. 36. 7), and in 308 B.C. with Iguvium (known only from this passage), Umbrian towns, as useful allies of Rome in operations towards Etruria. A conspicuous example in the Italian federation of a *foedus aequum* is that of Camerinum; Livy, xxxviii. 45. 20, after giving a list of volunteers for the African campaign of 205 B.C., says that Camerinum sent a cohort, although its *foedus* was *aequum*. On the field of battle at Vercellae (101 B.C.) Marius enfranchised two cohorts of allied troops from Camerinum for bravery in action. Plutarch, *Marius*, 28, says that a thousand men were enfranchised. See p. 622, note *c*.

iudices, L. Cornelius condemnari, ut non C. Mari factum condemnetur?

47 Exsistat ergo ille vir parumper cogitatione vestra, quoniam re non potest, ut conspiciatis eum mentibus, quoniam[1] oculis non potestis; dicat se non imperitum foederis, non rudem exemplorum, non ignarum belli[2] fuisse; se P. Africani discipulum ac militem, se stipendiis, se legationibus bellicis eruditum, se, si tanta bella legisset,[3] quanta gessit et confecit, si tot consulibus meruisset, quotiens ipse consul fuit, omnia iura belli perdiscere ac nosse potuisse; sibi non fuisse dubium, quin nullo foedere a re publica bene gerenda impediretur; a se ex coniunctissima atque amicissima civitate fortissimum quemque esse delectum; neque Iguvinatium neque Camertium foedere esse exceptum, quo minus eorum civibus a populo Romano praemia virtutis tribuerentur.

48 XXI. Itaque, cum paucis annis post hanc civitatis donationem acerrima de civitate quaestio Licinia et Mucia lege venisset, num quis eorum, qui de foederatis civitatibus esset civitate donatus, in iudicium est

[1] quem iam *Halm-Reid.*
[2] bellici iuris *Halm-Baiter-Reid.*
[3] egisset MS.

---

[a] With Iguvium and with Camerinum.
[b] He served with distinction under P. Cornelius Scipio Aemilianus (the younger Africanus) in Spain, in the Numantine War (Plutarch, *Marius*, 3).
[c] Marius died on 13 January 86 B.C., in his seventh consulship.
[d] According to Asconius (p. 68 Clark) the *lex Licinia*

Cornelius be condemned, gentlemen, without the action of Gaius Marius being condemned ?

Let that great man therefore stand before you for 47
a while in your imagination, since he cannot do so in reality, that you may see him with your minds, since you cannot see him with your eyes ; let him tell you that he was not ignorant of the treaty,[a] not unversed in precedents, not unacquainted with war ; that he was a pupil of Publius Scipio and a soldier under him [b] ; that he had received his training in the field and as a legate in war ; that if he had only read in books about such great wars as he waged and brought to an end, if he had only served under consuls as many in number as his own consulships,[c] he could have acquired a thorough knowledge and understanding of all the laws of war ; that he had never doubted that any treaty could prevent him from acting for the advantage of the State ; that from a people that was most united and devoted to us he had chosen every bravest citizen ; that in the treaty neither with Iguvium nor with Camerinum was there any saving clause stipulating that rewards of valour should not be bestowed upon their citizens by the Roman People.

XXI. And so, when a few years after this gift of 48
citizenship by Marius, the question of citizenship was subjected, under the Licinian and Mucian Law,[d] to an investigation of the utmost severity, was anyone of those from the allied states, upon whom citizenship had been bestowed, ever brought to trial ? Titus

Mucia, 95 B.C., precipitated the Social War, 91–88 B.C. By it Latins and Italians (*socii*) who could not justify their presence in Rome were expelled from the city, and the claims of those who passed as Roman citizens were subjected to searching scrutiny.

vocatus? Nam Spoletinus[a] T. Matrinius unus ex iis, quos C. Marius civitate donasset, dixit causam ex colonia Latina in primis firma et illustri. Quem cum disertus homo L. Antistius[b] accusaret, non dixit fundum Spoletinum populum non esse factum (videbat enim populos de suo iure, non de nostro fundos fieri solere), sed, cum lege Appuleia[c] coloniae non essent deductae, qua lege Saturninus C. Mario tulerat, ut in singulas colonias ternos cives Romanos facere posset, negabat hoc beneficium re ipsa sublata[d] valere debere.

49 Nihil habet similitudinis ista accusatio; sed tamen tanta auctoritas in C. Mario fuit, ut non per L. Crassum, adfinem suum, hominem incredibili eloquentia, sed paucis ipse verbis causam illam gravitate sua defenderit et probarit. Quis enim esset, iudices, qui imperatoribus nostris in bello, in acie, in exercitu dilectum virtutis, qui sociis, qui foederatis in defendenda re publica nostra spem praemiorum eripi vellet?

---

[a] In 241 B.C. an important Latin colony was planted at Spoletium, in southern Umbria, on the line of the later Via Flaminia (220 B.C.) to Ariminum.

[b] A man of this name was tribune in 58 B.C. and, according to Suetonius (*Div. Iul.* 23), prosecuted Caesar. But it is more likely that P. Antistius, tribune 88 B.C., is meant, for Cicero, *Brutus*, 226, while discussing P. Antistius, says that P. Antistius successfully prosecuted Gaius Iulius.

[c] L. Appuleius Saturninus, in his second tribunate (100 B.C.), introduced a measure for the foundation of colonies in various provinces, Sicily, Achaia, and Macedonia being mentioned. These colonies were almost certainly intended to enjoy the Latin citizenship, with (if the text is sound) three *cives Romani* in each as a small privileged class; and to be recruited not only from Roman citizens but in part at least from Italians (*socii*) also. See H. M. Last, in *C.A.H.* ix, p. 169.

[d] Saturninus' measures of 100 B.C. were declared invalid by the Senate immediately after his violent death on 10 December in that year.

Matrinius of Spoletium [a] was, in fact, the only one of those upon whom Gaius Marius had conferred citizenship, who had to defend himself, and he came from a Latin colony that was specially powerful and distinguished. His prosecutor, the eloquent Lucius Antistius,[b] did not say that the people of Spoletium had not "given their consent" (for he knew that peoples were in the habit of "giving consent" about legal points that concerned themselves and not us); but, since the colonies under the Appuleian Law, a law which Saturninus had passed in the interest of Marius empowering him to confer Roman citizenship upon three members of each colony,[c] had not been founded, he maintained that Marius' grant of citizenship should be invalid since the measure itself had been annulled.[d]

That prosecution [e] has no resemblance to our case. 49
But so great was the prestige of Gaius Marius, that, without employing the services of Lucius Crassus, his kinsman by marriage,[f] a man of surpassing eloquence, he himself undertook the defence and in a few words won the case by his own personality.[g] Who could there be, gentlemen, who would desire that our commanders should be deprived of the right of choosing out the bravest in war, in battle, and in our army, and that our allies and federate peoples should lose the hope of rewards while defending our State? But

[e] Of T. Matrinius, of Spoletium (§ 48).

[f] L. Licinius Crassus (consul 95 B.C.), the leading orator of his time (see p. 628, note *b*), was the father of Licinia, who married C. Marius the younger (consul 82 B.C.), adopted son of the elder Marius.

[g] Marius' grant of citizenship to Matrinius probably preceded the invalidation of Saturninus' law. But Matrinius' claim to citizenship was weakened by its dependence on a law which was subsequently annulled.

Quodsi vultus C. Mari, si vox, si ille imperatorius ardor oculorum, si recentes triumphi, si praesens valuit aspectus, valeat auctoritas, valeant res gestae, valeat memoria, valeat fortissimi et clarissimi viri nomen aeternum. Sit hoc discrimen inter gratiosos cives atque fortes, ut illi vivi fruantur opibus suis, horum etiam mortuorum, si quisquam huius imperii defensor mori potest, vivat auctoritas immortalis.

50 XXII. Quid? Cn. Pompeius pater rebus Italico bello maximis gestis P. Caesium, equitem Romanum, virum bonum, qui vivit, Ravennatem foederato ex populo nonne civitate donavit? Quid? Cohortes duas universas Camertium C. Marius?[1] Quid? Heracliensem Alexam P. Crassus, vir amplissimus, ex ea civitate, quacum prope singulare foedus Pyrrhi temporibus C. Fabricio consule ictum putatur? Quid? Massiliensem Aristonem L. Sulla? Quid? Quoniam de Gaditanis agimus, idem servos novem[2] Gaditanos? Quid?

[1] C. Marius *added by Lange.*

[2] erosnovem Gaditanos MS.; heros *some edd.*; servos novem, *Reid's conjecture, is followed.*

---

[a] This is illustrated by a famous incident in a dungeon at Minturnae related in Plutarch, *Marius*, 39.

[b] On 1 January 104 B.C. Marius (consul ii) triumphed over Jugurtha; in 101 B.C. he triumphed (consul v), with Catulus, over the Cimbri and Teutoni.

[c] Cn. Pompeius Strabo, as *legatus* in 90 and consul in 89 B.C., crushed the rebel movement in Picenum during the Social War by his long siege and capture (on or before 17 November 89) of Asculum. For his enfranchisement of the *Turma Salluitana* see p. 623, and p. 653, note *d*.

[d] The *foedus* of Ravenna, an important port in Cispadane Gaul, is known only from this passage. If, as seems probable, Ravenna obtained Roman citizenship in the settlement following the Social War, it is difficult to understand why Caesius had to depend on Pompeius Strabo for his citizen-

if the countenance of Gaius Marius, if his voice, if the flash of his commanding glance,[a] if his recent triumphs,[b] if the sight of his bodily presence, had such power, let his authority, let his achievements, let our memory of him, let the everlasting name of that most courageous and most illustrious hero have the same power now! Let us make this distinction between citizens who are personally popular and those who are courageous, that the former in their lifetime shall enjoy their own influence, while the prestige of the latter, even after their death—if any defender of this Empire can ever die—shall live and remain immortal.

XXII. Again, did not Gnaeus Pompeius,[c] the 50
father of Pompeius, after great exploits in the Italian War, bestow citizenship upon Publius Caesius, a Roman Knight, a worthy man still living, who was a citizen of Ravenna and a member of a federate state?[d] Again, did not Gaius Marius confer the same upon two whole cohorts from Camerinum?[e] Again, did not that eminent man Publius Crassus[f] bestow it upon Alexas of Heraclea, a member of that state with which an almost unique treaty is thought to have been concluded in the time of Pyrrhus during the consulship of Gaius Fabricius?[g] Again, did not Lucius Sulla bestow it upon Aristo of Massilia? Again, since Gades is our theme, did not he also bestow it upon nine

ship. May not this citizenship have been conferred by Pompeius Strabo on Caesius, under the *lex Iulia*, as a reward for distinguished service in the field? Alternatively, Ravenna may have received Roman citizenship from Julius Caesar in 49 B.C. To P. Caesius Cicero probably wrote a short letter in 46 B.C. (*Epp. ad Fam.* xiii. 51).

[e] Plutarch, *Marius*, 29. See p. 687, note *e*.

[f] P. Licinius Crassus, consul 97 B.C. See pp. 678-679, note *f*.

[g] See p. 650, note *a*.

Vir sanctissimus et summa religione ac modestia, Q. Metellus Pius, Q. Fabium Saguntinum? Quid? Hic, qui adest, a quo haec, quae ego nunc percurro, subtilissime sunt omnia perpolita, M. Crassus, non Aveniensem foederatum civitate donavit, homo cum gravitate et prudentia praestans, tum vel nimium parcus in largienda civitate?

51 Hic tu Cn. Pompei beneficium vel potius iudicium et factum infirmare conaris, qui fecit, quod C. Marium fecisse audierat, fecit, quod P. Crassum, quod L. Sullam, quod Q. Metellum, quod M. Crassum,[1] quod denique domesticum auctorem patrem suum facere viderat? Neque vero id in uno Cornelio fecit. Nam et Gaditanum Hasdrubalem ex bello illo Africano et Mamertinos Ovios[2] et quosdam Uticenses et Saguntinos Fabios civitate donavit. Etenim cum ceteris praemiis digni sunt, qui suo labore et periculo nostram rem publicam defendunt, tum certe dignissimi sunt, qui civitate ea donentur, pro qua pericula ac tela

[1] quod M. Crassum *inserted by Baiter.*

[2] obvios *MS.*; Ovios *Baiter. For* Fabios *others have* fabros.

---

[a] A Spanish town put under Roman protection about 231 B.C., before the Second Punic War. In the Sertorian War it remained loyal to Rome when Sertorius overran Spain. See p. 652, note *b*. See p. 679, note *g* for Q. Metellus.

[b] For Avennio (now Avignon) in Gallia Narbonensis see *C.I.L.* xii, pp. 130-135; P.-W. ii. 2281 (Ihm). Originally dependent on Massilia, it received the Latin citizenship, probably from Julius Caesar. See Strabo, iv. 1. 11 (position) and Pliny, *N.H.* iii. 36 (citizenship). The form Avennio is preferable to Avenio.

[c] Cn. Pompeius Strabo, consul 89 B.C. See p. 692, note *c*.

[d] In 81 B.C., against a Marian refugee Cn. Domitius Ahenobarbus and a Numidian leader Iarbas.

[e] The Mamertines (" Sons of Mamers, a Campanian war-

slaves of Gades? Again, did not Quintus Metellus Pius, that most righteous man, most scrupulous, most law-abiding, bestow it upon Quintus Fabius of Saguntum? [a] Again, did not this man here before us, by whom all that I am now touching upon lightly has been elaborated in great detail,—did not Marcus Crassus bestow it upon an inhabitant of Avennio,[b] a federate city, himself a man distinguished for his force of personality and his wisdom and even over-sparing in granting citizenship?

Do you, in this Court, endeavour to invalidate a 51
favour, or rather a decision and a deed of Gnaeus Pompeius, who did what he had heard Gaius Marius had done, what he had heard Publius Crassus, Lucius Sulla, Quintus Metellus, Marcus Crassus had done, and, lastly, that for which he had authority in his own house in what he had seen his father do? [c] Nor did he bestow citizenship in the instance of Cornelius alone. For he bestowed it also upon Hasdrubal of Gades after that war in Africa,[d] upon the Ovii descendants of the Mamertines,[e] and upon certain Fabii of Utica [f] and of Saguntum. In fact, if those who defend our State at the cost of their own toil and danger are worthy of other rewards, then assuredly are they most worthy to be presented with that citizenship, to defend which they have braved dangers and the weapons of war.

god") were Campanians and Bruttians formerly under Agathocles of Syracuse, who, on his death in 289 B.C., occupied Messana and by plunder and massacre set out to seize N.E. Sicily. The Roman alliance with them in 264 B.C. precipitated the First Punic War.

[f] To mention Utica as a *civitas foederata* may be a slip of Cicero's; according to the *lex agraria*, 79 (111 B.C.), it was a *civitas libera*. See L.C.L. *Remains of Old Latin*, iv, pp. 424-425.

subierunt. Atque utinam, qui ubique sunt propugnatores huius imperii, possent in hanc civitatem venire et contra oppugnatores rei publicae de civitate exterminari! Neque enim ille summus poeta noster Hannibalis illam magis cohortationem quam communem imperatoriam voluit esse:

> Hostem qui feriet mihi erit Karthaginiensis
> Quisquis erit: quoiatis siet,

id habent hodie leve et semper habuerunt.[1] Itaque et cives undique fortes viros adsciverunt et hominum ignobilium virtutem persaepe nobilitatis inertiae praetulerunt.

52 XXIII. Habetis imperatorum summorum et sapientissimorum hominum, clarissimorum virorum, interpretationem iuris ac foederum. Dabo etiam iudicum, qui huic quaestioni praefuerunt, dabo universi populi Romani, dabo sanctissimum et sapientissimum iudicium etiam senatus. Iudices cum prae se ferrent palamque loquerentur, quid essent lege Papia de M. Cassio Mamertinis repetentibus iudicaturi, Mamertini publice suscepta causa destiterunt. Multi in civitatem recepti ex liberis foederatisque populis sunt; nemo[2] umquam est de civitate accusatus, quod aut

[1] *The above reading is Baiter's, except that he has* cuius civitatis sit (*so Reid*) *and* hodie (*Halm*) *for* hoc.

[2] Multis in civitatem receptis . . . nemo *Reid, who deletes* sunt.

---

[a] The quotation is from Ennius. See *Remains of Old Latin*, vol. i (L.C.L.), *Ennius and Caecilius*, by E. H. Warmington, pp. 102-103.

[b] It is very doubtful whether there was a special court for trying cases of citizenship.

[c] A *lex Papia* (64 B.C.) made all non-citizens liable to eviction from Rome, but in practice was mainly directed against the unenfranchised residue of Italians, *e.g.* Transpadane

And would that those who, wherever they may be, defend this Empire, could be admitted to our citizenship, and that, on the contrary, those who attack our State could be expelled from the community! For that greatest poet of ours did not intend that that exhortation of Hannibal to his soldiers should be his rather than one common to all commanders:

> He who shall smite the foe, shall be for me a Carthaginian,
> Whoever he may be, whatever his country. . . .[a]

To what country he belongs, commanders regard to-day as a trifling matter, and have always done so. And so they have both taken in as citizens brave men from every country, and have very often preferred merit without birth to nobility without energy.

XXIII. You see how the greatest generals and 52
the wisest men, how the most illustrious personages interpret the law of treaties. I will also put before you a decision of jurors who were appointed to investigate cases of this kind[b]; I will put before you a verdict of the whole Roman People; I will put before you a most righteous and wise decision of the Senate also. When the jurymen clearly showed and openly spoke of the verdict they proposed to give in the case of Marcus Cassius, when the Mamertines were claiming restitution under the Papian Law,[c] the Mamertines gave up the case although the prosecution had been officially undertaken. Many members of free and federate peoples have been admitted to our citizenship, but no one of them has ever been prosecuted for his assumption of citizenship, either

Gauls. See pp. 618-619. The Mamertines, here, were the people of Messana, descendants of the discharged mercenaries who seized the city after Agathocles' death in 289 B.C. See § 51.

populus fundus factus non esset, aut quod foedere civitatis mutandae ius impediretur.

53 Audebo etiam hoc contendere, numquam esse condemnatum, quem constaret ab imperatore nostro civitate donatum. Cognoscite nunc populi Romani iudicium multis rebus interpositum atque in maximis causis re ipsa atque usu comprobatum. Cum Latinis omnibus foedus esse ictum Sp. Cassio Postumo Cominio consulibus quis ignorat? Quod quidem nuper in columna ahenea meminimus post rostra incisum et perscriptum fuisse. Quo modo igitur L. Cossinius Tiburs, pater huius equitis Romani, optimi atque ornatissimi viri, damnato T. Caelio, quo modo ex eadem civitate T. Coponius, civis item summa virtute et dignitate (nepotes T. et C. Coponios nostis), damnato C. Masone civis Romanus est factus?

54 An lingua et ingenio patefieri aditus ad civitatem

---

[a] The evidence for this *foedus Cassianum* of 493 B.C. is as good as evidence for the early fifth century in Italy can be. Since Livy, ii. 33. 9, refers to it as *foedus cum Latinis in columna aenea insculptum*, and as Dionysius of Halicarnassus, vi. 95. 2, gives the terms (but not completely), it seems certain that the inscribed column existed in their time and had been removed from its site in the Forum behind the Rostra (to some temple ?) when structural changes were made at the western end of the Forum by Sulla. For these changes see E. B. van Deman, "The Sullan Forum" (*J.R.S.* xii, pp. 1-31), where a new Senate House and a new Rostra are attributed to Sulla.

[b] He probably fell in 73 B.C. in the war against Spartacus when serving as a *legatus* under a praetor P. Varinius (Plutarch, *Crassus*, 9).

[c] Tibur, whose status was governed by the *foedus Cas-*

because his own people had not "given its consent," or because his right to change his citizenship was debarred by a treaty.

I will even go so far as to maintain that no one has ever been condemned, when it was clear that citizenship had been conferred upon him by one of our commanders. And now let me inform you of a verdict of the Roman People, which has been declared on many occasions and confirmed in fact and practice in most important cases. Who does not know that a treaty was struck with all the Latins in the consulship of Spurius Cassius and Postumus Cominius, which not so long ago we remember was engraved and written out upon a column of bronze standing behind the Rostra? [a] How then did Lucius Cossinius [b] of Tibur,[c] father of this Roman Knight here present, a most excellent and distinguished man, become a Roman citizen after the condemnation of Titus Caelius; how did Titus Coponius also of the same city, a man likewise of the highest merit and position (you know his grandsons Titus and Gaius Coponius [d]), become a Roman citizen after the condemnation of Gaius Maso? [e] 53

Could a way of entry to citizenship be opened up by 54

sianum, remained after the dissolution of the Latin League in 338 B.C. a powerful and autonomous Latin state, until it was enfranchised by the *lex Iulia* (90 B.C.).

[d] The Coponii, mentioned in *Pro Caelio*, 24 (see Austin's second edition, pp. 76-77), were close friends of Dio, an Academic philosopher, who was murdered in Rome (probably in 57 B.C.) when leading an embassy of Alexandrians (see pp. 402-403). C. Coponius was possibly praetor in 49 B.C. (Cicero, *Epp. ad Att.* viii. 12a. 4; Caesar, *Bell. Civ.* iii. 5).

[e] Under Roman criminal law citizenship, among other rewards, could be conferred on the successful prosecutors of certain classes of offenders.

potuit, manu et virtute non potuit? Anne de nobis trahere spolia foederatis licebat, de hostibus non licebat? An, quod adipisci poterant dicendo, id eis pugnando adsequi non licebat? An accusatori maiores nostri maiora praemia quam bellatori esse voluerunt? XXIV. Quodsi acerbissima lege Servilia principes viri et gravissimi et sapientissimi cives hanc Latinis, id est foederatis, viam ad civitatem populi iussu patere passi sunt neque ius est hoc reprehensum Licinia et Mucia lege, cum praesertim genus ipsum accusationis et nomen et eius modi praemium, quod nemo adsequi posset nisi ex senatoris calamitate, neque senatori neque bono cuiquam nimis iucundum esse posset, dubitandum fuit, quin, quo in genere iudicum praemia rata essent, in eodem iudicia imperatorum valerent? Num fundos igitur factos populos Latinos arbitramur aut Serviliae legi aut ceteris, quibus Latinis hominibus erat propositum aliqua ex re praemium civitatis?

55 Cognoscite nunc iudicium senatus, quod semper iudicio est populi comprobatum. Sacra Cereris,

---

[a] Certainty is here difficult, if not impossible. The law may be either (1) the *lex Servilia Caepionis* (106 B.C.), which restored to the Senate complete control of, or granted it a share in, the *quaestio repetundarum*, which the *lex Acilia* (122 B.C.) had reserved for *equites*; or (2) the *lex Servilia Glauciae* (? 104 or 101 B.C.), which restored sole control to the *equites*. The latest commentator on this difficulty (E. Badian, *The Classical Review* (New Series), iv. 2, pp. 101-102), prefers the *lex Servilia Caepionis*, and explains *acerbissima* by the fact that whereas the *lex Acilia* offered to any non-Roman the reward of citizenship for a successful prosecution in the *quaestio repetundarum* (see *Lex Acilia*, 76, 77, 78 in L.C.L. *Remains of Old Latin*, iv, pp. 366-369), the *lex Servilia Caepionis* restricted this privilege to Latins. For

eloquence and talent, but not by exploits and valour? Was it lawful for federate peoples to take spoils from us and not from our enemies? Was it unlawful for them to win by fighting what they could acquire by eloquence? Did our fathers intend that greater rewards should be assured to a prosecutor than to a warrior? XXIV. But if, under that most harsh measure the Servilian Law,[a] our leading men and our most influential and sagacious citizens left this way to citizenship open to Latins, that is, to federated allies[b] by a resolution of the Roman People; and if this privilege was not revoked by the Licinian and Mucian Law,[c] and that too although the very nature of the accusation, although its name, and although a reward which could be won only by the ruin of a senator, could not be too pleasing either to a senator or to any honest man, could there be any doubt that, in a matter in which rewards conferred by jurymen were allowed validity, in that same matter the decisions of commanders should be of equal force? Are we then to think that the Latin peoples "gave their consent" either to the Servilian Law or to other laws, under which a reward of citizenship for some reason or other was offered to individuals of Latin status?

Let me now tell you of a decision of the Senate 55
which has always been confirmed by one of the

this difficulty see also: *C.A.H.* ix, pp. 162-163; Balsdon, *P.B.S.R.* xiv, pp. 98-113; Hill, *The Roman Middle Class*, pp. 122-123.

[b] Except Lavinium the Latin states were not *foederati* in the normal sense of the word. See Sherwin-White, *The Roman Citizenship*, pp. 91-92, who calls Cicero's words "a rhetorical malpractice . . . for the purpose of his case."

[c] See note on § 48, pp. 688-689.

iudices, summa maiores nostri religione confici caerimoniaque voluerunt; quae cum essent adsumpta de Graecia, et per Graecas curata sunt semper sacerdotes et Graeca omnino nominata. Sed cum illam, quae Graecum illud sacrum monstraret et faceret, ex Graecia deligerent, tamen sacra pro civibus civem facere voluerunt, ut deos immortales scientia peregrina et externa, mente domestica et civili precaretur. Has sacerdotes video fere aut Neapolitanas aut Velienses fuisse, foederatarum sine dubio civitatum. Mitto vetera; proxime dico ante civitatem Veliensibus datam de senatus sententia C. Valerium Flaccum praetorem urbanum nominatim ad populum de Calliphana Veliense, ut ea civis Romana esset, tulisse. Num igitur aut fundos factos Velienses aut sacerdotem illam civem Romanam factam non esse aut foedus et a senatu et a populo Romano violatum arbitramur?

56 XXV. Intellego, iudices, in causa aperta minimeque dubia multo et plura et a pluribus peritissimis esse dicta, quam res postularet. Sed id factum est, non

---

[a] According to Dionysius of Halicarnassus (vi. 17. 2) in 496 B.C., at a time of famine in Rome, a dictator L. Postumius vowed a temple to Demeter, Dionysus and Kore, which in 493 B.C. was dedicated by the consul Sp. Cassius to Ceres, Liber and Libera, with whom the Greek deities were identified. The temple, on the slope of the Aventine, near the west end of the Circus Maximus, was of political importance, as the worship of Ceres was essentially plebeian. See Platner and Ashby, *A Topographical Dictionary of Ancient Rome*, pp. 109-110.

[b] See note on § 21.

[c] Velia (Elea), on the coast of Lucania, was founded about 535 B.C. by Phocaeans who, after a defeat at sea, had been ousted from their colony of Alalia in Corsica, founded about 560 B.C., by the Carthaginians and Etruscans. Velia was

People. It was the wish of our fathers, gentlemen, that the rites of Ceres should be performed with the strictest reverence and ceremonial; and since they were introduced from Greece, they were always performed through Greek priestesses and all the terms in use are Greek.[a] But, although they chose from Greece a woman who should expound and perform that Greek rite, yet they saw fit that she should be a citizen when she performed rites on behalf of Roman citizens, so that she might offer prayers to the immortal gods with knowledge that was foreign and from abroad, but in a spirit that was of our own home and citizenship. I observe that these priestesses were nearly always from Neapolis[b] or Velia,[c] which were undoubtedly federate cities. Passing over instances from ancient times, I say that quite recently, before citizenship was conferred upon the people of Velia,[d] Gaius Valerius Flaccus, as city praetor,[e] in accordance with a resolution of the Senate, expressly submitted a proposal to the People that Calliphana of Velia should be made a Roman citizen. Do we then believe either that the people of Velia "gave their consent," or that that priestess was not made a Roman citizen, or that the treaty was violated both by the Senate and by the People of Rome?

XXV. I am aware, gentlemen, that in a case which 56
is so clear and admits of such little doubt far more matters have been discussed and by more learned counsel than the case required. But the purpose of

brought into alliance with Rome in 272 B.C. She supplied ships (Polybius, i. 20. 14; Livy, xxvi. 39. 5).

[d] Under the *lex Iulia*.

[e] In 96 or earlier. He was consul in 93 B.C. (Broughton, *op. cit.* p. 628). See note on § 40.

ut vobis rem tam perspicuam dicendo probaremus, verum ut omnium malevolorum, iniquorum, invidorum animos frangeremus; quos ut accusator incenderet, ut aliqui sermones hominum alienis bonis maerentium etiam ad vestras aures permanarent et in iudicio ipso redundarent, idcirco illa in omni parte orationis summa arte aspergi videbatis, tum pecuniam L. Corneli, quae neque invidiosa est et, quantacumque est, eius modi est, ut conservata magis quam correpta esse videatur, tum luxuriam, quae non crimine aliquo libidinis, sed communi maledicto notabatur, tum Tusculanum, quod Q. Metelli fuisse meminerat et L. Crassi, Crassum emisse de libertino homine, Soterico Marcio, ad Metellum pervenisse de Vennoni Vindici bonis non tenebat. Simul illud nesciebat, praediorum nullam esse gentem, emptionibus ea solere saepe ad alienos homines, saepe ad infimos, non legibus tamquam tutelas
57 pervenire. Obiectum est etiam, quod in tribum

---

[a] In *Epp. ad Att.* vii. 7. 6 (December 50 B.C.) Cicero mentions disapproval of Balbus' gardens (*horti*, on the outskirts of Rome, given him by Pompey) and of his villa at Tusculum. See also *Epp. ad Att.* ix. 13. 8.

[b] Probably Q. Metellus Pius, consul 80 B.C. See note on § 40.

[c] Probably L. Licinius Crassus, consul 95 B.C. See note on § 49.

[d] Possibly an artist whose carvings were mentioned by Seneca, but not with approval (Gellius, xii. 2. 11).

[e] Otherwise unknown. May he have been a house-agent like the Vettius mentioned in the following note?

[f] Such properties were alienable, not entailed. In *Epp.*

this was not that we might by what was said prove to you what was so obvious, but that we might overcome the hostility of all those who are malevolent, unjust, and envious. That, in fact, the prosecutor might excite them further, and that certain idle talk of people who lament over the good fortune of others might also trickle its way to your ears and flood the Court with its influence, was the reason why you saw those accusations sprinkled with consummate art throughout his speech: now the wealth of Lucius Cornelius, which is not such as to make him an object of dislike, and, however great it is, is of such a kind that it would appear to be the result of careful management rather than ill-acquired; now his extravagance against which no particular charge of profligacy but mere general slander was brought forward; now his villa at Tusculum,[a] which the prosecutor remembered once to have belonged to Quintus Metellus [b] and to Lucius Crassus,[c] remembered that Crassus had bought it from a freedman, Sotericus Marcius,[d] but did not remember that it had come into the hands of Metellus from the ownership of Vennonius Vindicius.[e] He also did not know that such properties do not belong to any particular clan, that by purchase they often come into the possession of strangers, often to men of the very lowest rank, and do not devolve like wardships by the rules of law.[f] His admission into 57

ad Att. iv. 5. 2 (after the Conference of Luca) Cicero complained that some nobles resented his owning a town house which had once belonged to Q. Lutatius Catulus, consul 102 B.C. (and later to Sulla), but did not reflect that he had bought it from a house-agent called Vettius, socially as much Cicero's inferior as Catulus was his superior. Vettius belonged to the family of Vettius Scato, a leader of the Marsi in the Social War.

Clustuminam pervenerit; quod hic adsecutus est legis de ambitu praemio minus invidioso, quam qui legum praemiis praetoriam[1] sententiam et praetextam togam consecuntur. Et adoptatio Theophani agitata est, per quam Cornelius nihil est praeterquam propinquorum suorum hereditates adsecutus. XXVI. Quamquam istorum animos, qui ipsi Cornelio invident, non est difficillimum mitigare; more hominum invident, in conviviis rodunt, in circulis vellicant,
58 non illo inimico, sed hoc malo dente carpunt. Qui amicis L. Corneli aut inimici sunt aut invident, ii sunt huic multo vehementius pertimescendi. Nam huic quidem ipsi quis est umquam inventus inimicus aut quis iure esse potuit? Quem bonum non coluit, cuius fortunae dignitatique non concessit? Versatus in intima familiaritate hominis potentissimi in maxi-

[1] senatoriam *Halm.*

---

[a] Although the incorporation of Crustumerium, a Sabine town, is attributed to Tarquinius Priscus (Dion. Hal. iii. 49. 6) and Livy (ii. 21) implies that the *tribus Clustumina* (the 21st), the first to bear a geographical name, was in existence by 495 B.C., Crustumerium can hardly have fallen to Rome before the conquest of Fidenae (425 B.C.). Membership of a rustic tribe was considered more honourable than that of the four urban tribes. The *tribus Clustumina*, highly aristocratic, included Pompey as a member (Dessau 8888).

[b] Illegal canvassing, or bribery at elections, had been recognized as an offence since the *lex Poetelia* of 358 B.C. The penalties under Sulla's *lex Cornelia de ambitu* had been increased by the *lex Calpurnia* (67 B.C.) and by Cicero's law, the *lex Tullia* (63 B.C.).

[c] Promotion to a higher grade in the Senate might be won by successful prosecutors. Members of the various grades, *consulares*, *praetorii*, *aedilicii*, *quaestorii*, were called upon to speak by the presiding magistrate in that order. The white wool of a toga was distinguished by a purple border

the *tribus Clustumina*[a] has also been cast in his teeth; a distinction which he won by privilege of the law concerning illegal canvassing,[b] one less invidious than is theirs who secure by privilege of the laws the right of giving their opinion amongst the praetors and of wearing a purple-bordered toga.[c] His adoption also by Theophanes was severely criticized; but by it Cornelius gained nothing but the right to inherit the property of his own relatives.[d] XXVI. To assuage, however, the feelings of those who envy Cornelius himself is not the most difficult of tasks. They show their envy as people usually do; they backbite him at dinner-parties, pull him to pieces in society, attack him with the tooth not of enmity but of slander.[e] It 58
is those who are either the enemies of the friends[f] of Lucius Cornelius or are envious of them who are much more seriously to be dreaded by him. For, as to my client himself, who has ever been found to be his enemy, or who could justly have been so? To what worthy citizen did he not show respect, to whose good fortune and position did he not show deference? Associated on most intimate terms with a most power-

for curule magistrates and for youths till they reached manhood. See vol. i, p. 233, note *d*.

[d] For Theophanes see p. 616. The meaning of the words *per quam . . . adsecutus* is obscure. Two possibilities are: Theophanes may have married into the family of Balbus; or Theophanes had somehow acquired property which had once been in the family of Balbus and which, by the adoption, returned to the family.

[e] The full force of *illo* and *hoc* can hardly be expressed in translation except at the cost of circumlocution. Cicero seems to mean: "They attack Balbus not with the tooth of envy which you all know and which I do not mean here, but with the tooth of slander which I *am* indicating here."

[f] Pompey and Caesar.

mis nostris malis atque discordiis neminem umquam alterius rationis ac partis non re, non verbo, non vultu denique offendit. Fuit hoc sive meum sive rei publicae fatum, ut in me unum omnis illa inclinatio communium temporum incumberet. Non modo non exsultavit in ruinis nostris vestrisque[1] sordibus Cornelius, sed omni officio, lacrimis, opera, consolatione omnes me absente meos sublevavit.

59 Quorum ego testimonio ac precibus munus hoc meritum huic et, ut a principio dixi, iustam et debitam gratiam refero speroque, iudices, ut eos, qui principes fuerunt conservandae salutis aut dignitatis meae, diligitis et caros habetis, sic, quae ab hoc pro facultate hominis,[2] pro loco facta sunt, et grata esse vobis et probata. Non igitur a suis, quos nullos habet, sed a suorum, qui et multi et potentes sunt, urguetur inimicis; quos quidem hesterno die Cn. Pompeius copiosa oratione et gravi secum, si vellent, contendere iubebat, ab hoc impari certamine atque iniusta con-

60 tentione avocabat. XXVII. Et erit[3] aequa lex et nobis, iudices, atque omnibus, qui nostris familiaritatibus implicantur, vehementer utilis, ut nostras inimicitias ipsi inter nos geramus, amicis nostrorum inimicorum temperemus. Ac, si mea auctoritas satis

[1] vestris nostrisque *MSS.*; nostris lacrimisque *Madvig*, *who omits* lacrimis *below*. *For* sordibus *Reid has* discordiis.
[2] huius *MSS.*; hominis *Müller*; eius *Reid*.
[3] erat *MSS.*; erit *Müller*.

[a] Caesar.
[b] The illegality of Caesar's methods in 59 B.C. and the opposition of the Senate to his coalition with Pompey and Crassus.
[c] The senatorial party.
[d] Cicero's virtual exile from March 58 to September 57 B.C.

ful man [a] at a time of our greatest troubles and disagreements,[b] he never at any time offended one who held different views or belonged to the opposite party [c] either by word or deed, or, in fact, even by a look. It was my destiny, or the destiny of the State, that upon me alone [d] fell all the weight of those critical times which threatened us all. Far from exulting in my downfall and your distress, Cornelius, by every kind of service, by his tears, his efforts, his sympathy, brought relief in my absence to all who were dear to me.

It is upon their evidence and at their entreaty that 59
I return this service, and, as I said at the beginning, repay him the debt of gratitude that is his due, and I hope, gentlemen, that, as you love and cherish those who were foremost in championing my welfare [e] or my honour, so what has been done by him as far as a man could, and as his position [f] allowed, will meet with your esteem and approval. It is not, then, by his own enemies that he is attacked, for he has none, but by the enemies of his friends,[g] who are both many and powerful; whom Gnaeus Pompeius yesterday, in his eloquent and weighty speech, bade attack himself, if they wished, and whom he endeavoured to draw away from this unequal contest and unjust struggle. XXVII. And it will be an equitable rule, 60
gentlemen, and one of very great advantage both to us ourselves and to all who are bound to us by ties of intimacy, that we should confine our enmities to ourselves, and show moderation in dealing with our enemies' friends. And, if my advice had sufficient

[e] With special reference to Cicero's recall from exile.
[f] His friendship with Caesar.
[g] Especially of Pompey and Caesar.

apud illos in hac re ponderis haberet, cum me praesertim rerum varietate atque usu ipso iam perdoctum viderent, etiam ab illis eos maioribus discordiis avocarem. Etenim contendere de re publica, cum id defendas, quod esse optimum sentias, et fortium virorum et magnorum hominum semper putavi neque huic umquam labori, officio, muneri defui. Sed contentio tamdiu sapiens est, quamdiu aut proficit aliquid
61 aut, si non proficit, non obest civitati. Voluimus quaedam, contendimus, experti sumus ; obtenta non sunt. Dolorem alii, nos luctum maeroremque suscepimus. Cur ea, quae mutare non possumus, convellere malumus quam tueri ? C. Caesarem senatus et genere supplicationum amplissimo ornavit et numero dierum novo. Idem in angustiis aerarii victorem exercitum stipendio adfecit, imperatori decem legatos decrevit, lege Sempronia succedendum non censuit. Harum ego sententiarum et princeps et auctor fui neque me dissensioni meae pristinae putavi potius adsentiri quam praesentibus rei publicae temporibus et concordiae convenire. Non idem aliis videtur. Sunt fortasse in sententia firmiores. Reprendo neminem, sed

---

[a] Cicero, having urged that it was unfair to attack Balbus because of political opposition to his friends, now suggests that " they " (*illi. i.e.* the supporters of this attack on Balbus) might do well to follow his own example, and in the public interest give up their opposition, especially to Caesar. The *Pro Balbo*, therefore, was delivered after the *De provinciis consularibus*.

[b] *Vir* and *homo* are variants here due to a desire for variety, as in *Pro Caelio*, 68. See Reid on *Pro Archia*, 16.

weight with them in this matter [a] (especially since they see that I have now learned much from change of circumstances and actual experience), I would endeavour also to draw them away from these more serious feuds. For to engage in political controversy, when defending the cause which you think best, I have always thought to be distinctive of brave and great men,[b] nor have I ever been found wanting in performing this task, this duty, this obligation. But such participation is only prudent so long as it is either of some advantage, or, if not advantageous, if it is not injurious to the State. I desired 61
certain ends, strove for them, did my best: they were not secured. While others were sad at heart, I mourned and grieved.[c] Why do we wish rather to overthrow what we cannot change than to uphold it? The Senate has honoured Gaius Caesar with a public thanksgiving in a most distinguished form, and for an unprecedented number of days. It has also provided pay for his victorious army in spite of the exhaustion of the Treasury, sanctioned ten legates for its commander, voted that he should not be superseded under the Sempronian Law. I introduced and moved these proposals,[d] nor did I think it more advisable to be swayed by my old disagreement with Caesar than to adapt myself to the present needs of the State and to promote concord.[e] Others do not think the same. They are, perhaps, men who hold their opinions more resolutely. I blame no one, but I

[c] Reid, *op. cit.* p. 96, explains the difference between *dolor*, *luctus* and *maeror*; see also Cicero, *Epp. ad Att.* xii. 28. 2.

[d] Cicero, *De prov. cons.* 28; *Epp. ad Fam.* i. 7. 10. See pp. 530-531.

[e] See *De prov. cons.* 43.

adsentior non omnibus neque esse inconstantis puto sententiam tamquam aliquod navigium[1] atque cursum
62 ex rei publicae tempestate moderari. Sed si qui sunt, quibus infinitum sit odium, in quos semel susceptum sit, quos video esse non nullos, cum ducibus ipsis, non cum comitatu adsectatoribusque confligant. Illam enim fortasse pertinaciam non nulli, virtutem alii putabunt, hanc vero iniquitatem omnes cum aliqua crudelitate coniunctam. Sed si certorum hominum mentes nulla ratione, iudices, placare possumus, vestros quidem animos certe confidimus non oratione nostra, sed humanitate vestra esse placatos.

63 XXVIII. Quid enim est, cur non potius ad summam laudem huic quam ad minimam fraudem Caesaris familiaritas valere debeat? Cognovit adulescens; placuit homini prudentissimo; in summa amicorum copia cum familiarissimis eius est adaequatus. In praetura, in consulatu praefectum fabrum detulit; consilium hominis probavit, fidem est complexus, officia observantiamque dilexit. Fuit hic multorum illi laborum socius aliquando; est fortasse nunc non nullorum particeps commodorum. Quae quidem si huic obfuerint apud vos, non intellego, quod bonum cuiquam sit apud tales viros profuturum.

[1] *Reid conjectures that an infinitive like* dirigere *has fallen out.*

---

[a] The rendering of " obstinacy " may be illustrated from words scratched on a sling-bullet found in 1878 at Apsoro on the island of Cherso, south of Fiume (*C.I.L.* i². 887, p. 564), *pertinacia vos radicitus tollet.*

do not agree with everybody, nor do I think it a mark of inconsistency to direct my opinion and course, as one might a ship, according to the weather which the State encounters. But if there be any, of whom I see 62
there are several, who cherish eternal hatred against those whom they have hated once, let them fight with the leaders themselves, not with their attendants and adherents. For the former course some will perhaps consider as obstinacy,[a] others as virtue, but all will consider the latter as injustice, with some admixture of cruelty. But if, gentlemen, there are no means by which we can appease the feelings of certain men, I am fully confident that your minds have been appeased, not by words of mine but by your own human feelings.

XXVIII. For why should not my client's friendship 63
with Caesar be regarded as crowning his glory rather than as causing him the least injury? When he was a young man he became acquainted with Caesar; he attracted a most discerning man; among Caesar's large circle of friends he ranked with his closest intimates. When praetor and when consul Caesar appointed him as his "Chief Engineer,"[b] he approved of the man's judgment, he appreciated his loyalty, he valued highly his services and his respect. At different times Balbus has shared in many of his toils; to-day, possibly, he shares in some of his advantages.[c] And if these matters should harm him in your eyes, I fail to see what advantage any man will gain from virtue with men such as you.

[b] See p. 615, note *d*. This post has no modern military equivalent. For this meaning of *detulit* see Tyrrell and Purser, *loc. cit.*

[c] With the gold of Gaul Caesar rewarded and bribed.

64 Sed, quoniam C. Caesar abest longissime atque in iis est nunc locis, quae regione orbem terrarum, rebus illius gestis imperium populi Romani definiunt, nolite, per deos immortales, iudices, hunc illi acerbum nuntium velle perferri, ut suum praefectum fabrum, ut hominem sibi carissimum et familiarissimum non ob ipsius aliquod delictum, sed ob suam familiaritatem vestris oppressum sententiis audiat. Miseremini eius, qui non de suo peccato, sed de huius summi et clarissimi viri facto, non de aliquo crimine, sed periculo suo de publico iure disceptat. Quod ius si Cn. Pompeius ignoravit, si M. Crassus, si Q. Metellus, si Cn. Pompeius pater, si L. Sulla, si P. Crassus, si C. Marius, si senatus, si populus Romanus, si, qui de re simili iudicarunt, si foederati populi, si socii, si illi antiqui Latini, videte, ne utilius vobis et honestius sit illis ducibus errare quam hoc magistro erudiri. Sed si de certo, de perspicuo, de utili, de probato, de iudicato vobis iure esse constituendum videtis, nolite committere, ut in re tam inveterata quicquam novi sentiatis.
65 Simul et illa, iudices, omnia ante oculos vestros proponite, primum esse omnes etiam post mortem reos clarissimos illos viros, qui foederatos civitate donarunt, deinde senatum, qui hoc iudicavit, populum, qui iussit,

---

[a] See p. 615, note *d* and p. 713, note *b*.
[b] See *Pro Sestio*, 1 and 9 and § 41.
[c] Pompey.

But since Gaius Caesar is so far away, and is at 64
present in places which, if we regard space, are the boundaries of the world, and, if we think of his achievements, are the boundaries of the Roman Empire, do not, gentlemen, in the name of heaven, do not suffer this sad news to be taken to him, do not let him learn that his "Chief Engineer," [a] a man most dear to him and his most intimate friend, has been ruined by your votes, not for any misdeed of his own, but because of his intimacy with him. Pity him who is on trial, at his peril,[b] not because of some offence of his own, but because of an act of this most eminent and most distinguished man [c] here in Court, not because of any accusation, but because of a point of public law. If Gnaeus Pompeius, if his father, if Marcus Crassus, if Quintus Metellus, if Lucius Sulla, if Publius Crassus, if Gaius Marius, if the Senate, if the People of Rome, if those who have acted as judges in similar charges, if states under treaty, if our allies, if those Latins of old were ignorant of this point of law, consider whether it is not more useful and more honourable for you to go astray with them as your guides than to be schooled with the prosecutor as your mentor. But if you are aware that you have to decide upon a point of law that is certain, obvious, valuable, approved, and established, beware of acting so as to form any new opinion about a practice so long established. At the same time, gentlemen, put before 65
your eyes all these considerations: first, that all those illustrious men who have bestowed our citizenship upon the inhabitants of states under treaty, are now on trial after their death; secondly, that there are also on trial the Senate, which has pronounced for that course, the People, who have ordered it, the

iudices, qui adprobarunt. Tum etiam illud cogitate, sic vivere ac vixisse Cornelium, ut, cum omnium peccatorum quaestiones sint, non de vitiorum suorum poena, sed de virtutis praemio in iudicium vocetur. Accedat etiam illud, ut statuatis hoc iudicio, utrum posthac amicitias clarorum virorum calamitati hominibus an ornamento esse malitis. Postremo illud, iudices, fixum in animis vestris tenetote, vos in hac causa non de maleficio L. Corneli, sed de beneficio Cn. Pompei iudicaturos.

[a] Caesar and Pompey.

Judges, who have approved it. Then also remember that Cornelius lives and has lived such a life, that although there are Courts of Inquiry for all offences, he is summoned to trial, not for the punishment of his sins, but for the reward of virtue. Remember also, that by your verdict in this case you are to decide whether you prefer that for the future the friendship of illustrious personages [a] shall be a calamity or a distinction for their fellow-men. Last of all, gentlemen, keep this fixed in your minds, that in this case you are about to judge, not whether Lucius Cornelius has committed an offence, but whether Gnaeus Pompeius has rendered a service.

IV. The Structure of the *Pro Balbo*

Cicero's defence of Balbus is based on two essential ideas [a]: no member of an allied state has ever been prosecuted for his assumption of Roman citizenship, on the ground that his state "had not given its consent," or that his right to change his citizenship was forbidden by a treaty; no one who had become a citizen by favour of a Roman general had ever lost this status by the verdict of a court of law.

Two scholars have expressed these ideas in words which may be appropriately borrowed. "Pompey had conferred the *civitas* on Balbus by virtue of the *lex Gellia Cornelia.* Balbus was a citizen of Gades, and it was argued that, just as the whole of the Gaditani could not become Romans unless a Roman law offering them the franchise had been definitely accepted by them, so an express acceptance of the *lex Gellia Cornelia* by the community was necessary to validate the gift of the *civitas* to Balbus. In other words, it was alleged that the municipality to which a non-Roman belonged had a right of veto on his acceptance of the Roman citizenship. This was of course untenable." [b]

"The doctrine of the *Pro Balbo* is that a man is free

[a] *Pro Balbo*, 52 and 53.

[b] J. S. Reid, "The so-called '*Lex Iulia Municipalis*,'" in *J.R.S.* v, p. 239, n. 4.

to change his *civitas* as he wishes. This law (the *lex Gellia Cornelia*) merely offered something to the *socii* as a gift from outside. Balbus by accepting it ceased to be a Gaditanus." [a]

Cicero dealt ably and effectively with what were presumably the prosecutor's arguments, and did not fail to urge every consideration which could influence the jury in favour of his client. The speech throws light upon the Roman law and practice of citizenship and upon relations with *civitates foederatae*. There is much intricate legal and constitutional argument. Yet while the *Pro Balbo* was a highly competent and successful speech, it cannot be said to be a moving one. Cicero was no longer a free agent: he was speaking to order. Fulsome compliments are of course paid to his masters, especially to Pompey (§§ 2-3; 9-16). In his *commiseratio* (§§ 63-65) Cicero appeals not only for Balbus but also for Caesar and Pompey. A conviction of the unpopular millionaire from Gades would be most unwelcome to his patrons. Cicero's speech lacks the undeniable fervour with which in the *De provinciis consularibus* he belauded Caesar's work in Gaul. We miss, naturally, the vigour and sparkle of the *Pro Caelio*. The defence of Balbus was an unwelcome task, but Cicero's ingenuity was to be still more severely taxed in his defence, two years later, of Gabinius and Vatinius.

The speech falls into four sections:

1. *Sections 1-19.*

These introductory sections, Cicero states, comprise his case. Their purpose is to create sympathy for Balbus, whose title to Roman citizenship conferred

[a] A. N. Sherwin-White, *The Roman Citizenship*, p. 162.

on him by Pompey is being attacked. It is Pompey, therefore, who should be on trial. But to accuse Pompey of any unlawful action is an absurdity ; he is incapable of it. "In my opinion my case is finished. But owing to the faults of our times rather than the nature of this trial, I shall have more to say."

2. *Sections 19-37.*

From Cicero's exposition of his legal arguments it appears that the prosecutor had attacked the enfranchisement of Balbus on three counts. First, he had contended that Pompey's enfranchisement of Balbus was illegal, on the plea that the *lex Gellia Cornelia* had not been adopted by Gades. Cicero's retort was that formal adoption of a Roman law by a community was necessary only when the internal affairs of that community were concerned, and that it was wrong to apply to the enfranchisement of an individual a principle applicable only to the enfranchisement of a whole community. In other words, that Gades should enjoy a right of veto on Balbus' acceptance of a gift from Rome was untenable. It was thus absurd to suppose that Rome was to be debarred from bestowing the honour of her citizenship on individual foreigners who had done her good service. Rome's principle, Cicero continued, governing change of citizenship was that a Roman citizen was free to change his *civitas* as he wished, save that no one could be a citizen of Rome and of other cities at the same time.

Next, Cicero deals with the prosecutor's second and third objections. The prosecutor had maintained that, as many *foedera* forbade any citizen of the *civitas foederata* concerned to become a citizen of

Rome, such a restriction must apply to the treaty with Gades, though not expressly mentioned in it. Cicero replied that such a restriction was not only not found in the treaty itself but would have been overruled [a] by the *lex Gellia Cornelia.* Lastly, the prosecutor submitted that the *lex Gellia Cornelia* contained a saving clause which denied its validity against any enactment by nature *sacrosanctum*, such as the treaty with Gades. Cicero's reply was that the treaty with Gades was not *sacrosanctum*, as it had never been formally ratified by the *populus Romanus.*

3. *Sections 38-55.*

Cicero reinforces his legal arguments by supplementary pleas. He stresses Gades' strong support of Balbus' case and Balbus' loyal interest in his native city. He then dwells at some length on recent enfranchisements of foreigners by Roman commanders: by Marius, whose experience and personality are invoked in aid of Balbus, and by others. Pompey ought not to be attacked for following the example of other commanders. All these grants of citizenship have been approved by our courts and our government. If Roman citizenship can be won as a reward for a successful prosecution, why penalize gallantry in the service of Rome?

4. *Sections 56-65.*

In his peroration Cicero passes to the personal and political setting of the prosecution. Although Balbus' wealth and social success have aroused envious detractors, he has no real enemies and his prosecution is nothing but a veiled attack on Pompey and Caesar.

[a] This is perhaps a dangerous assumption.

Political animus should not be carried to extremes, and political behaviour, as Cicero's own change of attitude towards Caesar had recently demonstrated, should be adapted to the needs of the moment. In enfranchising Balbus Pompey has merely followed admirable precedents, and Balbus should not be condemned either on that score or for having won the friendship of great men.

The following is a summary of the speech.

Sections 1-4.

Although, compared with the distinguished counsel who have already defended Balbus, I have little to offer, I can at least express gratitude to my benefactors (Pompey and Balbus). The brilliance of Pompey's speech was remarkable for one whose military career has denied him opportunity for the study of oratory.

Sections 5-10.

Balbus, who is fighting for the citizenship conferred on him by Pompey as a reward for distinguished services in the Sertorian War, is not charged with any offence. He is bearing the brunt of an attack which properly ought to be made against Pompey. But that Pompey is incapable of any unlawful action should be obvious from his brilliant military career, his ability, his high character.

Sections 11-13.

The legality of Pompey's actions is comparable with the financial integrity of Q. Metellus Numidicus. We should no more call in question Pompey's respect for laws and treaties than the Athenians could doubt the honesty of Xenocrates. The whole of our Empire would cry out in protest if Pompey were accused of violating a treaty wittingly.

Sections 14-16.

The prosecutor, however, suggests that Pompey acted unwittingly. But it is incredible that a man in Pompey's position should show ignorance of the treaty with Gades. Pompey in fact must be well informed of the treaty relations between Rome and foreign states, for his experience abroad must have taught him fully what study imperfectly teaches us at home. That finishes my case. But the ills of our time urge me to continue. Were Pompey a hero of early Rome, and were he now accused before us of breaking a treaty, the charge would be dismissed as absurd.

Sections 17-19.

The speeches of Crassus and Pompey have left nothing new to be said, but from a sense of duty I am complying with their wish that I should speak last for the defence. Since the source of the charge against Balbus is envy of his social success, I ask the jury to regard my client's distinctions as a help not a hindrance to his case.

Sections 19-22.

The source of this case is the *lex Gellia Cornelia* which confirmed a grant of Roman citizenship made by Pompey to certain individuals among whom was Balbus, a citizen of Gades, a *civitas foederata.* The prosecutor, by claiming that *civitates foederatae* were excepted from the operation of the *lex Gellia*

Cornelia unless they had adopted it themselves, argued that this grant of Roman citizenship to Balbus was invalid. I reply that *civitates foederatae* and the Latin states, enjoying an option to adopt such Roman laws as they liked, adopted the *lex Furia*, the *lex Voconia*, and many other civil laws. That such adoption was not compulsory is clear from the hesitation felt at Heraclea and Neapolis to accept Roman citizenship under the *lex Iulia* (90 B.C.). Formal adoption of a Roman law was necessary when its operation would affect the internal affairs of an allied state, but was not required when the interests of Rome alone were concerned. The privilege enjoyed by *civitates foederatae* of adopting Roman laws must in no way restrict the power of Rome to reward by citizenship any special services rendered to her by individual members of such states.

Sections 23-27.

It would be deplorable for Rome to be deprived of the aid in war of citizens of *civitates foederatae* like Massilia, Gades and Saguntum, and for the citizens of such states to be debarred from winning Roman citizenship, a reward which is open to members of tributary states, to enemies who have gone over to Roman commanders and even to the slave population. It is illogical to refuse the people of Gades that privilege of citizenship which we have made open even to our enemies. We should be resentful if Gades formally forbade its citizens to serve Rome at their own risks. But that is virtually the effect of the prosecutor's contention, for he would empower the people of Gades to prevent those who volunteer for Roman service from gaining their due reward.

Sections 27-31.

Our legal principle governing change of citizenship is that Roman citizens enjoy complete freedom to migrate and acquire citizenship in another state, save that no one can be a citizen of Rome and of other cities at the same time. For example, a Roman citizen can become a citizen of Gades by exercising the right of exile (*ius exsilii*), or by surrender of his Roman citizenship. Conversely, there is no reason why a citizen of Gades should not be allowed to become a citizen of Rome. The closer the political relations between Rome and foreign states, the more closely should these states be associated with us by the bonds of privilege, reward, and citizenship. But between Roman and foreign practice in this matter there is this difference that, whereas no Roman can be a citizen of Rome and of another city at the same time, a foreigner who is not a Roman citizen can hold the citizenship of many other cities. A citizen of a Greek city, for example, can at the same time be a citizen of other cities. A Roman citizen, however, on acquiring, say, Athenian citizenship, would lose his Roman citizenship unless he should recover it by exercising *ius postliminii*, the right of "subsequent return." Foreigners enjoy an unrestricted right to acquire Roman citizenship if Rome chooses to confer it. By the admission to Roman citizenship of members of Italian states, an admirable practice traditionally begun by Romulus, the power of Rome has been firmly established and extended. The conferment of Roman citizenship upon members of Italian states would not have been regarded as an infringement of any treaty concluded with them.

Sections 32-37.

On the analogy of treaties with some Gallic and Illyrian tribes which contain a clause forbidding Rome to confer citizenship on any of their members, the prosecutor argues that such a veto must apply to the treaty with Gades, though not specifically mentioned in it. I reply that such a restriction is not only not found in the treaty, but would have been overruled by the *lex Gellia Cornelia.* " But," says the prosecutor, " the *lex Gellia Cornelia* contained a clause providing that it should not be valid against an enactment which was in its nature *sacrosanctum,* such as the treaty with Gades." To this I reply that, even if this clause were taken literally, it could not apply to the treaty with Gades, which was not *sacrosanctum* because it had been informally negotiated by a Roman centurion, L. Marcius Septimus, and formally renewed or concluded (78 B.C.) by the Senate, not by the Assembly. Even if the treaty had been formally ratified by a vote of the Assembly, and thereby made *sacrosanctum,* there was no clause in it forbidding the conferment of Roman citizenship upon a citizen of Gades. The treaty contained two provisions [a] only : " There shall be a holy and everlasting peace (between Rome and Gades) " ; and, " Let them (the people of Gades) uphold the greatness of the Roman People in a friendly way." As for these two provisions I can disprove the prosecutor's interpretation of a word (*comiter*) contained in one of them.

Sections 38-44.

It is unnecessary to argue the point whether under

[a] An incomplete statement, for we know from Livy (xxxii. 2) of another provision.

the treaty with Gades Rome has no right to confer her citizenship upon Balbus, for the people of Gades support him enthusiastically. Despite their foreign origin they have nobly come to our aid both in war and in other times of hardship, and they have been true to their treaty. They demand that their bravest should be privileged to serve under us, and they would resent the exclusion of such men from citizenship as a reward. They support Balbus in every way, and they have condemned and fined his prosecutor. Balbus retains his affections for Gades and advances its interests in Rome. Caesar, when governor in Spain (61–60 B.C.), conferred many benefits upon Gades at the instance of Balbus. Leading men of Gades, therefore, have come to support a loyal champion of their city. I must reassure Gades itself, her citizens here in court and the jury, that the legal point now to be decided has never been in doubt.

Sections 45-51.

Since military commanders are more skilled than even the most practised lawyers in the interpretation of treaties, C. Marius must rank as a most competent interpreter. If Balbus is condemned, the action of Marius in enfranchising M. Annius Appius of Iguvium and two cohorts from Camerinum must also be condemned. That experienced commander, who never doubted that any treaty could prevent him from acting for the good of the State, declared that in the treaties with Iguvium and Camerinum there was no clause forbidding the enfranchisement of their citizens. Of those upon whom Marius had conferred citizenship T. Matrinius, of Spoletium, a Latin colony, alone was prosecuted under the *lex Licinia Mucia* (95 B.C.). His prosecutor did not claim that Spoletium had not "given consent," but maintained that Marius' grant of citizenship to Matrinius should be regarded as invalid because Saturninus' law (100 B.C.) empowering Marius to confer Roman citizenship upon three members of each colony to be founded under that law had been annulled by the Senate. Although the prosecution of Matrinius has nothing in common with that of Balbus, Marius won his acquittal by the force of his personality. May his memory and his prestige help to win Balbus' acquittal also!

Many other precedents also uphold Pompey's action in enfranchising Balbus: Cn. Pompeius Strabo, the father of Pompey, P. Licinius Crassus, L. Sulla, Q. Metellus Pius, and M. Licinius Crassus, one of Balbus' defending counsel, all of these commanders have enfranchised members of *civitates foederatae*. Pompey ought not to be attacked in this court for following the example of other commanders, among whom was his own father. He has enfranchised not only Balbus, but also Hasdrubal of Gades, the Ovii of Messana and certain Fabii of Utica and Saguntum. In fact, all men who have served Rome gallantly are worthy of her citizenship, whatever their country.

Sections 52-55.

Grants of Roman citizenship have always been upheld by our courts and our government. For example, information of a verdict which a Roman jury proposed to give dissuaded the people of Messana from an attempt under the *lex Papia* (64 B.C.) to evict from Rome M. Cassius as no true Roman citizen. Two citizens of Tibur, a city whose relations with Rome were based on the *foedus Cassianum* (493 B.C.), L.

Cossinius and T. Coponius, won Roman citizenship by successful prosecutions. If citizenship could thus be won by eloquence, why should bravery be a disqualification? If the *lex Servilia* (either of Caepio, 106 B.C., or of Glaucia, ? 104 or 101 B.C.) entitled Latins to win Roman citizenship as a reward for securing a conviction in a prosecution before the *quaestio repetundarum*, and if this privilege was not revoked by the *lex Licinia Mucia* (95 B.C.), should not an award of citizenship by commanders in the field be allowed the same validity as one arising from the verdict of a jury? Neither the *lex Servilia* nor the other laws offering citizenship to Latins for some similar reason were formally adopted by the Latin communities.

The rites of Ceres were always celebrated for us by Greek priestesses, generally from Neapolis or Velia, formerly allied cities. Recently (96 B.C. or earlier), before citizenship was conferred on Velia (90 B.C.), Calliphana of Velia was made a Roman citizen by vote of the Assembly on a resolution of the Senate, in order that she might officiate for Roman citizens as a Roman citizen. It is incredible that the people of Velia "gave consent" to this enfranchisement, or that the treaty with Velia was thereby broken both by the Senate and by the People.

Sections 56-65.

So thorough a defence of Balbus is intended to defeat those who are envious of his social success, and whose malevolence the prosecutor has sought to inflame. Wealth, extravagance, a villa at Tusculum, admission into the *tribus Clustumina*, adoption by Theophanes, all these have been cast in his teeth. Slanderers are easily dealt with; less so are the enemies of his friends. Balbus himself has no real enemies and, though he was associated with Caesar at a time of violent political conflict (59–58 B.C.), he never gave offence to any member of the senatorial party. During my exile Balbus was kindness itself to my family, a service which I am now repaying. His worst enemies are attacking Pompey through him, but, if I may speak from my own recent experience, they would be well advised to drop that unequal struggle. Political conflicts, commendable though they may be to a point, should not be carried to the disadvantage of the State.

I abandoned my unsuccessful opposition to Caesar, for I myself proposed the great distinctions which the Senate has recently conferred upon him. Political behaviour should be adjusted to the conditions of the moment. The enemies of Pompey and Caesar should not attack adherents like Balbus, but those leaders themselves. Balbus' friendship with Caesar, the reward of his services, should stand to his credit. Do not let Caesar hear that Balbus has been condemned, and not for any crime but for his association with him. Pompey's act of enfranchisement, for which Balbus is on trial, is strongly supported by precedents. Indeed this charge is an indictment of many famous commanders, some now dead, of the Senate, of the Roman People, of our jurors, of states allied with us. Save Balbus from condemnation, not for any offence but for having won the friendship of illustrious men. " You are about to judge, not whether Lucius Cornelius has committed an offence, but whether Gnaeus Pompeius has rendered a service."

V. The Later Career of L. Cornelius Balbus

Balbus' later career may now be traced. After his acquittal he continued as Caesar's agent in Rome, but occasionally visited him in Gaul, as for example in 54 B.C. when he made two journeys.[a] Cicero, who was then on the best of terms[b] with Balbus, was grateful to him for his interest in his brother Quintus,[c] then one of Caesar's officers, and in C. Trebatius Testa,[d] a young lawyer who was seeking his fortune in Gaul.

During the drift towards civil war Balbus still appears as a loyal Caesarian, and, though ready to expostulate with such leading Pompeians as Q. Metellus Scipio,[e] he was at the same time in friendly association with them.[f] On the eve of war his diplomacy was employed, but in vain, in seconding Caesar's efforts to win over Cicero.[g] In the war itself he took no active part, but continued to keep on good terms with both sides, and on better terms with the stronger. In spite of his obligations to Pompey and to Lentulus Crus (consul 49 B.C.), he was soon busy with Caesarian propaganda. Caesar's famous letter, proclaiming clemency and generosity as novel methods of victory in civil war, was addressed to Balbus and to his colleague C. Oppius, although it was intended for a wider circulation.[h] But the frequent letters which passed between Cicero and Balbus before the former left for Pompey's camp in June 49 B.C. show Cicero

[a] Reid, *op. cit.* p. 8. Tyrrell and Purser, *op. cit.* p. lxxiv.

[b] *Epp. ad Quintum fratrem*, iii. 1. 9.

[c] *Epp. ad Quintum fratrem*, ii. 10. (12 L.C.L.) 4.

[d] *Epp. ad Fam.* vii. 6. 1.

[e] *Epp. ad Fam.* viii. 9. 5.

[f] *Epp. ad Att.* vii. 4. 2.

[g] *Epp. ad Att.* vii. 3. 11.

[h] *Epp. ad Att.* ix. 7c.

as impervious to his attempts to win him to neutrality and, at long last, as angered by Balbus' ingratitude to Pompey and his open adoption of Caesar's cause.[a] Cicero's growing dislike of Balbus was intensified by his attempts to become a senator.[b] When, after Pharsalus, Cicero returned to an unhappy sojourn of eleven months at Brundisium, he received from Balbus little encouragement concerning Caesar's future attitude towards him.

During the remainder of Caesar's dictatorship Cicero tempered his dislike [c] of Balbus by the need to keep on good terms with him. Business dealings and the interests of friends are now the main topics of their correspondence. Since Caesar claimed that the Senate had refused to co-operate with him in public administration, he entrusted all business [d] to Balbus and Oppius as his personal representatives, although they had no rank in the government. Balbus was autocratic : in his hands were *condiciones pacis et arbitria belli.*[e] His activities were automatically ratified by Caesar.[f] It has been recently demonstrated [g] that Balbus, not the Senate, was in a

[a] *Epp. ad Att.* ix. 13. 8.

[b] *Epp. ad Att.* x. 11. 4 (May 49 B.C.). He was probably not a senator ; *cf.* Syme, *The Roman Revolution*, p. 81 ; *pace* Tyrrell and Purser, *loc. cit.* p. lxxvi. Münzer, *loc. cit.* 1266, suspends judgment.

[c] *Epp. ad Att.* xii. 2. 2 (May 46 B.C.) : " At Balbus aedificat ; τί γὰρ αὐτῷ μέλει ; verum si quaeris, homini non recta sed voluptaria quaerenti nonne βεβίωται ? "

[d] Gellius, *N.A.* xvii. 9. 1.

[e] Tacitus, *Annals*, xii. 60.

[f] *Epp. ad Fam.* vi. 8. 1 ; 18. 1.

[g] M. Grant, *From Imperium to Auctoritas* (Cambridge, 1946), pp. 5-6. Balbus' name appears in the abbreviation *BAL* on the earliest bronze Caesarian issue of coins minted at Corduba.

position to grant the right of coinage to Cn. Iulius, a quaestor of Further Spain.

On the murder of Caesar, Balbus temporarily left the scene, but, when Octavian appeared at Naples in April 44 B.C., Balbus was at hand and ready to be secured by Caesar's heir as agent and financier.[a] But we have no record of his services to Octavian, and for four years he disappeared from history.[b] But that he was appointed *consul suffectus* [c] at the end of 40 B.C. suggests that he thereby received a reward for undisclosed activity. According to Pliny [d] he was the first foreigner to attain this dignity.

The date of his death is unknown, but was probably not much later than that of Atticus, who died aged seventy-seven on 31 March 32 B.C.[e] Under Balbus' will a legacy of twenty-five denarii came to every citizen of Rome, a sum as large as Caesar had bequeathed.[f] It is probable that he suggested to A. Hirtius the completion of Caesar's *Commentarii de Bello Gallico*, the eighth book of which was dedicated to him. He left memoirs [g] from which a story told in Suetonius, *Div. Iul.* 81, was probably derived.

[a] *Epp. ad Att.* xiv. 10. 3.

[b] Syme, *The Roman Revolution*, p. 131, *pace* Reid, *op. cit.* p. 9 and Butler and Cary, Suetonius, *Div. Iul.* p. 141, who make him praetor early in the Second Triumvirate. Broughton, *The Magistrates of the Roman Republic*, ii, p. 550, denies him a praetorship.

[c] Dio Cassius, xlviii. 32. 1; Pliny, *N.H.* vii. 136; *C.I.L.* (ed. 2), i, p. 158. A dedication from Capua to Balbus as its *patronus* (*C.I.L.* x. 3854) dates to his consulship or later.

[d] Pliny, *N.H.* vii. 136.

[e] Nepos, *Vita Attici*, 21. 4. The last mention of Balbus is in Cicero, *Epp. ad Att.* xvi. 11. 8 (5 November 44 B.C.).

[f] Dio Cassius, xlviii. 32. 2.

[g] Called *Balbi ephemeris* in Apoll. Sid. *Ep.* ix. 14. 7.

This able Spaniard excelled in diplomacy. "In the last decade of the Republic there can have been few intrigues conducted and compacts arranged without the knowledge and the mediation of Balbus." [a] To him fell a full part in the making of contemporary history : he was employed in the formation of Caesar's coalition at the end of 60 B.C. ; the Civil Wars saw him active as a negotiator ; he figured in the introduction of Cabinet Government during the dictatorship of Caesar ; he served Octavian. He and Oppius were the predecessors of the civil servants of the Principate. The first foreigner who rose to a consulship, he was a portent of that later age when Trajan, a Spaniard married to a woman from Nemausus in southern Gaul, became the first emperor of provincial origin.

[a] R. Syme, *op. cit.* p. 72.

BIBLIOGRAPHY

I. Texts and Commentaries

Austin, R. G. *M. T. Ciceronis pro M. Caelio oratio.* Oxford (1933, 2nd edition, 1952).

Butler, H. E., and Cary, M. *M. T. Ciceronis de provinciis consularibus oratio ad senatum.* Oxford, 1924.

Clark, A. C. *M. T. Ciceronis orationes pro Sex. Roscio, etc.* Oxford (1905, new impr. 1908).

Holden, H. A. *M. T. Ciceronis pro P. Sestio oratio.* London (1883, 9th impr. 1933).

Klotz, A., und Schöll, F. *M. T. Ciceronis scripta*, vol. vii. Leipzig (Teubner), 1919.

Long, G. *Ciceronis orationes*, vols. iii, 1856, and iv, 1858. London.

Müller, C. F. W. *Ciceronis scripta*, ii. 3. Leipzig (Teubner), 1904.

Peterson, W. *M. T. Ciceronis orationes cum senatui gratias egit, etc.* Oxford, 1910.

Pocock, L. G. *A Commentary on Cicero in Vatinium.* London, 1926.

Reid, J. S. *M. T. Ciceronis pro L. Cornelio Balbo oratio.* Cambridge (1878, new impr. 1908).[a]

II. Principal Works consulted or referred to

Altheim, F. *Lex Sacrata: Die Anfänge der plebeischen Organisation.* Amsterdam, 1939.

Asconius Pedianus Q., *Orationum Ciceronis quinque enarratio.* A. C. Clark, Oxford, 1907.

[a] Professor J. S. Reid's widow presented to the Cambridge University Library an interleaved copy of this edition with full manuscript notes by the editor (Adv. d. 93. 3).

Badian, E. " *Lex Servilia.*" *Classical Review*, New Series, vol. iv. 2 (1954), pp. 101-102.

Balsdon, J. P. V. D. " The History of the Extortion Court at Rome, 123–70 B.C." *Papers of the British School at Rome*, xiv (1938), pp. 98-114.

" Consular Provinces under the Late Republic." *Journal of Roman Studies*, xxix (1939), pp. 57-73 ; 167-183.

" Roman History, 58–56 B.C. Three Ciceronian Problems." *Journal of Roman Studies*, xlvii (1957), pp. 15-16.

Barker, Ernest. *From Alexander to Constantine* (*Passages and Documents illustrating the History of Social and Political Ideas, 336 B.C.–A.D. 337*). Oxford, 1956.

Boyancé, P. " *Cum dignitate otium.*" *Revue des Études anciennes*, xliii (1941), pp. 172-191.

Broughton, T. R. S. *The Magistrates of the Roman Republic*, vol. ii (99–31 B.C.). New York, 1952.

Cambridge Ancient History (edited by S. A. Cook, F. E. Adcock, M. P. Charlesworth). Vol. ix, chapter xii. Cambridge, 1932.

Cary, M. *A History of Rome.* London (2nd ed. 1954).

" Asinus germanus." *Classical Quarterly*, xvii (1923), pp. 103-107.

Ciaceri, E. *Cicerone e i suoi tempi*, vol. ii. Rome, 2nd edition, 1941.

Cichorius, C. *Das Offiziercorps eines römischen Heeres aus dem Bundesgenossenkriege. Römische Studien*, pp. 130-185. Berlin, 1922.

Clark, A. C. *Cicero, Pro T. Annio Milone.* Oxford, 1895.

Cochrane, C. N. *Christianity and Classical Culture*, pp. 44-45. Oxford, 1940.

Cousin, J. " *Lex Lutatia de Vi.*" *Revue historique de Droit français et étranger*, 1943, pp. 88-94.

Denniston, J. D. *M. T. Ciceronis in M. Antonium Orationes Philippicae, Prima et Secunda.* Oxford, 1926. (Appendix iii, pp. 180-186.)

Dessau, H. *Inscriptiones Latinae Selectae.* Berlin, 1892, etc. Nos. 8888, 9461 (vol. iii. 2, 1916).

Drexler, H. " Zu Ciceros Rede *pro Caelio.*" *Nachrichten*

von der Akademie der Wissenschaften in Göttingen, Phil.-Hist. Kl., 1944, pp. 1-32.

Frank, Tenney. *Catullus and Horace*. Oxford (Blackwell), 1928.

Gelzer, M. *Die Nobilität der römischen Republic*. Leipzig-Berlin, 1912.

Grant, M. *From Imperium to Auctoritas*, pp. 5-6. Cambridge, 1946.

Greenidge, A. H. J. *The Legal Procedure of Cicero's Time*. Oxford, 1901.

Roman Public Life. London, 1901.

" The Repeal of the *Lex Aelia Fufia*." *Classical Review*, vii (1893), pp. 158-161.

Hardy, E. G. " The Transpadane Question and the Alien Act of 65 or 64 B.C." *Journal of Roman Studies*, vi (1916), pp. 77-82.

Cicero's Argument in Pro Balbo, 19-22, in *Some Problems in Roman History*. Oxford, 1924, pp. 326-330.

Haskell, H. J. *This was Cicero : Modern Politics in a Roman Toga*. New York, 1942 ; London, [1943].

Heinze, R. " Cicero's Rede *pro Caelio*." *Hermes*, lx (1925), pp. 193-258.

Heitland, W. E. *The Roman Republic*, vol. iii. Cambridge (1909, new impr. 1923).

Hill, H. *The Roman Middle Class in the Republican Period*. Oxford (Blackwell), 1952.

Holmes, T. Rice. *The Roman Republic and the Founder of the Empire*, vols. i and ii. Oxford, 1923.

Hough, J. N. " The *Lex Lutatia* and the *Lex Plautia de Vi*." *American Journal of Philology*, li (1930), pp. 135-147.

How, W. W. *Cicero, Select Letters*, vol. ii (notes). Oxford, 1926.

" Cicero's Ideal in his *De Republica*." *Journal of Roman Studies*, xx (1930), pp. 24-42.

Kroll, W. *Die Kultur der ciceronischen Zeit*, vols. i and ii. Leipzig, 1933.

Last, H. M. " The Servian Reforms." *Journal of Roman Studies*, xxxv (1945), esp. p. 32.

Marsh, F. B. *A History of the Roman World from 146 to 30 B.C.* 2nd ed. revised by H. H. Scullard. London, 1952.
The Founding of the Roman Empire. Oxford (2nd ed. 1927).
"The Policy of Clodius from 58 to 56 B.C." *Classical Quarterly*, xxi (1927), pp. 30-35.

McDonald, W. F. "Clodius and the *Lex Aelia Fufia.*" *Journal of Roman Studies*, xix (1929), pp. 164-179.

Meyer, E. *Caesars Monarchie und das Principat des Pompeius.* Stuttgart (3rd ed. 1922).

Münzer, F. *Römische Adelsparteien und Adelsfamilien.* Stuttgart, 1920.

Nisbet, R. G. *M. T. Ciceronis de domo sua oratio.* Oxford, 1939.

Oxford Classical Dictionary. Oxford, 1949.

Pauly-Wissowa-Kroll. *Real-Encyclopädie der classischen Altertumswissenschaft.* Stuttgart, 1894– .
Gelzer, M. *s.v.* "M. Tullius Cicero," No. 29. Vol. viiA, cols. 935-947.
Gundel, H. *s.v.* "P. Vatinius," No. 3. Second Series. Vol. viiiA 1, cols. 495-520.
Laqueur, R. *s.v.* "Theophanes," No. 1. Second Series. Vol. v, cols. 2090-2127.
Münzer, F. *s.v.* "Caelius," No. 35. Vol. iii, cols. 1266-1272.
s.v. "L. Cornelius Balbus," No. 69. Vol. iv, cols. 1260-1268.
s.v. "P. Sestius," No. 6. Second Series. Vol. ii, cols. 1886-1890.
Strasburger, H. *s.v.* "Optimates." Vol. xviii. 1, cols. 773-798.
Weinstock, St. *s.v.* "Obnuntiatio." Vol. xvii, cols. 1726-1735.
Wissowa, G. *s.v.* "Auspicium." Vol. ii, cols. 2580-2587.

Peterson, W. "Cicero's *Post Reditum* and other Speeches." *Classical Quarterly*, iv (1910), pp. 166-177.

Platner, S. B., and Ashby, T. *A Topographical Dictionary of Ancient Rome.* Oxford, 1929.

Pocock, L. G. " Publius Clodius and the Acts of Caesar.' *Classical Quarterly*, xviii (1924), pp. 59-64.
" A Note on the Policy of Clodius." *Classical Quarterly*, xix (1925), pp. 182-184.
Reid, J. S. " The so-called '*Lex Iulia Municipalis*.'" *Journal of Roman Studies*, v (1915), p. 239, n. 4.
Remy, E. " *Dignitas cum otio*." *Musée Belge*, xxxii (1928), pp. 113-127.
Richards, G. C. *Cicero, a Study*. London, 1935.
Scullard, H. H. *Roman Politics 220–150* B.C. Oxford, 1951, pp. 27-28 and Appendix iv, pp. 290-303.
Sherwin-White, A. N. *The Roman Citizenship*. Oxford, 1939.
Shuckburgh, E. S. *The Letters of Cicero*, vols. i and ii. London, 1899.
Sihler, E. G. *Cicero of Arpinum*. Yale Univ. Press, 1914.
Skutsch, O. " Cicero, *Pro Sestio*, 72." *Classical Review*, lvi (1942), pp. 116-117, and *ibid.* lvii (1943), p. 67.
Smith, R. E. *The Failure of the Roman Republic*. Cambridge, 1955.
Stevenson, G. H. " Cn. Pompeius Strabo and the Franchise Question." *Journal of Roman Studies*, ix (1919), pp. 95-101.
Strachan-Davidson, J. L. *Cicero and the Fall of the Roman Republic*. London (1894, 2nd ed. 1925).
Problems of the Roman Criminal Law, vols. i and ii. Oxford, 1912.
Suetonius Tranquillus, C. *Divus Iulius*. Butler, H. E., and Cary, M. Oxford, 1927.
Syme, R. *The Roman Revolution*. Oxford, 1939.
Taylor, L. R. *Party Politics in the Age of Caesar*. Berkeley, 1949.
Tucker, G. M. " Cicero, *Pro Sestio*, 72." *Classical Review*, lvi (1942), p. 68.
Tyrrell, R. Y., and Purser, L. C. *The Correspondence of Cicero*, Dublin, vols. ii (2nd ed. 1906), iii (2nd ed. 1914), iv (2nd ed. 1918), v (2nd ed. 1915).
Valeton, I. M. J. " De modis auspicandi Romanorum." *Mnemosyne*, vols. xvii and xviii, 1889–1890.

Warde Fowler, W. *Social Life at Rome in the Age of Cicero*. London, 1909.
Warmington, E. H. *Remains of Old Latin*. Loeb Classical Library. London. Vols. i (1935), ii (1936), iii (1938), iv (1940).
Webster, T. B. L. *Cicero, Pro L. Flacco*. Oxford, 1931.
Wegehaupt, H. *Die Bedeutung und Anwendung von dignitas*. Diss. Breslau, 1932.
Weinstock, S. " Clodius and the *Lex Aelia Fufia*." *Journal of Roman Studies*, xxvii (1937), pp. 215-222.
Wilkinson, L. P. *Letters of Cicero : a New Selection in Translation*. London (Bles), 1949.
Willems, P. *Le Sénat de la République romaine*, vols. i and ii. Paris, 1878.
Williams, W. Glynn. *Cicero, The Letters to his Friends*. Loeb Classical Library, vols. i-iii. London, 1927–1929.
Winstedt, E. O. *Cicero, The Letters to Atticus*. Loeb Classical Library, vols. i-iii. London, 1913–1919.
Wirszubski, Ch. *Libertas as a Political Idea at Rome during the Late Republic and Early Principate*. Cambridge, 1950.
" Cicero's *Cum Dignitate Otium* : a Reconsideration." *Journal of Roman Studies*, xliv (1954), pp. 1-13.

III. Translation

A free translation in French of these five speeches is to be found in *Collection des auteurs latins avec la traduction en français publiés sous la direction de M. Nisard : Œuvres complètes de Cicéron*, vol. iii, Paris, 1852, pp. 54-170.

Additions to the Bibliography

Austin, R. G. *M. T. Ciceronis pro M. Caelio Oratio.* Oxford (3rd edition, 1959).

Badian, E. *Foreign Clientelae (264–70 B.C.).* Oxford, 1958.

Balsdon, J. P. V. D. "*Auctoritas, Dignitas, Otium.*" *Classical Quarterly* (liv), N.S. x. 1. May, 1960, pp. 43-50.

"*Roman History, 65–50 B.C.: Five Problems.*" *Journal of Roman Studies*, lii (1962), pp. 134-141.

Cousin, J. Cicéron : Discours : Tome xv, "*Pour Caelius, sur les Provinces Consulaires, pour Balbus,*" Texte établi et traduit. Collection des Universités de France. Association Guillaume Budé (Paris, Société d'Édition " Les Belles Lettres," 1962).

Dorey, T. A. "Cicero, Clodia and the *Pro Caelio*" (*Greece and Rome*, 2nd series, v, 1958, pp. 175-180).

Lacey, W. K. "Cicero, *Pro Sestio*, 96-143." *Classical Quarterly* (lvi), N.S. xii. 1. May, 1962, pp. 67-71.

Nisbet, R. G. M. *In L. Calpurnium Pisonem Oratio.* Edited with text, introduction, and commentary. Oxford, 1961.

"Cicero, *De provinciis consularibus*, 6." *Classical Review* (lxxv), N.S. xi. 3. Dec. 1961, p. 201.

Shackleton Bailey, D. R. "*Sex. Clodius–Sex. Cloelius.*" *Classical Quarterly* (liv), N.S. x. 1. May 1960, pp. 41-42.

INDEX

Fairly full references to persons, places and certain topics are given, the footnotes being covered as well as the text. Persons are entered under their gentile names (*e.g.* for Crassus, *see under* Licinius Crassus), and the years of their most important tenures of office are supplied. References to the following have been excluded from the Index: Table of Events in Roman Politics from 60 B.C. to 56 B.C. (pp. xv-xxiv); The Structure of the *Pro Caelio* (pp. 508-515); Summary of the *De provinciis consularibus* (pp. 604-610); The Structure of the *Pro Balbo* (pp. 718-730).

The numbers refer to pages.

Bona Dea, 377, 569 n.
Bosporus, 546
Brundisium, 449 n., 732
Bruti, 678
Bruttians, 456 n.
Byzantii, Byzantium, 390, 543 n., 544, 545 n., 546

Caecilius Metellus Celer, Q. (praet. 63, cos. 60), 378-384, 400, 446, 447 n., 478-482, 485 n.
Caecilius Metellus Creticus, Q. (cos. 69), 379
Caecilius Metellus Delmaticus, L. (cos. 119), 563 n.
Caecilius Metellus Macedonicus, Q. (praet. 148, cos. 143), 542 n.
Caecilius Metellus Nepos, Q. (trib. 62, praet. 60, cos. 57), 379, 392-395, 481 n., 566
Caecilius Metellus Numidicus, Q. (cos. 109), 563 n., 630 n., 636
Caecilius Metellus Pius, Q. (cos. 80), 614, 624, 630, 631 n., 679 n., 694, 704, 714
Caecilius Metellus Pius Scipio, Q. (cos. 52), 518, 731
Caecilius Statius, comic dramatist, 450 n., 452 n., 511
Caelius, T., 698
Caelius Rufus, M. (trib. 52), 398-507 *passim*, 515-522, 617
Caelius Rufus, the elder, 398-399, 408, 426
Caesernius, C., 494, 495 n., 496
Caesius, P., of Ravenna, 624, 692, 693 n.
Calidius, M., 518
Calliphana, of Velia, 623, 702
Calpurnia, fourth and last wife of Julius Caesar, 548 n.
Calpurnius Bestia, L. (trib. 62), 400, 404-405, 407 n., 414 n., 424 n., 436, 437 n., 463 n., 476 n., 500 n., 502 n., 568 n.
Calpurnius Bibulus, M. (cos. 59), 381, 383, 391, 444 n., 537, 584 n., 596 n., 597 n., 598 n., 599 n., 601 n.
Calpurnius Piso Caesoninus, L. (cos. 58), 384, 388, 480 n., 533-536, 538 n., 540, 543 n., 544-548, 552 n., 554-560, 568, 569 n., 586, 593 n.
Calventius, maternal grandfather of L. Calpurnius Piso, 547 n.
Camerinum, 622, 687 n., 688 n.
Camertes, of Camerinum, 622, 675 n., 686, 687 n., 688, 692
Camilli, 456
Campania, Campanian land, 383, 519, 526-527, 532, 624
Campus Martius, 503 n.
Camurtius, M., 494, 495 n., 496
Caninius Gallus, L. (trib. 56), 620
Cannae, battle of, 654 n.
Capua, 383, 395, 449 n., 676 n., 733 n.
Carthage, Carthaginians, 668, 670, 678, 702 n.
Carthago Nova, 613-614, 630
Cascellius, a broker, 686

Printed in Great Britain by R. & R. Clark, Limited, *Edinburgh.*

THE LOEB CLASSICAL LIBRARY

VOLUMES ALREADY PUBLISHED

LATIN AUTHORS

Ammianus Marcellinus. J. C. Rolfe. 3 Vols.
Apuleius : The Golden Ass (Metamorphoses). W. Adlington (1566). Revised by S. Gaselee.
St. Augustine : City of God. 7 Vols. Vol. I. G. E. McCracken. Vol. II. W. M. Green. Vol. III. D. Wiesen. Vol. IV. P. Levine. Vol. V. E. M. Sanford and W. M. Green. Vol. VI. W. C. Greene.
St. Augustine, Confessions of. W. Watts (1631). 2 Vols.
St. Augustine : Select Letters. J. H. Baxter.
Ausonius. H. G. Evelyn White. 2 Vols.
Bede. J. E. King. 2 Vols.
Boethius : Tracts and De Consolatione Philosophiae. Rev. H. F. Stewart and E. K. Rand.
Caesar : Alexandrian, African and Spanish Wars. A. G. Way.
Caesar : Civil Wars. A. G. Peskett.
Caesar : Gallic War. H. J. Edwards.
Cato and Varro : De Re Rustica. H. B. Ash and W. D. Hooper.
Catullus. F. W. Cornish ; Tibullus. J. B. Postgate ; and Pervigilium Veneris. J. W. Mackail.
Celsus : De Medicina. W. G. Spencer. 3 Vols.
Cicero : Brutus and Orator. G. L. Hendrickson and H. M. Hubbell.
Cicero : De Finibus. H. Rackham.
Cicero : De Inventione, etc. H. M. Hubbell.
Cicero : De Natura Deorum and Academica. H. Rackham.
Cicero : De Officiis. Walter Miller.
Cicero : De Oratore, etc. 2 Vols. Vol. I : De Oratore, Books I and II. E. W. Sutton and H. Rackham. Vol. II : De Oratore, Book III ; De Fato ; Paradoxa Stoicorum ; De Partitione Oratoria. H. Rackham.
Cicero : De Republica, De Legibus, Somnium Scipionis. Clinton W. Keyes.

CICERO: DE SENECTUTE, DE AMICITIA, DE DIVINATIONE. W. A. Falconer.
CICERO: IN CATILINAM, PRO MURENA, PRO SULLA, PRO FLACCO. Louis E. Lord.
CICERO: LETTERS TO ATTICUS. E. O. Winstedt. 3 Vols.
CICERO: LETTERS TO HIS FRIENDS. W. Glynn Williams. 3 Vols.
CICERO: PHILIPPICS. W. C. A. Ker.
CICERO: PRO ARCHIA, POST REDITUM, DE DOMO, DE HARUSPICUM RESPONSIS, PRO PLANCIO. N. H. Watts.
CICERO: PRO CAECINA, PRO LEGE MANILIA, PRO CLUENTIO, PRO RABIRIO. H. Grose Hodge.
CICERO: PRO CAELIO, DE PROVINCIIS CONSULARIBUS, PRO BALBO. R. Gardner.
CICERO: PRO MILONE, IN PISONEM, PRO SCAURO, PRO FONTEIO, PRO RABIRIO POSTUMO, PRO MARCELLO, PRO LIGARIO, PRO REGE DEIOTARO. N. H. Watts.
CICERO: PRO QUINCTIO, PRO ROSCIO AMERINO, PRO ROSCIO COMOEDO, CONTRA RULLUM. J. H. Freese.
CICERO: PRO SESTIO, IN VATINIUM. R. Gardner.
[CICERO]: RHETORICA AD HERENNIUM. H. Caplan.
CICERO: TUSCULAN DISPUTATIONS. J. E. King.
CICERO: VERRINE ORATIONS. L. H. G. Greenwood. 2 Vols.
CLAUDIAN. M. Platnauer. 2 Vols.
COLUMELLA: DE RE RUSTICA, DE ARBORIBUS. H. B. Ash, E. S. Forster, E. Heffner. 3 Vols.
CURTIUS, Q.: HISTORY OF ALEXANDER. J. C. Rolfe. 2 Vols.
FLORUS. E. S. Forster; and CORNELIUS NEPOS. J. C. Rolfe.
FRONTINUS: STRATAGEMS AND AQUEDUCTS. C. E. Bennett and M. B. McElwain.
FRONTO: CORRESPONDENCE. C. R. Haines. 2 Vols.
GELLIUS. J. C. Rolfe. 3 Vols.
HORACE: ODES AND EPODES. C. E. Bennett.
HORACE: SATIRES, EPISTLES, ARS POETICA. H. R. Fairclough.
JEROME: SELECT LETTERS. F. A. Wright.
JUVENAL AND PERSIUS. G. G. Ramsay.
LIVY. B. O. Foster, F. G. Moore, Evan T. Sage, A. C. Schlesinger and R. M. Geer (General Index). 14 Vols.
LUCAN. J. D. Duff.
LUCRETIUS. W. H. D. Rouse.
MARTIAL. W. C. A. Ker. 2 Vols.
MINOR LATIN POETS: from PUBLILIUS SYRUS TO RUTILIUS NAMATIANUS, including GRATTIUS, CALPURNIUS SICULUS, NEMESIANUS, AVIANUS, with "Aetna," "Phoenix" and other poems. J. Wight Duff and Arnold M. Duff.

OVID: THE ART OF LOVE AND OTHER POEMS. J. H. Mozley.
OVID: FASTI. Sir James G. Frazer.
OVID: HEROIDES AND AMORES. Grant Showerman.
OVID: METAMORPHOSES. F. J. Miller. 2 Vols.
OVID: TRISTIA AND EX PONTO. A. L. Wheeler.
PETRONIUS. M. Heseltine; SENECA: APOCOLOCYNTOSIS. W. H. D. Rouse.
PHAEDRUS AND BABRIUS (Greek). B. E. Perry.
PLAUTUS. Paul Nixon. 5 Vols.
PLINY: LETTERS, PANEGYRICUS. B. Radice. 2 Vols.
PLINY: NATURAL HISTORY. 10 Vols. Vols. I-V and IX. H. Rackham. Vols. VI-VIII. W. H. S. Jones. Vol. X. D. E. Eichholz.
PROPERTIUS. H. E. Butler.
PRUDENTIUS. H. J. Thomson. 2 Vols.
QUINTILIAN. H. E. Butler. 4 Vols.
REMAINS OF OLD LATIN. E. H. Warmington. 4 Vols. Vol. I (Ennius and Caecilius). Vol. II (Livius, Naevius, Pacuvius, Accius). Vol. III (Lucilius, Laws of the XII Tables). Vol. IV (Archaic Inscriptions).
SALLUST. J. C. Rolfe.
SCRIPTORES HISTORIAE AUGUSTAE. D. Magie. 3 Vols.
SENECA: APOCOLOCYNTOSIS. *Cf.* PETRONIUS.
SENECA: EPISTULAE MORALES. R. M. Gummere. 3 Vols.
SENECA: MORAL ESSAYS. J. W. Basore. 3 Vols.
SENECA: TRAGEDIES. F. J. Miller. 2 Vols.
SIDONIUS: POEMS AND LETTERS. W. B. Anderson. 2 Vols.
SILIUS ITALICUS. J. D. Duff. 2 Vols.
STATIUS. J. H. Mozley. 2 Vols.
SUETONIUS. J. C. Rolfe. 2 Vols.
TACITUS: AGRICOLA AND GERMANIA. Maurice Hutton; DIALOGUS. Sir Wm. Peterson.
TACITUS: HISTORIES AND ANNALS. C. H. Moore and J. Jackson. 4 Vols.
TERENCE. John Sargeaunt. 2 Vols.
TERTULLIAN: APOLOGIA AND DE SPECTACULIS. T. R. Glover; MINUCIUS FELIX. G. H. Rendall.
VALERIUS FLACCUS. J. H. Mozley.
VARRO: DE LINGUA LATINA. R. G. Kent. 2 Vols.
VELLEIUS PATERCULUS AND RES GESTAE DIVI AUGUSTI. F. W. Shipley.
VIRGIL. H. R. Fairclough. 2 Vols.
VITRUVIUS: DE ARCHITECTURA. F. Granger. 2 Vols.

THE LOEB CLASSICAL LIBRARY

GREEK AUTHORS

Achilles Tatius. S. Gaselee.
Aelian: On the Nature of Animals. A. F. Scholfield. 3 Vols.
Aeneas Tacticus, Asclepiodotus and Onasander. The Illinois Greek Club.
Aeschines. C. D. Adams.
Aeschylus. H. Weir Smyth. 2 Vols.
Alciphron, Aelian and Philostratus: Letters. A. R. Benner and F. H. Fobes.
Apollodorus. Sir James G. Frazer. 2 Vols.
Apollonius Rhodius. R. C. Seaton.
The Apostolic Fathers. Kirsopp Lake. 2 Vols.
Appian's Roman History. Horace White. 4 Vols.
Aratus. *Cf.* Callimachus.
Aristophanes. Benjamin Bickley Rogers. 3 Vols. Verse trans.
Aristotle: Art of Rhetoric. J. H. Freese.
Aristotle: Athenian Constitution, Eudemian Ethics, Virtues and Vices. H. Rackham.
Aristotle: The Categories. On Interpretation. H. P. Cooke; Prior Analytics. H. Tredennick.
Aristotle: Generation of Animals. A. L. Peck.
Aristotle: Historia Animalium. A. L. Peck. 3 Vols. Vols. I and II.
Aristotle: Metaphysics. H. Tredennick. 2 Vols.
Aristotle: Meteorologica. H. D. P. Lee.
Aristotle: Minor Works. W. S. Hett. "On Colours," "On Things Heard," "Physiognomics," "On Plants," "On Marvellous Things Heard," "Mechanical Problems," "On Indivisible Lines," "Situations and Names of Winds," "On Melissus, Xenophanes, and Gorgias."
Aristotle: Nicomachean Ethics. H. Rackham.
Aristotle: Oeconomica and Magna Moralia. G. C. Armstrong. (With Metaphysics, Vol. II.)
Aristotle: On the Heavens. W. K. C. Guthrie.
Aristotle: On the Soul, Parva Naturalia. On Breath. W. S. Hett.
Aristotle: Parts of Animals. A. L. Peck; Movement and Progression of Animals. E. S. Forster.
Aristotle: Physics. Rev. P. Wicksteed and F. M. Cornford. 2 Vols.

THE LOEB CLASSICAL LIBRARY

Aristotle: Poetics; Longinus on the Sublime. W. Hamilton Fyfe; Demetrius on Style. W. Rhys Roberts.
Aristotle: Politics. H. Rackham.
Aristotle: Posterior Analytics. H. Tredennick; Topics. E. S. Forster.
Aristotle: Problems. W. S. Hett. 2 Vols.
Aristotle: Rhetorica ad Alexandrum. H. Rackham. (With Problems, Vol. II.)
Aristotle: Sophistical Refutations. Coming-to-be and Passing-away. E. S. Forster; On the Cosmos. D. J. Furley.
Arrian: History of Alexander and Indica. Rev. E. Iliffe Robson. 2 Vols.
Athenaeus: Deipnosophistae. C. B. Gulick. 7 Vols.
Babrius and Phaedrus (Latin). B. E. Perry.
St. Basil: Letters. R. J. Deferrari. 4 Vols.
Callimachus: Fragments. C. A. Trypanis.
Callimachus: Hymns and Epigrams, and Lycophron. A. W. Mair; Aratus. G. R. Mair.
Clement of Alexandria. Rev. G. W. Butterworth.
Colluthus. *Cf.* Oppian.
Daphnis and Chloe. *Cf.* Longus.
Demosthenes I: Olynthiacs, Philippics and Minor Orations: I-XVII and XX. J. H. Vince.
Demosthenes II: De Corona and De Falsa Legatione, C. A. Vince and J. H. Vince.
Demosthenes III: Meidias, Androtion, Aristocrates, Timocrates, Aristogeiton. J. H. Vince.
Demosthenes IV-VI: Private Orations and In Neaeram. A. T. Murray.
Demosthenes VII: Funeral Speech, Erotic Essay, Exordia and Letters. N. W. and N. J. DeWitt.
Dio Cassius: Roman History. E. Cary. 9 Vols.
Dio Chrysostom. 5 Vols. Vols. I and II. J. W. Cohoon. Vol. III. J. W. Cohoon and H. Lamar Crosby. Vols. IV and V. H. Lamar Crosby.
Diodorus Siculus. 12 Vols. Vols. I-VI. C. H. Oldfather. Vol. VII. C. L. Sherman. Vol. VIII. C. B. Welles. Vols. IX and X. Russel M. Geer. Vols. XI and XII. F. R. Walton. General Index. Russel M. Geer.
Diogenes Laertius. R. D. Hicks. 2 Vols.
Dionysius of Halicarnassus: Roman Antiquities. Spelman's translation revised by E. Cary. 7 Vols.
Epictetus. W. A. Oldfather. 2 Vols.

EURIPIDES. A. S. Way. 4 Vols. Verse trans.
EUSEBIUS: ECCLESIASTICAL HISTORY. Kirsopp Lake and J. E. L. Oulton. 2 Vols.
GALEN: ON THE NATURAL FACULTIES. A. J. Brock.
THE GREEK ANTHOLOGY. W. R. Paton. 5 Vols.
THE GREEK BUCOLIC POETS (THEOCRITUS, BION, MOSCHUS). J. M. Edmonds.
GREEK ELEGY AND IAMBUS WITH THE ANACREONTEA. J. M. Edmonds. 2 Vols.
GREEK MATHEMATICAL WORKS. Ivor Thomas. 2 Vols.
HERODES. *Cf.* THEOPHRASTUS: CHARACTERS.
HERODIAN: C. R. Whittaker. 2 Vols. Vol. I.
HERODOTUS. A. D. Godley. 4 Vols.
HESIOD AND THE HOMERIC HYMNS. H. G. Evelyn White.
HIPPOCRATES AND THE FRAGMENTS OF HERACLEITUS. W. H. S. Jones and E. T. Withington. 4 Vols.
HOMER: ILIAD. A. T. Murray. 2 Vols.
HOMER: ODYSSEY. A. T. Murray. 2 Vols.
ISAEUS. E. S. Forster.
ISOCRATES. George Norlin and LaRue Van Hook. 3 Vols.
[ST. JOHN DAMASCENE]: BARLAAM AND IOASAPH. Rev. G. R. Woodward, Harold Mattingly and D. M. Lang.
JOSEPHUS. 9 Vols. Vols. I-IV. H. St. J. Thackeray. Vol. V. H. St. J. Thackeray and Ralph Marcus. Vols. VI and VII. Ralph Marcus. Vol. VIII. Ralph Marcus and Allen Wikgren. Vol. IX. L. H. Feldman.
JULIAN. Wilmer Cave Wright. 3 Vols.
LIBANIUS: SELECTED WORKS. A. F. Norman. 3 Vols. Vol. I.
LONGUS: DAPHNIS AND CHLOE. Thornley's translation revised by J. M. Edmonds; and PARTHENIUS. S. Gaselee.
LUCIAN. 8 Vols. Vols. I-V. A. M. Harmon. Vol. VI. K. Kilburn. Vols. VII and VIII. M. D. Macleod.
LYCOPHRON. *Cf.* CALLIMACHUS.
LYRA GRAECA. J. M. Edmonds. 3 Vols.
LYSIAS. W. R. M. Lamb.
MANETHO. W. G. Waddell; PTOLEMY: TETRABIBLOS. F. E. Robbins.
MARCUS AURELIUS. C. R. Haines.
MENANDER. F. G. Allinson.
MINOR ATTIC ORATORS. 2 Vols. K. J. Maidment and J. O. Burtt.
NONNOS: DIONYSIACA. W. H. D. Rouse. 3 Vols.
OPPIAN, COLLUTHUS, TRYPHIODORUS. A. W. Mair.
PAPYRI. NON-LITERARY SELECTIONS. A. S. Hunt and C. C.

Edgar. 2 Vols. LITERARY SELECTIONS (Poetry). D. L. Page.

PARTHENIUS. *Cf.* LONGUS.

PAUSANIAS: DESCRIPTION OF GREECE. W. H. S. Jones. 5 Vols. and Companion Vol. arranged by R. E. Wycherley.

PHILO. 10 Vols. Vols. I-V. F. H. Colson and Rev. G. H. Whitaker. Vols. VI-X. F. H. Colson. General Index. Rev. J. W. Earp.

Two Supplementary Vols. Translation only from an Armenian Text. Ralph Marcus.

PHILOSTRATUS: THE LIFE OF APOLLONIUS OF TYANA. F. C. Conybeare. 2 Vols.

PHILOSTRATUS: IMAGINES; CALLISTRATUS: DESCRIPTIONS. A. Fairbanks.

PHILOSTRATUS AND EUNAPIUS: LIVES OF THE SOPHISTS. Wilmer Cave Wright.

PINDAR. Sir J. E. Sandys.

PLATO: CHARMIDES, ALCIBIADES, HIPPARCHUS, THE LOVERS, THEAGES, MINOS AND EPINOMIS. W. R. M. Lamb.

PLATO: CRATYLUS, PARMENIDES, GREATER HIPPIAS, LESSER HIPPIAS. H. N. Fowler.

PLATO: EUTHYPHRO, APOLOGY, CRITO, PHAEDO, PHAEDRUS. H. N. Fowler.

PLATO: LACHES, PROTAGORAS, MENO, EUTHYDEMUS. W. R. M. Lamb.

PLATO: LAWS. Rev. R. G. Bury. 2 Vols.

PLATO: LYSIS, SYMPOSIUM, GORGIAS. W. R. M. Lamb.

PLATO: REPUBLIC. Paul Shorey. 2 Vols.

PLATO: STATESMAN, PHILEBUS. H. N. Fowler; ION. W. R. M. Lamb.

PLATO: THEAETETUS AND SOPHIST. H. N. Fowler.

PLATO: TIMAEUS, CRITIAS, CLITOPHO, MENEXENUS, EPISTULAE. Rev. R. G. Bury.

PLOTINUS. A. H. Armstrong. 6 Vols. Vols. I-III.

PLUTARCH: MORALIA. 16 Vols. Vols. I-V. F. C. Babbitt. Vol. VI. W. C. Helmbold. Vol. VII. P. H. De Lacy and B. Einarson. Vol. VIII. P. A. Clement, H. B. Hoffleit. Vol. IX. E. L. Minar, Jr., F. H. Sandbach, W. C. Helmbold. Vol. X. H. N. Fowler. Vol. XI. L. Pearson, F. H. Sandbach. Vol. XII. H. Cherniss, W. C. Helmbold. Vol. XIV. P. H. De Lacy and B. Einarson. Vol. XV. F. H. Sandbach.

PLUTARCH: THE PARALLEL LIVES. B. Perrin. 11 Vols.

POLYBIUS. W. R. Paton. 6 Vols.